Single Markets

Single Markets

Economic Integration in Europe and the United States

Michelle P. Egan

OXFORD
UNIVERSITY PRESS

OXFORD

UNIVERSITY PRESS

Great Clarendon Street, Oxford, OX2 6DP,
United Kingdom

Oxford University Press is a department of the University of Oxford.
It furthers the University's objective of excellence in research, scholarship,
and education by publishing worldwide. Oxford is a registered trade mark of
Oxford University Press in the UK and in certain other countries

First Edition published in 2015
Impression: 1

Published in the United States of America by Oxford University Press
198 Madison Avenue, New York, NY 10016, United States of America

British Library Cataloguing in Publication Data
Data available

Library of Congress Control Number: 2014944413

ISBN 978–0–19–928050–6

Printed and bound by
CPI Group (UK) Ltd, Croydon, CR0 4YY

Preface

In 1889, a traveling salesman found himself in circuit court in Montgomery County, Missouri for violating the law by going from place to place, in a cart or spring wagon, selling Singer sewing machines, without having a license as a peddler. The Missouri Supreme Court ruled that it was a valid exercise of the power of the state over persons and business within its borders. The fine was $50. We might not call them drummers, hawkers, or peddlers in Europe these days, but the story of the traveling salesman in Missouri shows how firms seeking new markets for their products faced challenges in selling in a single market. To me, the peddlers of sewing machines symbolize the journey towards single markets in both Europe and the US.

The primary focus of this book is on drawing together two disparate fields of European integration and American Political Development to understand how markets are constituted into broader territorial units. Although the focus is on the transformation of market forces by largely internal rather than external stimuli, building on the work of American Political Development, the processes of American state- and market-building have been tied to issues of industrialization, sectionalism, professionalization, organized interest mobilization, and jurisdictional competition that bear many resemblances to how scholars have studied the European integration process. These contributing factors should not underestimate the power of states—or public authorities—in shaping the developments in law and political economy to foster market consolidation as both polities seek to integrate into larger economic units.

Market integration in both polities generated concerns over the centralization of authority, the distributional consequences of market integration, and the impact of the *jural* state in shaping economic and societal outcomes. Yet all too often, the narrative in the US is often focused on liberalism, exceptionalism, and weak states, even as contemporary historiography challenges such assumptions about state power and its role in American political history and economic development. In much the same way European scholars are questioning the progressive European narratives, whether in terms of rhetorical devices and concepts used, or by viewing European integration as a model to imitate. How we recount the past has sometimes given us cognitive dissonance where historical rhetoric and contemporary political reality seem at odds, as we try to discern and understand patterns of authority, governance, and control, to account for European and American Political Development.

Given the sheer historical scope of the project, the narrative is broken up into a discussion of key elements shaping market integration followed by four specific cases on the free movement of goods, capital, services, and labor in both contexts. Each case study follows a similar format and strives to highlight critical developments, and to allow for comparison across cases as well as across polities. Thus it seemed appropriate to look at the consequences of economic integration on political development in the American context in the nineteenth century, and the lessons that the American experience provides for European governance. Just as the US polity has engaged in a political project to create a national market, wresting control over money from subnational authorities, removing interstate commercial barriers, and extending authority over business practices through anti-trust and regulatory policies, so have the dynamics in the EU context generated similar policy developments.

The title of the book indicates its intention. Certain elements in the processes of market integration in Europe have captured my attention in particular: the relationship between democracy, governance, and economic integration; the redefinition of the role of the state and constraints on national policies in various domains particularly welfare, monetary, and fiscal issues; and the extent to which states have remained the focus of democratic political organization and collective identity. Studying the American experience in terms of its own domestic efforts to consolidate markets in the nineteenth century gave me a different vantage point to study developments in the European case. This has led me to delve deeper into historical processes of market formation, and to relate the importance of sectional and economic cleavages, law and regulation, and territorial expansion to the political and economic development of divided power systems.

I wish to thank both the German Marshall Fund for a Research Fellowship which enabled me to begin the initial research and writing for this book, as well as the Howard Foundation at Brown University for a research fellowship to enable me to move towards completion while on sabbatical leave. Special thanks go to my various colleagues who have provided advice and support on this project. Any book that seeks to cover such a broad topic in a single volume owes a debt to many scholars. I can only acknowledge their influence through various citations of their work. I am indebted to Alberta Sbragia, whose own work on comparative federalism and American public finance has proved to be an important reference for my own work on political economy. My thanks extend to James Goldgeier, Susanne Schmidt, Kalypso Nicolaïdis, Pam Camerra-Rowe, Phil Brenner, Stephen Silvia, Randy

Henning, Virginia Haufler, Kate McNamara, Jacques Pelkmans, Andrew Moravcsik, Guy Peters, Craig Parsons, Robert (Bob) Pastor as well as the anonymous referees at Oxford University Press for comments and suggestions. The Institute for International Economics and Syracuse Maxwell School working group provided many stimulating discussions, as did the Globalization and Governance Seminar at the University of Maryland. My thanks to various capable research assistants for tracking down numerous and often obscure references: Jeannette Buchner, Monica Knapp, Robertus Anders, Maia Lowell, Andy Marshall, and Brian O'Hanlon. As always, Dominic Byatt, Commissioning Editor at Oxford University Press, provided strong support for this project and his patience is much appreciated. Thanks are also due to Susan Frampton and Olivia Wells for working with me on the production of this volume.

Special thanks to my family for their support in writing this book. To my parents, Gill and Ted, who have always provided significant support and have encouraged me. To my children, Georgina, Declan, and Daniel, who have provided much joy and welcome distractions. And to my husband, Bill, who has read and commented on the entire manuscript, and provided critical insights on both the European and American cases.

Contents

List of Tables

List of Abbreviations

ABA	American Bar Association
AMA	American Medical Association
APD	American Political Development
BRRD	Bank Recovery and Resolution Directive
CAP	Common Agricultural Policy
CCP	Central Counterparty Clearing House
CEE	Central and Eastern Europe
CRD	Capital Requirements Directive IV
CRR	Capital Requirements Regulation
EBA	European Supervisory Authority for Banks
EC	European Commission
ECJ	European Court of Justice
ECSC	European Coal and Steel Community
ECU	European Currency Unit
EFSF	European Financial Stability Facility
EFSM	European Financial Stabilisation Mechanism
EFTA	European Free Trade Association
EIOPA	European Supervisory Authority for Insurance and Occupational Pensions
EMIR	European Market Infrastructure Regulation
EMU	Economic and Monetary Union
ERDF	European Regional Development Fund
ERT	European Round Table
ESMA	European Supervisory Authority for Securities and Markets
EU	European Union
ICC	Interstate Commerce Commission
OECD	Organisation for Economic Co-operation and Development
OEEC	Organisation for European Economic Co-operation
NATO	North Atlantic Treaty Organization

List of Abbreviations

SEA	Single European Act
SLIM	Simpler Legislation for the Internal Market
TEC	Treaty on European Community
TEEC	Treaty of Rome (Treaty establishing the European Economic Community)
TEU	Treaty on European Union
TFEU	Treaty on the Functioning of the European Union
UCIT	Undertakings for the Collective Investment of Transferable Securities
UNCTAD	United Nations Conference on Trade and Development
WEU	West European Union

1

States, Democracies, and Single Markets

We could learn a lot from America about how to utilize and develop a single market.

EU Commissioner Vivian Reding[1]

Introduction

Comparisons of American and European political development have proliferated in recent years broadening lines of inquiry into the past. Part of this
research has focused on understanding the durable shift in political authority
and governance, in terms of identity politics, welfare state formation, sovereignty and statehood, federalism and market relations, that have accompanied
their respective shifts from singular states to unions (Glencross, 2007; Fabbrini,
2007, 2005, 2003, 2004; Nicolaïdis and Howse, 2001; Moravcsik, 2002b; Menon
and Schain, 2006; Sbragia, 1992a; Donahue and Pollack, 2001; Egan, 2008;
Keohane, 2002). One of the most interesting consequences of these broad
comparative and historical studies is the need to more adequately historicize
the American state to use as a comparison with the European Union (Novak,
2008; King and Lieberman, 2009). Challenging the "myth of the weak state,"
where the American state is conceptualized in terms of constitutional restraints
such as federalism, limited government, and separation of powers, these studies
provide new avenues for comparison with the European Union (hereafter EU)
through narratives and interpretations that historicize political and economic
developments across time to compare the nature and role of political institutions
(Novak, 2008).

For many scholars, increased concern about fostering democratic legitimacy
in Europe has focused particular attention on decision-making and constitutional development in the early US, as enshrined in the Philadelphia convention
and the constitution it produced. Much less attention has been paid to the
influence of American capitalism and economic development in relation to

constitutional jurisprudence, federalism, separation of powers, equal protection, and preferred freedoms (Gillman, 1999; Scheiber, 1975). Yet it is important to give both democracy and capitalism, the two major products of the American Revolution, full credit in shaping the economic and political options available to policymakers (Moore, 1966). The need to manage an industrializing society shaped many of the decisions in Philadelphia. While one of the central concerns of the constitutional convention was the security and structure of a new form of government, the framers were also concerned with the development and working character of market institutions. Significant sections of the US Constitution focus specifically on economic rights and the regulations and institutions needed to facilitate business and commercial activity. From Philadelphia onward, the historical vitality of American market capitalism has been profoundly and continually linked to the constitutional structure and institutional design of the American state.

This book examines the evolution of the American single market in the nineteenth century and the corresponding political and societal struggles that ensued as a means of comparison with the efforts in postwar Europe to foster market integration and create a single market. The politically successful adoption of single markets represents one of the most interesting issues in comparative political economy. By examining how—and how successfully—markets are consolidated in two regions, this book analyzes the politics of economic integration in the EU and the US, the two largest advanced economies that have broadly integrated single markets. What accounts for the political success or failure in creating integrated markets in their respective territories? What institutional rules and norms are necessary for promoting and legitimizing market integration? Are compensatory mechanisms for garnering support crucial in advancing integration?[2] Can social discontent threaten market integration with a populist backlash, and if so, what needs to be done to create political support for market integration? And what variation in the processes and outcomes of market integration are evident in comparing the two regions? These questions have broad significance, as efforts to create an integrated market economy and the politically successful adoption of regionally integrated trade blocs has become an important area of study in the field of comparative politics and political economy (Duina, 2006; Pastor, 2011; Mattli, 1999; Chase, 2005; Mansfield and Milner, 1997).

While some scholars have focused on how single markets have been instituted in other historical periods, drawing on examples from nineteenth-century German unification and integration (Hallerberg, 1996; Henderson, 1981) and nineteenth-century American consolidation and expansion (Egan, 2008; Bensel, 1990; North, 1966), a study of the historical processes of market consolidation can provide a useful starting point to understand the contemporary situation in Europe. Yet European integration has rarely been tied to research on the spread of the market economy and interregional flows of goods, services, and productive factors in the US (see North, 1966; Sbragia, 1992). This is surprising since both Europe and the United States were able to make a feasible and persuasive case about the gains from increased trade and productivity explicitly using ideology to persuade society of the necessity of expanding and securing their markets (North, 1981; Schmidt, 1939; Cecchini, Catinat, and Jacquemin 1988; Emerson, 1988).

In comparing two economic unions, the book addresses larger debates about organizing the polity and the economy. Using nineteenth-century America as a comparative analogy, the consolidation of markets in the US took place in conjunction with the expansion of state regulatory power and the pressures for democratic reform. Emphasizing the economic nature of EU identity, as the core element in the integration process, the process of market integration has to some degree mirrored that of the US where market freedoms are "guaranteed by public power in order to become institutionalized and develop" (Fabbrini, 2002: 8; Fligstein, 2001). Unlike the historical experience of state- and market-building among Europe nation-states, the formation and consolidation of a "common market" in the US emerged from a different structural and institutional context in which a federalist heritage of power sharing among the states and the national government stretched back to the nineteenth century (Johnson, 2009: 89). Partisan, institutional, and ideological struggles emerged from this complex mixture of state- and market-building in the US and the corresponding efforts to balance the conflicting demands of democracy, order, economic stability, and economic development (John, 1997; Novak, 1996; Weibe, 1967). This fragmented polity has often been viewed as exceptional in terms of political development (Lipset, 1996; cf. King and Lieberman, 2009; Fabbrini, 2003). That distinction is increasingly challenged by scholars from Europe and the United States, who have focused on systematic comparison of both polities. These scholars have focused on a variety of lessons and experiences drawn from comparative politics, public and constitutional law, international relations, and public policy generating theoretical and empirical analysis that no longer treats the EU as *sui generis*.

Part of this is driven by the expansion of research agendas in European integration where the dominant explanations in international relations have been supplemented and complemented by new perspectives. The basic divide has been between supranationalist and intergovernmental theories. The former, neofunctionalism, is based on a rational framework of analysis that draws on functionalist theories of international cooperation. Neofunctionalism requires positive results in the economic realm for its justification, so that providing welfare benefits and economic growth is generally seen as a way of legitimizing further spillover into other policy areas (Christiansen, 1997). By contrast, liberal intergovernmental approaches focus on the need for

3

cooperation as means to promote commercial exchange and enhance the credibility of interstate commitments, based on the rational calculations and relative bargaining power of national governments (Moravcsik, 1998). Market integration is viewed as the product of state power and interests where the material and distributional consequences of greater cooperation generate domestic support. More recently, constructivists rooted in sociological perspectives have focused on the influence of ideas, norms, identities, and ideologies on the economic practices of governments, firms, and societies (Fligstein, 2008). Constructivist political economy stresses ambiguity and uncertainty in driving economic outcomes rather than rational utilitarian approaches. In understanding how ideas about market integration emerge on the agenda, strategic constructivists focus on the power of political or economic ideas to explain how particular choices emerge (Jabko, 2006). Comparative politics scholars have focused on the functioning of the European polity, with interactions similar to those within national systems and especially federal ones (Hix, 1994; Jupille and Caporaso, 1999). They have drawn attention to the politics of identity formation, social movements and mobilization, party politics and democratic competition. The result has been the expansion of comparative and international relations perspectives that have suggested new lines of inquiry.

One major area of research has focused on comparing their respective federal systems, with emphasis on the institutional allocation of authority to assess their origins, durability, and performance (Börzel and Hosli, 2003; Hooghe and Marks, 2003; Sbragia, 2002, 2004; Scharpf, 1988; Kelemen, 2010). Scholars have evaluated federalism in terms of the trade-offs between the representation of functional and territorial interests on the one hand (Sbragia, 1992, 2004) and the optimal allocation of competencies and economic efficiency on the other (Scharpf, 1988). Both the economic and political dimensions of federalism have been used in relation to both polities, with arguments for both centralization and decentralization. Welfare economics and public choice approaches suggest that the logic of fiscal federalism and interjurisdictional competition would benefit from decentralization (Tiebout, 1956). Similarly, Barry Weingast (1995) has argued that "market-preserving federalism" provides a means for governments to commit credibly to rules that sustain a market economy. Thus, replacing a monopoly over economic policies at the center with jurisdictional competition stimulates "a diversity of policy choices and experiments" (Montinola, Qian, and Weingast 1995: 59). By contrast, political studies of federalism, such as Kelemen, focus on the "durability of federalism," notably the types of institutions and constitutional rules that effectively manage and sustain federations (Kelemen, 2007; Börzel and Hosli, 2003). Such studies highlight the tensions between decentralization and subsidiarity in Europe and the US, suggesting that these two polities can be examined in terms of how the institutional context—the logic of federalism—determines policy outcomes, or how its political feasibility and durability is determined by partisan politics, institutional rules, and other veto mechanisms.

A second area of comparative research has revolved around democracy and identity, and the implications for sovereignty and legitimacy in divided power systems. Both polities have confronted the need to legitimate the exercise of political authority. They have fought protracted struggles over the exercise of strong central state authority. For Moravcsik, the European integration experience, which has often been depicted as facing a crisis of democracy and legitimacy, may be less exceptional when viewed in terms of constitutional checks and balances, institutional delegation, and electoral participation in the US (Moravcsik, 2002a, 2002b). For Majone, the shift to non-majoritarian institutions which characterizes both polities can enhance efficiency which assumes that some policy areas do not require democratic legitimation as they focus on regulatory rather than redistributive issues (Majone, 1998, 1996, 2002). Yet the expansion of European competences has generated increased political contestation about the role of national sovereignty and identity, as European integration tries to create a political community that complements or transforms national territorial identities. For Hooghe and Marks, this has fundamental consequences for democratic competition as it has disrupted patterns of party political competition and allegiance in member states (Hooghe and Marks, 2009, 2004).

A third research theme has focused on (contemporary) institutional comparisons in terms of regulatory agencies and bureaucratic authority (Majone, 1994a, 1994b), the development of legislative rules and parliamentary procedures (Kreppel, 2006), the role of judicial politics and constitutional developments (Kelemen, 2011; Shapiro, 1992; Sandalow and Stein, 1982), and the presence of organizational interests and interest group dynamics (Mahoney, 2007) as key features of both polities. Comparing policy areas such as environmental policy (Kelemen and Vogel, 2010), immigration (Schain, 2006), monetary integration (McNamara, 2003, 2005; McKay, 1996), and competition (Damro, 2006) has highlighted both the philosophical and regulatory differences over modes of economic governance, and the strategies and opportunities for transatlantic regulatory coordination to strengthen economic cooperation where differences in the regulatory choices and domestic preferences can have significant trade impacts (Egan, 2005; Drezner, 2007; Damro, 2006; Young, Wallace, and Wallace, 2000). Comparative studies in this vein assess the supply of public goods and services in both polities to determine how this affects their trade and economic relations. But more broadly, the significance of trade has generated greater attention to the systematic influences and constraints of the global international economy on domestic economic constituencies, and conversely the "relative power of states stemming from asymmetrical interdependence" in shaping market outcomes (Moravcsik, 1998: 18). This has also led some scholars to focus on "market power" Europe to understand how the EU uses its regulatory and market strength to promote its internal policies to shape transatlantic and global markets (Damro, 2011). And similarly, scholars of American Political Development have also focused on the quest for overseas markets through imperial expansion, highlighting the role of finance capital in conjunction with state authority in shaping international economic policies as a means of understanding contemporary American "market" power (Moore, 2011).

In different ways, these comparative studies have focused on governance structures, rules of exchange, and issues of state sovereignty which bear directly on different elements of market consolidation, administration, and regulation (Fligstein, 1990; Egan, 2008). This has resulted in a significant expansion of the institutional capacity of the American state over two centuries with a similar discernible pattern of institutional development in Europe (Pollack, 2009). For some, the institutional basis for a market economy owes much to federalism as the territorial structure of government affects not only central–local relations but the shape of markets (Sbragia, 1996; Weingast, 1995). By contrast, rather than focus on internal political developments, other scholars have focused on the international dimension of markets with the significance of trade, war, and the struggle to secure borders, as key features of promoting and sustaining economic development (Katznelson, 2002: 9, 10, 15). Though the institutional capacity of the antebellum state was viewed as weak, both in terms of administrative and military capacity, in fulfilling its foreign obligations (Keohane, 2002), it was vastly strengthened after the Civil War, responding to pressures to increase its security requirements as military capacity was an essential element of state-building (Katznelson, 2002: 83). The international capacity of the state was in evidence as the military promoted the territorial expansion, trade, and security of the continent by shielding shipping lanes for commerce, settling territories, and protecting borders through land settlement and garrisons, which brings in the international dimension to understanding how the US integrated a diverse polity and extended its sovereignty through responding to domestic and international pressures to provide internal security and facilitate the growth of a "commercial republic" (Katznelson, 2002: 102–4).

Equally important, market transactions and commercial exchanges are often contested in Europe and the United States, so efforts to deal with negative externalities or market failures through regulatory action may have distributive or redistributive outcomes. The value of a single market has to have some form of utility or productive benefit for states to ensure that they accept the costs of compliance with market rules, and choose to exercise voice over exit in strengthening economic cooperation even if those political or economic conditions change (Hirschman, 1970). As such, market outcomes should strive for Pareto optimal choices, to meet the functional needs of integration, since this provides the best method of legitimating institutions (Majone, 1998, 1997). For others, socially acceptable outcomes are critical to balance democracy and markets given the constraints that market integration imposes on state autonomy in terms of redistribution and welfare. The need to offset the impact of increased market contestability requires an institutional response so that compensatory social and regulatory policies provide normative legitimacy, accountability, and support for the deepening of market integration (Scharpf, 1999b; Monti, 2010; Polanyi, 1944).

While these studies have generated a wealth of insightful contributions, few have related the European experience of consolidation and regulation of markets to processes of American state-building (see Skowronek, 1982; Novak 1996; Dobbin, 1994; Pollack, 2009). Like the growth of theoretical 'pluralism' in EU studies, American scholars have also offered new paradigms to understand the development of the American polity (Novak, 1994, 2008; Smith, 1993). Their critique pushes theoretical, normative, and empirical questions about democratic legitimacy, institutional allocation of power, and legal doctrine to the forefront of recent scholarship on the American state, especially in light of its current global hegemony. For these scholars, the characteristics of the state in the US generated a trajectory that was different than individual European nation-states, and institutionalized a regulatory state that differed from public control and nationalization in Europe (cf. Fabbrini, 2007). While most discussions of state-building focus on war and welfare, thus using the European nation-states as their model, some also consider market-building as part of state-building (Tilly, 1992; Dobbin, 1994; Fligstein, 1990; Fabbrini, 2003; Bensel, 1990, 2000). Mapping the development of American political economy, their studies of regulation, tariffs, banking, anti-trust, and other policies highlight the need to embed market relations in society as the structural changes driven by industrialization require the institutionalization and growth of state capacity to deal with the contradictions of market integration and foster its development through a combination of market-making, market-facilitating and market-regulating mechanisms (see Table 1.1; Polanyi, 1944).

Clearly the consolidation of the American single market has implications for how we think about the evolution and development of regulatory governance in Europe. The process of market integration in the US was contentious with significant periods of mass mobilization and opposition to changing economic conditions, with important implications for American Political Development (Noble, 1985). By focusing on partisan politics and the impact of strategies of governance in the nineteenth century, it shifts the focus of the "regulatory state" from the abstract to a situational context in which the struggles over territoriality and governance have relevance for the political and institutional dynamics in the EU. While political union initially led economic union in the US, with the reverse true in the EU, both have had to define and constantly reevaluate the relationship between political institutions and levels of political authority, market rules, economic interests, and societal actors.

State-Building and Market Integration: APD meets the EU

Although the US experience is instructive in terms of the pattern of American Political Development (APD) with its institutionalization of state power in terms of functional and territorial representation, and shared rule through the horizontal and vertical separation of powers, few studies have linked the work on American Political Development and European integration (Fabbrini, 1999; Egan, 2013, 2008; McNamara, 2003). Scholars of both polities are interested in several interrelated aspects of political development. One element is the critical reconstruction of political identities and political culture in the US and EU (Risse, 2010; Smith, 1993). While the American case focuses on challenging the assumptions based on Hartz or Tocqueville that American political identity is more contested and rooted in multiple traditions (Smith, 1993), the European case is also moving in that direction in that there are collective and distinct European identities depending on what resonates at the domestic level (Risse, 2010). A second element is the tension between different layers of authority and the impact of what Orren and Skowronek call the "durable shifts of political authority" across time (Skowronek and Orren, 2004: 132). The institutional allocation of power affects regulatory and distributive outcomes, and the institutional evolution of federalism in both cases has often been contested and challenged, whether through constitutional provisions, political opposition, or market actions. A third element is the "incurrence" between institutions and ideas involving both state and market. In this case, the simultaneous operation of different sets of rules, and how they are layered upon each other, may create incongruent patterns of authority and governance leading to recurrent or emergent patterns of change or pressures due to different perceptions of the polity or the economy (Skowronek, 1982; Orren and Skowronek, 2004: 17–19). Exploring this relationship requires us to draw together these distinctive areas of research along two dimensions. Scholars of American Political Development focus on the institutional conditions for market integration, viewing it as a political project, in which their economies have generated a set of policy innovations and administrative arrangements that are essential to provide stable conditions for market exchanges and transactions. They see market integration as a contextual variable shaping the incentives and actions of actors and institutions.

For scholars of American Political Development who focus on political economy, market integration is a core component of state-building (Bensel, 2000). The new historiography with its emphasis on state power in terms of rule of law, regulatory authority, and public–private modes of governance differs from our conceptions of European state-building but can nonetheless provide a version of the American state that is useful in thinking about the European integration project. More recent scholarship has argued that the American state has been consistently stronger, larger, more durable, more interventionist, and more redistributive than described in many earlier US historiographies (Novak, 2008; King and Lieberman, 2009).

Stephen Skowronek's analysis of the development of the administrative capacity of the American state has widely influenced the field of American Political Development (Skowronek, 1982). Richard Bensel has focused attention on the role of tariffs, fiscal stability, and state regulation as critical elements in the creation of a national commercial marketplace in the US (Bensel, 2000). John has explored the role of the state in the promotion and regulation of communications infrastructure, from the post office to the telegraph and telephone in the nineteenth century (John, 1995), Skocpol has documented the early origins of the welfare state (Skocpol, 1992), and Mashaw has highlighted the centralizing impact of national administrative law and the growth and development of national administrative statutory law (Mashaw, 2006, 2007; Mashaw and Perry, 2009). The formative powers of the state have also been examined in terms of land management and eminent domain (Scheiber, 1971), and the role of police powers in regulating social conduct and behavior (Novak, 1996). Long before regulatory agencies emerged in the late nineteenth century, national and state administrative capacity was substantial in interpreting a range of statutory measures, affecting health and safety, sanitation, public safety, and public property, resulting in a mode of governance that emphasized regularity and uniformity of practice (Mashaw and Perry, 2009). The expansive role for administrative discretion emerged under broad delegations of Congressional authority that generated substantial regulatory activity on the part of administrative agencies, contributing towards the consolidation and growth of state power, through permissive acceptance of administrative adjudicatory and enforcement authority.

These studies suggest that market consolidation in the US strengthened the role of the state as the expansion of public law and steady growth of regulation underpinned American political–economic development (Novak, 1996; Keller, 1977; Horwitz, 1977; John, 2008). As government intervention in the economy grew, in part due to the need to establish economic security and stability, reduce transaction costs, and respond to increased societal pressures and demands, the strengthening of administrative capacity and democratic reform measures undertaken suggests that the extent of state action and public economic policy in nineteenth-century America is indicative of the historical growth and power of the American state. And rather than view the US as an underdeveloped "weak" state in comparison to state formation in Europe (Hartz, 1955; cf. Fabbrini, 2003; Katznelson and Shefter, 2002), they emphasize how the political struggles over the organization of state power produced different state formations including a "decentralized" antebellum state, a coercive, "extractive" southern state directed towards war-related production and economic development, an interventionist "Reconstruction state" in the transition from slavery to free market economy and a more market-oriented post-Reconstruction state that paved the way for a more centralized "regulatory state" at the end of the nineteenth century (Bensel, 2000; Orren and Skowronek, 2004).

For many APD scholars, a single market contributes to the administrative and bureaucratic expansion of the state, although the balance between local authority and national control in the regulatory arena has evolved over time. Initially, states were able to pursue their varied individual policy preferences in response to economic and social change during the early nineteenth century (Novak, 1996; Childs, 2001). The mechanisms of regulation in the US are often more varied than portrayed, in part as a result of the shift from a "developmental" state to a "regulatory state" in which there was competition among regulatory regimes, as well as innovative governance structures that evolved to cope with changing economic, technological, and political developments. Not only was there strong debate regarding the legitimacy for government to regulate, to assure that resources and facilities would be available for "the common use" or public interest, but the public and private were never so rigidly segregated in understanding the overall pattern of economic development during these early decades of US market-building (Scheiber, 1981, 1984; Sbragia, 1996). Addressing economic pressures of a rapidly industrializing and urbanizing society, new ways of thinking about the role of the state, and new ways of thinking about the economic environment and its material and moral repercussions emerged (Hays, 1995). The evolution of political economy in nineteenth-century America is thus germane to the EU as both involved a restructuring of the relationship between territory and governance, with new forms of authority, new mechanisms of representation, and new demands articulated by societal interests about the regulatory and distributive costs and benefits entailed by economic growth, productivity, and competition. Rather than see particular trends in American politics as reflecting new solutions, new ideas, and new modes of governance, American Political Development seeks patterns and relationships between past and present, emphasizing the central incentives and constraints that have structured the political development of the American state (Egan, 2013; Orren and Skowronek, 2004).

Since its founding, practical questions about democratic governance and participation, notions of the public and private, and the structure of governing institutions have shaped discussion and debate about the American polity (Jacobs and Zelizer, 2003). These have also included sharply different conceptions about the market, property rights, and the economic role of the state, based on competing demands over the political economy of market integration as disagreements over tariffs, gold, and regulation reflected different regional economic interests (Bensel, 2000). Mapping out the underpinnings of American economic growth, with its multiple competing economic orders, the nineteenth-century American state is considered much more authoritative in regulating markets than earlier accounts generally concluded (King and Stears, 2011; King and Lieberman, 2008, 2009). Yet as policymakers and scholars renew a debate over the economic role of the state amidst a recession in the US, few have turned to historical precedents even though government regulation in the public interest was much more salient and typical in understanding American economic governance in the nineteenth century (Scheiber, 1997; Novak, 2009). The emphasis on market liberalization in the contemporary era needs to be placed in a broader context of public–private partnerships in social and economic policy development. How to think about the state–market relationship, the balance between public and private power, the relationship between legal institutions and the market economy, the conflict over national identity, and the patterns of democratic competition, in particular historical settings, is at the core of APD (Keller, 2007; Orren and Skowronek, 2004). By exploring the complex interrelationships between state and economy, and the ideas, policies, and institutions through which these are expressed, the American case allows us to see the current efforts to promote European market integration in a new light. Market consolidation is partly a collective effort to resolve different interests and preferences, which are often in conflict, but also an effort to enhance institutional capacity in order to make markets work effectively; and to reconcile different ideas about the constitutive nature of markets.

This also allows us to link recent scholarly developments on the causes, content, and impact of the European single market comparatively and historically, as this too has been the source of much contestation and contention over its institutional capacity in regulating, liberalizing and integrating markets. Much of this research has focused on the benefits allocated to particular interests in terms of gains from trade, the advantages derived from institutional cooperation and credible commitments, or the role of neoliberal ideas in driving market liberalization (Moravcsik, 1998; Parsons, 2003; Jabko, 2006). Some have argued that this is part of the political economy of

11

embedded liberalism at the supranational level (Caporaso and Tarrow, 2009) with the legitimacy of democratic capitalism maintained through the explicit compromise between markets and social protection (Polanyi, 1944). Others have critiqued this model of market integration as reflecting the dynamics of transnational capital and class struggle (Apeldoorn, 2000). In recent years, the focus has also shifted towards understanding the EU in terms of regulation in which the formalization and expansion of policymaking capacity can occur within a polity with limited fiscal and budgetary capacity (Majone, 1996a). While increasing international competition and deepening economic and monetary integration have resulted in a reduced role for the positive, interventionist state mode of governance and a corresponding increase in European regulatory governance, major features of the regulatory state borrow from the American state-building experience (Majone, 1996a, 1997). This is especially useful as both polities engage in policy formation, regulation, standard-setting, and enforcement as a means of promoting economic growth, dealing with market externalities, and fostering greater economic coordination. Since both rely on judicial power and bureaucratic rule-making, their histories and characteristics may offer significant promise in thinking about their respective political and economic developments across and through time (King and Lieberman, 2008; Skowronek, 1997).

Moreover, if the EU is committed to completing the single market and focusing more attention on promoting reliable access for goods, capital, and services, combined with credible European governance by means of specific rules and institutions, amidst financial turbulence and debt problems, the American experience provides an important reference point for understanding not only the efforts at fiscal sustainability and budgetary compliance, but also the impact on the institutional allocation of power, intergovernmental relations, and patterns of governance (Sbragia, 1996; Elazar, 1964). Nineteenth-century American economic development also experienced debt crises, defaults, and debt limits, with new administrative capacities and policy instruments aimed at reducing state fiscal autonomy. Europe is experiencing a problem similar to that which the American economy wrestled with during the nineteenth century—averting the bankruptcy of constituent governments (Wallis, 2005; Sbragia, 1996). Because the defaulting states were part of a large and economically integrated nation, creditors could not enforce payment by imposing military or trade sanctions. Doing so would be difficult due to the freedom of trade among states in the US. In spite of the absence of sanctions, states repaid their debts in order to maintain access to capital markets (English, 1996; Wibbels, 2003). As one of the most traumatic periods in American public finance, with strong pressure for federal assumption of state debts, the market-preserving resolution to the debt crisis is a critical model for Europe.

In the wake of this financial crisis, US states began in the mid nineteenth century to enact laws through legislative or constitutional means to restrict state borrowing (Sbragia, 1996; Wallis, Sylla, and Grinath, 2004). Defaults stimulated institutional innovation, and the actions of federal and state governments have shaped the development of markets and federalism across time. As Europe faces the prospect of destructive fiscal policy pursued by individual countries, the historical experience of the US shows how law-based and market-based strategies are important in understanding that past historical choices over the appropriate role of both national and local and public and private governance shape and constrain market integration (Egan, 2001: 212; Sbragia, 2000). Market integration in nineteenth-century America was one of volatile market transition, heavily dependent on well-defined legal mechanisms for resolving interstate conflicts that were often contested. The legacy of the past means that the US federal government is not responsible for state debt nor does it exercise surveillance (Sbragia, 1996). The market does. But as several economic historians have noted, the emergence and subsequent reduction of Civil War debt ultimately proved to be a significant impetus to postwar growth (Williamson, 1974; James, 1984). As policymakers assume new responsibilities for responding to economic crises in Europe, the conflict over public finances is tied to the future direction of European political economy.

Modes of Governance and Differentiated Integration

Building on this analysis, this book argues that markets are social institutions, created and sustained by competing values and interests; and that "single markets" have specific attributes, embedded in the governmental mechanisms which define and protect different legal, political, and economic rights. Specifically, effective state institutions are crucial for making markets work. As both the American and European examples show, the need for an effective state exists not only during the process of market integration but also after the market system has been instituted. The building of a productive, growing economy requires creation of a mutually re-enforcing relationship between business, government, and society, in which government accepts responsibility for establishing a clearly defined and uniformly enforced "playing field" for economic actors, for sustaining the vitality of markets (Carstesen, No Date). Governments must wrestle with the problems that emerge from the rapid expansion of market transactions such as the concentration of private economic power, and the dilemmas of uneven development. In the US, sectional conflict fundamentally shaped the nature of industrialization, market consolidation, and state formation, and produced growing inequality through

13

the disproportionate and deliberate exclusion of rights along race, ethnic, and class lines. In these circumstances, according to Skowronek, "the foundations of the modern American state were forged in the vicissitudes of this scramble" (Skowronek, 1982: 169). Similarly, the EU is an arena of deep economic integration characterized by non-exclusive territoriality, where sovereignty is functionally limited and integration is an extension of administrative governance aimed at dealing with changing patterns of production beyond the nation-state. Although there has been an expansion of competences in Europe to address market externalities and regional disparities, the growth of administrative power generates tension between the procedural arrangements of democracy due to the trade-offs between accountability and performance that result from bureaucratic delegation across an increasing range of policy areas at the European level.

Since governments have to articulate coherent answers to these problems to preserve and even strengthen markets, they have adopted a variety of mechanisms to meet these challenges. For example, it is crucial to have effective governmental regulation of privatized enterprises, and reliable guarantees of property rights. Table 1.1 provides the three broad categories of government responses in order to distinguish different patterns of governance that are evident in the case studies. Governments can introduce *market-facilitating* measures in order to provide information, reduce transaction costs, and promote efficient markets. They typically adopt regulations to improve market competition and facilitate business transactions. This can include the codification and formalization of rules, as well as legal and administrative reform. They may also delegate regulatory responsibility to private enforcement bodies through legislative mandates which they do in order to cope with the growing complexity of markets and the information costs associated with regulatory oversight.

Government has also played a critical role historically in investment in infrastructure and human capital. Private firms have enjoyed much government encouragement and protection, whereby governments may intervene in some instances to favor specific industries, usually national champions, provide industry subsidies, and discourage the entry of foreign competitors. Governments may also introduce competition, by maintaining entry for new competitors or participants in areas where there are often concentrations of power in the form of oligopolies or monopolies. Such *market-correcting* measures may result in specifying the conditions of mergers and acquisitions, levying fines, or having the authority to break up companies. Governments may offset the impact of increased competition by designating specific welfare provisions and benefits for certain particular interests. Such market correcting policy interventions serve to complement the more familiar market integration and liberalization measures by constraining and modifying the effects of

Table 1.1. Market coordination measures

Market facilitating	Standardizing weights and measures
	Standardizing monetary units
	Licensing of professionals
	Investment in infrastructure and human capital
	Property rights and contracts
Market correcting	Antitrust laws
	Welfare benefits
Market regulating	Regulatory commissions/regulatory agencies
	Government ownership and control

market competition (see Scharpf, 1999a). Governments may institute *market-regulating* measures in order to exercise control over specific industries and sectors. In some instances, firms remain privately owned and managed, but are subject to regulatory oversight by public commissions or regulatory agencies. The alternative is government ownership where government directly owns and operates large-scale industries where there is often a strategic imperative or economic interest in managing large-scale investments.

However, if the gradual expansion of policy competences and administrative power has some parallels across issue areas, especially in relation to economic governance, as both have allocated formal regulatory powers at different levels over time, (Donahue and Pollack, 2001: 109; Weatherill, 2012), research on market-making in Europe has been more attentive to the constitutive impact of different modes of governance on internal developments and processes (Héritier and Rhodes, 2011). While scholars of APD have been attentive to the configuration of formal political institutions, less attention has been given to informal modes of governance. Yet both Europe and the US have used both formal and informal policy instruments to shape domestic political regimes, covering a wide range of tools including reciprocity mechanisms, uniform laws, and decentralized enforcement of standards. For example, the uniform-law process conceived in the late nineteenth century has much in common with harmonization in Europe, although the former was not federal in contrast to the latter. Comity between states has resulted in either mutual recognition of rules and standards in Europe or state administered compacts, interstate administrative agreements and other forms of mutual reciprocity in the US (Zimmerman, 2010, 2006; Pelkmans, 2007).

In each case, both coercive mechanisms as well as more coordinative soft-power instruments have been used to shape public welfare and private market behavior (see Table 1.2). Though EU scholars have increasingly focused on "non-hierarchical modes of coordination and the involvement of non-state actors in the formulation and implementation of public policies," (Börzel and Risse, 2010: 113) so too have American historians begun to focus on the different configurations of American governance, which were often public in form and private in substance (Balogh, 2009). Such modes of governance "have occurred with surprising frequency in American history," in ways similar to the EU, where efforts to build state capacity have created particular institutional arrangements that allow private actors to play a central role in the administration of policies, highlighting ways that market integration can be pursued "outside of the confines of formal state institutions" (Moore, 2011: 34).

Not all states shared the same state-building goals, and cognizant of the organizational and institutional limitations of reaching political agreement, both polities have structured relations to accommodate diversity, whether through more differentiated integration models such as interstate compacts, interstate administrative agreements, comity measures, opt outs, or selective membership (Zimmerman, 2002; Nugent, 1999; Dyson and Sepos, 2010). In Europe, the customs union, common external trade policy, and the single market have been the core of unitary integration, based on a model of legal uniformity. There has, however, been a shift towards more differentiated integration by a subset of states to foster agreement through collective action due to the greater diversity of membership and the increasing scope of policies that have become Europeanized. Differentiated integration is part and parcel of state-building, and it remains part of the internal process of consolidation of power within states, as well as to European integration (Dyson and Sepos, 2010: 10).

In Europe, the opt outs on monetary union, and selective membership in the eurozone, raise concerns about asymmetric effects for both insiders and outsiders. Labor market restrictions generate problems of discrimination and exclusion, in sharp contrast to the possible "free-rider" gains from opting out of social policy or financial supervision. At the same time, differential integration has accompanied American state-building. Though the American federal system appears to be symmetrical, there is substantial territorial differentiation and constraints imposed on federal and state governance. In the US, there are non-state components that are part of the polity, as well as concurrent legal systems within the US tribal lands and territories, and sovereign proprietary claims exercised over states in the West, that provide a distinctive historical context to American state-building and market activities. The existence of internal, dependent nations within the country's border, in the case of Indian tribal lands and the extensive federal control of Western lands, has created distinct federal relations within the broader polity.

By examining the ways in which the American and European political systems integrated and consolidated their markets, the book provides important insights into the interplay between law and political forces in the context of capitalism, and the emergence of the administrative and regulatory state in response to the functional requirements of a market economy. More surprising

Table 1.2. Comparing Modes of Governance in the US and EU

Modes of Governance US	Modes of Governance EU
Interstate compacts	Mutual recognition
Administrative Agreements	Harmonization
Partial mutual recognition and reciprocity	Open method of coordination
Uniform state legislation	Decentralized enforcement
Federal–State compact	Delegation to private actors
Public–private partnerships	Voluntary accords

is that these two experiences in market-building, which offer such rich cases in political, regulatory, and economic action, have not been the subject of a detailed comparative study. This book addresses that challenge, drawing out the relationship between market and state institutional transformations, and the effects of administrative, legal, and regulatory changes on the legitimacy and accountability of the political system.

Methodology

The present study pursues a cross-regional comparison which includes historical background, development level, economic structure, and political–institutional framework. The regions selected have a number of factors in common in terms of the relationship between market-building and institutional development, making it easier to acknowledge the impact of differences—such as the role of political parties, colonization, and slavery, on the political processes and outcomes of market integration and consolidation. The chapters that follow bring out commonalities across regions, while also highlighting variation in legal, political, and regulatory developments that affect how a market economy is constituted.

Based on in-depth qualitative research using a case-oriented approach, the book provides a longitudinal analysis of the efforts to consolidate and integrate markets. The goal is to assess the conditions that promote economic integration by focusing on the operation of specific causal factors at certain points in time (Bartolini, 1993). While research on regional integration initially started with a historical and comparative focus, and acknowledged that regional integration processes are affected by different degrees of economic development and state capacity, societal pluralism and interest mobilization, there has been much less attention in recent years to broad comparisons with processes and developments elsewhere (Caporaso, 1997; Marks, 1997; Duina, 2006; Mattli, 1999).

In comparing the political conditions and effects of market integration, understanding how they evolve and are implemented requires specific cases to illustrate the dynamics of market integration. Thus the book focuses on substantive issues that balance rights of establishment and free movement of factors of production against the provision of public goods and mitigating market externalities. While this provides us with a selection of case studies, it does not provide the causal interferences that large statistical analysis can demonstrate. The methodological approach of American Political Development, with its systematic consideration of temporality and its emphasis on conceptualizing historical processes of change, fits with the historical turn in EU studies, unraveling the "teleological assumptions" of earlier studies to reexamine traditional themes about state power, bureaucratic capacity, ideological conflict, and market behavior (Orren and Skowronek, 2004: xi, 123; Parsons, 2003; Hooghe and Marks, 2009). While the study is small in comparison, it does speak to concerns about the treatment of the EU as a distinctive single case, by focusing on the broader themes in comparative politics about the relationship between capitalism and democracy, and the institutional powers and organizational processes needed to foster and maintain a functioning market economy. For "there are uncanny similarities and persistent tendencies—regularities and recurrences"—in the logic and processes of American market integration that suggest structural features and historical insights that can alter our usual narratives that tend to depict the American state, with its multiple centers of public authority, intergovernmental bargaining, and federal-type structure as similar to the European integration experience without addressing the transformation and changes inherent in American Political Development that have shaped the logic and pace of market integration (see Novak, 2010: 797). While European integration has offered different theoretical explanations about the complex relationship between sovereignty, integration, and power, the rationale and conditions under which new policies and practices emerge, or the constitutional, federal, or compound nature of the EU, the nature of the American polity is often viewed in terms of federalism, separation of powers, or constitutionalism, with less attention paid to the historical rise of the mechanisms of legal, political, economic, corporate power, or change over time in American state- and market-building (Novak, 2010; Gerstle, 2010; Johnson, 2009).

The issue of constitutional and institutional reform has been debated at length over the past decade in Europe, often generating historical analogies with the founding of the American Constitution. Many of these comparisons have focused on the atypical development of the American compound Republic with its horizontal and vertical separation of powers, sectional balance of powers, and fragmented sovereignty (see Siedentop, 2001; *Economist*, December 15, 2001; *European Voice*, 8, 8: February 28, 2002). Being acutely sensitive to the division of powers and competencies between federal and state governments, the American Founding Fathers debated distinctly different conceptions of the

American polity and state. Focusing on broad political considerations regarding the role of the national government in American politics, the original design specifically demarcated the boundaries, dividing and organizing power to create a structure of mutual balance and influence between the two levels of government (Beer, 1978; Elazar, 1964). The purpose of this institutional allocation of authority was a solution to the problem of representation for the American polity. Since then, the growth of the public sector and the evolution of new structures of decision-making and representation within the public sector have generated renewed concerns about the legitimacy and accountability of the American polity (Beer, 1978; Lowi, 1979). Ironically, this has not dispelled interest among proponents and critics of European integration alike in using the US as a comparison in terms of fundamental questions concerning the distribution of sovereignty, and related issues of governance, representation, and legitimacy (Nicolaïdis and Howse, 2001; Ansell and Di Palma, 2004; Fabbrini, 2004, 2005; Sbragia, 1992a; Scharpf, 1999a; McKay, 1996, 2001; Moravcsik, 2002b). While contesting the nature of EU power, both in normative and structural terms, they have not engaged with the state-centered analyses of American political and economic development, which has shifted from a philosophical and theoretical premise of a "weak" state due to the broad distribution and fragmentation of power via multiple levels of governance, into one where the formative powers of the state(s) in different areas was critical for American political economy (Bensel, 2000; King and Lieberman, 2009; McCraw, 1981). These new directions suggest that the work on American Political Development can shed light on the creation of a national and subsequently regional marketplace, and the interrelated development of state intervention and market expansion.

Case Selection

The book follows a case-study approach through a detailed comparison of the so-called four freedoms: namely the removal of border controls and the largely unrestricted transfer of goods, services, and capital across different jurisdictions. Using these categories that are the core objectives of the European founding document, it is then possible to establish a functional equivalence with the US, since most observers recognize that economic integration requires the removal of restrictions to trade in goods and other factors of production. Each case-study chapter provides a comprehensive overview of the efforts in both the US and EU at consolidating markets through the removal of restrictions to trade liberalization, through the constraint of at least some domestic policy instruments, and the irrevocable transfer of some rules and instruments to the federal or European level. This allows us to compare the process of integration across markets, and compare the EU with the US polity at the macro level, while at the same time comparing micro-level cases to provide substantial empirical analysis and explore patterns of commonality.

The book also acknowledges that there are differences in terms of the cases chosen, since the depth and scope of many transactions, the trade patterns, and the configuration of different economic instruments may change and vary over time. The volume of trade within the US is much smaller than that of the EU; there are fundamental differences in the nature of their trading relationships. European states, operate in an increasingly interdependent international system in which international institutions play a key role in trade liberalization, monetary cooperation, and financial stability. Though the US economy was inextricably linked with foreign as well as domestic policy objectives, and also had to cope with external constraints imposed by the European powers, the efforts to oppose attempts to restrict American commerce in the early nineteenth century were replaced with sectional trade patterns in which foreign trade become less important in the North and West, and was critical for the South (Keohane, 1983: 47). Moreover, the type of cross-border trade is different in that intra-industry trade is a significant factor in Europe, and has no precedent in the nineteenth-century US case. The nature of financial flows is different since contemporary financial flows are dominated by short-term investments whereas capital flows during the nineteenth century were for long-term investment for infrastructure and public debt. Yet capital flows were a major factor in promoting economic integration. Other factors include the major shifts in the relative importance of agriculture, and the growth of services in postwar Europe. As a result, the research recognizes that the same language may not be strictly analogous. Although labor, goods, and capital flows were dominant features of the nineteenth century, both internally within the US and as part of the Atlantic economy, trade in services is a more recent phenomenon. However, the book focuses on transportation services, to illustrate the importance of services to economic growth and regional development, and the central role of the state in the provision of public services.

The case studies provide additional evidence concerning the contextual changes promoting market integration, as well as the evolution of political processes and institutions to support—or hinder—the growth of the single market and its ancillary policies (Frost et al., 2002). They draw together the work of business, legal, and political historians, with that of more contemporary work in political science and public policy. Arguably, the US and EU share enough similarities to carry out a cross-regional study on the politics of market integration. By using a comparative approach, this study brings together two closely related but largely unacquainted bodies of scholarship in the US and EU and seeks to contribute to our understanding of the policies required and political support necessary to build and sustain a single market.

Overview of the Book

The first section focuses on the general dynamics of market integration. It draws on research on political and economic development, and examines the factors that foster market consolidation, the types of tools and strategies that promote integration, and the legal, political, and economic conditions that characterized both polities in the nineteenth and twentieth century. The second section of the book is comparative case studies of market integration across issue areas. This involves a paired comparison of the four markets, since most observers recognize that economic integration requires the removal of restrictions to trade in goods and other factors of production.

Chapter 2 provides a historical comparison between the American and European cases, illustrating that a comparison between these political systems is possible. While differences in the two cases come readily to mind, the chapter draws attention to some important shared features that shape their respective political developments and drive towards market integration. The chapter outlines the constitutional underpinnings of market integration and specific institutional developments, the respective economic development and structure of their political economies, and the impact of war and reconstruction and expansion and enlargement in shaping their overall economic development and market consolidation. It stresses that the allocation of authority between different levels of government, the tension that this can generate between those levels, and patterns of uneven regional development have all been features of both polities.

Chapter 3 describes the circumstances in the nineteenth and twentieth century, respectively, for the emergence of a trade doctrine supporting internal market integration, and offers some generalizations about economic development and the dynamics of legal change in fostering an ever closer union. In doing so, it offers four of the fundamental explanations developed by contemporary integration theory, namely the role of law, interest group mobilization and business influence, distributive politics, and the centralization of regulatory activity. The chapter discusses the relationship between law and markets, and the role of courts in providing the constitutional principles and jurisprudence that was instrumental in overcoming local resistance to interstate business and thereby shaping government–business relations as well. Other factors driving the dynamics of market integration including the mobilization of business interests, the side payments and the politics of compensation and distribution, and the developmental politics of the respective regulatory states are discussed.

Chapter 4 on the free movement of goods compares the US Commerce Clause, police powers, and Fourteenth Amendment with the free movement provisions in the Treaty of Rome. In both cases, well-defined legal and judicial mechanisms are considered crucial in promoting a single market in goods, and particularly in shaping the boundaries between legitimate and illegitimate economic activity. Chapter 5 on the free movement of capital examines the wide range of domestic regulatory measures that can be imposed on short- or long-term capital flows to protect domestic or local capital markets, and to control domestic monetary expansion. The chapter then analyzes the corresponding pressures and efforts to promote capital mobility. Chapter 6 on the free movement of services recognizes that the notion of a service economy is relatively recent. It uses the notion of "public services" and conceptions of a public interest function to compare policy developments in transport services. This sector is characterized by extensive state intervention and monopolization, only to be later replaced by efforts to promote greater competition and liberalization. Chapter 7 on the free movement of labor focuses on efforts to foster labor mobility without discrimination, using the movement of professions as a case study for the degree of market mobility in both polities, and to illustrate differences in how national labor markets are regulated, which can create subtle market-entry barriers.[3]

In sum, chapters 4, 5, 6, and 7 are the core empirical chapters that compare EU and US market integration in each of the four freedoms. They have a common structure in examining the barriers to trade that hinder internal commerce, the prevailing market structure and how it evolved in response to interest group pressures for integration and consolidation, the regulatory strategies undertaken to integrate fragmented markets, and the role of law in shaping market integration. Each provides a comprehensive overview of the efforts in both the US and EU at consolidating markets through the removal of restrictions to trade liberalization, through the constraint of at least some domestic policy instruments, and the irrevocable transfer of some rules and instruments to the federal or European level. Taken as a whole, these chapters argue that the contentious politics between governments over the boundaries of regulatory authority is shaped, in large part, by pressures emanating from the courts and business. They also offer evidence that the instruments used to promote market integration, though sometimes differing in name or political usage, are in fact similar in terms of their rationale and objectives.

The conclusion brings together both the common and distinctive features that underpin the efforts by the US and EU to construct integrated markets. In particular, it focuses on the interplay between institutions, ideas, and interests in shaping the relationship between the state and the market. And of course, emphasis is given not only to the responsibility of government for creating and sustaining markets—of nurturing individual economic choice and of creating a supportive environment for enterprise—but also in generating socially and politically acceptable solutions. The promotion of competitive markets is qualified by the need to sustain public support for integration, with very substantial but well-defined and limited power, in order to maintain political legitimacy. The concluding chapter assesses the degree to which the four different markets have been consolidated in both the EU and US. This illustrates how uneven the development of the single market has been in both cases, drawing attention to constraints on factor mobility and free trade that continue to persist in the US and Europe. It highlights the importance of understanding not only the institutional and regulatory arrangements that govern markets, but also how the very growth of government, even when the objective is wholly appropriate, can result in a backlash against further concentrations of power. The efforts to restructure their political and administrative institutions have not fully addressed problems of legitimacy, transparency, and control.

Highlighting the tensions over regulatory authority and sovereign control, as well as the efforts at economic coordination in divided power systems such as the United States fits with ongoing interest in Europe about the emerging system of multiple and overlapping governance. As such, the literature on the construction of the American single market, which is tied to analyses of industrialization and state-building, offers a complementary set of categories, concepts, and causes of market consolidation that is helpful in illustrating the mechanisms of political and institutional change—and continuity—that has characterized European integration (see McNamara, 2001a; Marks, 1997). The study of American market integration is more than mere historical interest. The emphasis of APD on conceptualizing historical processes of change to connect past and present has contemporary relevance as concerns about governability have increased in salience in the US and EU (Orren and Skowronek, 2004). As such, market integration can be understood as part of a broader process of political development in which the transformation of state and administrative capacity in response to changing market conditions and economic ideas, constitutional doctrines and practices, social power and political mobilization can and does reconstitute governance, thus altering market practices and political behavior. *Single Markets* is a study of market integration and the resulting institutional change, resistance, and adaptation, as well as an exercise in comparative analysis.

Notes

1. As quoted in *New York Times*, July 8, 2011, Kevin O'Brien "Europe Explores Passage of Consumer Rights Bill".
2. Similar questions were raised as part of a working group Lessons from a Globalizing World: European and US Experiences in Market Integration, sponsored by Maxwell School at Syracuse. See E. Frost, C. Parsons, J. D. Richardson, and M. Schneider,

"Lessons for a Globalizing World: European and U.S. Experiences in Market Integration," September 2002 (unpublished mimeo).

3. Scholars have focused on the disjuncture between the internationalization of the European political economy and the continuance of national welfare regimes tied to different conceptions of economic citizenship and social rights. Cross-border mobility of labor is designed to enable workers to move in and out of labor markets as easily as movement within them, rather than harmonization of national systems. See Scharpf (1999a, 1999b), and Moses (2011).

2

Foundational Politics

Benjamin Franklin wrote to his European friend Rodolphe-Ferdinand Grand in 1787, just after the American Constitution was signed:

> I send you enclos'd the propos'd new Federal Constitution for those States.... If it succeeds, I do not see why you might not in Europe [do the same] by forming a Federal Union and One Grand Republick of all the different States and Kingdoms by means of a like Convention; for we had many Interests to reconcile. (Franklin, 1787)

Although the states of Europe did not heed his advice at the time, the advent of European integration and promotion of an ever closer union has renewed interest in the American experience that two hundred years ago seemed to be a compromise of "dissimilar interests and inclinations" (Hamilton, 1961 [1788]).

Traditionally, American Political Development has been viewed as the antithesis of European state-building due to its political fragmentation, creating a system of governance characterized by often contradictory pressures resulting from the diffusion of power, radical democratic governments, and selective curtailment of liberties and rights (see Jacobs and King, 2009). Particular attention has been given to the role of regions, parties, courts, and ideologies in shaping political developments, with the development of the American state often described in both exceptional yet paradoxical terms (Lipset, 1996). If we treat American state-building in the early Republic on its own terms, the power of states with overlapping jurisdictions across economic, social, and political affairs, provided both public welfare as well as the suppression of rights, market access, and freedom through state laws and regulations (Gerstle, 2009, 2010). Yet Americans also sought active governance at the federal level over the course of the nineteenth century, much less visible than their European state counterparts, through intervention in political economy, to achieve economic gains from trade, effective rule of law, and legitimacy for business transactions (Balogh, 2009). The expansion of state power reflected a mixture of constitutional forces, interest group pressures, and Congressional developments as the federalist tradition of power-sharing among the states and the national government stretched back to the nineteenth century. Equally important, as we shall see in subsequent chapters, American market-building relied on the state—both via indirect and direct means—through a myriad of institutions, jurisdictions, rules, norms, and practices, which was a constitutive element for successful market consolidation (Johnson, 2009; Egan, 2008; Balogh, 2009). As markets and transactions, corporations and communications became national in scope, the construction and maintenance of a national market gave rise to new governmental arrangements, linking state-building, market consolidation and democracy, as state and local governments, professions, interest groups, and private corporations played a key role in shaping economic governance (Balogh, 2009; Hays, 1995). National market integration was first and foremost a *political* construction.

The simultaneous transformation of the market and polity generated substantial protest about prevailing economic and democratic conditions that reverberate in the current debates in Europe. Nineteenth-century integration in the US generated a wide range of regulatory and administrative mechanisms that shaped economic development and market consolidation, allowing us to see the institutional complementarities between the nature of American Political Development and contemporary European governance. This period in American history also highlights other commonalities and differences stemming from concerns about democratic and constitutional legitimacy, market activities, and corresponding industrial developments, and durable inequalities that have persisted in modernized market-polities. As Europe enters a period of prolonged fiscal austerity, with weak economic growth across the region, just like its American counterpart, the fact that the single market has proved resilient does not mean it is complete, nor does it mean that eroding public support and constitutional challenges will lessen the pressure for dealing with economic imbalances and social inequality (see Monti, 2010).

Some scholars have compared the rationale for market integration in terms of the strategic calculus of economic costs and benefits, the presumption being that economic gains outweigh costs (Moravcsik, 1998c). Others have emphasized the institutional design of divided power systems, and the impact of federalism in influencing not only intergovernmental politics and sovereign relations, but in securing public goods such as consolidated markets and common security (Ziblatt, 2004: 70). In addition to the management of a heterogeneous polity and the consolidation of territory, others have compared broader changes in democratic practice including an erosion of trust and legitimacy in political institutions that has resulted in pressure for reform, heightened by concerns about growing economic insecurity and social change (Rittberger, 2009; Riker, 1964). This chapter provides some comparable insights into the market integration process while also drawing attention to important historical differences between the US and Europe. What is being attempted by the EU in such a short period of time, by historical measure, is reminiscent of efforts by the US to consolidate local and regional markets, bind states into a single economic unit, and link the development of an integrated economy to the development of a polity with a distinct political identity. Similar accomplishments in terms of a single market, single currency, and single bank required one and a half centuries for completion in the US.

The chapter begins with the constitutional and legal underpinnings of market integration in the US and EU, and then focuses on their respective economic development. This is followed by a comparison of the institutional and democratic features of their political systems to highlight areas of differentiation and congruence in their overall political and market development including their fiscal extractive power, instruments of representation, and governance mechanisms. The chapter highlights two crucial developments that shaped the nature of both polities, namely the impact of war and reconstruction and expansion and enlargement which are seen as constitutive elements of state-building. The resulting combination of coercion and compromise shapes the dynamics of market integration (Katznelson, 2002a: 82; Tilly, 1992; Marks, 1997; Ziblatt, 2004).

Constitutional and Legal Foundations of Market Integration

Both the American Constitution and Treaty of Rome provide the legal framework for the creation of a single market. These documents set out the formal provisions that have become the basis for their efforts to integrate diverse economies into an economic entity that is neither homogenous nor completely free of restrictions to interstate commerce. While the original European Economic Community Treaty of Rome has undergone substantial revisions over the past fifty years,[1] significantly expanding the Community's reach with respect to market integration, the US Constitution has not undergone major changes in the provisions related to market integration. In both cases, the founding documents contain a mixture of express provisions and restrictions, and thus constitute efforts to promote both negative integration, in terms of the removal of discriminatory barriers between economies, and positive integration, in terms of agreement on common economic policies for the future (Tinbergen, 1954b).

The American Founding Document

The United States Constitution was drafted in light of the weaknesses of the Articles of Confederation. Part of the problem was the weakness of central authority, and a precarious financial situation in which the lack of common currency and unsecured paper monies impaired both intrastate and interstate commercial activities (Hoke, 1992: 856). Lack of authority to compel states to comply with laws and treaties, or provide resources for dealing with public emergencies also hampered the American system of governance. The US Constitution sought to address some of these problems, providing for the promotion of a limited number of common policies, and the creation of a customs union through the guarantee that duties, imposts, and excises shall be uniform throughout the US (see Article I Section 8). The possibility of the federal state raising new revenues is expressly granted in the Constitution, with the power of taxation vested in Congress.

The Constitution also provides Congress with the sole authority to coin money, regulate its value, and fix the standards of weights and measures. However, this was not a mandate for a single currency or central bank (Hurst, 1973). In addition to promoting the harmonization of common standards for commercial transactions, the Constitution provides Congress with the most crucial provision with regard to the formation of a single market, the power to regulate commerce. This involves both the regulation of foreign economic relations, and internal regulation of commerce between states and with Indian tribes (Article 1 Section 8). Together with Sections 9 and 10, the Constitution prohibits states from imposing restraints—financial or otherwise—on interstate trade. No area generated more detail than provisions related to the market (Hurst, 1982: 11). Yet the broad power to regulate commerce generated little discussion at the Constitutional Convention, in part because it was designed to remedy prior problems of destructive trade wars and promote the general welfare of the Union (Conant, 1991: 89).

In fact, the Framers of the Constitution envisioned the allocation of services and goods in the American economy to be private decisions, and the Commerce Clause, Due Process Clause and other articles were evidence of that commitment (Hovenkamp, 1992a). The negotiations indicate that the private market was considered the essential institution in the social order, and consequently there are certain prohibitions on states regarding activities that affect the functioning of markets (see Hurst, 1982). While states are expressly prohibited from coining their own money, they are given more leeway in being able to impose restrictions upon commerce to uphold their inspection laws. This allowed states to regulate through their "police powers" for purposes of advancing health, safety, and welfare goals (Hurst, 1977; Novak, 1996). These efforts to serve communal values or societal interests in the area of eminent domain and police powers were also designed to promote the public good in a society undergoing rapid social and economic change (Scheiber, 1988: 141; Scheiber, 1984). The interpretation of these clauses required judicial intervention to determine, on one hand, the balance between independent prerogatives and the independence of markets and, on the other, the sovereign power and rights to interfere and regulate markets (Hovenkamp, 1992a).

The basis of authoritative competencies at the national level is now well established in the US, with the most significant domestic activities settled. These functions, including a national banking system, single market, and single currency, were settled in the nineteenth and early twentieth century, in the aftermath of the US Civil War and other, less bloody, but similarly contentious political and judicial conflicts. From this perspective, the devolution of power to state and local levels appears to involve a relatively narrow range of issues, largely related to the welfare state. Yet the balance between local autonomy and central state power was politically charged throughout the nineteenth century, and federal actions were largely related to tariff policies, land management, and banking and monetary policies. None of these policies required substantial administrative or fiscal resources, and hence the overall impact of tax policy and revenue collection was minimal. The redistributive effects of such a small federal budget were also small, and certainly not comparable to the current levels of federal budget expenditures that characterize the modern American economy or that of postwar European nation-states.

Despite the efforts to limit the intervention of public power in many market domains, the framers also managed to take the most threatening and divisive issue off the agenda. Provisions in the US Constitution tied to the issue of slavery ensured that the migration or importation of labor by individual states would not be hindered or prohibited by Congress. This politically charged and divisive issue defined the fault lines of US politics during much of the nineteenth century even though the provisions of the Constitution placed discussions out of bounds of both the national and federal levels (Ellis, 2000: 16).

The European Founding Document

The Treaty of Rome is much more explicit than the Constitution in advocating the creation of a single integrated market. Unlike the American Constitution, the negotiations focused on internal trade liberalization and the Treaty outlined specific goals and timetables to achieve economic integration, covering an extremely wide area of activities (Bertrand, 1956). Initially, this meant the establishment of a common market and the harmonization of economic policies of the member states, with a view to raising the standard of living and promoting closer economic relations to ensure peace and stability. The specific obligations and tasks were laid out in Article 3: the removal of obstacles to the free movement of goods, persons, services, and capital; the creation of common policies in agriculture, fisheries, and transport; the approximation of laws of the member states to assist in the functioning of the common market; the establishment of a common external tariff and commercial policy; and the creation of a European Social Fund and a European Investment Bank to improve the employment opportunities and economic development of the Community (see appendix).

The main emphasis was on the progressive elimination of tariffs and quantitative restrictions. Although the Treaty envisaged that customs duties within the common market would be abolished over a period of twelve to fifteen years, there were disagreements over the timetable resulting in three stages of liberalization for the elimination of internal tariffs. The stress on liberalization was also a reflection of the greater confidence of national governments in the efficacy of market mechanisms (Tsoukalis, 1997: 19). The inclusion of competition policy, and the emphasis on policing the market through the abolition of state aids and anticompetitive practices pointed to a liberal economic approach in which efforts were made to restrict the latitude of national economic planning (Von der Groeben, 1987: 24). By contrast, policies requiring intervention such as industrial policy and regional policy were the subject of few explicit provisions. Specific exemptions were written into the Treaty, in case member states experienced substantial economic difficulties and needed to take corrective measures before continuing their commitment to liberalization. Such provisions are absent in the US Constitution.

The negotiations surrounding the Treaty clearly also placed a priority on trade liberalization in goods rather than other factors of production. Though most member states were committed to the free movement of labor and capital, and this is reflected in the emphasis on the "four freedoms," struggles behind the scenes meant that the Treaty provisions in these areas were more limited than might be expected (see Laurent, 1970). The Treaty does not provide for a Community-wide social policy, with related articles restricted to social regulation and coordination. At the outset, social policy was largely concerned with the problem of reducing restrictions to labor mobility (Articles 48–50) and freedom of establishment (Articles 52–58). Specific provisions on social security for migrant workers and on vocational training were also included in the Treaty. National welfare states were, however, to remain the primary institutions of social policy.

If labor issues and the cross-border movement of people were as salient for the US as it remains for the EU, the issue of capital and currency has been no less important in promoting economic interdependence and institutionalizing political ties across sovereign territories (Marcussen, 1999; McNamara, 1998). Though freedom of capital is one of the conditions necessary for achieving an integrated market, the Treaty makes clear that capital should be liberalized "as far as necessary." There are a number of caveats and restrictions that allow member states to retain some control over this aspect of economic policy (Article 67) as the local impact of capital mobility may impact liberalization. Freedom of establishment and freedom to provide services are also essential elements of the single market. Aimed at providing freedom of choice over location, the Treaty provisions were based on principles of non-discrimination and market access.

However, national governments were less willing to transfer fiscal and monetary powers to the European level, especially with their goal of attaining the objectives of full employment domestically (Tsoukalis, 1997: 21). While there was initially no intention in the Treaty to set up a regional currency, this changed with the 1992 signing of the Maastricht Treaty, which outlined the rules governing economic and monetary union (EMU), including the establishment of a European Central Bank and the introduction of the Euro. The single market is considered a key reason for the drive towards a single currency, as it provided the momentum for restructuring the public expenditures of member states to meet the criteria for economic and monetary union. To prevent free-riding, fiscal rules to prevent excessive deficits were created and mechanisms to monitor compliance enacted; similar to state balanced-budget rules that emerged in the US in the nineteenth century (Schelkle, 2009b; Sbragia, 2001).

Initially, the EU did not have the same fiscal authority set out in the US Constitution, in which the power to levy and spend taxes is retained at each level of government. The Treaty of Rome provided for no such taxing authority. The EU is distinctive in that it originally lacked an autonomous source of revenue, as "the structure of taxation and spending was left for national governments to decide" (Schelkle, 2009b: 4, 2009a; Laffan, 1998). While the development of new revenue-raising possibilities on the part of the American federal state increased dramatically due to the pressures of waging war and the expenditures entailed during the Civil War, the same imperatives have not been present in the EU.[2] The lack of budgetary resources explains why regulation is the main instrument of market integration and public power in the Union. While the EU is severely constrained in the fiscal area, since it cannot impose direct taxation, run deficits, or issue public debt, its limited extractive power until recently had much in common with the US in the antebellum era.

In the US, much of the influence of the national government at the state and local level is derived from fiscal transfers, supplementing the resources of states and local authorities (taxing and borrowing) through grants in aid which have taken different forms over time and varied in the degree of conditionality imposed. While the simple act of bargaining itself places the national government in a position of authority, the situation in the nineteenth century was much different and more closely comparable to the EU. In the US, states provided the bulk of promotional and public investment activities, distributing public largesse to specific groups and regions, and following independent fiscal policies and capital investment activities. Like the federal experience in the nineteenth century, the EU institutions were not in a position to use fiscal transfers as a means of influencing member states and their constituent units (Henning and Kessler, 2012).[3] Because of this, the EU has, until recently, struggled to address the sovereign debt crisis, credit crunch, and collapse of export markets, as they were forced to rely on indirect measures to promote structural reform because they lacked an effective fiscal apparatus (Henning and Kessler, 2012). Given large internal imbalances and massive external borrowing, the weak fiscal framework proved wholly inadequate to deal with the economic crisis, requiring political elites to recapitalize the banking sector, coordinate a fiscal stimulus, and enhance fiscal governance.

Economic Governance, Political Development, and Democratic Pressure

The EU and the US in the nineteenth century can be described as custom unions engaged in sustained efforts to integrate their markets. On the surface, the most striking difference between the US and EU appears to be the level of economic development. The early US was an agrarian economy, engaged in both modernization and industrialization, while the EU, though recovering from World War II, was industrialized with a modern economy. Yet subtle similarities exist in the two cases as "both had a significant agricultural base, with varying levels of economic development among states" (see McNamara, 2001a: 5). The most striking feature in the US and Europe was the gap between the more industrialized north and west, and the more agricultural and underdeveloped south. Concern about the polarization effects of integration, potentially impeding the laggard regions and creating a division of production between labor-intensive and capital-intensive economies is a feature common to both (Hirschman, 1970). In the American case, the Southern economic region grew, although it did not develop a substantial commercial and industrial sector, as it was dependent on slave labor. The South experienced "growth without development" (Keohane, 1983: 47) as the economic position of the South in the international division of labor meant that it exploited its economic advantage in cotton production through slave labor (Keohane, 1983: 47). Following the Civil War and abolition of slavery, the state-sponsored program of economic development did little to bridge the growing gap between North and South, since the region had a small indigenous capital stock and attracted little investment from the East Coast or Europe.

The European economies also experienced substantial growth, those with prior industrial development experiencing greater productivity, and those with less wartime disruption making rapid progress (Eichengreen, 2008: 89–90). However, Britain, Belgium, and Ireland performed poorly both in absolute and relative terms, stagnating relative to their peers. While many economies in Europe faced regional problems of underdevelopment, the different regional levels of economic development in Italy are similar to the economic dualism that divided the American North and the South. Despite national measures showing growth in exports and productivity, capital was poured into the industrialization of southern Italy, and tax breaks were used to encourage investment and foster national champions, the southern economy subsisted largely on net income transfers and the regional balance of payments was continually in deficit (Putnam et al., 1993; Barzanti, 1965). Despite large-scale emigration from the south, unemployment remained a significant concern, making Italy the laggard among the original six in terms of regional disparities.

Both the US and Europe made striking advances in the overall development of their respective economies aided by a range of government interventions. High rates of growth were characteristic of both post-World War II Europe and the nineteenth-century US. On the eve of the Civil War, the US had undergone rapid and sustained economic expansion (North 1966: v).[4] Barriers to free movement of goods, services, and productive factors were being relaxed, and there was a shift away from dependence on the Atlantic economy towards the internal economy as the mainspring for expansion and growth (North, 1966: 66–7; Schmidt, 1939: 798). Conditions also improved in terms of the transport facilities that connected the East and West, and a new market developed for agricultural imports from the West to the rapidly urbanizing East. Canal and railroad construction, land sales, and the influx of the first big wave of immigration all contributed to economic growth and development (North, 1966; Bruchey, 1990). American industrial development continued to blossom in the late nineteenth century as the rate of capital investment in firms and the value of production increased rapidly (Bensel 2000: 24; Keohane, 1983). While foreign capital proved crucial at specific times, notably 1815 to 1818, 1832 to 1829, and 1850 to 1857, domestic savings rates increased dramatically. Capital investment from the North and Midwest funded the settlement and development of the agricultural and mining economy in the West. The shift from labor-intensive to capital-intensive production, rapid technological innovation as well as the expansion of employment opportunities in a wide variety of local trade and manufacturers signaled a process of modernization (McPherson, 1982: 13–23).

Just as the nineteenth-century American economy provided a fertile environment for economic growth, so the European economies experienced rapid expansion in productivity and output in the 1950s and 1960s. The twenty-five-year period following World War II was one of sustained growth, with shifts from agriculture to industry, as well as moderated wage demands and the adoption of mass production methods and commercial technologies (Eichengreen, 2008). Economic growth was sustained by governments through the expansion of state activity including the extension of government welfare provision.[5] There was considerable variation in economic development strategies (Shonfield, 1965). Though the principle of planning gained considerable support, a general consensus emerged around a model of economic development mixing private and governmental activity in various disguises including price and wage controls and nationalization over key sectors of the economy (see Shonfield, 1965). While markets were increasingly regulated and controlled, the widespread acceptance of Keynesian economic policy meant that government regulated the economy through policies of supply and demand. Government promoted full employment in order to enhance demand, consumption, and productivity. Abundant supplies of labor, as well as stable exchange rates, and pressures for reduction of trade barriers also played an important role. High rates of capital accumulation also fed economic growth, driven in part by the continuation of high taxation inherited from the war, and tax relief granted by governments for industrial reinvestments that would otherwise have gone towards dividends (Shonfield, 1965: 6). Investment continued to grow due to the prospects of rising demand, the absence of recession, and constantly rising prices (Maddison, 1976: 477–86). Consequently, those whose trade had been geared towards other European economies were willing to provide further weight to that export orientation through commitment to European integration (Eichengreen, 2008: 130).

Exceptions did exist to the foregoing generalizations regarding economic growth, productivity, and modernization. While attention has been given to the institutional environment that provided the opportunities for economic growth, changes in the socioeconomic environment also "wiped out losers, and there were lots of them" (North, 1990: 136), including farmers on the frontier, shipping firms that lost comparative advantage, or laborers that suffered wage competition from surges of immigrant labor (North 1990: 136). Even with these exceptionally long periods of growth, the nineteenth-century American economy suffered from recession, panics, and defaults which brought economic dislocation for labor and farmers, generating intense class conflict that had different characteristics in different regions (Bensel, 1984; Sanders, 1999). Northern and Midwestern manufacturing saw violent labor stoppages, strikes, and lockouts, whereas the South experienced struggles between sharecroppers and tenant farmers, planters, and merchants over cotton contracts, so that agrarian class grievances were bound up with racial tensions. Populist attack on monopolies and land speculators in the West, and the appeals for government intervention in Eastern labor conflicts, were indicative of social and market cleavages that spilled over into the domain of parties, states, and courts. Increasingly, ideological and social conflicts shaped economic policy and the rules governing the market as local-oriented businesses sought to protect themselves and their communities from outside foreign interests as "smaller and weaker market interests turned against mercantile and corporate capitalists" using the legal system (Freyer, 1994: 14) which initially generated beneficial outcomes for the weaker participants in the market (Freyer, 1994: 25). For others, significant regulatory practices exercised by state and local governments created innumerable social welfare provisions providing public welfare in response to changing economic and social conditions (Novak, 1996). Yet there was also curtailment of privileges and rights, as efforts to regulate labor-market practices and conditions were legally suppressed in the late nineteenth century as contravening interstate commerce (see Gillman, 1996). The heightened conflict across enterprises, regions, ethnicity, and market position resulted in disaggregated responses as the specific economic protections sought varied with economic circumstances and conditions (Noble, 1985: 317–20). The costs of growth resulted in asymmetrical bargaining power, with those exploited having limited access to remedies.

Like the US, Europe faced rising tensions when economic conditions changed with sharp polarization in some states between business and trade unions. With two recessions in the wake of oil shocks, economic problems also beset Europe beginning in the 1970s, as wages rose faster than productivity and currency instability created mounting strain. This threatened the export-led growth model, even as the rapid expansion of trade continued to make the common market attractive for potential new members (Eichengreen, 2008: 234; Tsoukalis, 1997). Chronic payment problems, pressure on wages, increasing inflation, and declining growth were compounded by the collapse of the international monetary regime, as fluctuating exchange rates impacted European competitiveness and trade (Eichengreen, 2008: 253). The failure of Keynesian economic policy was not simply due to a particular set of macroeconomic policies, but also the failure of the postwar compact (Hooghe and Marks, 1997: 4). Although corporatist economies succeeded in restraining wage growth and limited the initial rise in unemployment, the growth of government spending generated massive public debts. While dissatisfaction with conventional politics was in evidence in some countries that sought more radical policies, generating labor unrest, the economic crisis generated different policy responses across member states (Boltho, 1982). This made achieving a common consensus at the EU level more difficult, as different conceptions about the operation of the market economy generated marked differences in macroeconomic policies. Eichengreen suggests that wage bargains in Germany generated less social conflict and strife when trade conditions deteriorated as business and labor were conscious of macroeconomic constraints and sought to promote increased productivity (Eichengreen, 2008). Italy, France, and Britain had more difficulties imposing incomes policy as grievances spilled over into industrial conflict. For political expedience, the latter opted for either generous welfare provisions or indiscriminate bail-outs of businesses through ill-conceived national industrial policies increasing public indebtedness over the long term (Hall, 1986; Pearce, Sutton, and Batchelor, 1985). Given trade deterioration and rising protectionism across Europe, the divisions over economic strategy sparked concerns about the unraveling of the European common commercial policy and the prospects for sustaining social welfare bargains (Hager, 1982; Kahler, 1985). As trade deficits soared, and Europe stagnated, attention focused on the completion of the single European market as a remedy for the problems, given that cross-border trade and capital flows made deeper integration the requisite government response to deal with their declining position at the beginning of the 1980s (Tsoukalis, 1997; Egan, 2001; Colchester and Buchanan, 1990). Whatever the failure or success of institutional arrangements and market practices, policy prescriptions reflected competing intellectual currents about how to minimize barriers to economic exchange and promote the collective benefits of an integrated market while managing the costs derived from the institutional framework that exploited specific groups that lacked sufficient bargaining power (North, 1990: 136–7).

Intergovernmental Relations

Despite their differing starting points, certain features of the American polity suggest that institutional comparisons have much more in common with the dynamics of European integration than is commonly assumed (See also McNamara, 2001a; Sbragia, 2001; Fabbrini, 2002). They have evolved through coercion and compromise as their efforts to balance territorial interests and divide policy responsibilities between constituent units at different levels has been often sharply contested. Debates over intergovernmental relations and competencies are characteristics of both political systems (McNamara, 2001a: 9; Deudney, 1995; Keohane, 1983; Schütze, 2009). In the US, the relationship between the national government and its constituent units was not well defined under the Tenth Amendment or reserved powers clause. While stating that "the powers not delegated to the United States under the

Constitution, nor prohibited to it by the States, are reserved to the States respectively, or to the people," little guidance was given as to how power is to be *shared* between the constituent units of the federal system. From this perspective, nineteenth-century American federalism would seem to offer many parallels to the ongoing debates in Europe about the division of competencies between different levels of government and across institutions. Notions and precepts of supremacy and preemption are not exclusive to the US. The European Union has also grappled with jurisdictional claims and inter-institutional conflicts, as well as adopting supremacy and other legal provisions such as direct effect that determine the rights and obligations of governments and individuals within the European polity.

Initially, American federalism was a "mosaic" in which each constituent state had its own specific policies and preferences (Scheiber 1975: 97). The result was a system in which each state promoted its own growth in competition with other states, and there was significant economic and political diversity within the American polity. This would fit with the circumstances facing the EU at its foundation with different languages, political traditions, and institutions, coupled with distinct state preferences and separate national identities. But more importantly, the Union of American States was considered atypical. Described as a "novelty and compound" in much the same way that the EU has been described by those trying to categorize a political entity that is neither a sovereign state nor intergovernmental agreement, comparisons with the early American policy, as Deudney concludes, render the EU less of an anomaly in international relations and comparative politics (Deudney, 1995; Sbragia, 1992a; Caporaso, 1996; Schmidt, 2001). The US was founded as an alternative to the hierarchically organized European Westphalian state, since it was based on formal state equality, division of power, and popular sovereignty which is further discussed later in this chapter in relation to the EU (Deudney, 1995: 193; De Tocqueville, 1969). In that respect, they may have more in common if we consider them as constituting alternative modes of governance, sovereignty, and authority, both of them have proved to have a malleable but adaptable institutional structure.

In terms of formal state equality, both the US and EU provide for equal representation for constituent units, going to extraordinary lengths to address the concerns of small states. While the US Senate allowed "equal vote to each state ... as a constitutional recognition of the portion of sovereignty remaining in individual states, and an instrument for preserving residual sovereignty,"[6] the House was based on proportionality in terms of population to satisfy the more populous states of New York and Virginia. The balance is evident in the EU as well, with formal equality in terms of membership in the Court, Commission, and Council, along with a weighted voting system that encourages coalition formation in the Council, coupled with additional weighting of votes in

Council and Parliament roughly on the basis of population (Rittberger, 2009).[7] States subsequently admitted join on an equal footing with the same powers, representation, and prerogatives as the original thirteen in the US and six in the EU. But they do not have the same discretion in constitutional design since member states vote when treaties are ratified in the EU. The European institutions may offer their opinions but they do not have direct political authority. Sbragia explains the significance of this difference:

> National governments . . . can disregard developments in one area of policy when they negotiate treaties in other areas. . . . Whereas amendments to a constitution resemble a continuing dialogue with previous political and constitutional developments, the formulation of new treaties can differentiate among whatever institutional innovations were made in previous treaties. Treaties allow for much greater discontinuity in institutional development, a disjuncture that permits national governments to control the timing and shape of institution building relatively closely. . . . The process of creating institutions by treaty maximizes the power of the executive within all national governments concerned. (Sbragia, 1992a: 273)

Even in the US, where the national Senate and state legislatures play important roles in amending the Constitution, this has been done infrequently and never in a manner to significantly alter the basic precepts of that document.

The division of competencies and efforts to determine the optimal allocation of authority is prevalent in both polities. There has been contentious debate in defining the specific concepts of republican government, federalism and states' rights in the US. Some of these American debates have been compared to that of subsidiarity in the EU where attention has focused on the proper level of government action for a number of policy issues.[8] While the trend towards devolution in the US appears to share many similar elements, "subsidiarity was, and is, an unknown expression in American political history," but it touches on issues of enduring concern to the federal balance in the US, especially when proponents of devolution believe that responsibility for the design and implementation of public policy should be returned to states if possible (Hackett, 1994; Berman, 1994: 340). However, the political terms of this debate have very different results and implications in the EU and US contexts. The basic institutions and policies of the US economic system (such as the single market) are not subject to the devolution debate and open to challenge.[9] Such is not the case in the EU where the principle of subsidiarity even in the context of the internal market is legally contested, making judicial assessments of the appropriate level of governance to deal with transaction costs and cross-border externalities as well as substantive claims of authority based on solidarity or common purpose necessary to define Community powers to integrate markets (Halberstam, 2009; Pelkmans, 2005).

Both have developed modes of differentiated integration, where competencies and functions differ across component units in the US, and across policy areas within the EU (Tarr, 2008; Dyson and Sepos, 2010). In the US, associated territories and Indian reservations are treated differently under the Constitution, with negotiated agreements between the federal government and these non-state units changing over time. They have been variously dealt with as semi-sovereign entities, dependent wards, and independent polities, where commercial transactions were neither foreign nor domestic, but subject to federal oversight (Tarr, 2008). These asymmetric relationships were devised by and imposed by the federal government, whereas in the European case, differential integration has emerged due to state choice and preference for non-inclusion or non-membership in specific policy areas such as defense, monetary union, and unrestricted border travel arrangements (Dyson and Sepos, 2010). Constitutional autonomy is expressed by state actions in the EU, choosing different rights and obligations when unitary agreement or collective action is not possible, whereas it is not a legal entitlement for component units, such as territories or tribes in the US, as these political arrangements have been devised or imposed by the federal government often with subordinate constitutional protections and rights.

The contrast between the political foundations of the US and EU is nowhere more apparent than in the development of democratic institutions and electoral practices. In the US, democratic institutions and electoral practices were far from perfect in the nineteenth century with widespread violence, fraud, and disenfranchisement (Noble, 1985; Wiebe, 1967). Groups were excluded from direct participation, as a racially and culturally bounded citizenship emerged. But the growth and integration of the American economy was tied to the impact of popular opinion, political parties, and electoral outcomes. Conflicting demands by the electorate over elements of industrialization, including the monetary system, tariff protection, and changing forms of production, led to widespread demands for social and political reform to address the impact of increased market competition (Bensel, 2000). While urban reformers sought to articulate the demands of workers seeking rudimentary welfare measures and relief, social reformers sought a more rational and ethical order imposed upon market society through non-partisan boards and commissions eschewing popular participation in decision-making. Agrarian reformers sought enhanced state power to solve problems of corporate power and monopoly, as pressure on government at all levels put party politics under considerable scrutiny as wide segments of the public expressed skepticism about the ability of the political system to respond to the multitude of demands (Noble, 1985). There were vigorous efforts to check the power of courts, reform the patronage system, and promote electoral change with direct primaries, secret ballots, popular senatorial elections, and referendums and recalls fuelling pressure for popular sovereignty during the Progressive Era.

For Europe, the integration process was one in which the "permissive consensus" enabled institutional coordination as a means of overcoming nationalism and partisanship, assuming that public support was acquiescent. The weakness of direct representation and the absence of European-wide democratic institutions meant that representational legitimacy was subordinate to that of territorial state-based representation (Marks, 1997). Within this particular context, market citizenship was important, as economic incentives shaped the protection of commerce and fashioned laws, and thus contributed to the constitutional "asymmetry" in Europe in which the social deficit has deepened due to the pursuit of market competition (Scharpf, 2002). Europe's "economic" constitution has fostered public distrust in light of changes in the socioeconomic environment, creating tensions based on state, class, region, and market position, reflecting efforts to resist, or at least be cautious about, continued market integration (Imig and Tarrow, 2001). Against this background, the debates on Europe's democratic deficit and legitimacy shortfalls has emerged, as different arguments have evolved about whether the liberal constitutional principles that apply to nation-states are evident at the European level (Follesdal and Hix, 2006; Moravcsik, 2002a, 2002b). Thus, constitutional checks and balances on the exercise of power, as well as guarantees of political rights, and competitive elections, are viewed as measures to evaluate whether the EU has a democratic deficit, and how it can, like its American counterpart, undergo political reforms to foster engagement generating a spate of proposals from enhancing (European) parliamentary power to promoting civil society and fostering citizens initiatives (Rittberger, 2009: 148–50). Such governance dilemmas resonate with earlier American efforts, as the search for a "well-regulated" society, with strong pressures to promote efficiency and order, shifting the method of making decisions by delegation to experts in order to transcend politics (Novak, 1996; Wiebe, 1967). This resonates with debates in Europe that more decisions should be taken by non-majoritarian institutions that are insulated from democratic pressures (Majone, 2006). From this perspective, the governance of the polity should be based not on democratic legitimacy but on efficient outcomes. Given mounting criticism about the democratic deficit in Europe, Americans were also concerned about the market society they wanted, and the nature of the social democratic and institutional power arrangements that resulted from "an ever closer union" (Scharpf, 1999b; Licht, 1995).

Despite the importance attached to the creation of an internal balance-of-power system and democratic norms, the American system emerged as both Republican and nationalist with a commitment to popular (albeit truncated) sovereignty (Deudney, 1995; McNamara, 2001a). The American polity—with strong expressions of individual statehood—left room for the creation of a national identity that was to be distinguished by its separation from Europe and its entangling alliances. To build such an identity, the US focused on domestic affairs including the expansion of commerce and industry, the enlargement of territorial boundaries to the West, and the settlement of the continent (Onuf, 1990). The political ideas that shaped the emerging American polity belie the fact that disagreements surfaced over whether sovereignty resided with states or people. In choosing the notion that a single sovereign power, the people of the US, provide the juridical basis of the American polity (see Madison's Federalist Papers No. 46, 1788), the framers rejected the compact theory of government based on the notion of extensive state rights. And here perhaps is where the trajectory of European political development bears watching. Though the US started out with a plurality of identities, and sought to create a polity constituted by distinct territorial units, in the same way that the EU has evolved, the expectation that integration would shift loyalties and create a distinct European identity did not materialize as expected by early integration theorists (Haas, 1958). Yet European integration has become increasingly contentious in the last two decades in terms of party competition, elections, and referendums as integration has impacted domestic politics (Hooghe and Marks, 2007, 2009). Like its American counterpart, European integration replaced local and functional boundaries, bringing pressure for more democratic governance due to concerns about the impact on cultural traditions and national identities, of changes wrought by the expansion of European policymaking (Hooghe and Marks, 2009). For some, European integration is destabilizing national identities, promoting greater political contestation, and undermining democratic processes, whereas for others, there seems to be a semblance of European identity emerging, complementing collective national identities (Risse, 2010; Hooghe and Marks, 2009; Caporaso and Kim, 2009).

War and Reconstruction

Paradoxically, war seems to be both the common element in shaping the American and European efforts at consolidation, yet also reflects the sharpest differences between them. In each case, the problem confronting state authorities was the need to revitalize and reconstruct devastated economies. War shaped the economic development of both the early American and EU polities. The mobilization of resources to finance their respective conflict left both the US and Europe heavily indebted. The recasting of political relationships after the war also served to promote a specific type of political economy. The politics of productivity and the spread of market-oriented relations were viewed as crucial to economic recovery in Europe and economic growth and development in the US. Both political systems rejected a specific economic regime and relied heavily on capital formation to propel growth and modernization.

In the case of the US, the feudal system of slavery was replaced by state-driven modernization that was uneven in effect, and favored a growing and prosperous agricultural sector outside of the plantation economy in the West and vibrant commercial and manufacturing sector in the North. In the Reconstruction era, the central state focused on creating a national economy based on the removal of regional and local trade barriers, the integration of capital markets, and the construction of a physical and financial infrastructure that was nothing less than an effort to "make a state" (Foner, 1988: 364). In Europe, the renunciation of communism was aided by political pressure and foreign assistance to promote economic recovery and stability that would restrain class conflict, maximize currency stability, and restore international trade (Maier, 1977). The conviction that Europe needed to promote a common market which would coordinate fiscal and monetary policies, harmonize economic policies, end protective restrictions, and limit government aid in order to ensure free and fair competition was nothing less than an effort to "remake states."

Although both had to overcome deep political divisions, the means used and the prospects of further integration were very different. The imperatives of the Cold War promoted reconciliation and the establishment of security guarantees in Western Europe. Although the US had dictated the terms of economic assistance, six European states had voluntarily agreed to move towards broad economic integration, and laid the foundation for Franco-German reconciliation. In the American South, the policy preferences of the North were imposed through military occupation. The decisions to go forward with a single currency, single market, and to develop strong and integrated financial markets were taken at a time of deep political division in the US. While the Civil War forced the South to remain part of the American nation, the development of the American single market was completed through the exercise of central state authority against local and state challenges (Bensel, 2000: 209). In Europe, negotiations surrounding the creation of a single market, and subsequently economic and monetary union, were agreed by and not forced upon states that were all equal participants in the discussions.[10] In the aftermath of war and Reconstruction, both the US and Europe shifted from physical occupation to a solution of embedding the major problems (Southern separatism and a resurgent Germany) within a centralized framework.

Sectionalism and Civil War

Considerable attention has been given to the economic issues that caused sectional divides and ultimately the Civil War in the United States (Stampp, 1965; Beard and Beard, 1927: 1–10). For the United States, the War of Independence was followed by the War of 1812, and culminated in the Civil War (1861–65). In its effort to achieve a collective national identity, the United States struggled to overcome internal and external challenges to its sovereignty and authority. Initially, concerned about violent disorder and revolution within the states, the solution was to create a tiered government in which states were constrained and embedded within a larger framework of governance (Deudney, 1995). States retained a militia, as well as policing and law enforcement functions, while the Constitution bound the states beyond a mere confederacy into a federal union. The US was aided by geographic isolation from European powers, which meant that they were not embroiled in aggressive territorial disputes or balance-of-power entanglements in the formative period of political development.

The major threats to the US came from sectional divisions within the domestic polity. The sectional rivalry between New England, the Mid-Atlantic States and the South intensified, during the nineteenth century, as interregional competition for control of the national political economy continued unabated (Key, 1964). As Bensel notes, "at stake for each region [was] its immediate economic welfare, and in the long run the preservation of social and political institutions which sustain(ed) the regional economy" (Bensel, 1984: 4). What emerged was a geographic division of labor between the economically advanced North and the underdeveloped Southern and Western peripheries. For the South, with its close ties to Britain, emphasis was placed on an export-oriented economy, and advocacy of low tariffs and competitive conditions in banking and shipping. The South opposed federally financed internal improvements, as the area was well supplied with rivers to carry Western produce to the South, and Southern cotton to the sea (Bruchey, 1990: 203). The agrarian economy of the South and West continually clashed with the North over tariff protection which unquestionably benefited Eastern manufacturing interests, as well as railroad companies that gained from tariff protection or exemptions with federal rail subsidies and other benefits.

These sectional rivalries also pitted Northern nationalists against Southern advocates of state rights. Concerns about disunion were high: if the Union could not convince the South to stay, then it was possible that the West would follow, and the country would be "as bad as the German states," in the words of a contemporary observer (McPherson, 1982). The rate of expansion of the US in the early nineteenth century also precipitated the crisis. While thirteen states were originally included in the early Republic, and were geographically concentrated along the Atlantic Coast, the Union had expanded by the outbreak of the Civil War to the Pacific Coast to include thirty-three states. The effect had been to redistribute power between the different sections of the Union which had important consequences for the balance of power between slave-holding and free states. While earlier compromises had depended on the concurrent inclusion of a free state and slave state, the parity became difficult to uphold as new Western free states sought to shift the balance of power and erode the position of the South. This was driven by politics but more importantly by economics—the cotton and other crops prevalent in the South, requiring slave labor, were simply not exportable to many of the Western territories now applying for statehood.

The prospect for disintegration seemed real. With Southern secession, the prospect was not simply "between one nation and two but between one nation and many" (Bensel, 1990: 62). While the balance of power had been so carefully constructed in the original constitutional design, there had been no device to prevent secession and the fears that "the dis-United States would fragment into a dozen petty, squabbling fiefdoms" grew more intense (Lincoln in McPherson, 1982). Only with the military defeat and occupation of the South was the national unity, which the constitution anticipated, finally achieved. The outcome transformed the American polity from a collective US, described in the plural, to one described in the singular (McNamara, 2001a: 5). In essence, "the old decentralized republic, in which the post office was the only agency of national government that touched the average citizen, was transformed by the crucible of war into a centralized polity that taxed people directly and created an internal revenue bureau to collect the taxes, expanded the jurisdiction of federal courts, created a national currency and a federally chartered banking system, [and] drafted men into the army" (McPherson, 1996: 64; McPherson, 1982). While the North experienced unprecedented prosperity during the Civil War, this effort had also mobilized the resources of the Union with profound economic consequences. The government had not only created a national paper currency and national banking system, but it had also generated an enormous national debt. The Civil War had restructured the way funds were loaned and borrowed (Sbragia, 1996: 106). Links to foreign lenders were weakened, and the emergence of a new class of domestic financiers fueled industrial expansion and economic development (Bensel, 1990).

Nationalism, Reconstruction, and the Cold War

The US had sought to expand national authority, create a national market, and overcome sectional divisions in the aftermath of war. A century later, several European states sought to experiment with an alternative system of governance in which the reformist impulse was deeply rooted in postwar politics. There was growing conviction among European federalists that the nation-state was no longer viable and that a new initiative might help the turbulent continent overcome its internal difficulties (Laqueur, 1992: 117). Over a period of seventy years, war had brought tremendous devastation and demonstrated the costs of nationalism. In each war, France and Germany were at the core of the disputes. The impact of the conflict on national economies was devastating with extensive damage to the industrial and agricultural sectors and the communications and transportation infrastructures, and lengthy disruptions to international trade and payments (Brusse, 1997; Eichengreen, 2008).

Like the US at the end of the Civil War, European indebtedness in the postwar period was substantial. Both the US and Europe were, to different degrees, in classically dependent situations where capital investment was concerned (see Keohane, 1983). Beginning with the American aid taken in the form of the Lend Lease Agreement in 1941, several European states had agreed to eliminate tariff and other protectionist trade barriers including the colonial preference system. This was followed by a massive injection of American aid under the Marshall Plan which transferred thirteen billion dollars in aid (De Long and Eichengreen, 1991). Known as the European recovery program, it was, in some ways, viewed as a means of forestalling the necessity for future American intervention. In forcing the European nation-states to coordinate their economic activities, the US was also driven by its own economic and strategic objectives (Maier, 1977). Without restored European economies, the US had little outlet for its huge export surplus. Fearing further economic deterioration, the US succeeded in fostering mutual dependence among West European states, and rapidly achieved its economic goals of promoting trade liberalization and currency convertibility.

The US was also concerned by the security implications of a strengthened Soviet Union and the problem of reforming and reintegrating Germany. Punitive policies that were proposed towards Germany, based on deep-seated opposition to restoring full sovereignty and to a full reindustrialization through the French Modernization Plan and the Morgenthau Plan, gave way to plans for economic recovery and gradual national rehabilitation. The net effect of Allied policies was to merge three occupied zones, cement the division of Germany, and determine German reparations. West German economic recovery proceeded rapidly, especially after the all-important currency reform of 1948. What later become known as the economic miracle resulted in a massive increase in foreign trade, low unemployment, and demand for foreign guest workers. This outcome, shaped by international developments, established a social market economy based on foreign trade and domestic demand that was conceived and nurtured by the strategic objectives of the West (Kreile, 1978: 195).

The question of German political participation was also dealt with quite differently than in the postwar South. Growing concern over Soviet expansion fostered a far greater degree of European unity than thought possible, and brought about a lasting involvement of the US in European affairs (Laqueur 1992: 108). A long-term policy of Western containment meant that an Atlantic Alliance would be necessary to bolster the military weakness of Europe, and in doing so also resolved the question of German participation. The agreement for collective defense—the North Atlantic Treaty Organization (NATO)—provided further experience in collaborative and collective decision-making, and extended membership to the new German state, as the focus on containing communism meant that a defensive equivalent to the Marshall Plan was necessary to thwart Soviet intentions and expansion. Efforts to prevent the renewal of German aggression through the creation of a European Defense Community (EDC) that would prevent German military parity failed in 1952 leading Europeans to fall back onto the 1948 Treaty of Brussels in seeking some form of defense coordination. The resulting compromise, now called the West European Union (WEU), shifted the focus towards advancing German claims for equality, and ensured a degree of intergovernmental collaboration.

The desire to minimize the potential for a revival of hostilities was also a motivating factor for European integration, as expressed in the European Coal and Steel Community (ECSC) in 1952 and the signing of the Treaty of Rome in 1957 (Dinan, 1999). Although the wars in Europe were about annexation rather than secession, the European project was envisaged as a means to bind Germany and its former enemies into a quasi-federal union. Thus, six nation-states (Belgium, France, Germany, Italy, Luxembourg, and the Netherlands) came together as equals, with the implicit idea of ceding some elements of sovereignty to a supranational authority, but without an explicit commitment to a federation or single European entity. The states began an experiment with a set of institutions and policies to promote integration and reconciliation—an experiment watched by other European neighbors that had declined to participate.[11]

Enlargement and Expansion

Enlargement obviously contributes to the expansion of interregional trade and economic diversification. The US and EU have expanded their geographic borders through annexation and accession, respectively. This has occurred in successive waves as states have applied for admission in the European context, and have been incorporated through purchase or conquest in the American context. In Europe, states must apply for membership and meet specific requirements in terms of a functioning market economy, the adoption of European laws (*acquis*), and stable democratic institutions in terms of rule of law, human rights, and democratic norms (European Council, 1993). In the US, territories must also apply for statehood since the federal government cannot unilaterally create a state. Although the promise of statehood to the new territories was premised on the assumption that the political formula and governing structures chosen for the original thirteen territories would in fact be the *acquis* offered to new territories, the constantly recurring statehood process during the nineteenth century did allow for a degree of fluidity in framing state constitutions, which in fact demonstrated changing attitudes toward government activity and practices (Still, 1936; Sbragia, 2003). The process of territorial expansion is also related to the issue of security and stability in both Europe and the US. Though the expansion of investment and markets is often a key factor driving states to seek greater association or membership, there are also defensive or strategic motives at the heart of the enlargement process (see Riker, 1964).

US Territorial Growth

Early American movement westward was concerned with the search for markets and profitable investment outlets for labor, capital, and entrepreneurship, and the drive to secure borders (Fowke, 1956: 463). The Constitution gave Congress complete and unrestricted power to dispose of any territories in the US, and for the admission of new states into the Union (Article 4 Section 3).[12] The Northwest Ordinances (1787) had established the terms under which newly settled land became part of the American political system, and stipulated that the state be accepted on the basis of equality with existing states (Atack et al., 2000: 291). Eastern states had ceded to the Union Western lands they had previously claimed under colonial charters, and "the federal government claimed land ownership over land within a territory even when that territory became a state" (Sbragia, 2001: 77; Nettels, 1962).

Initially, Congressional policy in terms of federal acquisition of public land in the Western territories was less about economic development than security concerns stemming from European conflicts and their international effects. The search for national security meant that, by the mid nineteenth century, negotiations (such as the Louisiana Purchase) and expeditions (such as Lewis and Clark) had secured almost all of the present continental boundaries of the US (Fowke, 1956: 670). Only later did Congress focus on the disposal of those lands and their settlement for economic development reasons. Beginning with the first sale of public lands, Congress sold numerous acres to large landholding companies at established minimum prices to raise money for the public treasury (Pope, 2000). Yet the commodification of the West, in which vast tracts of land were made available from the public domain, did not mean the federal government consciously guided Western development. While more land came under cultivation in the two decades after the Civil War than in the previous two centuries, and thirty-one states were created from the public domain by 1880, Western states have radically different conceptions about the impact and functions of federalism, and the effect of the federal government on their political economies.[13] Though it was politically impracticable for the national government to serve as a landlord for vast territories, the federal government did retain a significant portion of lands in Western states.

Westward expansion was also a crucial political issue that had tremendous social and economic implications. The North had originally viewed the West as a threat to the abundant labor markets and property values that were factors promoting the growth of its regional economy. While the North saw public land revenues as a means to reduce national debt, the South saw the same revenues as an alternative to higher tariffs and the prospect of extending the plantation and slave-holding economy (Fowke, 1956). A realignment of interests in the 1850s was accompanied by changes in the economic significance of the West. The surge of westward expansion and the shift from self-sufficiency to a market-oriented economy played a key role. As frontier communities developed to the point where surpluses could be produced and ties to distant markets were established through investment in transportation, the West become increasingly important in providing food staples for rapidly growing urbanized areas. For the North, the issue of ready labor and property values paled in comparison to the prospects generated by an enlarged market for goods and services. Increasingly, the development of the West was also tied to the international mobility of capital and labor. Massive emigration from Europe, aided by capital investment in railroad and inland water transportation, proved to be the catalyst in settling frontier lands (see Goodrich, 1956). For the South, railroad construction, which linked the North Atlantic Seaboard and the West, challenged the commercial primacy of Southern ports. More importantly, the promotion of free homesteads undermined the prospects for extension of the Southern political economy regime of plantation–slavery (see Gates, 1936).

Public land policy and railroad development were the twin factors responsible for the subsequent enlargement and incorporation of the West into the national economy. While the Homestead Act of 1862 was a political commitment to allow free homesteads for settlers in the West, and is often seen as the mechanism by which rapid settlement occurred, a significant portion of the public domain was placed outside of the reach of the Homestead Act through grants to states, land grants to colleges, and tribal concessions (Gates, 1936).

The policy of granting lands to railroads for construction also struck at the principle of free homesteads. Railroad construction absorbed significant investment capital, reduced transportation costs, and helped establish a vast national market. It also led to large concentrations of land ownership generating substantial agrarian discontent over land prices, railroad credits, tax exemptions, and other market distortions. Enlargement thus became embroiled in controversy that involved conflicting public and private interests and objectives (see Fowke, 1956). Throughout the nineteenth century, there was continual conflict over distribution of resources as security considerations gave way to economic exploitation of the West. Enlargement brought competing economic claims on the government, with corporate interests opposed by farmers, laborers, and freed blacks in seeking to shape the rapid expansion and development of the West. The resulting populist backlash and contentious politics in the nineteenth century is an important reference for the increasing politicization in Europe as Americans sought major changes in governance to cope with modernization, industrialization, and economic integration.

Membership and Association

While the EU has altered its territory as its boundaries have shifted due to successive enlargements, territorial differentiation persists within the European polity and its neighborhood giving rise to new strategies of territorial engagement that range from association to accession and membership. Like the US, the EU has greatly expanded the territorial reach of its polity, driven by geopolitical security concerns during the Cold War to create a Euro-Atlantic Alliance (Wallace, 2002). Although enlargement has been a central preoccupation since the Community's foundation, serving as a key element of foreign policy, it has gradually become more institutionalized through a set of rules, principles, and practices that have evolved intermittently over its history. Unlike the US, the concepts of conditionality and burden of adjustment, coupled with the formalization in the Copenhagen criteria of rules on democracy, rights, and markets (1993) have resulted in routine procedures and actions that have developed incrementally through successive enlargements over five decades (Pentland, 2009: 183–4; Schimmelfennig, 2001).

The negotiations are often protracted and contentious as the object is to influence the applicant states' domestic structure and policies, and so their legal and political systems, societies, and culture are subject to pressure to change to meet the *acquis*, the European body of accumulated laws and practices (Pentland, 2009: 181; Grabbe, 2001). Acceptance of all new members must be by unanimous vote of existing members, giving each veto power. Notwithstanding the exercise of a veto twice against Britain by France, the enlargement process has promoted domestic adjustments, and increasingly referendums on membership which have thus far resulted in only Norway rejecting the terms and conditions of entry. To date, secession has only occurred in the case of the remote and tiny population of Greenland, that had progressively been given more autonomy from Denmark, and whose impact has been marginal on the European polity.

Following the first wave of enlargement with Britain, Denmark, and Ireland, the subsequent southern enlargement, aimed at promoting democratic institutions in Portugal, Greece, and Spain after the collapse of authoritarian regimes, was to some degree a strategic calculation by member states to deepen democracy in its neighborhood, and foster explicit foreign policy goals through offering prospective membership (Vachudova, 2005; Schimmelfennig, 2009). For Austria, Sweden, and Finland, the interest in membership was partly the deepening of economic integration, which provided incentives for a stronger institutional relationship as well as the transformation in the security environment at the end of the Cold War (Schimmelfennig, 2009: 46). The internal market provided a strong pull, and the development of a consolidated market in which investment and trade might be diverted, provided a strong push towards creating contiguous economic boundaries for Nordic states (Keating, 2010: 54; Schimmelfennig, 2009: 46). As the EU became more confident about its long-term political ambitions, the prospect of remaining outside of the Community became even less attractive for those countries that had deliberately remained part of the European Free Trade Association (EFTA) and non-members in the EU (Ingebritsen, 1998).

While enlargement links with trade, development, and other goals such as border management, security concerns have remained central to enlargement. Even as the EU expanded to three neutral states, it sought to embark on eastward expansion involving up to ten Central and East European members. For the EU, this was partly driven by the need to manage the neighborhood at the end of the Cold War as the collapse of communism, and the breakup of multinational states, generated significant challenges in the region with political instability, and in some instances ethnic conflict and war (Pentland, 2009: 181; Tesser, 2003). While prospective members expressed a sense of belonging to, and a desire to be recognized as part of Europe, the need to fill the institutional vacuum pushed the EU into managing the transformation of Central and Eastern Europe (CEE), in order to stem further instability and crisis (Schimmelfennig, 2001; Sedelmeier and Grabbe, 2009; Keohane et al., 1993). Given the dependence of Central and Eastern Europe on trade and investment from the EU, the economic rationale for expansion was markedly different than that of the US, although both extended their direct influence into the new states. In the EU case, the range and pervasiveness of intervention is unprecedented across a range of policy areas, taking place before the accession negotiation even begins (Vachudova, 2005; Grabbe, 2001). Whether favoring specific institutional outcomes, protecting minorities, or shaping market economies, the EU has been able to shape economic and political governance of CEE much more than in current member states, and the conditionality requirement for accession extends the reach of the EU more deeply into domestic policymaking in CEE than it has done in the past in areas such as taxation and social policy and civil–military relations for example (Egan, 2001; Grabbe, 2001). Though requiring direct assistance, as well as "derogations" or transition periods, enlargement in Europe has restricted policy options and guided accession, in ways that seem more similar to Western expansion in the US than commonly thought. While enlargement to the Western states in the US is characterized by "asymmetrical federalism," enlargement to eastern states in Europe is currently one of "asymmetrical integration," in which acceptance of European rules and obligations takes place both simultaneously and sequentially across different chapters, and often leads to extended transition periods where the *acquis* is deferred upon accession.[14]

Enlargement has become more dynamic and ambitious, with trade liberalization and market access assuming an important place in this process. The market power of the EU has acted as a magnet for applicant states, anticipating economic growth and trade creation, extending the boundaries both physically and economically as the US absorbed Western frontiers in the nineteenth century (Onuf, 1990; Damro, 2011; cf. Fowke, 1956). Unlike the US, where the prospect of secession held out much deeper prospects of disunion, the EU has not yet faced such threats of withdrawal to destabilize the Community. European integration has become more contentious, measured by increased Euroscepticism, across member states, as partisan conflict has intensified as market integration has deepened. While the backlash against European institutions and specific policies varies over time, it seems unlikely that governments would terminate membership, although this is a salient issue in current British debates, where it has gained increased traction. Despite general discontent about the resulting pressures on national economies and identities deriving from greater political and economic integration, there are new territorial and economic cleavages emerging in Europe, with declining levels of trust and satisfaction with European integration which are highly affected by context, notably economic stagnation, increasing inequality, rising unemployment, and weak growth prospects (Hooghe and Marks, 2007, 2009). To some degree, the diverging interests of creditors and debtors in Europe that is creating this ideological and territorial cleavage between North and South is one that is familiar to those focusing on sectional conflicts in the US.

Conclusion

The political and economic conditions surrounding the single market in the US and EU suggest that helpful insights can be drawn by linking the historical development of market integration across the nineteenth and twentieth centuries, while also recognizing some distinctive features in terms of colonialism, slavery, structure of trade patterns, forms of production, and so forth. Seeing the European and American cases in terms of political development and economic integration is instructive, as they both grapple with some of the same issues of governance, legitimacy, coordination, and authority (Hooghe and Marks, 2003: 234). Even if the polity that evolves is not the traditional model of centralized and hierarchical control in the European sense of state-building, there are still some critical commonalities they face in terms of boundaries and membership, effective legal authority and enforcement of laws, along with different elements in terms of levels of coercion and control, fiscal capacity and extractive power in both political systems (Fabbrini, 2003). The power to tax, along with the power to borrow in order to meet the threat of war or other national emergency was considered essential for the viability of the young American Republic. By contrast, the lack of extractive power and monopoly over security on the part of the EU (even now) is distinctive when compared to the historical processes of state- and market-building in the US (cf. Deudney, 1995). Irrespective of whether the EU establishes a stronger security framework, however, the provision of external security and foreign economic policy issues has been a preoccupation of both polities since their foundation. Geopolitical stabilization through the maintenance of safe borders has also been a crucial factor in promoting the expansion of their respective territories (see Wallace, 2002; Marsh and Rees, 2012). Both European and American efforts were attempts to turn back the tide of war as states needed to cooperate to foster a peace settlement under profound insecurity, with the threat of external intervention, internal competition, and territorial and partisan cleavages (Deudney, 1995).

Equally significant are the contested nature of political authority and the constraints of coordinating multiple jurisdictions that often produced a decentralized and competitive economic structure (cf. Goldstein, 1997; Hooghe and Marks, 2003: 239). Struggles over the balance between different levels of government were characteristic features of both polities. Certain differences in terms of instruments of representation or popular sovereignty, consent and representation between the EU and US as political systems are readily apparent, although both have struggled to create "member states" and with it a sense of common identity as compared to local, regional, and national identities. In both cases, protecting borders, extending territories, expanding markets, and dealing with economic diversity generated new institutional ideas. The following chapter focuses on the causal conditions that promote the consolidation of distinct economies into a larger economic unit, and the actual regulatory tools and organizational strategies that turn this into a reality. This is especially timely as the financial and economic crisis provides unprecedented challenges for the single market and economic governance in Europe.

Notes

1. See the Single European Act (1987), Maastricht Treaty (1993), Amsterdam Treaty (1999), Nice Treaty (2003), and Treaty of Lisbon (2009).
2. Not until the Sixteenth Amendment passed in 1916 did the emphasis on intergovernmental transfers emerge in its modern form with the use of taxing and spending powers to advance national policies. The Sixteenth Amendment provides that the Congress shall have power to lay and collect taxes on incomes, from whatever source derived, without apportionment among the several states, and without regard to any census or enumeration.
3. Henning and Kessler (2012) argue that the balanced-budget rules and constitutional debt limitations of US states operate differently than that envisaged in the eurozone and that stabilizing banking systems is federal in US whereas in Europe bank rescues and recapitalization are still national as harmonization of banking regulations is still incomplete.
4. North stresses the role of agricultural exports in providing the initial key take off for the growth of the colonies during the first half of the nineteenth century (see North, 1966).
5. Government spending on goods and services in the postwar period amounted to about 15% of GNP, and transfers and subsidies about 20% of GNP see Maddison (1976).
6. James, Madison, Federalist Papers No. 62.
7. The voting procedure is based on three conditions: a) majority of states; b) weighted voting system with qualified majority voting; and c) majority support based on population. The new "double majority" rule is comprised of a) 55% of the member states vote in favor, b) 65% of the total population, and c) a blocking majority must include at least four members representing 35% of the population of the EU.
8. Subsidiarity was included in the Maastricht Treaty as follows: "In areas which do not fall within its exclusive competence, the Community shall take action ... only if and in so far as the objectives ... cannot be sufficiently achieved by the Member States and can therefore ... be better achieved by the Community."
9. This is not to deny the role of devolution in the US where the role of policy innovation by states, allows local preferences to often prevail and become models for the federal level. See Gray (1973); Walker (1969).

10. I am grateful to McNamara (2001a) for this point.
11. EFTA was an alternative form championed by Britain and included Austria, Britain, Denmark, Norway, Portugal, and Sweden.
12. Article IV, Section 3 of the Constitution, in empowering Congress to admit new states to the Union, implicitly allows Congress to establish the conditions under which states will be admitted.
13. I am grateful for Alberta Sbragia for this point.
14. The term is taken from Sbragia (1992a).

3

Market Dynamics and Integration

The Intersection of Law, Politics, and Markets

Few could imagine the economic, political and social changes that would result from the transformation of small, fragmented economies to larger economic units in the US and Europe. Their respective developments offer important and sometimes complementary interpretations of the political dynamics and challenges of market-building. In the US, changes in economic organization challenged the legal precepts by which the public and private sector operated, and generated both support for and opposition to the reorganization of economic life and rise of a national economy. Though production, investment, and trade increased throughout the nineteenth century, the industrial economy produced greater economic inequalities and regional disparities as the US consolidated into a national market. As Europe faces a deep economic crisis, with growing income inequality, rising unemployment, and a backlash against further market integration, increased attention is placed on identifying particular factors that provide insights into how the crises developed, and whether we can learn "policy lessons" from other periods to stabilize markets (Mattihjs, 2013; Eichengreen and O'Rourke, 2010; Henning and Kessler, 2012).

As Europe confronts mass protest and reaction to budget constraints and ongoing economic crises, multiple comparisons can be made to the turbulence in the late nineteenth century in the US, which was also a period of social ferment, with injunctions, strikes, and pitched battles over labor rights and working conditions (Robertson, 2000; Sanders, 1999). Despite similar fears about effects of foreign labor on wage rates, wage convergence took place within some parts of the US during the nineteenth century, and unemployment was relatively widespread, while in Europe today unemployment is concentrated on the least skilled, youngest, and non-white segments of the labor force (King and Rueda, 2008; Rosenbloom, 1996). In Europe, the current two-tier labor market in which some workers are highly vulnerable to economic fluctuations, while others are insulated from economic shocks, differs from the US experience where a system of property rights over labor had long-term implications for economic development (Wright, 1978). The two-tier labor market in the US between the South and North resulted in distinctive labor market regimes for decades. The largely isolated labor-market regime in the American South differed from the more geographically integrated Northeast and Midwestern regions, in terms of technological innovation, legal framework, and rising volume of European immigration that provided a continuous labor supply (Rosenbloom and Sundstrom, 2009: 14–15; Rosenbloom, 1996).

Both the US and EU have faced recurring crisis and dislocation stemming from market integration. They have addressed the compound problems of anonymity, complexity, and concentrations of power through government action (Carstensen, No Date). Each of these problems has threatened to derail the consolidation of markets, requiring governments at different levels to articulate answers and preserve market integration, which has often had unintended effects on corporate structure, competition, and the market itself (Weingast, 1995). The growth of market size, scope, and complexity has created challenges as commercial transactions have increased in terms of frequency and rapidity, and often over greater distance, creating problems of anonymity for consumers in terms of knowledge of those providing goods and services. Many processing, distribution, and production networks are distant from local consumption, generating a greater need for market surveillance.

As products and services have become increasingly complex, the result has been greater levels of government regulation to guarantee consumer confidence and to preserve trust in markets. Without such guarantees, markets may falter. However, the corresponding urbanization, industrialization, outsourcing, and mass production also results in increased dependence on others, so that governments are expected to provide assurances about quality, reliability, and safety through a raft of laws, regulations, and standards that are reciprocal or mutually equivalent to generate cross-border trade and transactions. Consolidation of markets has raised additional challenges created by concentrations of power, fostering monopolies in certain industries and services, with efforts to assert public control through commissions, agencies, and nationalization efforts. Governments either create a corresponding public concentration of power, seeking to control private power with government regulations or nationalization, or promote the breakup of monopolies, the restructuring of industries, and the facilitation of new market entrants.

Understanding the evolution of market integration in both the American and European contexts has generated divergent explanations among historians, economists, lawyers, and political scientists. Often this research has focused on different elements of market integration, to illustrate the substance, impact, and enforcement of rules in fostering integrated labor, services, goods, and capital markets, as well as the origins, institutions, workings, and even desirability and benefits of a single market (Kox and Lejour, 2005; Pelkmans, 2010; Mustelli and Pelkmans, 2013a; Anderson, 2012). Without neglecting the role of the judiciary in American and European governance, legal historians have focused on legal ideas and their subsequent reception, as well as the role of administrative rule-making to shed light on the dynamics of market integration (Lindseth, 2010; Davies, 2012; Hurst, 1971, 1982; Boerger-de Smedt, 2012). For economists, the emphasis has been primarily on the effects on trade in goods, and the resulting effects of market integration on competition, price convergence, and productivity (Scitovsky, 1956; Buiges et al., 1990; Notaro, 2011). In contrast to the attention given to both product and financial market integration, the emergence of an integrated labor market has been relatively neglected in both the US and European context. And the internal market in services has not yet contributed much to the European economy because of the differences and levels of national regulations, so that research has lagged behind that for trade in goods (Kox and Lejour, 2005; Kox et al., 2004). As the eurozone states are preoccupied with promoting growth, economists focus on service productivity and dealing with the anticompetitive nature of services markets as a means of boosting growth (Mustelli and Pelkmans, 2013a). The closest historical parallel is Williamson and O'Rourke's analysis of international economic integration where the implementation of improved transport technology aided commodity trade as transport costs fell, and capital and labor flowed across national borders in unprecedented quantities in the late nineteenth century, especially to the US (O'Rourke and Williamson, 1999).

For political scientists, both the US and EU have faced the constraining effects of national identity on integration, with political discontent emerging over immigration, emerging out of a mix of perceived economic effects on wage rates, and growing nativist sentiments leading to specific constraints on labor mobility directed against particular ethnic groups or nationalities. Thus, the US case anticipated many of the problems experienced by European efforts to deal with and respond to changing global conditions, including continuing challenges arising from contradictory pressures for protectionism and liberalization of markets, and differing demands arising from public policy and business strategy. Rather than assess the costs and benefits of market integration, the goal in this chapter is to focus on the explanations and concepts derived from scholars of American Political Development and European integration, and then highlight the mechanisms used to promote interstate economic cooperation and market consolidation. This complements earlier chapters focusing on the contextual background for market consolidation and integration in the US and European cases.

In reviewing the historiography of market evolution in both contexts, four important driving factors seem to resonate in terms of the causes, content, and timing of market integration: (1) the expansion of regulatory authority, (2) the constitutionalization of law, (3) the mobilization for and expansion of collective and individual rights, leading to (4) contested and often conflicting redistributive and regulatory goals (Novak, 2008; Weiler, 1981: Imig and Tarrow, 2001; Keller, 1977; Egan, 2013; Majone, 1996a, 1999). The debates among American legal and business historians explaining the conditions for economic development have much in common with those in Europe. Both highlight the relationship between law and markets, the entrepreneurial energy to enhance the productive power of the economy, and the mobilization of interests in shaping market integration. Though there is a diverse body of scholarship on the conditions driving market integration, it has not produced a dominant explanation but rather different conceptual and empirical explanations. Although market integration generates obligations on the state to manage competition and enforce rules and laws, exogenous pressures from societal actors who both share and oppose the substantive objectives of enhanced market coordination, reduction of trade barriers, and facilitating market access are also important in shaping the governance patterns that emerge.

Law and Markets: Judicial Activism and Economic Order

The instrumentality of law in creating and regulating the conditions for the consolidation of the market economy is widely recognized by scholars from diverse standpoints. As Novak concludes, "whether it is the so-called 'commonwealth historians' who have demonstrated the active role of law in the nineteenth-century state in establishing, promoting, and regulating the socioeconomic infrastructure through public works, subsidization, corporate charters, public lands policies, eminent domain, mixed enterprises, and police power" (Novak, No Date: 15; Scheiber, 1981, Lively, 1955; Horwitz, 1977) or the seminal work by European constitutional lawyers focused on the transformation of EU jurisprudence to promote greater market integration through a doctrinally bold set of rulings (Weiler, 1991; Stein, 1981; Alter, 2010; cf. Rasmussen, 2013), markets are profoundly dependent on the legal order (Hurst, 1982). The conscious jurisprudence fostered by the Court of Justice, outlined by the new legal historians in the EU matches the US where the prolific instrumental role of public and private law generated new conceptions of sovereignty and administration that created a foundational legal revolution (Weiler, 1981; Novak, No Date). A stream of case law served to challenge state protectionism in the US and subsequently the EU (McCurdy, 1978; Freyer,

1979; Egan, 2001; Caporaso and Stone Sweet, 1998). The Supreme Court had only 253 cases pending before it in 1850, but in 1890 the docket had swollen to an unmanageable 1,800 appellate cases, necessitating judicial reform and expansion (Frankfurter and Landis 1928: 60 and 86 as quoted in Novak, No Date; Gillman, 2002). The European Court of Justice generated a similar explosion in preliminary rulings, with more than 5,425 cases between 1961 and 2005, leading to the creation of more flexible compositions of judicial hearings through chambers or panels (see Kelemen, 2011; Caporaso and Stone Sweet, 1998).

Acting when other institutions were unable or unwilling to address trade barriers and commercial restrictions, Shapiro argues that courts have played a key role in shaping ideas about the market and in the expansion of market relationships (Shapiro, 1968). They have played a strong role in shaping the boundaries between national, local, and regional markets, though the transition was gradual and uneven, and necessitated changes in legal and constitutional doctrines in response to the transformation of the economy. This was not inevitable, nor was it accepted without a degree of political protest as efforts to constrain perceived court activism and resist rulings frequently occurred (Freyer 1994; 1979; Goldstein, 1997; Alter, 1998). If the courts were to exert their influence, they would have to assert their legitimacy as the arbiter of disputes between different governments, and reconcile acceptance of federal authority with local interests and preferences (Weiler, 1991).

In the US, the Court sought to promote a national market through negative rather than affirmative action, by applying a judicially enforceable restriction on state legislation that explicitly or by effect discriminated against interstate commerce, or put an undue burden on such commerce. The Court sought to distinguish between permissible and impermissible regulations, and to delineate trade into interstate and local components (Bensel, 1990: 327; Kommers and Waelbroeck, 1985). Constant adjudication was required to police the boundaries, and the constitutional jurisprudence that emerged saw the Court engaged in interpretative techniques and sometimes esoteric statutory construction (Frankfurter, 1937: 20). Consequently, constraints on state economic activity produced some uneven effects. Though curbing state discriminatory practices, the Court also allowed states to play an active role in regulating the economy by expanding their reserve powers. As a result, public rights doctrines existed alongside private vested rights in shaping the operation of the market. This meant that the prerogative of deciding what constituted public interest belonged to the courts. The effect was to enhance judicial activity in the construction and maintenance of the national market, although the doctrines and principles articulated by the courts were not uniform, constantly challenged, and revised in response to changing terms of trade. The Supreme Court struck down numerous clauses regulating business, drawing on the newly adopted Fourteenth Amendment in 1868 to transform the original intent of the amendment to protect Southern blacks from being deprived of "life, liberty or property without due process of law" into one in which any regulation that prevented a person or corporation from earning a reasonable return on invested capital was unconstitutional (Bensel, 2000: 334). The extension of such economic rights, did not parallel the extension of market and social rights that some have argued and advocated for in the EU, but rather allowed corporations to challenge state regulatory policies across a spectrum of constitutional provisions.

The relationship between the Supreme Court and American capitalism is crucial in understanding the formation of a national economy (Gillman, 1996). While the Court has come to occupy a central position in determining the appropriate constitutional limits of government intervention in the market, its systematic pragmatic bias in promoting the productive power of the economy meant that nineteenth-century litigation generated important tensions in the structure and scope of American governance (Hurst, 1964). While the Court determined the scope of state and federal regulatory powers, the doctrines that emerged were not always consistent nor were they always supportive of free trade at the expense of states' rights. The Court was sensitive to the political reality of the time, and sought to navigate a path that maintained its political legitimacy by recognizing local interests and pressures. This included the nineteenth-century notion of dual sovereignty that tended to undercut the strong centralizing pressures implicit in the notion of an ever closer union (Kommers and Waelbroeck, 1985: 169). However, the law faced new challenges in the late nineteenth century with the consolidation of business enterprises, and the decisions regarding regulation and anti-trust shifted towards consideration of competition. Much litigation ensued, reflecting the changing nature of commerce that forced the legal system to grapple with the evolving jurisdictional power of different governments to regulate markets and the challenges that nationalization posed to inherited doctrines and their premises (see also Scheiber, 1997: 861).

The means by which European law has shaped the dynamics of the single market and affirmed the saliency of legal doctrines in shaping the polity and economy has much in common with the American experience. The European Court of Justice, armed with a substantive interpretation of the treaty provisions, forged new doctrines that both liberated the market and transformed the way in which markets are regulated (Maduro, 1997, 1998, 2010). While there are more numerous provisions in the European treaty with regard to prohibiting intra-community trade compared to the American Constitution, there are also legitimate exceptions and derogations available to member states invoking them as a means of retaining national regulations. The Court sought to distinguish between arbitrary discrimination and protectionist practices from legitimate non-discriminatory legislation. This legal practice, known as the test of proportionality in Europe, meant that the Court often engaged in what American scholars called a balancing standard, and thus evaluated the degree to which state regulations discriminated on the basis of the least restrictive means possible (Shapiro, 1992; Egan, 2001).

Like the US, the EU has often experienced clashes over the reserved powers of constituent units. The territorial balance is not judicially fixed, since the Court has been concerned about preserving regional and local diversity while constructing a more centralized economic order. Some of the same tensions are also evident in the decisions of the European Court of Justice. Although it did not have the same federal characteristics or enumerated powers of the American Constitution, the Court has proceeded from its fragile jurisdictional base and "arrogated to itself the ultimate authority to draw the line between Community law and national law" (Stein, 1981: 1). Moreover, it has established and obtained acceptance of the broad principle of direct integration of Community law into the national orders of the member states and of the supremacy of Community law within its limited but expanded area of competence, thereby promoting judicial review and legally extending authority over national actions (Stein, 1981; Alter, 1998; Alter 2009; Weiler, 1991). The ECJ subsequently moved closer to the American constitutional system, by supplying national courts with stronger guarantees for the effectiveness of European law through the doctrines of indirect effect and government liability, making member states liable for damages for non-compliance with European law (Kelemen, 2011). According to Alter, the Court at times chooses to play, "a more minimalist role, interpreting the law narrowly," especially if there is not broad social or political support (Alter, 2010: 1). Thus, the law responds to the political context in which it operates, can redistribute social costs and benefits, and can be activated by others to deal with contestation over different objectives as the scope of economic activities has widened and deepened.

Regulation and Interests: Mobilization and Business Pressure

Another major factor in promoting the American and European single market was the pressure from business to create the conditions conducive to economic growth and industrial expansion. While neofunctionalist scholars predicted that the mobilization of interest groups, social movements, and subnational governments would mobilize to advance their interests in the European context, historians have highlighted how this transnational mobilization emerged in different sectors in the formative period of integration (Kaiser and Henrik, 2013; Kaiser et al., 2010). Such action in support of market integration mirrors the US, where big business sought to overcome barriers to trade that restricted their freedom of movement through advocating for the uniformity of rules, laws, and standards (Nugent, 2009). In both cases, interest groups organized their efforts at the national and regional level, and engaged in effective lobbying strategies to promote the importance of the single market and common commercial practices, uniformity, and standardization.

Although such action is well known in contemporary politics, the growth of commercial and trade associations, chambers of commerce, and other professional associations really began in the late nineteenth century, providing an important example of societal action in promoting substantive objectives of market integration. Seeking changes in government policy, the costs of creating such a national organization at the time were significant (Davis and North, 1971). Businesses adopted a diversity of political strategies and used multiple channels of influence to seek federal laws to replace the diverse and often discriminatory state laws that impeded interstate trade, although they faced competing industrial demands for protection during economic downturns, as well as from industries under severe pressure from foreign competition (Mansfield and Busch, 1995: 727; Coen, 1997; Woll, 2008; Freyer, 1979; Nugent, 2009). Many American businesses, frustrated by continued protectionism, formed a variety of trade and business associations to lobby for and assist the passage of particular legislation in the post-Civil War period. Among the most important targets were discriminatory licensing laws and commercial practices that favored in-state producers and creditors. The combination of business pressure for legislative intervention and redress picked up in the second half of the nineteenth century as laws regulating business increased dramatically. Sales associations, wholesalers, and boards of trade generated grassroots support to tackle interstate barriers that were becoming increasingly ill-suited to an integrating economy. But mobilization works both ways as concerns that new marketing methods and traveling salesmen would undermine traditional local sales generated a wave of legislative intervention and restrictions, both at the municipal and state level (Hollander, 1964). Restrictive laws were also tied to concerns about spreading abolitionist sentiment, diminishing tax revenues, and threatening local suppliers. To promote cross-border sales, US companies also engaged in "forum shopping" in which the politics of legal jurisdiction played a key role. Since the substantive laws of the states differed, this required federal courts to prefer certain rules over others in such cases as routine commercial contracts and property rights, as well as such controversial issues as slave-trade and bank oversight. The extent to which judges exercised their federal jurisdiction defined the opportunity for lawyers and their business clients to promote the relationship between law and a growing national market as federal courts offered a forum for greater predictability and uniformity for business transactions (Freyer, 1992: 543–4, 1994).

Major companies exerted pressure for uniform legal regulation; they repeatedly challenged state law in the courts and were often caught in a crossfire of retaliatory state laws as they argued that many statutes were used to maintain the competitive position of local producers (Keller, 1963; Whitney, 1885).

American business in the nineteenth century also engaged in collective efforts to shape markets through concerted action. For railroads, this involved a number of strategies including informal agreements to determine prices, allocate markets, and control production using pools, trusts, and intercompany cooperation. Shippers responded to such collusive practices by filing complaints, promoting alternative transportation routes, and lobbying for improvements in inland waterways to promote viable commercial river traffic routes. Though these concerted practices generated public opposition and were subsequently abandoned in the face of legal challenges, businesses sought to exercise their influence and shape public opinion by hiring professional public relations staff to counteract negative attitudes towards big business (Hays, 1995: 74). Similarly, trade unions, merchant associations, and farm cooperatives sought to mobilize and advocate for their particular interests. In many instances, they sought relief through government intervention to promote their economic interest or conversely seek protection from the effect of foreign competition, industrialization, or economic change (Bensel, 2000: 208, 233–4).

Substantial political opposition came from those threatened by increased market competition, with farmers voicing populist criticisms and demands for redress about bankers and railroads, state politicians resisting federal control and encroachment, and declining industries seeking protectionism through tariffs and other controls (Bensel, 2000; cf. Irwin, 2001).[1] Professionals such as doctors and lawyers organized themselves in the nineteenth century to establish specific standards and reduce fraudulent practices to deal with what they perceived as ruinous competition (Licht, 1995: 194). These new professional societies sought to push government to tighten statutory provisions, resulting in the vesting of regulatory authority in non-governmental organizations. Such self-regulation by these societies limited access to their ranks and subsequently entrenched their privileged new professional position in the marketplace (Balleisen, 2009).

In Europe, transnational political activities of firms were initially rather limited, as they channeled their demands through national federations (Kaiser et al., 2010). While national federations did not actively lobby for the creation of a single market, often reacting defensively to specific policy initiatives, the persistence of such diffuse national interests made European-wide coordination difficult (Sidjanski, 1967; Greenwood and Aspinwall, 1998; Pollack, 1997; Gorges, 1996: 63). When impacted by specific trade barriers, large firms often enlisted the assistance of national governments to exert pressure on another member state. Small businesses threatened by transnational production and collaboration often "requested protection, sometimes vociferously, in parliamentary committees, professional organizations, and from national government agencies" (Haas, 1958; Feld, 1970: 90–3). Throughout the early period of integration business networks often sought specific concessions, based on perceived business needs, including advocating for uniform standards, like their American counterparts (Kaiser, et al., 2010). In the mid 1970s, multinational businesses and particularly American firms began to press for the removal of barriers and constraints that impacted their ability to operate effectively across borders (Feld, 1970: 219). Part of this stemmed from regulatory actions related to European-wide collective bargaining that would allow greater scrutiny of management decisions, as well as recognition among European companies that nationally federated companies were inefficient in practice (Cowles, 1995; Egan, 2001). Later, firms lobbied for the harmonization of fiscal policies and technical standards, the creation of a European company statute, and the liberal application of competition laws to allow for increased business collaboration through financial investment, joint ventures, and strategic alliances that were not constrained by national market barriers (Feld, 1970). Firms also opted for legal action to address trade barriers that were not effectively addressed through legislative action by European institutions, using the preliminary reference procedure to rule on the validity of national barriers to free movement (Fligstein and Stone Sweet, 2002).

While historians highlight business networks in shaping policy choices in the formative period of integration, political scientists focus on the business lobbying efforts that increased dramatically in the 1980s, in response to the changing institutional environment in Europe and passage of the Single European Act and 1992 program, as European companies began arguing for unification of fragmented markets in the EC to be able to compete globally (Sandholtz and Zysman, 1989: 206; Mazey and Richardson, 1993: 3–5). For Cowles, the European Round Table (ERT) was critical, focusing specifically on the removal of non-tariff barriers, promoting new industrial strategies, and creating a European regulatory framework to compete successfully in a global market (Cowles, 1995). More formal industrial forums in areas such as telecommunications, energy, and transport also emerged to promote greater innovation and competitiveness (Coen, 1997; Cowles, 1995). These industrial forums did not run into the same problems of collusion as their American counterparts, as European business in the postwar period had found it harder to sustain cartels in face of American pressure, and had gradually accepted a more competitive environment where a common market would be undermined by private restrictive practices (Rollings and Moguen-Toursel, 2012; Brusse and Griffiths, 1997). Business mobilization in both cases was, however, backed by material resources providing opportunities for influence, in sharp contrast to the more diffuse consumer and environmental interests that were less effectively organized and mobilized much later to press their specific interests (Pollack, 1997; Gorges, 1996: 75–7; Hays, 1995; Cowles, 1995).

What is striking in these mobilization efforts is the asymmetry between business and labor activities in both cases. In the US, as labor mobilized in the post-Civil War period, the growth of national labor organizations focused on working conditions and collective bargaining as state governments actively regulated the employment relationship. This approach differed from European unions who at the time were more engaged in the political arena and advocated for extensive state-sponsored social reforms (Hattam, 1993: 3). Labor in Europe has focused more on working conditions, collective bargaining, and social rights than European-wide political activism. At the EU level, the outcome was more in line with their American counterparts, as Streeck argues that European social policy reflects business-inspired neo-voluntarism rather than social promotion of labor demands. The resulting "new social legislation" or "industrial legislation" generated a host of statutory measures that amounted to what Majone has described in the European context as social regulation, rather than social welfare or broader social reforms (Majone, 1993). Just as European legal jurisprudence initially focused on market citizenship rather than social protection, echoing the response to industrialism in the US, both initially imposed sharp restrictions on recipients, based on a hierarchy of rights and benefits around the concept of citizenship. While the EU initially focused on social rights and benefits to European citizens excluding non-citizens, and the US imposed sharp restrictions by gender, race, and ethnicity, in terms of mobility, freedom, and property rights, this resulted in highly different rules of membership, status, and access to social provisions. Both polities have subsequently extended their safety nets well beyond the original intentions in the EU and the US through the constitutionalization of rights to include previously marginalized groups (Egan, 2013; Caporaso and Tarrow, 2009).

Regulation and Markets: From the Developmental State to the Regulatory State

A crucial feature of European and American Political Development is the role of the state in the economy. One of the most important features of nineteenth-century American economic development is the role of public capital investment at both the state and local level (Sbragia, 1996). Railroads, canals, and banks were all treated as proper areas for public enterprise, and the "internal improvements" undertaken in the US were the product of public rather than private investment, and the development of economic policy was often the product of state involvement in business enterprises (Hartz, 1955; Goodrich, 1956; Sbragia, 1996: 20). Resource allocation by governments—particularly at the state level—was aided by fierce sectional rivalries that opposed a strong role for federal government in capital investment, since it might encourage further incursions into other areas. State and municipal governments were at liberty to expand and continued to maintain an active presence in the economy through building, lending, borrowing, and regulating throughout the nineteenth century that suggested a *dirigiste* tradition (Shonfield, 1965: 303; Lively, 1955).

States were also developing a legal framework to support their economic development activities. Even with the growth of private capital, especially after the Civil War, states still exercised a degree of leverage over the private enterprise through their distribution of legal privileges and immunities, which could provide such tangible benefits as tax exemption and limited liability. The most important feature was eminent domain, with states authorizing land seizure under the guise of economic development, on the assumption that business could claim they were fulfilling a public purpose (Scheiber, 1975: 65; Merkel, 1984). Upheld by state courts, such developmental practices were a characteristic feature of early nineteenth-century American economic development. However, the institutionalization of limits to restrict state borrowing and impose debt limits, from the 1840s, was the first step in a shift in law and governmental operations (Sbragia, 1996; Dove, 2012). Initially, the developmental strategies suited the relatively decentralized character of the economy and the jurisdiction of states was congruent with decentralized promotional and regulatory powers (Scheiber, 1980a: 680; Novak, 1996). The subsequent shift towards greater centralization signaled the slow but steady enlargement of federal authority and the expansion of the jurisdiction of federal courts contributed to the growth of the American regulatory state (Scheiber, 1980a: 680). Driven by the ever-growing number of firms extending their business operations across state lines and into foreign markets (Sklar, 1988: 51), states sanctioned the rights of companies of interstate holdings and assets which then weakened state restrictions on corporate action and placed them under the commercial jurisdiction of the federal government (Sklar, 1988: 52).

As states struggled to contain and regulate the growth of large-scale national corporations, they began to develop their own anti-trust policies to promote greater control, order, and accountability of firm activities. The increased number of business failures, the problems of overproduction, and changing conceptions about property and the market in the late nineteenth century meant that jurisprudence and legislation related to the regulation of market activity and restraint of trade became increasingly contentious (Sklar, 1988: 4; Keller, 1977). The effort to bring tighter control over private sector business activities led to new federal institutions that began with the passage of the

Interstate Commerce Act covering railroad regulation in 1887 and then anti-trust regulation under the Sherman Act in 1890. Although the movement towards an administered market stabilized railroad rates, the first federal regulatory agency, the Interstate Commerce Commission, was constrained in its enforcement powers and largely irrelevant to the consolidation of the national railroad system. The effort to regulate railroads was undermined by the Supreme Court, which struck down many state and federal regulations, and effectively stripped the Interstate Commerce Commission of its authority to set rates and other issues. While cut-throat competition between rival lines and rate regulation sapped the financial strength over railroads that often went into receivership, and were reorganized into more efficient systems (Bensel, 2000: 314), the conflicted regulatory policymaking and multiplicity of rules meant that pressures for the extension of regulation were counterbalanced by pressures for its limitation (Freyer, 1994: 465).

The emergence of large industrial corporations in the late nineteenth century was even more central than railroad expansion to the expansion of the single market as the organizational revolution led to collective efforts to manage production and distribution. The concentration and integration of firms through vertical integration resulted in heavy industry consolidation that allowed companies to generate greater economies of scale through mass production and distribution. Continued pressure of falling prices forced companies to organize to regulate supply and prices. Through price agreements, and subsequently trusts, the assignment of market shares and guaranteed prices generated state, and subsequently federal law against such restraint of trade (Sklar, 1988: 34). The Sherman Anti-trust Act reflected the desire to promote competition and restrain monopoly but it failed to provide effective rules about what actually constituted restraint of trade.

Though anti-trust policy was adopted at the federal level after a long and bitter conflict, the result was more symbol than substance (Sbragia, 2001; Keller, 1981). The number of anti-trust cases brought against large firms was quite limited. However, the act was to have an enormous unexpected impact. The legislation had the paradoxical effect of making combinations of small units illegal but led other businesses to consolidate their trusts into a new form of corporate organization or holding companies that actually encouraged the swift growth of big business in manufacturing and distribution (Chandler and Salsbury, 1968). While the concern over the effects of advanced industrialism resulted in both economic and social regulations such as anti-trust policy to mitigate the effects of the market, the same regulations were used to suppress labor organizations and welfare provisions. The effort to address market competition and prevent the monopoly of trade was frequently applied to regulate and intervene in labor disputes far from the original intention of prosecuting industrial trusts and collusive business practices.

Government shifted from subsidizing enterprise activities to governing them at the end of the nineteenth century, as big business rather than central government became the dominant concern (Merkel, 1984). Regulation became the central thrust of politics, with demands by one sector of the economy that it be advanced or that another be restrained (Hays, 1995: 133). Despite efforts to extend control over large-scale business enterprises, constitutional obstacles stood in the way. The Supreme Court, which had played such a crucial role in promoting the consolidation of a national market by addressing discriminatory state practices and acting as final arbiter in these matters, opted for the same strategy with regard to regulatory policy setting. In determining that the structure and activities of a corporation came under the jurisdiction of the state that chartered it, the Court provided a serious setback to federal regulation under the Sherman Act (McCurdy, 1978; Keller, 1977). The Court interpreted the boundaries between public and private markets through such devices as substantial due process and reasonable or unreasonable restraint of trade, following a complicated pattern of anomalies and inconsistencies that advanced public rights doctrines and controls but also furthered private market transactions and freedom of contract on the other (Scheiber, 1997: 861; Sklar, 1988). This resulted in different interpretations of the meaning and impacts of legal decisions, and continuous tension between competing legal doctrines throughout the nineteenth century—an era of rapid technological change and economic integration, and one in which successive new challenges to the law and inherited doctrines shaped the governance of the economy (Scheiber, 1997: 861).

In Europe, a similar view held that the "developmental" state could act as entrepreneur, planner, and provider of services in the postwar period (Majone as quoted in Egan, 2001: 20). To promote economic growth and modernization, many states implemented "internal improvement" policies that required sustained intervention through indicative planning and industrial policy along with fiscal and monetary policies, periodic price and wage controls (Ward, 1976; Goodrich, 1956). State intervention also increased with the growth of the welfare state and the nationalization of strategic sectors and industries (Beer 1965). An intricate system of economic controls, selective incentives and credits provided advantages to domestic business, protecting them from the pressures of competition and effectively insulating markets (Shonfield, 1965; Hall, 1986).

The manipulation of macroeconomic variables to alleviate unemployment and provide public goods came under increasing strain in the 1970s and 1980s as budget deficits soared and stagflation undermined the economic management favored by member states. What may have been appropriate action in the 1950s and 1960s became increasingly problematic as the capacity of states to manage domestic economies was undermined by changes in the transformation in the international economy, the collapse of Keynesianism, and the failure of the corporatist model (Hooghe and Marks, 1997). As states struggled to contain import restrictions, with continued recourse to discriminatory trade practices in the 1970s and early 1980s, there was a "temptation to replace national *dirigisme* by its supranational equivalent" (Majone, 1998: 96). This encouraged efforts to promote European-wide industrial activity and economic growth through a comprehensive industrial policy, aimed at broadening the workings of the single market, coordinating economic policies, and promoting techno- logical development (European Commission, 1972). But it reflected conflicting goals between promotion of competition and industrial reorganization and intervention, reflecting the absence of any discernible convergence in national industrial policies (Hodges, 1983: 268–9). While European industrial adjustment was carried out in specific crisis sectors such as steel and textiles, states curtailed their developmental and interventionist practices and replaced them with pol- icies of retrenchment aimed at shedding public burdens. States opted for struc- tural reforms such as privatization, deregulation, and devolution, increasingly shifting from subsidizing business activities to governing them.

There was no comparable public concern over the trust/monopoly question that had been evident in the US. Even though the Treaty provided for rules to prevent distortions to competition within the single market, as well as any distortions resulting from special provisions and exclusive rights for state- owned enterprises, the need for rigorous application of competition rules remained far short of treaty objectives (Hodges, 1983; McGowan, 2000; Smith, 2005). This was often justified on the basis that such practices, "pro- tected jobs, fostered innovation and prevented damaging competition" (McGowan, 2000: 118). As states struggled to find effective substitutes for domestic rules on market concentrations resulting from mergers and strategic alliances, the effort to regulate corporate activity shifted to the European level, strengthened by influential court decisions. Growing concern among firms about multiple jurisdictions meant that firms pressured for greater European regulatory authority to provide a single set of rules to govern the internal market, and thereby reduce transaction costs (Majone, 1996a: 69). Unlike the American experience, where the Court infringed on the expansion of regula- tory competencies by states, particularly in relation to anti-trust policies, the ECJ reinforced the activist stance of the European Commission allowing it to play a stronger role in determining the competition criteria of the single market (McGowan, 2000; Schmidt, 2008). Competition policy emerged as an important mechanism for extending the single market into areas that were hitherto protected from competition under the premise of broad public interest goals (Schmidt, 2008; Nicolaïdis and Schmidt, 2007). Opening up utilities, transport, banking, and media markets to greater competition through liberalization is not dissimilar to pressures and developments in the

US (see Scheiber, 1975; McGowan, 2000). The growing presence and salience of EU legislation for the provision of public services has led to the emergence of regulatory agencies, driven partly by the privatization of activities formerly undertaken through state ownership. It is also a response to problems that cannot be resolved exclusively by member states through intergovernmental cooperation, since it is often difficult to know if there is a credible commitment and that agreements are properly enforced (Majone, 1995; Lodge, 2008). As the European effort follows the American path, such regulatory emulation through sector-specific agencies has "partially displac(ed) an earlier emphasis on public ownership, public subsidies and directly provided services" (Hood et al., 1999: 3) by providing a further extension of the state through new regulatory instruments and mechanisms (Lodge, 2008; Majone, 1997, 2009).

Although arguably the American regulatory state was aimed at curtailing corporate power at its inception, and subsequently dealing with market externalities, making its origins somewhat different, it too shifted from state to federal level to foster better compliance and ensure credible commitments, similar to Europe where national regulators do not always take account of the repercussions of their policy choices for the single market (Majone, 1995). Both polities faced some similar dilemmas. Each has sought to recognize the importance of services having a public interest as requiring special treatment, as the US with its emphasis on contracts, private property, and economic freedoms balances notions of the public interest and a sense of community obligation through law, corresponding to public services connotations in Europe. American market ideology has alternatively endorsed both private property rights and public intervention as part of its legal and political history in much the same way that Europe has also dealt with and accommodated different models of capitalism to deal with problems of complexity, dependency, and ensuring credible commitments (Scheiber, 1973, 1981; Majone, 1996a; Lodge, 2008). In providing rules and the means for their enforcement, states reduce the problems of predatory or rent-seeking behavior (Fligstein and Stone Sweet, 2002: 1207). Both polities have shifted from creating an appropriate environment for business transactions and economic development to addressing a variety of challenges arising from market integration, monitoring public and private actions to regulate and govern markets.

Regulation and Compensation: Unequal Development and Distributive Politics

The politics of side-payments and distributive bargains are important in understanding how political support for certain public policies was mobilized in both the US and EU cases. Substantial differences among regions in terms of population growth, urbanization, and agricultural developments were a characteristic feature of the American economy in the nineteenth century (Schmidt, 1939; North, 1966). Although the growth rate increased rapidly for a long period, chiefly a result of the expansion of factors of production (Gallman, 2000), the Civil War and its aftermath negatively impacted growth as shares in world trade fell dramatically and the near-term indebtedness of the American economy increased substantially (Lipsey, 2000: 725; cf. North, 1966). On the whole, through most of the nineteenth century per capita incomes were high, savings and investment increased, and the reorganization of industry in response to technological developments contributed to economic growth. Yet the nineteenth century was also a period of increasing inequality that generated political struggles over the distribution of income and wealth (Pope, 2000). While providing opportunities for many to enter, relocate, and shift occupations, it also generated regional battles over slavery and tariff policy, as well as conflicts over land distribution, and rising discontent of farmers against the perceived threats from big business. While struggles over the economic effects of land policy and settlement, slavery, tariff policy, and the gold standard were especially prominent, the transfer of resources and compensation mechanisms to generate political support for the integration of a national economy targeted certain interests and constituencies at the expense of others.

In the US, debate over tariffs reflected party divisions (Bensel, 2000). Raw materials and food represented a large portion of US exports at the beginning of the nineteenth century. The export of cotton in particular meant that Southern states depended heavily on exports and free trade, while the Northern states were import dependent and more favorable to protectionist legislation. Setting tariff rates was thus the subject of intense and often bitter Congressional debate (Engerman and Sokoloff, 2000: 399). Though impacting only a few industries, notably cotton, steel, and iron, the general trend towards increased tariffs in the early part of the nineteenth century generated a backlash and subsequent compromise towards Southerners until the outbreak of the Civil War (Engerman and Sokoloff, 2000: 399). The revenue needs of the war generated sharp increases in tariffs, and the breadth of imports subject to tariffs increased over the course of the nineteenth century. Since the benefits conferred on those manufacturers exposed to competition were not politically strong enough to sustain the tariff, it was broadened to selective agricultural products (Bensel, 2000: 457). The revenue from tariffs also provided a vast pension scheme for union veterans so that protectionism and pensions provided a formidable coalition of interests as benefits were distributed to a small number of industries, sectors, and regions (Bensel, 2000: 459). Distributing benefits to almost every Northern and Western district at the expense of the South, the demands for tariff protection generated thousands of petitions whenever tariff revision became a serious possibility (Bensel, 2000: 459). While the terms of trade were set against the agricultural interests of the South and West, substantial side-payments to unrelated groups such as sheep farmers and union veterans, along with auxiliary policies, softened the impact of protectionism and served to reinforce the relationship between nationalism and tariff protection (Bensel, 2000: 507; Skocpol, 1992).

The tariff was marginal in economic terms compared to the gold standard which was crucial in stabilizing exchange rates, and thus encouraging foreign investment and domestic profits in the industrial sector (Bensel, 2000: 516). Yet the fight over the currency, in particular the relative worth of gold, bimetallism, and silver, generated substantial political conflict (Bensel, 2000; Bryan, 1896). While denominating the dollar in gold meant that the government could appear independent from Britain, it also carried the economic advantage that adherence to the gold standard would bring in integrating the US into foreign capital markets. This enhanced American financial credibility by enabling federal, state, and local bonds to be purchased overseas. Adherence to such a conservative monetary policy generated conflict between those who wanted silver or paper substitutes to inflate the dollar against those who supported gold as a means of continued industrial expansion. The impact of the gold standard clearly benefited the bondholders, wealthy creditors, and capital-exporting Northeast region, who viewed the development of financial markets as crucial for industrial growth. In the case of the gold standard, there were no corresponding side-payments to unrelated groups. Having much less popular appeal, the gold standard was the most politically vulnerable policy, since it generated popular opposition. Controls over banking, the money supply, and the gold standard influenced prices, borrowing terms, and the availability of funds (Engerman and Sokoloff, 2000: 391).

Not surprisingly, different positions on the gold standard reflected differences in interregional capital flows, with the resulting clash between debtors and creditors figuring strongly. For much of the economy deflation was not problematic; for debtors, especially farmers, deflation increased the costs and terms of repayment on mortgages (Rockoff, 2000). With falling commodity prices and spiraling debts only compounding their financial distress, opposition to the gold standard increased. The powerful silver mining interests in the West argued that there was an inadequate money supply in circulation. Third party agrarian movements, such as the Grangers in the Midwest, the Farmers Alliance in the South and Midwest, and the Populists of the Great Plains and Far West protested the effects of economic policies on agricultural development. While regional differences in terms of output and specialization in agriculture clearly emerged, the protest movements representing farmers with long-term mortgages opposed the gold currency standard, in addition to wanting greater regulation of corporations, and greater government intervention in the marketing of commodities, through commodity exchanges and set transportation rates (Kirkland, 1956). Their efforts to gain relief through a variety of measures, including, ironically, the establishment of farming trusts and holding companies to counter industrial trusts, received limited attention. The lack of credence given to their demands coupled with the absence of federal agricultural policy meant that American agriculture was dependent on the prosperity of the industrial economy (Saloutos, 1948: 156). Despite the mobilization of farmers' organizations to lobby for specific economic and political issues, they were less influential in shaping the direction of the economy than industrial and commercial groups, and received limited compensation or adjustment measures to alleviate the effects of uneven development and economic modernization. This is in marked contrast to the postwar European experience where the Common Agricultural Policy was a central element in convincing specific states to support and maintain their commitment to economic integration, given the concentrated pressure from domestic farmers to gain commercial benefits (Moravcsik, 1998b; Germond, 2013).

Given the regional gap between different levels of economic development in Europe, and the relative differences in manufacturing and agriculture within national economies, the first concrete efforts to tackle economic disparities evolved during initial Treaty negotiations. The resulting concessions, compromises, and protocols resulted in active measures "to temper to the needs of the less thriving economies" and promote "equitable possibilities of development" (Deniau, 1961: 55–6). Specific initiatives were aimed at promoting economic and social parity, although issues of distribution were initially considered marginal to the overall development of integration in which anticipated benefits would occur through common policies (Wallace, 1983: 81–2). Concern that market forces would increase rather than decrease inequalities between regions, as industrial production, capital, and almost all other economic activities would gravitate toward certain areas that provided the best return (Myrdal, 1957), the Treaty provided a transition period for the weakest economic sectors and regions before facing the full brunt of competition from more competitive member states (Barzanti, 1965: 345).

Specifically, the Community addressed social dislocation through the European Social Fund which supported employment training to promote the geographic mobility of workers and provide the abundant supply of unskilled labor with new employment opportunities (Hodson, 2012). The European Investment Bank served a similar function in trying to promote economic development through the promotion of specific projects for less developed regions (Lankowski, 1995). Such aid was crucial in compensating for the limited credit available for underdeveloped regions, and initially covered a range of sectors including agriculture, textiles, transport, and energy, in an effort to deal with the increased competitive pressures from market liberalization. The most important compensatory welfare mechanism was the Common Agricultural Policy (CAP) which replaced widespread government intervention at the national level with intervention at the Community level. Powerful national farm lobbies promoted their interests effectively despite the subsequent decline of agriculture relative to other industries and sectors (Pearce, 1983; Germond, 2013; Patterson, 1997). Since the CAP was designed to solicit support for the common market from farmers, it provided a common agreement among the original six regarding the need for increased productivity, stable markets, and livable wages for farmers via policies that guaranteed price and production levels. What differed among member states was the means by which this would be achieved based on different commercial interests (Moravcsik, 1998). However, the crippling burden of such welfare provisions on the overall budget resulted in successive reforms of the CAP which generated fierce and prolonged disagreements, as well as concessions for different farm sectors in response to the demands of member states as a means of dealing with the shift away from price-support guarantees (Patterson, 1997; Garzon 2007).

Each expansion of the Community has brought new demands for compensatory mechanisms. With the accession of Britain and Ireland, the British had sought for changes in the financial distribution of Community resources, bolstered by support from the Irish and Italians, so that the resulting European Regional Development Fund (ERDF) was an effort to grant access to Community resources, although both France and Germany were reluctant to promote a common regional policy. Though the ERDF was limited in terms of its scope and financial resources (Wallace 1983: 88ff; Hodson, 2012), it drew attention to regions that suffered from industrial rather than agricultural decline, expanding the scope of compensatory policies and instruments to deal with the changing economic environment. Similarly, the accession of Spain and Portugal also resulted in pressures to compensate the poorer Southern areas, and the resulting Integrated Mediterranean program was designed to modernize the socioeconomic structure of the region to aid their integration into the European market, and provide the Mediterranean regions of France, Italy, and Greece with a stronger regional policy platform (Yannopoulos, 1989; Smyrl, 1997, 1998). These distributive issues have revealed sharp differences in perspective, as member states such as Ireland and Greece sought a positive transfer of resources to poorer members, whereas others such as Britain sought a stronger commitment towards a more equitable allocation of fiscal and other economic benefits (Wallace, 1983: 106–7).

From the outset, regional policy has been criticized as distributing too little money to too many regions (Hodson, 2012). Though economists have been divided over the impact of the EU in reducing economic disparities, with different views about the role of economic geography, economic openness, and good governance in impacting institutional efforts, EU regional policy continues to play a role in promoting social cohesion. Proponents of regulated capitalism have constantly sought a variety of inclusive mechanisms to generate broad political support for the single market. The resulting efforts to promote economic and social cohesion, consumer and environmental protection, and rural development were narrower than the traditional social market philosophy and distinct from the traditional *dirigiste* policies of state ownership and control. The global financial crisis has reinforced the importance of regional policy, as it is being promoted as a means to offset fiscal austerity and low growth for southern states in the eurozone in particular (Hodson, 2012).

Conclusion

This chapter has reviewed the causal and distributive dynamics of market integration. First, economic integration owes much to the "developmental" role of the state in promoting economic and social development (Evans, 1995). Yet such efforts to foster new channels of commercial and economic activity generated social and economic conflict among different classes and sectors. In the US, in the midst of such socioeconomic transformation in the late nineteenth century—when class distinctions and public burdens were clearly accelerating—the actual power and policies of the American "regulatory state" expanded and increased (Novak, 1996; Lowi, 1984; McCraw, 1984; Keller, 1977). The result was that different mechanisms emerged at different levels of government, including states and municipalities as well as the federal government, to regulate market behavior. Such multilevel governance arrangements meant that the activities of government in the nineteenth century were largely shared activities, mirroring more recent scholarship on the EU (Elazar, 1964: 249; Beer, 1978; Hooghe and Marks, 2010). The resulting system of multilevel governance has been built "in response to demands for increased regulatory capacity" in which power has been diffused both horizontally and vertically to deal with the need to manage, administer, and govern the market commensurate with its functional and constitutional reach (Lindseth, 2010: 1–3).

Establishing the structure of governance in the nineteenth century also meant that the state defined, regulated, and used the private sector in achieving public goals and objectives. The delegation of regulatory power to private institutions, the role of self-regulation of various professions, and the private enforcement of public law provides important illustrations of the different modes of governance inherent in regulating and administering markets in the US (Novak, 2003). The public powers of the state suggest that the pattern of intergovernmental public management and the intersection between the public and private sector are indicative of a system of "networked governance" that is not unfamiliar in describing the European polity (see Kohler-Koch, 2003). European governance has also drawn on the private sector to achieve regulatory objectives, delegated authority to regulatory agencies, and fostered modes of intergovernmental cooperation in administering market activities, in areas ranging from competition to regional policy. The EU has expanded its regulatory capacity given that until recently it has had limited fiscal and budgetary capacity as a means of coordinating markets, replacing the interventionist state with new modes of regulatory governance (Majone, 1996a, 1997). In both cases, state institutions not only provide rules and norms that constrain economic behavior, they also create boundaries of institutional authority that determine the role of the state and market, and the allocation of regulatory authority among different levels of government.

Second, economic integration is also aided by legal doctrine and judicial decisions which have facilitated and constrained market processes. Competing interests have used the courts to advocate for specific interests and enterprises, while also creating new doctrines that have restructured legal monopolies, increased competition, and transformed governance, often generating heated debate about the legitimacy and accountability of administrative and legal power (Maduro, 2010: 1–10; Maduro, 1997; Lowi, 1979). As markets become more regulated, so the legal arena in which private firms and public agencies operate also changes. The experience with new forms of business organization, new business practices, and the commercial realities of cross-border trade and services, depends on the legal system to provide legitimacy for new contractual relations. The intersection of national law with federal constitutional law in Europe has clear parallels in the American experience, where local common law was displaced by federal constitutional law in the post-Civil War period with corresponding legal mobilization and resistance, and concerns about the balance between enumerated rights, state autonomy, and constitutional tolerance. Constitutional practices were as unsettled in nineteenth- and twentieth-century America as in postwar Europe.

Third, there was widespread demand for social and political reform to address the impact of increased market competition. Though they may have taken different forms, addressing concerns about socioeconomic modernization has been key to the success of market integration. In the US, it was not the result of a "permissive consensus." The US tried to manage economic interdependence and ameliorate the possibilities of market failure through public sector intervention to modify or supplement the operation of markets. The process of market integration was contentious with significant periods of mass mobilization and opposition to changing economic conditions. This necessitated changes in legislation and governance that appear to have sustained and reinforced its legitimacy. While integration in Europe has led to an unbundling and reorganization of aspects of national economies and political systems, the process has considerable societal effects, not least efforts to resist or challenge continued market integration with corresponding social and political mobilization (Imig and Tarrow, 2001). The loss of access to counter-cyclical monetary and fiscal policies in Europe and the tensions between structural reform, fiscal consolidation, and local models of protection have generated deep concerns about constitutional asymmetry in Europe (Scharpf, 2002; Scharpf, 1999b; Moses, 2011; cf. Caporaso and Tarrow, 2009). The US provided a limited range of compensating policies through regulatory protection or social welfare guarantees, including voluntary self-organization and selective state actions in response to changes wrought by market society (Skocpol, 1992). If as many argue, the logic and functioning of the single market is one in which social protection is decoupled from market integration in Europe, then the American market-building effort is one in which state-based social welfare models were limited but social market regulations evolved to address market externalities (Law and Kim, 2010: 9). Such a "well-regulated society" (Novak, 1996) mirrors the argument of Majone (1993) about the focus on social regulation in Europe, with a similar absence of social welfare and social distribution at the European level to compensate and protect against intensified market competition. However, the fiscal crisis in Europe especially in the eurozone has exacerbated governance problems in the EU. Over the next four chapters, the challenges it faces in creating, managing and maintaining markets are compared with the US experience across the four factors of production—goods, services, labor, and capital to illustrate the coordination and implementation dilemmas common to multilevel systems of governance.

Note

1. There is a substantial debate about US growth and its relationship to a protectionist international policy in the nineteenth century. Despite caution about the causal relationship between trade policy and economic performance, important substitution policies have continued to be viewed positively in nineteenth-century history. Cf. Irwin (2001).

4

Interstate Commerce and Free Movement of Goods

What is ultimate is the principle that one state in its dealings with another may not place itself in a position of economic isolation. . . . Restrictions so contrived are an unreasonable clog upon the mobility of commerce.

Cardozo in *Baldwin* v. *Seelig* 294 U.S. 511 (1935)

Contemporary debates about trade have drawn attention to the impact and consequences of globalization, with rapid growth of trade flows, technology transfer, and financial movements leading many states to feel that they are losing their ability to manage prices, interest rates, and markets. The increasing vulnerability to financial crises and industrial slumps has led to pressure for protection for specific sectors and industries, coupled with greater demands to address the sources of inequality. Although globalization is increasingly used to characterize the evolution of the modern economy, in terms of the diminished significance of geography to trade, the nineteenth century also witnessed a similar convergence of capital and labor flowing across national boundaries in unprecedented quantities. As trade in goods also increased in response to sharply declining transportation costs and changing tariff levels (see O'Rourke and Williamson, 1999: 280), forces promoting an open economy were considered crucial factors in explaining patterns of relative growth. While much of the attention has focused on the political economy of globalization in terms of the removal of trade barriers between nation-states, the lowering of internal barriers to trade and opportunities created by the consolidation of local markets into national or regional markets is also crucial.

The removal of trade barriers should increase the scope for exploiting comparative advantage and further extend the possibilities for specialization and exchange in both the American and European economies in the nineteenth and twentieth/twenty-first centuries respectively. A single market in goods means a) free and unencumbered trade, b) no additional market entry barriers or market access restrictions, and c) policies of non-discrimination against out-of-state products. The elimination of restrictions to cross-border trade can result in entry and expansion into other markets that were previously highly protected, rationalization of production, and increased manufacturing efficiency as firms are able to exploit economies of scale. Those industries with relative cost advantages and other factor endowments will gain as the removal of barriers to trade decreases transaction costs and may also encourage innovation as new market entrants have more incentive to promote new processes and products than those with investments in established products and technologies. Beyond the benefits occurring from an integrated product market, it is important to examine the legal and political changes that have pushed such market consolidation. The strategies undertaken are important in determining the ability of states to adopt measures which are more or less thinly disguised protectionism favoring local industry and business.

The focus of this chapter is the emergence of interregional trade in goods and the removal of restrictions to interstate commerce. Since protectionist measures involve a range of restrictive practices, it covers a variety of managed trade mechanisms that limit cross-border trade, including tariffs and customs duties, import prohibitions, quotas, and other explicit quantitative restrictions. Other restrictive measures such as voluntary export restraints, anti-dumping duties, price controls, certificates of origin, or other administrative controls protect domestic or local markets. In some cases, the impediments to trade might appear to have legitimate public policy objectives such as health and safety standards, but can often be used to protect local industries and merchants by creating subtle barriers to entry. The latter include licensing marks, quality seals, quarantine restrictions, and labeling requirements, which can become a serious impediment to trade by imposing additional or discriminatory requirements on out-of-state producers and suppliers (see Hillman, 1991; Curzon and Curzon, 1970; Johnsen, 1940; Abel, 1947b, 1948; Egan, 2001; Novak, 1996; Grieco, 1990; McCurdy, 1978; Stone Sweet, 2005).

For the realization of a common market, state impediments had to be curtailed and made subordinate to a uniform (inter)national system of governance. How did an integrated product market emerge in the US and EU? What effect has the integration of product markets had on patterns of economic behavior and strategies of firms? How then do the US and EU ensure that welfare objectives were legitimate measures and not disguised restrictions to trade? In understanding how trade barriers are addressed, what is striking in the two cases is that interregional trade and commerce in goods is not simply about negative integration or the removal of barriers to trade, but also about positive integration or the construction of regulatory mechanisms and provisions to ensure reciprocal market access. Though this could take various forms—from harmonization and approximation of state legislation to reciprocity statutes and mutual recognition of state laws—the choice of instruments can reduce state authority and competence through preemption and the horizontal transfer of sovereignty, or expand state authority through delegation and enforcement powers (Nicolaïdis, 1993, 1997; Zimmerman, 2002).

This chapter first traces the American experience, focusing on the growth of interregional trade, and the barriers affecting internal commerce in both the antebellum and postbellum period. The second section examines European efforts to address trade barriers, both in the early period of integration, along with later developments in the context of the single market program and beyond. The final section evaluates the impact of the single market in goods on corporate strategies and patterns of economic behavior. It concludes with a comparison of strategies and methods used to integrate the US and EU markets.

American Interregional Trade

Prior to the adoption of the Constitution, interstate commerce was a branch of foreign commerce with each state enjoying full sovereign authority to tax, restrict, or prohibit commercial transactions (Grant, 1937: 34). Under the Articles of Confederation, trade barriers were quickly erected among several states, and commercial competition and rivalry resulted in the imposition of tariffs, duties, and fees designed to protect local markets. Such trade barriers and commercial rivalries between states were among the root cause of the weakness and disruptions of the Confederate government (Kutler, 1984). It is not surprising that states sought legislative barriers when the colonies became independent, as the spirit of mercantilism was still dominant when the Revolution made each of the colonies a sovereign nation (Conant, 1991: 88).

Important questions about the precise boundaries between the authority of state governments and that of the federal government were of considerable importance during the 1787 Constitutional Convention. The effects of the postwar depression had fueled efforts by the New England states that Congress be granted comprehensive powers to regulate commerce. The Southern states, who wished to expand territorially, acquiesced in these demands for Congress to regulate trade, if concessions were made regarding representation that would allow the growing influence of the South in national government (Crosskey, 1953). Thus, "the Northerners wanted a diversified national economy and a Congress fully empowered to establish an American commercial system. The Southern states, by contrast, were committed to an agricultural economy based upon slavery, and were opposed or indifferent to the northern petitions regarding commerce" without concessions based on representation (see Krash, 1984: 969). The pressure to regulate interstate commerce was based not merely on complaints about commercial practices and trade barriers, but driven by the fears emerging from recession where pent-up demands, rising unemployment and debt, falling incomes, and fears of disunion and insurrection, generated calls for Congressional power to regulate trade (Krash, 1984: 973). In their efforts to reach political accommodation, these sectional economic differences were to play a major role in the pace of industrialization and development throughout the nineteenth century (Bensel, 1984).

The result was specific provision in the Constitution giving Congress the right to regulate commerce with foreign nations, tribes, and among the states, and denying states the right to levy import or export duties. Other specific provisions to promote free trade included provisions forbidding Congress to levy export duties, forbidding states to deny privileges and immunities to citizens of other states,[1] or levy import or export duties unless for revenue purposes related to state inspection laws.[2] The authority given to Congress was direct but vague about precisely what was meant by commerce. The fact that there was "no constructive criticism by the states of the commerce clause as proposed to them" meant that the jurisprudence evolved without substantial guidance or restrictions from the Convention or ratification process (Frankfurter, 1937: 12). National power was to be shared with states, so any conflicts would have to be resolved by the supremacy clause. As a result, the power of the federal government to regulate commerce between states has generated diverging interpretations. Some argue that the Commerce Clause specifically limits state power over commerce, whereas others view states as free to regulate and tax until specific restraints are introduced by Congressional action (Moseley, 1895: 30).

In the early period, foreign commerce was the predominant interest, and internal commerce was initially limited to the Atlantic and Gulf coasts (Schmidt, 1939: 798). The growth of American cotton–textile manufacturers made it the leading export sector between 1808 and 1815—followed by the growth of the iron and steel industry in the 1840s—resulting in the development of a more diversified manufacturing sector (Keohane, 1983: 63). The predominant view is that there was considerable development of internal commerce as a result of a territorial division of labor and regional specialization among the South, West, and East (Schmidt, 1939 and North, 1966).[3] This "marked the transition from a colonial to a national economy," and the relative importance of different commodities had an important effect on the political and economic development of the national economy (Schmidt, 1939: 798). The heavy demand, both foreign and domestic, for cotton, tobacco, and sugar led the South Atlantic and Gulf States to focus exclusively on these staples and allowed the West to engage in other types of agricultural production such as grain and livestock (Schmidt, 1939; North, 1966). The

South and West were tied together by other interests, linked by navigation systems and geographically separate from the Atlantic Seaboard (Schmidt, 1939). Extension of direct transportation to the Midwest diverted commerce and traffic from the South, and tied the West and East closer together. The struggles for control of trade routes shifted commercial centers and meant that merchandise from the East was in return supplied by staple Western agricultural products (*Hunt's Merchants' Magazine,* 1840 as quoted by Schmidt, 1939).

However, Fishlow contends that the trade between the South and West was relatively small and that it failed to keep pace with the trade patterns between the West and East (Fishlow, 1964; see also Taylor, 1951, 1964). This rapidly growing commerce between East and West played a significant role in promoting internal commerce (Fishlow, 1964). Most Western products were shipped to the South, but little was retained for consumption and was instead shipped to foreign ports or Northern cities. Eastern imports of Western products exceeded local production by 20 percent, and Eastern demands furnished Western expansion as by 1860 Western imports accounted for 53 percent of Eastern consumption (Fishlow, 1964: 193; see also US Congress, 1887). The per capita production of the South also indicates widespread self-sufficiency and local sale of foodstuffs, so that Southern states were far from dependent on Western products. While the sheer size of the Southern market and its export role in the antebellum period gave it a key role in economic development, its high consumption of foreign imports blunted its demands for domestic products and services.

Fishlow contends that interregional trade flows were less integrated and interdependent than is commonly assumed in the antebellum period. Taylor, however, suggests that the integration of the West into the national economy and the rapid expansion of the market are due to institutional and technological changes and the process of capital accumulation and investment. He also stresses urbanization and the growth of commercial–industrial cities that fueled economic growth and linked regional markets. The result for the Southern economy, highly specialized in export agriculture, and dependent on forced labor, meant that the antebellum South developed a thin and poorly articulated internal market for manufactured goods (Carlton, 1990: 447). This view came under challenge as regional manufacturing comparisons have indicated that the Southern economy in the aggregate was prosperous, despite its economic base and industrial condition, and had similar levels of output as Western states (Bateman and Weiss, 1975: 183). But the region became truly peripheral to the modern industrial economy after the Civil War, trapped in a downward spiral of poverty and near colonial dependence (Sanders, 1999: 113).

"One of the earliest estimates of the total value of domestic commerce was made by a writer in *Hunts' Merchants' Magazine* in 1843, who placed it at

$900,000,000... while the treasury, making an estimate in 1846 reported that the value of American production exceeded $3,000,000,000... of which that 'interchange' among the several states of the Union was $500,000,000" (Taylor, 1951: 174). The surge of industrialization in the postbellum period was part of the larger development—the consolidation of a national market— as mass production increased and distributional networks developed rapidly beyond local and regional boundaries. Prior to this, the full effects of industrialization were not apparent, let alone realized (Fishlow, 1964). While the credit market was becoming increasingly national and the money supply grew to meet business demands (as discussed in detail in Chapter 5), the national market for goods and services was achieved through the rapid construction of canals, turnpikes, and especially the railroad that spanned the continent and built tracks into virtually every part of the country at a frenzied pace. By 1840 there were about as many miles of railroad in operation as canals (Taylor, 1951: 79). Railroad mileage increased from 3,328 in 1840 to 8,879 by 1850 and reached 30,626 by 1860 to register "an increase about four times that achieved during the previous ten-year period" (Taylor, 1951: 85, 79). Along with the technological advances such as refrigerated cars which facilitated the movement of products to primary and secondary markets, the intense competition forced reduction in costs and the concomitant lowering of rates further influenced the expansion of the national market (Hacker, 1940: 241).

The literature on trade flows and interstate commerce has offered a number of explanations to account for the development and expansion of trade flows and commercial transactions. North stresses the importance of external trade and the growth of foreign demand as crucial for economic development (North, 1966). Frankel suggests that the development of manufacturing production was tied to embargoes and war in Europe, preventing European protagonists from trading even with neutrals, and enabling American infant industries to develop and later seek protection from foreign competition (Frankel, 1982: 291, 301–2). Freyer argues that the progressive integration of product markets produced conflict between a local and national market structure, generating different legal attitudes towards commerce in the antebellum period, and the emergence of two jurisprudential traditions (Freyer, 1994). Later on, structural changes in American manufacturing and the growth of transportation networks certainly lowered the costs of production and facilitated the growth of internal trade flows as large-scale businesses tapped into larger and larger segments of the domestic market (O'Rourke and Williamson, 1999: 4). McCurdy illustrates how the jurisprudence evolved in the postbellum period, in response to these changes, with the Supreme Court imposing limits on states whose actions restricted the formation of a national commercial market (McCurdy, 1975, 1978; Hovenkamp, 1991). There is general consensus that interregional trade had to overcome considerable impediments and restrictions imposed by states on doing business within their borders throughout the nineteenth century.

Barriers to Trade in the United States

Studies of economic growth and trade have often distinguished between the antebellum and postbellum period to describe changes in the economic landscape, especially with regard to marketing, distribution, and production. Since consolidation of a single market for manufactured goods continued throughout the nineteenth century, the development of internal commerce is examined in both periods. Of crucial importance is the impact of changing business structures and organization, and the scale on which goods were produced, distributed and consumed, which in turn depended on the willingness of the federal judiciary to accept and defend interstate commerce against local pressures.

Although the development of American manufacturing took place almost entirely within the private sector, the effect of government policies often had a significant impact on encouraging as well as restricting industrial activity (Engerman and Sokoloff, 2000: 390–1). The creation of a national market for goods raised questions of the powers allocated between the federal government and the states, the proper scope and interpretation of the Commerce Clause, and the degree to which state laws were protectionist. While countless state statutes were aimed at promoting public welfare, by protecting the public against fraud and deceit, the transformation of the market meant that these subsequently became subject to scrutiny, as measures taken in certain states to curb the exportation of natural resources or limit the sale of products from out of state for example created discriminatory trade practices (Novak, 1996).

By virtue of their proprietary interests, states confidently wielded their regulatory powers to constrain private rights in the name of public interest using their police powers, resulting in a tension between sovereignty, public rights, private claims, and other constitutional doctrines such as states' rights and national supremacy in the nineteenth century (Scheiber, 1997: 833–4). Though ostensibly designed to promote specific public policy objectives, they have often protected and insulated domestic producers and industries. State legislations designed to foster public morality, protect public health and safety, or promote certain socioeconomic interests have been subject to judicial scrutiny to determine their impact on interstate commercial transactions, and whether they are more restrictive than necessary. State prohibitions and enforcement measures are increasingly reviewed to determine whether they create an undue burden on commerce. Market integration has meant that balancing the national interest in a common market with more specialized local needs requires constant adjudication (Kommers and Waelbroeck, 1985). There would inevitably be conflict regarding trade between the delegated powers to Congress at the federal level, and the reserved powers of states that enabled them to use their police, proprietary, license, and tax powers to affect internal commerce (Zimmerman, 1996: 118; Conant, 1991: 87). The notion that states have residual powers (often termed police powers) generated several interpretations about the accommodation between the interacting concerns of state and nation, and resulted in the crafting of a set of judicial principles through which boundaries between state and federal regulatory authority were continuously debated and established (Frankfurter, 1937).

Antebellum Developments

During the antebellum period, federal law was not as voluminous as it would become after the Civil War. Impediments to unrestricted movement across state lines continued to grow in form and extent as the wide array of economic regulation that had begun in the colonial period continued unabated during the antebellum era.[4] Although they varied widely, they generally involved three practices: a) regulatory action, b) protection or subsidy of particular interest, and c) participation and promotion of industrial activity (Taylor, 1951: 378).

Antebellum era states enjoyed considerable regulatory authority to regulate not only the terms and conditions of trade, but also modes of production across a range of social and economic areas (see Novak, 1996). States and municipalities issued statutes and ordinances affecting internal trade within their own borders, but these increasingly posed important restraints on cross-border trade in goods and services (Zimmerman, 2003, 2006; Abel, 1947b; Hurst, 1956). If the contract clause protected corporate development against undue state interference during this period, the Commerce Clause as a means of creating a national free-trade area was not initially promoted as a means of restricting state power over commerce (Moseley, 1895: 30; Abel, 1947a: 121). In the antebellum period, there were few challenges to the numerous state or municipal regulations, and while comparatively few state or lower federal courts referenced the Commerce Clause, this was in part due to the widespread belief that the issues involved did not warrant invoking the Commerce Clause (Abel, 1947a: 171).

Obstacles to economic integration as a result of incompatible standards and laws certainly existed. Trade laws were practical and tailored to specific needs. Local inspection, product and licensing laws were justified in terms of public welfare—and the problems of high prices, fraud, unsanitary conditions, and adulterated food necessitated a degree of control and regulation of the market. Statutes in Maryland, Ohio, South Carolina, Michigan, and Massachusetts reveal numerous laws inspecting the quality of butter, bread, salted meat and fish, with strict controls on packaging, inspection, and certification, and fixing of prices charged by ferries, pawnbrokers, chimney sweeps, and bakers (see Scheiber, 1997: 841). As markets outgrew local limits, state regulation became of increased importance, and legislatures became increasingly involved in setting standards for weights and measures, licensing slaughterhouses, auctioneers, taverns, and vendors, setting prices for hackneys, bridges, and bakers, and regulating the transportation of goods, largely but not exclusively through provisions in corporate charters. Yet despite widespread state and municipal regulation of markets, including some that reflected reform pressures such as prohibitions on lottery tickets and alcoholic sales, and others that reflected economic pressures such as debtor protection, interstate commerce was also affected by the lack of uniformity in local laws. This generated uncertainty with regard to private transactions and constituted a barrier to economic development (Freyer, 1994: 20). While the bulk of statutes and laws affected commerce within their own locality, the question of allowable control by states over the business of transporting goods and persons across state lines and permissible extent of state taxation of business enterprise brought greater scrutiny of the effects of state legislation upon national commerce.

Furthermore interstate rivalry meant that state legislatures confronted pressures for an immediate response to out-of-state competition, often providing special assistance or subsidies to specific interest groups within their own localities. During this period, agricultural interests gained specific support with New York loaning state funds directly to farmers on mortgage security and Maine providing agricultural subsidies and farm relief. In the manufacturing sphere, Vermont made generous provisions for tax exemption for local manufacturing firms, Ohio exempted iron, glasswork, and textile mills from taxation during economic downturns, and Southern states provided numerous tax exemptions to encourage iron manufacture (Taylor, 1951: 380–1). Louisiana and Alabama targeted shipbuilding, and California offered generous subsidies to projects to hasten the completion of the transcontinental telegraph lines that would connect with Eastern lines and networks. New York imposed high transportation charges on foreign salt to exclude imported products from interior markets, and similar efforts to stimulate local production through discrimination against foreign and out-of-state competitors were common (Taylor, 1951; Hartz, 1955). There was, however, "no end to the ingenuity or persistence of state interests in seeking to fence off markets for themselves" (Hurst, 1956: 78).

Because the commercial policy objectives of states were broad, "state governments acted freely"—and in many instances the interstate ramifications were ignored—despite the fact that the Commerce Clause had divested them of powers they had previously held under the Articles of Confederation

(McCurdy, 1975: 635). So long as there was decentralization of significant promotional and regulatory policies, state policies continued to shape the overall government structure. Many areas of public policy, including labor relations, corporate charters, and expropriation of private property under the laws of eminent domain for state transport programs, as well as for the encouragement of manufacturing and other enterprises signified the considerable influence of states on economy policymaking (see Chapter 6). Only with the changing scope and power of corporations in the postbellum period did the ineffectiveness of state policies become increasingly apparent. As interregional markets expanded, driven in part by the spread of mass production, distribution, and marketing, the economy required new mechanisms to address the growing anonymity of markets and business transactions.

As a result, the boundaries between states and federal authorities over the regulation and policing of the market became increasingly subject to dispute requiring constant adjudication. While law provided the momentum or what Hurst referred to as the "release of energy," mutual reinforcing factors brought about significant changes in behavior. The growth of industrial investment and productivity, greater efficiency in farm production, improvements in transportation, as well as legal instruments and subsidies, were bound up with the excessive localism in which the force of private pressures emerged in a federal context in which the public interest was also contested in the courts.

Integration through Law

"Left to their own devices, states would have erected significant barriers to the consolidation of the national market" (Bensel, 2000: 321). But the courts played a crucial role in striking down many legislative barriers, so basic principles of free trade and the state–federal relationship became primarily a product of judicial elaboration. The fate of many state and local enactments hinged on judicial action during the nineteenth century, as judicial rulings on the Commerce Clause played a key role in the political construction of the national market (see Bensel, 2000: 321ff). The federal government took early action for the regulation of ships and cargoes from foreign countries and passed licensing laws for vessels engaged in coastal trade. Although many of these cases were in fact dealing with foreign policy (Friedman, 2005), there were also domestic motives in centralizing such policies. Although federal authority was growing in response to the emergence of commerce across state borders, Congress took virtually no positive action for the control of interstate commerce. State legislative practices continued unabated because Southerners feared that the use of the power might eventually extend to the regulation of slavery and resisted federal oversight (Freyer, 1994: 26). The lack of federal intervention and consistent rules and regulations generated considerable restrictions on commerce. As a result, federal abstention in the adjudication of commerce questions left significant power with the states (Scheiber, 1975: 883).

The nature of the Commerce Clause was not tested until the seminal *Gibbons* v. *Ogden* case in 1824. Though this initial Supreme Court judgment did not indicate that federal power over interstate commerce was exclusive, it did cut down the power of the states to pursue independent policies on trade. States did have the right to enact laws based on their police powers, even though such laws might have an influence on commerce. The power of the federal government was put forth negatively rather than affirmatively; federal power was aimed at restraining excessive state authority rather than providing affirmative national regulation. Building on this, *Brown* v. *Maryland* in 1827 upheld federal authority over interstate commerce, but the courts did not have many opportunities to define the scope of state regulatory authority prior to the Civil War (see Prentice and Egan, 1898; Bensel, 2000).[5] In fact, the general trend in the antebellum period was to extend the acquisition of powers of states under dual federalism, and permit states to exercise concurrent power to regulate commerce (*Willson* v. *Black-Bird Creek Marsh Co.*, 1829).

As both McCurdy and Scheiber note, "the protectionist impulses of states were not easily curbed" and there were counter-movements to the centralizing tendencies of legal doctrine (McCurdy, 1978: 641; Scheiber 1975: 84). The continuing litigation of cases concerning regulatory statutes on various quarantine, licensing, and commercial rules signified the persistence with which states asserted their authority even if it impinged on interstate commerce (Scheiber 1975: 85).[6] There was not judicial agreement on the precise line between the right of states to exercise their police power and whether the commerce power was concurrent or exclusive under so-called "Passenger Cases" (*Smith* v. *Turner; Norris* v. *Boston*, 48 U.S. 283 (1849). State sovereignty marked out certain subjects as the exclusive jurisdiction of states, and states carved out mercantilistic policies through their police powers, as well as concurrent power over interstate commerce. Legal judgments channeled the dynamics of the market in the antebellum period, developing precedents that sought to remove impediments to the market. At the same time, however, a countering legal tradition sought to control rather than liberate the economic environment (Keller, 1979: 296). This became an increasingly prominent feature in the late nineteenth century, as the organizational complexity of commercial life demanded a balance between those that sought legal protection from the judiciary for local economic interests, and those that sought the promotion of a national economy (Freyer, 1979).

The balance of power shifted in the post-Civil War period, as the trend towards increasing centralization meant the federal courts played an increasingly important role in determining the scope of state legislation, often preempting state policy through judicial doctrines that supported federal intervention (Scheiber, 1975: 100). Conflicts over the structure and regulation of the economy continued throughout the entire period.[7] The Supreme Court, armed with an enlarged jurisdiction and three new constitutional amendments in the aftermath of the Civil War, used the opportunity to forge new doctrines and boundaries between the public and private sectors (McCurdy, 1975: 971). In the postbellum period, the Court reconsidered the scope of state police powers and eminent domain and restricted the range of mechanisms that states employed for subsiding private business (Scheiber, 1971). The incompatibility between types of intervention of various subnational governments and a legal commitment to promote interstate commerce subsequently generated greater centralization as a substitute for local market control (Heller and Pelkmnans, 1986: 399). The crusade against state and local trade barriers began with *Welton* v. *Missouri* in 1876, which allowed out-of-state firms to engage in interstate commerce on equal footing with local firms (see McCurdy, 1975, 1978). The Court ruled that the license tax imposed on persons selling products from out of state was a restraint on interstate commerce. Subsequent state efforts to impose licensing fees on sales agents were also rebuffed as a burden on interstate commerce (*Robbins* v. *Shelby County Taxing District*, 1887). Though these rulings appear to be consistent with a general trend in American law during the postbellum era to allow increased freedom for private corporations, in striking down such state regulations, the judiciary also affirmed the rights of federal intervention. As states struggled to control the growth of large-scale corporate enterprises, the Court interpreted the Commerce Clause in favor of increased federal power by the 1880s.

The Court also widened the scope of its scrutiny of state regulation using the Fourteenth Amendment. The Court shaped the economic landscape through the due process provisions of that Amendment, asserting its right of judicial review with regard to discriminatory taxation, promoting the dormant power clause to ensure national union and upholding Congressional statutes while continuing to strike down harmful state actions (McCurdy, 1975; see *Smith* v. *Turner; Norris* v. *Boston*, 48 U.S. 283 (1849). The limitations imposed upon the powers of states and municipalities, through the tight rein held on public finances and their restriction to the barest necessities of health, safety, and education, meant that states were subject to scrutiny under a substantive interpretation of the due process clause that complemented the judicial doctrine of dual sovereignty (McCurdy, 1975). Such constitutional barriers to economic regulation prompted the consolidation of ever-larger corporations. Despite hostility to the creation of monopolistic conditions, very few monopolies were dismantled.

The outcome, as McCurdy concludes, was a constitutional revolution that set government–business relations on a new legal footing (McCurdy, 1975: 971). Although states had actively used their police powers to regulate corporate behavior and commercial activity, the conflicting trends in constitutional interpretation resulted in a reduction in state regulatory authority. Yet the Court was also taking steps to bring an increasingly integrated national market under federal control as the caseload, jurisdiction, and policy agenda of the Court all expanded rapidly after the Civil War (Gillman, 2002). Issues under litigation such as shipment of lottery tickets and taxes on oleomargarine, while often pedestrian, provided the foundation for the subsequent growth of federal police powers and regulatory authority. However, it meant that the court was constantly defining the boundaries between federal and state authority, and retaining for itself the power to distinguish in each individual case.

Postbellum Period

The establishment of a national market for goods and services reflected a significant change in the structure of the economy in the postbellum period. Prior to the consolidation of manufacturing, transportation, and commercial operations, interstate commerce had been limited, and only when the states repeatedly attempted to control and tax corporate activities after the Civil War did the issue of state legislative restrictions rise onto the agenda, consuming much of the energy and attention of the Supreme Court. Persistent challenges by local and regional interests to the authority of federal courts in creating a business system that transcended state lines continued throughout the period (Freyer, 1979). The courts were constantly required to deal with local interests that continued to challenge and restrict out-of-state commercial enterprises (see McCurdy, 1978; Hollander, 1964). States often attempted to pass laws that required licensing or taxing of merchants that were known as commercial travelers, drummers, or peddlers to protect local interests, and curbed non-resident insurance company efforts to foreclose on farm mortgages. Such local licensing laws and ordinances made it costly, and sometimes prohibitive, to gain a license, under the guise of contributing to the local tax burden (Hollander, 1964: 481). In some instances, the legislation provided moieties or rewards to report unlicensed peddlars and hawkers (Hollander, 1964: 485). Many state courts upheld the constitutionality of such licensing and restrictive practices, even though they interfered with interstate commerce (Hollander, 1964). Although such discrimination against non-residents had supposedly been ruled unconstitutional in *Ward* v. *Maryland* (1871), local and state courts from Missouri to West Virginia continued to impose fines throughout the nineteenth century, even while commercial associations petitioned for relief. Invariably, if appealed, state law was subsequently held unconstitutional under the Commerce Clause as federal courts were instrumental in overcoming states' resistance to the emergence of national business entities (Freyer, 1979: 344). Some state legislatures tried to exclude corporations incorporated in another state. Many tried to establish criteria for out-of-state corporations; this often required incorporation in the "host" state which would subject them to the regulations of that state (Freyer, 1979). State legislatures and courts had been dealing with corporations for decades over the conduct of business affairs through their status as chartered entities by states. But as corporate activity extended beyond state lines, as participants in the flow of national, interstate commerce, this realm of business activity became increasingly a concern for the federal judiciary (Keller 1979: 299–300; Keller, 1977). States sought to hinder the activities of non-resident companies, often forcing them to incorporate or bargain away their right to sue in federal courts. Such efforts to restrict corporations to litigate only in state courts targeted federal judicial review itself (Bensel, 2000: 324).

While state and local governments often impeded the creation of a national economy, and had an array of legal devices for controlling corporations within their territory, the juridical principles on which this was based were progressively dismantled in the late nineteenth and early twentieth century (McCurdy, 1975; *United States* v. *E. C. Knight Co.*, 156 U.S. 1 (1895)). The Court read into the due process clause an entirely new meaning to protect private business from public regulation. Through its interpretation of the interstate Commerce Clause, the Court removed restrictions to the free movement of goods to allow for interstate marketing and distribution, but at the same time allowed states to regulate firms that conducted business in their territories. As McCurdy concludes, "the court protected the mobility of foreign goods but not the mobility of foreign firms" thus deducing new rights from the Commerce Clause (McCurdy, 1979: 314). This crucial distinction between commerce and manufacturing allowed firms to gain competitive advantages through marketing and distribution, but still subjected them to state control over their structure and operations in order to protect the public interest.

Corporations often attempted to use the Commerce Clause both ways in order to escape regulation, arguing that their operations were not commerce and therefore not subject to federal supervision under the Commerce Clause, and not production, and thus not subject to state supervision (*United States* v. *E. C. Knight Co.*, 156 U.S. 1 (1895)). Businesses also sought to circumvent controls by creating holding companies, avoiding state regulation of internal corporate activities through national corporate entities (McCurdy, 1979; see also Merkel, 1984). The net effect was to create regulatory competition among states in which weak regulatory practices prevailed. This abdication of public authority meant that one state after another gravitated toward lax regulation, and thus a "race to the bottom" occurred.

Because many large commercial and industrial corporations that emerged during the late nineteenth century operated across state lines, states also responded by seeking common action. Sensing the problems were increasingly national in scope but before federal judicial and political authority had adapted to the changing circumstances, the emergence of the uniform state laws movement was an attempt to rejuvenate dual federalism by getting state governments to address social and economic problems and obviate the need for federal involvement (Nugent, 1999). Such efforts in the US in the late nineteenth century, of trying to pass an identical law in all the states, while laborious, were premised on the notion of dual sovereignty. The uniform state laws process in the late nineteenth century cannot be said to have succeeded to nearly the degree to which its proponents had hoped. Yet it emerged in part due to the absence of Congressional intervention to exercise its own authority over interstate commerce. As a means of facilitating interstate commerce through the removal of legal impediments (Zimmerman, 2006: 187) and promoting common judicial interpretations to resolve problems created by firms operating in multiple states, the process suffered from weak enforcement and implementation, despite constitutional authorization of interstate compacts that would have fostered harmonization.

Subsequently, there was a centralization of regulatory authority in response to the changing commercial realities, with expanded federal regulation of commercial practices, as well as the introduction of federal police powers and regulatory agencies. At the turn of the century, the progressive mood of Congress expanded federal law by regulating railroads, enacting food and drug requirements, establishing farm credit programs, regulating large corporations through anti-trust measures, and controlling currency through the Federal Reserve. While the American regulatory state expanded, it meant that the changing roles of market and state during the nineteenth century signaled a realignment of economic and political power. The development of a national market raised new challenges in which modern corporate capitalism and concentrations of power necessitated the growth of the administrative state. In particular, regulation, administration, and organization became hallmarks of a polity increasingly committed to controlling and influencing the market (Novak, No Date).

American government at the local and federal level shifted from promoting economic activity towards bolstering market control. Agencies were created and policies implemented which sought to curb and check market power through a variety of governance mechanisms. Industrialization stimulated the growth of public administration in stages. While the first effort was federal land policy, which initially had emphasized rapid distribution for economic development, new policies arose to reserve lands for public management and conservation. More significantly, the growth of regulation of railroads and corporations became the foundation for new federal powers and activities during the early twentieth century. The rise of corporate capitalism was also tied to broader forces of social reform, as rival claims of efficiency, growth, prosperity, security, and social justice emerged (Sklar, 1988; Noble, 1985). The dynamics of electoral politics also played a role, as the Republicans saw the Court as a suitable vehicle to promote economic nationalism, by passing a series of laws expanding federal court jurisdiction, including several statutes designed to promote access to the federal courts for interstate business interests. As a result, the functional and instrumental problem of the distribution of political powers and economic resources in society was intimately bound up with the normative and constitutional issues of legitimacy, democracy, and political reform (Novak, No Date, 2008).

Lessons from the US for the EU

The national product markets and interregional trade that emerged gradually from the integration of local and regional markets in the US have important policy implications for the EU. Based on the early American Republic, the subsequent effort to prohibit states from erecting barriers to interstate commerce was the product of a variety of legal, political, and economic developments that shaped market consolidation. Leaving aside the general welfare effects from the efficiency of larger markets, the American single market was largely a product of struggle over the terms of trade within the national economy (Bensel, 2000). Politically, the gains from free trade were uneven as regional specialization provided specific comparative advantages to the West and North. The single market also owed much to the legal rules that cleared away impediments to interstate commerce. Federal courts sought to circumvent state protectionist practices by determining the scope of state regulatory activity, while balancing local preferences against the demands for greater market liberalization. Released from the tight confines of local segmented markets, business was able to exploit both managerial and technological economies of scale. As the nineteenth century progressed, the responsibility of government for creating and sustaining markets increased as the legitimacy of the market was increasingly challenged. Consequently, there was a countering legal trend that sought to control the economic environment. As issues of monopoly and control became more salient, government acquiescence was replaced by an expansion of state activities through the positive public deployment of legal and regulatory power.

Taken together, the interactions between courts and economy at different levels had a significant effect on the configuration of the business system, and also on the regulatory dynamics between different levels of government. Deepening trade and investment generated pressure from business to address the mismatch between economic reality and regulatory administration, especially in the postbellum period. The transaction costs of different state regulations, administrative systems, and other regulatory impediments hindered the effective operation of an integrating market. For state governments, the resulting regulatory competition meant that they fell short in their efforts to protect welfare, since they continued to develop discrete sets of market-correcting and market-regulating policies in which it was more difficult to enforce local or state compliance. Efforts to promote uniformity of laws across states also failed to reach their objectives, mirroring the seemingly incompatible desires for national action and local autonomy that have made similar efforts at harmonization difficult to achieve in Europe. Yet the effort to successfully reduce restrictions to interstate commerce does provide an important precedent for the EU. In America, the intersection of law and markets shaped the nature of policy responses, with tensions between public rights and private claims often resolved in the courts. Since similar barriers to commerce exist in Europe, it is important to compare the strategies pursued in relation to the free movement of goods, identifying similarities and differences in their efforts to consolidate and create a common market.

Europe

The foundation of European economic integration is internal trade liberalization. Multilateral trade liberalization prepared the ground for an increasingly interdependent economic system in Western Europe. The early European liberalization efforts concerned the abolition of trade barriers, tariffs, and quotas. Like the US, the creation of the common market was in part due to economic necessity. To tackle economic protectionism, the EU sought expansion of markets through the creation of a customs union in which the participants removed all trade barriers between themselves and established a common tariff against third parties. However, tariff reduction was not merely a common market issue, culminating in the European Economic Community in 1957. Rather, tariff and trade negotiations took place simultaneously through a variety of different international institutions and with a variety of goals and outcomes.

Although the initiatives under the auspices of the Organization for European Economic Cooperation promoted economic cooperation, negotiations were often difficult due to the reversal of liberalization occurring when economic or monetary difficulties emerged. Early efforts including the European Coal and Steel Community and the Benelux Customs Union show how active commercial diplomacy was in Europe, and illustrate how difficult it was to promote economic integration among relatively interventionist economies (see Milward, 1984: 235, 279ff). Yet despite repeated setbacks, and isolated calls for deeper economic cooperation, these initial efforts at multilateral and bilateral liberalization turned out to be quite successful in laying the groundwork for subsequent European integration (Brusse, 1997).

Against this background, the negotiations leading to the Treaty of Rome sought to provide a framework for industrial free trade, among the six original members. The intergovernmental committee that embarked on negotiations promoted trade liberalization as well as fair competition and concern for equitable development (Laurent, 1970; Spaak Report, 1956). The resulting Spaak Report provided for extensive provisions for a common market that had three central elements: the promotion of competition through the elimination of protective barriers; the curtailment of state intervention and monopolistic conditions; and the harmonization of state legislation. Clauses covering the free movement of goods were at the heart of this effort. Provisions seeking the elimination of customs duties (Articles 12–17) were accompanied by the establishment of a common external tariff (Articles 18–20) so that the negotiations would result in a customs union (see Articles 9–37), with a limited number of sectoral policies regulated at the European level. Emphasis was placed on the elimination of quantitative restrictions among member states, although member states were allowed important derogations from the free movement of goods (Article 36), allowing member states to have reserve powers over trade in a similar manner to the dormant Commerce Clause in the US.[8] The Treaty addressed the inherent problems created by derogations from free trade by providing for the approximation or harmonization of laws and regulations. This would reduce the impact of protective measures through the uniform enforcement of common trade rules.

A number of concessions during the negotiations impacted efforts to address both tariff and non-tariff barriers. A relatively long transition period for tariff liberalization was agreed upon, to accommodate the relatively weak position of certain industries, along with mechanisms to offset the pressures of competition including the alignment of agricultural prices and social assistance for economic development (see Bertrand, 1956). Despite the overall emphasis on free trade, the treaty is rife with conditional requirements that hinder the creation of an internal market for goods.[9] These include across-the-board special subsidies and special import charges for certain states to avoid balance of payments difficulties. In the free movement of goods title of the Treaty there is no mention of quotas vis à vis third countries (Pelkmans, 1984). Thus, member states retained old prerogatives to maintain national protection for specific products against third countries. This ensured the emergence of disputes over the scope of national regulations and the degree to which they constituted discriminatory restrictions to trade.

Interregional Trade Flows

One of the major objectives of post-World War II international economy policy was liberalization of trade from the constraints of high tariffs, quantitative restrictions, and specifically the abolition of preferences and discrimination. The Treaty focused not only on the elimination of state interventions at the border, such as customs duties and quantitative restrictions, but also the differences in national laws and regulations and all forms of discrimination that occur behind the border and impact interstate commerce (Von der Groeben, 1987). Although the Treaty of Rome is more explicit in prohibiting impediments to cross-border trade than the Commerce Clause, the American experience served as an instructive example in terms of the broad variety of distortions caused by both public and private behavior (Pelkmans, 1984). The expected gains in productivity, efficiency, and competitiveness were premised on the American experience of a large integrated economy (Owen, 1983).

Initially, emphasis in the literature was on the trade and welfare effects of the change from national tariff protection to a customs union. Economic studies of the formative period of the European Community found that the effect of the customs union was immediately apparent (Viner, 1950). The extent of trade diversion is striking; the relative expansion of intra-EC trade was almost wholly at the expense of developing countries in agriculture, and at the expense of the rest of Europe and the US in manufactured goods (Pomfret, 1986, 1981). While a customs union shifts demand as the abolition of import restrictions and internal tariffs increases trade within the group at the expense of certain domestic protected groups, such effects also increase overall efficiency. Most calculations found that the changes in flow-of-trade patterns resulted in trade creation which exceeded trade diversion (Owen, 1983).

Since trade creation and trade diversion both augment intra-European trade, early trade liberalization did help to increase the share of intra-regional trade as a portion of total trade. The rapid expansion of foreign trade constituted an exchange of manufactured products among countries with a similar industrial structure and output (Zacchia, 1976: 314). Sustained growth rates in output coupled with the achievement of full employment allowed for the progressive elimination of barriers to trade. The total foreign trade of Western Europe increased rapidly between 1955 and 1972 by about ten percent per year (Saunders, 1975: 15). In 1960, the members of the EC conducted about one-third of total trade with each other. By 1962, this had risen to 40 percent, and by 1968, when internal tariffs were abolished, it had risen to 48 percent. In 1972, on the eve of the first enlargement, it had risen to 50 percent (Saunders, 1975). The share of overall trade aided by successive enlargements also contributed to the growth of intra-European trade as these new members diverted trade from non-member states. On the whole, the postwar period in Europe was a period of unprecedented growth of trade, with volume expanding more rapidly than output. More significantly, trade between West European states rose faster than trade with the rest of the world. The rise of so-called "intra-industry trade" (Grubel and Lloyd, 1975) differed from international trade in the nineteenth century as it involved trading similar types of goods—mainly manufactured products among industrial countries.

These results were affected by a variety of direct and indirect impacts on market integration. In particular, market integration took place against the background of mixed economies and governments prone to intervene in markets, not only through tariffs but also state aids and subsidies, divergent monetary policies, promotion of full employment policies as well as other actions that shaped market behavior and shielded domestic industries from competition (Pelkmans, 1984; Shonfield, 1965). For their part, firms operated as nationally federated companies, with separate marketing, distribution, and production systems within member states, although the competitive effect of a single market was expected to weaken domestic protectionist practices among firms (Franko, 1974: 289; 1976).

The virtuous cycle of postwar trade growth ended in the early 1970s, as external economic shocks and accompanying protectionist policies contributed to economic recession, undermining efforts to promote liberalization and integration. The conflicting political pressures and social demands within member states meant that various forms of protectionism emerged to deal with the competitive challenge emerging from the US and Japan. Many sectors were subject to protection through indirect measures, as the rate of growth of international trade declined significantly in marked contrast to the earlier postwar era (Boltho, 1982; Smith and Ray, 1992). Protectionism also impacted intra-Community trade as member states adopted a variety of non-tariff barriers that undermined the common market, and hampered the free movement of goods and services during this period (Egan, 2001; Nicolaïdis, 1993; Messerlin, 2001).[10]

Barriers to Trade in the EU

A variety of controls and restrictions affect the free movement of goods within Europe. These measures can include tariffs and production quotas, safeguard measures, and price supports that shield domestic agriculture and manufacturing industries, segment markets, and increase transaction costs. Governments can employ a variety of mechanisms to protect markets, including border delays and administrative formalities, as well as unnecessary and costly differences in standards and regulations that create impediments to the operation of a single integrated market. Separate national licensing systems and inspection regimes can block and delay imports, and foreign ownership restrictions and content quotas protect specific industries from competition. Governments can also exempt certain sectors and industries from trade agreements, and impose voluntary export restraints to protect domestic industries. These regulatory strategies create impediments to the operation of a single integrated product market, and hinder the flow of goods and commerce across borders (see Pelkmans and Winters, 1988; Egan, 2001; Pearce, Sutton, and Batchelor, 1985; Armstrong and Bulmer, 1998). In practice, the free movement of goods requires a mixture of basic rules and coordinated policies in the context of trade liberalization (Sun and Pelkmans, 1995).

Promoting an integrated product market means addressing different barriers to determine the most appropriate and effective ways to reduce or eliminate the negative impacts of such divergent regulatory systems. Not only must the integration of industrial product markets overcome the problem of disparate domestic interventions, but also the resistance of firms that seek to reduce competition and protect national markets (Frieden, 1991). The resulting local monopolies, price discrimination, and other methods that restrict intra-European trade are as much a problem of the internal market as they are of competition policy. The removal of barriers to trade also requires the prohibition of practices that maintain or create divisions within the European market. The mutual reinforcing character of these two policy instruments is crucial for removing a broad variety of distortions to interstate commerce caused by public or private action.

There is general consensus that the trade-impeding effects of discriminatory trade practices across Europe were considerable (see Cecchini et al., 1988; Flam, 1992). Though the estimated gains from market integration have been widely debated, the resulting efficiency improvements and scale advantages were expected to induce significant economic benefits (Cecchini et al., 1988) and allow member states to capitalize on internal liberalization.[11] Seeking to link loss of competitiveness with market fragmentation, the EU focused attention on the costs arising out of divergent national regulatory frameworks. The costs of border controls were estimated at between 8.4 and 9.3 billion European Currency Units, or ECU (the EC's unit of account at that time), with about 7.5 billion ECU due to administrative costs for cross-border trade.[12] Similarly, discrimination in public purchasing meant only 2 percent of contracts were awarded outside the home country, despite potential savings of between 8 and 19 billion ECU from procurement-market integration. Although the estimated gains have been treated with caution, the abolition of barriers to trade due to different regulations and standards was considered the number one obstacle to intra-European trade among industrialists surveyed. The cost of barriers on production was estimated at 2.4 percent of EU GDP, and would yield significant economies of scale and efficiency gains.[13] The overall goal was to enhance welfare and growth by reducing trade costs and prices, increase the variety of products, and promote innovation through the dismantling of customs formalities and trade barriers, primarily in goods and capital markets. When public or private market interventions are restrictive, without a proper justification for market failure, such policies tend to have an adverse effect on the functioning of cross-border trade. While the integration of product markets will remove market entry barriers and increase the contestability of markets, such efforts take place in the context of imperfect markets where governments act strategically to impact trade flows and increase national welfare (Egan, 2001: 45). The removal of trade barriers is about the evolution of rules for market access that are uniformly accepted, and the prevention of distortions to trade from (re) occurring through the creation of commitments and compliance mechanisms to which governments have acquiesced. This is also tied to efforts at preventing the substitution of public barriers by private barriers, which may endanger the common market. To ensure the proper functioning of the common market, competition policy must serve to remove restrictive business practices that can form effective barriers to trade. A common competition policy is also part of the regulatory process to ensure that distortions do not affect the competitive workings of the internal market (Pelkmans, 1984; Armstrong and Bulmer, 1998). Both the US and the EU sought to address the ways in which competition can be distorted through control of agreements and monopolies. Yet the efforts to correct distortions were much broader in the European case since it also includes the controlling of state aids and subsidies, which were deemed incompatible with the common market, in sharp contrast to the American experience (Lively, 1955).

The Early Formative Period: The 1960s to the 1970s

The key feature of the proposed European common market was the creation of a customs union among the six countries. While this would entail the removal of different kinds of intra-European barriers, it was to be achieved through a mixture of liberalization, approximation, and common policies. The creation of a common market was viewed as an essential element in promoting the overall economic growth and modernization of member state economies.

Sensitivity to various arguments and misgivings about the common market led to specific concessions and agreements that shaped the underlying motivation and philosophy behind the Treaty (see Laurent, 1970; Camps, 1959). Since the transitional stages leading to the reduction of tariffs caused considerable concern for France, it explains their caution as high customs tariffs and balance of payment deficits, along with prices estimated to be 20 percent higher than in other countries, meant that emphasis was placed on cushioning against radical change at the outset. In Benelux, there was in existence low duties so the reduction had very little effect in regards to other member states

(Deniau, 1961: 129). The Treaty advocated that customs duties would be eliminated within twelve years, or fifteen if there were necessary reasons to extend the deadline. The method for lowering tariffs allowed for flexibility so that governments could postpone the most difficult areas until the end. However, it was based on the understanding that all tariffs must be zero by the agreed-upon deadline to ensure that the customs union was irreversible (Bertrand, 1956). It was intended that the common tariff would come into effect at the same time as the progressive reduction of tariffs among the six. While the focus of attention was on the removal of quantitative restriction to trade, less attention was given to the use of restrictions in the case of balance-of-payments difficulties even though these were impacted by the renunciation of import restrictions (see Pelkmans, 1984).[14]

Early liberalization efforts resulted in the elimination of quantitative restrictions and customs duties in 1958 and the introduction of a common external tariff in 1968.[15] To avoid large-scale dislocation, the Treaty provided for a transitional period representing a substantial difference between agricultural commodities and industrial products.[16] The extension of tariff reduction to non-members minimized the discriminatory effects of the customs union, particularly in the early formative period of the European Community. The implications of economic interdependence were inextricably entangled with foreign as well as domestic policy objectives. American support for European integration depended on the progress towards free non-discriminatory trade and convertibility of currencies. A common market based on such provisions would be consistent with American support of such arrangements as the General Agreement on Tariffs and Trade and International Monetary Fund, both of which have as their objective the expansion of non-discriminatory multilateral trade (Brusse, 1997).

With the progressive establishment of the customs union, distortions of competition based on differing national laws and administrative provisions acquired increased significance. In spite of explicit legal provisions, violations of free-trade provisions continued. While substantive results had been achieved in relation to traditional trade barriers, firms were constrained by the widespread barriers to market entry that prevented them from engaging in cross-border competition. The intrinsic difficulties in trying to achieve the free movement of goods continued to plague the European Community throughout the early period. Distortions of competition due to differences between the various national laws and administrative provisions acquired increased significance, especially as it was increasingly difficult to determine between those regulations that reflected legitimate interests and those that served protectionist purposes (see Egan, 2001; Kelemen, 2011). The Commission responded by issuing Directive 70/50.[17] This sought to address those national measures that applied equally to both domestic and imported goods, which on the surface did not appear to discriminate but in practice restricted market access for imported goods through domestic preference or special measures.

Although the European Commission drew attention to the possibilities of a large common market, member states continued to protect and promote domestic industries and refused to allow the Commission greater authority to promote a coordinated economic policy. Unable to exercise any leverage over industrial planning due to its limited treaty competence, the European Commission turned its attention towards the problems of non-tariff barriers. Directive 70/50 expanded its regulatory authority and ability to address member state practices. Opting for harmonization of member state regulations as a solution, the Commission began to focus on several areas including foodstuffs, veterinary and phytosanitary standards, pharmaceuticals and motor vehicles in an effort to address barriers to trade (Welch, 1983). This was supplemented by efforts to push harmonization in new areas such as company law, mergers, and fiscal policy in order to expand policy competences at the European level.

The bulk of regulatory activity, however, focused on dealing with non-tariff barriers in the agricultural and product market sector. The European Commission began cautiously by choosing to harmonize products where national laws were relatively similar. The European Commission began to integrate markets with its first proposal in 1960 on agricultural products, which was selected in part due to the emphasis that had been placed on the Common Agricultural Policy. Addressing certain trade barriers in agricultural markets was followed by several other directives in sectors with marginal trade impacts, in an effort to tackle uncontroversial barriers in the early stages. Much of the initial success came from harmonization of specific products or practices, rather than those directives that attempted to specify design or composition agreements. Even then, common standards were often difficult to agree upon, and member states were left with a significant amount of discretionary authority in determining rules for market access. The European Commission was further constrained by the scope and quantity of national regulations, which made it difficult to fully promote an integrated market. Member states continued to adopt national regulations without regard for the implications for internal trade liberalization at the European level. Provisions to prevent new barriers from occurring were hard to enforce, and it was difficult to detect what constituted an illegitimate barrier to trade.

The European Commission faced substantial difficulties in promoting harmonization (see Dashwood, 1983). The slow progress meant that many agreements remained stalled or were simply shelved for consideration at a later date, often reflecting different national patterns of consumption, production, and culture. The Commission sought to remedy the problem with a general program for the elimination of technical barriers to trade in 1968.

Designed to proceed in stages, following earlier efforts at removing quotas and tariffs, the expectation was that non-tariff barriers would be removed by the scheduled deadline. Yet many key sectors such as telecommunications and pharmaceuticals were excluded from the program. Though armed with a variety of ways to address barriers to trade, the European Commission often found it difficult to get common agreement. Barriers could be removed through harmonization, mutual recognition, or reference to standards, as alternative means of coordinating different rules, but the program was modified repeatedly with meager results. Few directives were adopted that addressed the pervasive restrictions that hindered the free circulation of products.[18] By the time the deadline for the general program was reached in December 1970, only nine directives from the original one hundred and fifty had been adopted. Not surprisingly, seeking to standardize bread or beer had meager results, often stemming from prohibitions due to local customs and practices, whether it was food composition and ingredients, or more general restrictions due to differences in production and processes across a range of products.

Member states continued to prohibit certain products and processes at the national level, protecting their domestic industries, or made it difficult to access markets, arguing that protective regulations were necessary for public health and safety reasons, in much the same way that nineteenth-century notions of public economy and the well-ordered market were often espoused to justify public welfare. There were increasing complaints from industry about the complexity of many of the new Europe-wide legislative rules. Such a protracted process taxed Community resources, and frequently such efforts were vetoed through the unanimity requirement for such decisions concerning the single market. Like the American experience, many states continued to adopt their own regulations with little consideration of the intra-Community effects. As there were relatively few restrictions placed on domestic regulatory activities, the efforts to promote internal free trade became mired in confusion under the contradictory pressures of protectionism and liberalization.

Considerable misunderstanding also existed regarding the impact of harmonization on national cultures and traditions. Many companies encountered barriers in the absence of a common definition of specific content or process requirements, resulting in inconsistencies for labeling and production and often different import levies being charged for the same product. Fears remained that many areas of social and environmental policy would be whittled down to the lowest common denominator. Notwithstanding the limited political commitment towards harmonization, any further efforts to promote internal liberalization were stalled by the strains created by declining economic conditions and severe recessions in the 1970s and early 1980s. Many firms focused on retaining national market share, unable to benefit from the possibilities of a large common market. Plagued by rising inflation, high unemployment, and declining growth, member states pursued a variety of unilateral policies, which included every conceivable device short of tariffs and quotas. Far from being fully integrated, many remaining barriers were the result of only partial implementation of Treaty provisions and the absence of common policies, which was made worse during the prolonged periods of economic recession (Tsoukalis, 1997: 77). Weak enforcement of prohibition of certain state aids and sectoral policies in agriculture and steel also contributed to further distortions in intra-European trade, preventing market integration from being fully realized.

Throughout most of the 1970s and early 1980s, governments devised a host of restrictive rules and regulations (Page, 1981). France required the importation of electronics to clear customs at the small town of Poitiers, a long way from any border, in order to restrict foreign imports. Germany maintained strict beer purity laws, religiously enforced on the domestic market, which inhibited the importation of foreign beers made with additives or preservatives. Competition was further limited by selective delivery and distribution contracts that blocked out many competitors from entering the market. Specific requirements for Italian vinegar or pasta impeded imports from other member states. Belgian packaging regulations concerning margarine, ostensibly to distinguish margarine from butter, also prevented many other member states from marketing their own differently packaged products (see Slot, 1975). Similar efforts to stimulate local production through discrimination against foreign and out-of-state competitors were common across Europe. Such policies skewed trade balances and curbed competition. Yet national efforts to contain import competition and stabilize industries failed to stem the tide as trade deficits soared. With national governments seeking more regulatory protection to counteract the effects of increased imports, market integration stalled. These attempts to maintain aggregate levels of economic activity undermined trade relations in Europe through the constant emergence and perpetuation of trade disputes. The failure of national economic policies and the strains on Keynesian economic policy in many European states forced a search for alternative policies to promote economic growth (Hooghe and Marks, 1997). Pursuing market integration and the completion of the internal market again became a central focus, although not without struggles behind the scenes over its scope and function (see Moravcsik, 1998a; Hooghe and Marks, 1997; Egan, 2012b; Jabko, 2006). Like the US, the process reflected competing conceptions about organizing the economy, and different patterns of contention in response to changing economic conditions.

The 1980s: Renewed Momentum of the Single Market Program

Efforts to remove restrictions to internal commerce and trade to create an internal market in Europe advanced in the mid 1980s. For Cowles, market liberalization was supported by business groups, with corresponding efforts to promote market-supporting and market-correcting policies to mitigate the impact of increased competition and redistribute resources to garner broader support for market integration (Cowles, 1995). Though waning competitiveness led business to focus on the accumulation of rules which increased costs and discouraged investment, their calls for a collective strategy matched the increasing inclination of politicians to shift from internal domestic controls towards market-oriented policies as selective member states fully embraced neoliberal ideas (Moravcsik, 1998c). For Moravcsik, the single market program was the result of intergovernmental bargaining among states as economic interdependence influenced state strategic interests and preferences towards economic management through policy coordination. The potential of a single market became increasingly evident, and those sectional interests adversely affected by increased competition found special measures devised to help them deal with the deepening of the European market (see Hooghe, 1998; Allen, 2000; Héritier 1997b).[19]

The European Commission pushed its vision in a June 1985 White Paper entitled "Completing the Internal Market" (European Commission, 1985; Pelkmans and Robson, 1987). The Commission argued that national protectionism had reduced competition, slowed market adjustments, and weakened incentives to diversify or innovate. To promote efficiency and growth, the Commission emphasized the importance of market access and the need to remove restrictions to cross-border trade. The White Paper presented a two-part strategy to promote free movement of goods, the removal of border controls and other trade frictions combined with the coordination of national economic policy measures, and an overall goal of ensuring market access through a combination of regulation and competition policies.

The free movement of goods was the core of the single market project. Though the bulk of proposals were concerned with non-tariff barriers, it was the subsequent Treaty reforms that provided the critical basis on which to complete the internal market. This was helped by the explicit definition of a single market as an area without internal frontiers, in which the economic aims of the Treaty were clearly laid out in the revisions to the Treaty of Rome. As a result, the Single European Act played a key role in changing the negotiating dynamics (Pryce, 1987). The new additions provided for more qualified majority voting on internal market issues, which made it more difficult for recalcitrant member states to block proposals. The reforms also changed the instruments of market integration by establishing a more flexible strategy aimed at promoting liberalization, approximation, and common policies. A key element was mutual recognition, which proved to be an important addition to the regulatory efforts to ensure a fully functioning single market.[20] This requires measures to harmonize rules so the scope for differences among states is small, with member states committing themselves to the principle of mutual recognition of their respective products. The reform of the European regulatory strategy in response to the problems inherent in the traditional harmonization approach proved a key factor in addressing the restrictions to internal commerce (see European Commission COM (85) 19 Final; Bieber et al., 1988; Pelkmans, 1987).

The European Commission began with the abolition of customs formalities, inspections, and administrative requirements between the borders of member states. In 1992, the Commission issued a common customs code, and customs barriers were finally abolished by December 1992. This was supplemented by efforts to address regulatory impediments to the operation of a single market. The widespread adoption of regulatory standards, from product safety to pollution to business competition, improved the flow of goods and services. The European Commission also put a new strategy in place to prevent new barriers to trade from arising through regulatory preemption. Aware that previous "voluntary" efforts had failed, the Mutual Information Directive (83/89) sought to function as an early warning system, by preventing member states from adopting new regulations without informing the European Commission. This allowed the Commission to assess pending regulatory activity, seek some form of standstill on any potential restrictions, and thus prevent new barriers that might result from public or private actions (Pelkmans, 2012). The adoption of the directive was the first step in strengthening community oversight over the regulatory activities of member states, as well as the activities of many private sector bodies whose standards often serve as barriers to market entry through specific product requirements (Schepel, 2005).

More importantly, the European Commission pushed for a new regulatory strategy in 1985 which sought to address the variety of technical barriers long considered as a major factor behind the fragmentation of the European market (Pelkmans, 1987). The process of harmonization had proven both inefficient and ineffective in addressing the problem, so the European Commission placed greater emphasis on the mutual recognition of regulations to allow the unrestricted flow of goods throughout the Community. This innovative regulatory framework shifts away from the old pattern of harmonization, and limits such means of integration to essential health and safety requirements where national differences remain too distinctive and harmonization is thus not feasible. Private standards bodies would provide the necessary rules to meet EU regulatory requirements, allowing business the option to innovate if desired, and to play an active role in shaping the rules of market access on a

European-wide basis (Egan, 2001; Büthe and Mattli, 2011). Designed to make it easier to operate on a European-wide basis, as well as provide for common standards for market entry, the new approach was crucial to promoting regulatory convergence.

Between 1985 and 1992, twenty so called "new approach" directives, were adopted via mutual recognition, along with several flanking policies to support the mutual recognition of licensing and inspections through a so-called "global approach." However, even at the end of 1992, the stated deadline goal of the Commission's single market program, many elements of the legislative program were not completed or required further legislative action. Not only did the continued persistence of trade obstacles warrant further action to make the single market work effectively, problems continued in implementation and compliance that discouraged the free flow of goods across borders (Egan and Guimarães, 2012; Pelkmans, 2007). The European Council requested continual review of the functioning of goods and capital markets in order to monitor market developments (European Commission, Cardiff Report, 2002b). Well aware of the problems still facing the single market, the Commission continued to develop single market measures as part of a broader strategy of economic reform.

The European Commission generated a series of new initiatives that began with the Single Market Action Plan in 1997 and the regulatory simplification initiative (SLIM) in 1996 to do less in "order to do better." These were followed by the Regulatory Action Plan in 2002, and the Better Regulation Initiative in 2005.[21] These set out priority areas to improve the functioning of the single market by focusing on problems encountered in mutual recognition, the simplification of single market legislation, as well as overly restrictive national technical regulations, lack of standards in certain sectors, and discrimination against non-national enterprises that undermined the effectiveness of the internal market (Pelkmans, 2007). Efforts to take stock of how the single market is working place emphasis on ensuring better enforcement and compliance, as well as the realization that the single market context has changed from that of economies of scale and mass standardization to a knowledge and service-based economy with more product differentiation (Liddle and Lerais, 2007; Lejour, 2008). The changing nature of competition puts a premium on innovation and adaptability, making the challenge one of competition in the global marketplace. Shifting the focus from removing internal barriers, the new internal market strategy focuses on managing globalization through recognizing the need for greater differentiation between sectors, regulatory flexibility, and greater coordination with other policies, especially trade, competition, and labor (Pelkmans, 2008).

With market surveillance increasingly important for the functioning of the single market, the EU has developed a number of formal and informal enforcement mechanisms to address both current and potential barriers to trade (Pelkmans and de Brito, 2012; Egan, 2008). While new flexible modes of governance have emerged that are less legalistic and more subject to member state cooperation and peer pressure, these instruments have not replaced the more formal judicial measures (Pelkmans and de Brito, 2012; Anderson, 2012). Despite such measures as the Internal Market Scoreboard, and the Single Market Assistance Plans,[22] the EU still uses more formal judicial enforcement measures, including infringements proceedings, although this is increasingly seen as slow and costly (Egan and Guimarães, 2012; Pelkmans and de Brito, 2012; Kelemen, 2011).[23] Problems of implementation of rules in a correct and timely manner, coupled with the lack of competition and liberalization in key markets highlight the unexploited potential of further market integration (Monti, 2010; Guimarães and Egan, 2014; Mustelli and Pelkmans, 2013a; Howarth and Sadeh, 2010). With unfinished work in a number of internal market areas, some of these involve politically difficult issues such as tax policy and company law and tend to drop on and off the EU's agenda (Donnelly, 2010; Mustelli and Pelkmans, 2013b; cf. Genschel and Jachtenfuchs, 2011).

Residual protectionist behavior remains, and conflicts are bound to arise between the basic requirements of a common market and the measures necessary to curtail national regulatory autonomy. National markets continue to demonstrate a substantial "home bias" with a tendency to spend on goods and services in the home country as well as domestic equity investment. The single market notwithstanding, Europeans still buy and invest locally despite measures to foster competition and industrial competitiveness. However, as Balta and Delgado (2009) point out, it is difficult to disentangle to what extent home bias is due to market imperfections that can be corrected by specific policies, or whether it is due to consumer preference for local product market characteristics or firms deciding to produce specifically for local markets.

Rules on the production, distribution, and exchange of goods are now predominantly set at the European level, and legal developments have further solidified the move towards goods liberalization. The emergence of judicial doctrine—and enforcement of legal norms—has greatly reduced the number of regulatory barriers to the internal market (see section following this). This has a strongly integrative effect in much the same way that corresponding principles emerged in the US to foster internal liberalization (see Kommers and Waelbroeck, 1985).

Integration through Law

Legal decisions have played a major role in shaping market integration. Like its American counterpart, the European Court of Justice (ECJ) struck down trade barriers among states while recognizing local diversity and needs

(Kelemen, 2011). In performing this balancing act, legal decisions have primarily looked at the aims of legislation to ascertain whether it serves a protectionist intent or promotes a legitimate local or national interest. Yet the jurisprudence of the Court of Justice (ECJ) was surprisingly limited until the mid 1970s despite the impact of trade barriers in undermining the single market. Few judgments were made on quantitative restrictions to trade, in spite of the strong treaty language in this area, and the Court rarely intervened in deciding the merits of state regulations, deferring to the activities of the Commission in pursuing harmonization. Although the Commission defined what constituted a trade barrier, expanding the notion of discrimination to those practices that were more restrictive than necessary, the Treaty articles allowed member states to enact legislative restrictions on commerce in the interest of legitimate policy goals (Article 36).

Since the 1970s, the European Court of Justice issued a number of landmark rulings determining the boundaries and scope of regulatory competence and what constitutes a legitimate or illegitimate restriction on trade.[24] In *Dassonville* (*Procureur du Roi* v. *Benoît and Gustave Dassonville*, 8/74) the judgment provided an expansive definition of what constituted a trade restriction so that it was not necessary that a measure actually restricts imports, only that it has the potential to do so. The principle that all trading rules are capable of hindering intra-European trade directly or indirectly meant that a range of measures came under Community purview in determining their ability to distort the functioning of the common market.[25] However, the European Court of Justice concluded that provisions governed by other Treaty rules such as customs duties, state aids, and internal taxation, fell outside the scope and scrutiny of quantitative restrictions, thereby imposing limits on what national measures restricting trade were subject to this type of judicial review.

In *Cassis*, the European Court of Justice determined the extent to which certain national measures that restricted trade were permissible. *Cassis* was a key decision as it struck down a national regulation that defined the alcohol content of liquor. Since the Treaty allowed certain derogations from free trade, the *Cassis* judgment (case 120/78 1979 ECR) shifted the focus away from the legitimacy of domestic regulatory measures to a comparison of regulatory measures across states to determine the degree to which national restrictions were allowable (Alter and Meneuir-Aitsahalia, 1994). *Cassis* has done much to open up the single market for goods (Barnard, 2004: 127) by establishing the legal basis for the presumption of equivalence, or mutual recognition, of rules. While still careful to acknowledge the regulation of local economies—in the sense of American police powers—when there is no Community law in place, the European Court of Justice has reserved the right to review these measures in so far as they may affect commerce (Egan, 2001: 99).

In subsequent judgments the Court consolidated its ruling in *Cassis*. Although the notion of mutual equivalence of regulations was the most widely publicized dimension of *Cassis*, derogations from free trade were possible for specific purposes such as public health and consumer protection, and were also extended to include national culture and environmental protection.[26] Like the efforts of the US Supreme Court, the ECJ has engaged in a "balancing standard" whereby state regulation toward interstate commerce can be upheld if it has a legitimate rationale and the burden imposed on interstate commerce and any resulting discriminatory effects are outweighed by state interest in maintaining such restrictive regulations (Egan, 2001: 97).[27] In doing so, the European judgments avoided some of the problems of the American Commerce Clause which had often charted an inconsistent course between different approaches, alternately embracing and rejecting state imperatives.

Yet the jurisprudence of the European Court of Justice has not always been consistent, with some of the same questions raised about the reserved powers of the states that have occurred in the American system (Maduro, 1998; Schepel, 2005). Although legal decisions have been pivotal in laying the groundwork for promoting free movement of goods, the jurisprudence of the Court has acknowledged state interests in exercising their right of regulation (so-called "police powers") where there is no European-wide legislation in place. Faced with so many challenges that obstruct cross-border trade, the European Court of Justice has also sought to distinguish those regulations that warrant review because of their impact on market access (Craig and de Búrca, 2003). Due to the increasing tendency of business to challenge any policy hindering their commercial freedoms, the Court sought to determine whether regulations had sufficient impact to require judicial scrutiny under the Treaty articles. In the *Keck* case, the Court addressed this increasing difficulty in determining the scope of regulatory jurisdiction by recognizing that the economic relationship between regulation and the market and the political relationship between member states and the union had advanced sufficiently to reduce the scope of judicial scrutiny, and acknowledging the importance of subsidiarity in areas where national laws had limited impact on intra-European trade (Maduro, 1998; Caporaso and Stone Sweet, 1998).

Like the American efforts, the ECJ has fashioned a legal regime to resolve interstate disputes. Law shaped boundaries between different territorial units, playing a critical role in determining the constitutional limits to state intervention in the market and the role of regulation in the economy. Both governments and firms sought to use the law to maximize their interests and enhance their market position. For some scholars, this reflects a strong intergovernmental tendency, with the Court ceding or avoiding critical decisions to avoid member state non-compliance with adverse judgments (Garrett, 1995; Garrett, Kelemen, and Schulz, 1998). However, this is in sharp contrast to others, who argue that in dealing with the discriminatory effects of barriers to trade in goods, the European Court of Justice has played an active role in determining those national policies that could be construed as distortions to market competition by measuring the outcome in terms of the reasonableness of public intervention (Caporaso and Stone Sweet, 1998). In doing so, the Court has sought to develop judicial governance based on balance and proportionality, placing a heavy burden on public authorities to defend their actions, and empowering their own position in framing trade rules (Shapiro and Stone Sweet, 2002; Egan, 2001; Alter, 2001).

Such parallel efforts in Europe and the US indicate that the law is important in resolving conflict between central and local units of government, thus rendering important support to market processes in dealing with discriminatory barriers to trade. However, the prospect of a largely case-law-based guarantee of a single market has practical limitations, in both polities, not least of which is the need to continually assess and balance different state regulations against their intent and impact on a case-by-case basis. Given the possibility of judicially created limitations on trade, the legal foundations of market integration have not always been consistent, reflecting the need to balance factors including the economic relationship between regulation and the market, and constitutional limits on state or public intervention in that market. While constitutional or legal provisions provide the foundation for pursuing free trade, the effectiveness and legitimacy of its decisions depend upon being sensitive to political reality and the crosscurrent of ideas regarding trade and commerce. Both the US Supreme Court and the ECJ have constantly defined and redefined such concepts as control of the market, and more crucially the market itself to meet new problems and issues and respond to new economic theories (Shapiro, 1968).

The Effects of Integration on Business Strategy and Market Structures

While much attention has focused on the corresponding efforts in Europe and the United States to forge an internal market, assessing the reactions of firms to market liberalization provides important indications about the impacts—intended and unintended—of product market integration on corporate strategies. Since reactions of firms may vary depending on market structure, including the number, size, and organization of firms, the potential advantage from greater economies of scale and the potential widening of markets can be very different across member states and sectors (Chandler, 1962: 209; Chandler and Salsbury, 1968). The political economy of protectionism may encourage different response patterns depending on the perceived distribution of costs and benefits of market liberalization.

Discriminatory practices in Europe and the United States that undermine cross-border trade have often served to segment markets, protect local industries and practices, and curb competition. In some instances, there was a noticeable tendency for big business to seek federal legislation in order to avoid the problems of adjusting to multiple state laws (see Lindsay, 1910). The counter-strategy in the US of securing uniform legislation in certain areas was a painstaking process, with often-limited results as the movement to adopt uniform laws often failed to overcome the impediments inherent in coordinating divergent legal and regulatory practices. In Europe, while allowing some leeway for states to exercise regulatory authority and avoid undue concentrations of power through mutual recognition and home country control, the harmonization process has also been rife with problems. Another strategy has been delegated governance.

Many businesses in late nineteenth-century America sought to rationalize and stabilize the economy through voluntary associations. The pooling arrangements and the organizing of trusts in terms of marketing and manufacturing, as well as the growth of other trade and commercial associations were intended to regulate market conditions (Kelly et al., 1991: 381). In Europe, the delegation of regulatory activities to private enterprise, though often controversial, has been a dynamic factor in the development of an integrated economy. Business and trade associations have sought to regulate market conditions through agreement on common standards and rules for market access, but unlike the American case this has led to increased competition and cross-border trade. Organizing themselves for regulatory purposes, the establishment of a functional relationship with business has enabled the EU to address many of the inherent problems caused by non-tariff barriers to trade.

However, as a political project, failure to stem the continual emergence of interstate trade barriers is a cautious reminder that implementation and compliance matters (Falkner et al., 2005). In Europe and the United States, individual states continue to use their regulatory powers in the form of licensing, taxation, and other means, in ways that impose burdens on commercial activity. For multinational corporations, this can become a serious problem, since it can hamper technological improvements in production and organization that accrue from the sheer size of a national or regional market. For corporations that dominate their particular sectors, the denial of access to markets through prohibitions and restrictions can enable them to exercise market power, and reduces the incentives for collective action, since any economic adjustment imposes costs as well as benefits. Business strategies and effects are thus dependent on the structure of government regulations, such as discriminatory taxation, licensing requirements, and subsidization on the one hand, and the level of diversification and competition in the sector or industry on the other.

The organizational choices of firms are thus an important indicator of the impact of market consolidation, providing evidence of how firms have transformed their structures and strategies in response to the changing terms of trade. In the American case, business in the postbellum period was characterized by consolidation into larger units in response to fundamental changes in the processes of production and distribution (Chandler, 1962; Chandler and Salsbury, 1968). Because large firms found the existing networks inadequate to distributing their products, firms integrated mass production with mass distribution in response to continuing and expanding markets. In practical terms, this allowed companies to market their products across state borders, but it did not resolve all local disputes about the distribution of legal competences in controlling and regulating industrial development. This was aided by the constant stream of litigation brought before the courts. Legal rulings struck down many laws constraining the national market which provided the opportunity for the rise of the modern industrial corporation.

Similarly, in Europe private actors had both the incentive and resources to litigate, drawing on legal doctrines that fostered integration (Stone Sweet, 2005; Conant, 2007). The Court provided for an expansive "economic constitution" in which the single market program rested on the premise that liberalization would increase economic restructuring and growth (Maduro, 1998). A marked increase in mergers and acquisitions, along with a surge of foreign direct investment, indicated that both investment behaviour and business strategies were influenced by the prospect of a single market. However, the effects of liberalization go beyond the removal of trade barriers to impact public intervention in the new regulatory environment as well. The consolidation of markets was the product of certain demand factors, such as business pressure and litigation, as well as the attempts to establish regulatory controls, by guaranteeing statutory rules as safeguards to protect the public interest. As a result, there have also been competing tensions among public rights and private claims that legal decisions have been forced to resolve, as well as tensions between local diversity and uniform laws. This has set the framework within which the principles of free trade have had to be defended (Bensel, 2000: 353).

Market Matters: The Politics of Commerce

Both polities needed to generate economic and political mechanisms that would forge a strong unified single market. They appreciated that constitutional arrangements could not by themselves suffice to bind distinct sovereign entities into a common market. Since the US and EU faced strong resistance from states unwilling to give up their sovereign control over trade and commercial issues, the promotion of a single market was not simply a matter of economic rationalization. The debate over commerce forced different states to define their respective interests. But the issue should not be framed simply in terms of relative commercial advantage (Matson and Onuf, 1990: 118). The recognition of differences on the proper balance between state and federal power over commerce and the economy in the US was matched by similar debates about the transfer of power and responsibilities over trade and commercial practices in Europe.

To function properly, the US in the nineteenth century needed to increase production, break down barriers to trade, and become a single market for home-produced goods (Garson, 2001: 33). Emphasis has often been placed on the constitutional provisions that encouraged a national market by regulating interstate commerce. Yet efforts to consolidate authority over commerce were difficult because many laws and practices had served to confirm the political authority of the states. Challenges often aroused local hostility with different interests using justifications for the decentralization of power at different times (McNamara, 2005; Goldstein, 2001). In other instances, specific industries sought political centralization as a means of economic surety. For them, differences in laws and rules adversely affected the interests of industry that sought to take advantage of the economic union.

The situation was similar in post-World War II Europe where efforts to ease entry into the commercial marketplace floundered in the face of fierce opposition to harmonization. The persistence of state laws was reinforced by customs and traditions that were widely accepted. Not surprisingly, the political development of a single market was extremely contentious since it brought to the fore the central issue of economic jurisdiction. In both cases, the resulting uncertainty about the locus of political authority was determined by judicial decisions. Law shaped and channeled the dynamics of the market in both cases. Judicial power helped to create integrated economies, often reflecting prevailing ideologies of the relationship between political authority and the market.

Conclusion

If we examine the formative efforts at promoting interstate trade and commerce, the deepening and broadening of local markets into a larger territorial unit is indebted to prior experience. The tendency of states to pursue their own interests and revive protectionist practices revealed the inadequacy of uncoordinated and often conflicting state responses to common problems.

The need for some restraints on the economic freedom of states resulted in bargaining and compromise that centered on the regulation of commerce.

While trade barriers were recognized as a key constraint on growth and efficiency, providing the effective instruments to remove such barriers was no easy task. States were profoundly conscious of their differences. State resistance to economic integration was expressed in reluctance to shift policymaking under the purview of central authorities (Goldstein, 1997; Matson and Onuf, 1990; Fabbrini, 2002). This is clear in the process of harmonization and effort to create uniform state laws. States recognized that a single market would ease economic transactions, but also determine the interactions between different governments in terms of the scope and locus of their respective political and legal authority. States were reluctant to cede economic authority, and often sought to regulate and intervene in the market to provide the necessary framework for market transactions. The divisions among states over the nature of market consolidation was in a sense about the lines of jurisdiction between the states and central authority, which invited further conflict over the relationship between markets and politics. The constant balancing of different values and the relationship between market regulation and market-promoting activities differed across states, based on their relative comparative advantages, as well as their different conceptions of political economy and economic development (Pisani, 1987; Parsons and Roberts, 2003; Bensel, 2000).

These dynamics in turn impacted the centralization of authority by provoking a strong counter-response on the part of states and setting the context for decisive judicial action. In both instances, the courts used the respective constitutional clauses to promote economic cohesion by restricting freedom to act—the so-called "dormant Commerce Clause"—even in the absence of federal legislation. By policing the boundaries between legitimate and illegitimate state laws, the judiciary shaped ideas about the market. Legal systems helped create the conditions—or preconditions—for allowing trade to cross borders by easing local restrictions. Attempting to reduce diversity through litigation proved too slow and uncertain to be a practical option in the US, and subsequently the EU (Pelkmans, 2007; Schofield 1908a: 418; Schofield, 1980b: 518–19). This necessitated new strategies to regulate and standardize interstate commerce and trade flows. Resolving commercial disputes resulted in innovative practices to promote regulatory cooperation and comity between states that are broadly equivalent in the US and EU. This combination of retained regulatory authority by states through mutual recognition and reciprocity on the one hand, and delegated authority from states to private trade associations and independent regulatory agencies on the other, promised a way of dealing with the practical needs of building an integrated market (Egan, 2008).

In establishing the parameters for economic regulation, the promotion of interstate commerce was a complex political project that created a regulatory framework within which state activity was curbed but not fully removed. State laws continued to exist alongside central efforts to establish regulatory authority to standardize and stabilize economic transactions. However, the process has encountered many problems. Effective enforcement and compliance with European-level regulations, limited scope of reciprocity and interstate compacts in the US, and continued adoption of state regulations that impede internal commerce have acted as a constraint on a truly internal market.[28] Business has often sought legal redress, and key litigation has sought to exercise limitations on state regulatory authority. In turn, these legal struggles set in motion constraints on the market activities of private actors, with working definitions of competition and regulation reflected in the institutionalization of controls over both commerce and corporations. This theme is taken up in the later chapter, on services, where the capacity of many large industries to restrain trade becomes a critical issue. While railroads and utilities were key industries promoted by government intervention and investment, the impacts of limited competition and monopolistic practices became increasingly salient as public service obligations clashed with established market mechanisms, as governments became the regulators and adjusters of market outcomes.

Notes

1. This provides non-residents with certain non-discriminatory provisions aimed at preventing barriers to interstate commerce and ensuring that they are unhindered by burdensome state restrictions and taxes.
2. Article 1 Section 10.
3. North uses tonnage passing through various ports and canals to demonstrate interregional trade patterns. See appendices in North (1966).
4. One of the earliest Congressional statutes adopted in 1796 prohibited the shipment of goods in interstate commerce in violation of state health and quarantine laws.
5. The result was that only five cases concerning the Commerce Clause came on to the docket of the Supreme Court, and only twenty-five between 1840 and 1870. See Prentice and Egan, 1898.
6. In a number of instances, states resisted the decisions of the higher court. See Scheiber, 1975; Goldstein, 2001 for specific cases of state intransigence.
7. See the discussion of *Swift* v. *Tyson* (1842) in Chapter 5.
8. The treaty articles on free movement of goods also allowed certain derogations from removing quotas and other measures for health and safety reasons (Article 36).
9. There are also a number of areas where the treaty is limited in application. The free movement of goods was not intended to apply to military goods; and hence dual-use technologies, for example.

10. Article 115 of the Treaty of Rome provides the most obvious escape clause mechanism for protection from imports.
11. Economies of scale improved efficiencies within companies and affected prices due to increased competition and new patterns of industrial competition based on comparative advantages and increased innovations.
12. See Ernst and Whinney, Border Related Control and Administrative Formalities, for the European Commission "Cost of Non Europe" project. Estimated as loss of 0.3% of GDP.
13. The Cecchini report on the "Cost of Non Europe" focused on both the direct effect of improved efficiency following the removal of protective measures by different national governments, and estimated the indirect effects from further EC-market integration and increased competition across a number of case studies of specific industries.
14. See Article 107–9 that covered a common concern about balance of payments and exchange rates.
15. The timing and percentages were prescribed in the first two stages, with flexibility built in to protect the costs of adjustment for sensitive sectors. Tariff reduction was automatic, across the board, and reintroduction of quotas was prohibited. The final reduction would be decided by the Council of Ministers on the basis of qualified majority.
16. Tariffs were reduced by 80% on industrial products and 65% on agricultural products during the same period.
17. Directive 70/50/EEC on the abolition of measures which have an effect equivalent to quantitative restrictions on imports and are not covered by other provisions adopted in pursuance of the EEC Treaty (OJ L 13, 19.1.1970).
18. Between 1967 and 1972 twenty-two directives were adopted; between 1972 and 1978 thirty-six directives were adopted, and between 1975 and 1978 fifty directives were adopted.
19. Economic and social cohesion was inserted into the Treaty in part as a political condition to allow the poorer members to agree to the 1992 program. It also reflected the general aims of the preamble of the Treaty.
20. Mutual recognition as a regulatory principle was given a central place in the single market project. The methods of integration were altered, and the conceptual framework of market liberalization applied to all areas thereby removing the dichotomy between goods and services in addressing barriers to trade.
21. See inter alia European Commission (1996a) "Communication on Simpler Legislation for the Internal Market (SLIM): A Pilot Project" COM (96) 204 Final, Brussels; European Commission (1996b) "Communication on the Impact and Effectiveness of the Single Market" COM (96) 520 Final, Brussels; European Commission (2002c) "Regulatory Action Plan" COM (2002) 278 Final, Brussels; European Commission (2005) "Communication on Better Regulation for Growth and Jobs in the European Union" COM (2005) 97 Final, Brussels.
22. European Commission, "Making the Single Market Deliver: Annual Governance Check-up 2011," Working Document, 2012.

23. The principal enforcement actions before the ECJ are actions brought either by the Commission on behalf of the EU or by another member state, and there is also state liability involved (see *Francovich* v. *Italy* (1990) C-6/90 for non-compliance with EU legal obligations).

24. For a detailed overview, see Egan (2001); Slot (1975); Barnard (2004); Oliver (1996).

25. The Dassonville formula was not new, as the ECJ had used the argument in a different way in its earlier judgments of Grundig and Consten under Article 85 covering competition issues.

26. See for example *Commission* v. *Denmark* ECR 4607 (1988).

27. The judgments were based on causality, proportionality, and substitution.

28. See the 1940 reports by Taylor et al., and also the EU as well.

5

Capital Flows and Financial Markets

Capital leads a complicated and curious life.

William Parker (as quoted in Bodenhorn, 2000)

While contemporary debates about capital markets have drawn attention to the problems created by "footloose capital," the rapid expansion of international financial activity challenged the powers of national governments to control their economies, even before the onset of the current global financial crisis (Strange, 1996; Garrett, 1995). Capital restrictions provided protection to conduct relatively autonomous monetary policies and at the same time maintain exchange rate stability by preventing massive capital flows, but market participants soon found new ways to circumvent exchange and credit controls (Bakker, 1994: 3; Sbragia, 1996). Speculative attacks against weaker currencies brought pressure for greater restrictions on capital mobility, although the new financial instruments and technology-driven innovations make efforts to exercise such regulatory controls increasingly difficult (Cerny, 1993). Capital liberalization has become an increasingly global phenomenon over the past two decades, affecting both advanced and developing countries and shifting attention to other policy domains including the role of central banks. Liberalization and regulation of capital movements are therefore tied up with discussions of banking and monetary policy in both Europe and the US (see McNamara, 2001a, 1999).[1]

The mobility and availability of capital flows is widely believed a crucial factor in economic development and growth. While Gerschenkron demonstrated that the institutional framework enabling the growth of capital mobility played a crucial role in industrialization in nineteenth-century Europe, it played a similar role in promoting an economic stimulus for America and Europe in the nineteenth and twentieth century, respectively (Gerschenkron, 1962). An integrated capital market requires that a) there is capital mobility across states and/or regions, b) that barriers to entry are reduced or eliminated in order to ensure competition and reduce monopolistic behavior, and c) that interest rate differentials are narrowed among different areas (Sushka and Barrett, 1984: 464). An integrated financial market is expected to result in an efficient and effective allocation of financial investments, since capital can move to where it receives the highest return. Although much attention has been given to the effects of capital mobility on interest rate convergence,[2] the legal, economic, and regulatory environment also shaped the evolution and operation of financial services, reflecting protracted struggle among different interest groups seeking to influence the structure of the industry (White, 1982: 33; Frieden, 1991; Woll, 2013).

This chapter focuses on the emergence of interregional capital mobility, and the integration of financial markets. Since the liberalization of financial services is linked to that of capital movements, it examines efforts to foster financial integration through measures to open up both banking services and capital markets.[3] Although the term capital controls is often used to depict restrictions on capital mobility, it masks a wide range of domestic regulatory measures used to hinder capital flows. Such restrictions can be imposed on short- or long-term capital flows to protect domestic or local capital markets, and control domestic monetary expansion. In some cases, impediments to trade are incidental to other objectives such as stemming speculative attacks, ensuring prudential lending, and keeping control over fiscal and monetary policies. In other cases it is difficult to avoid characterizing them as protectionist (Pelkmans and Winters, 1988: 46). The latter include discrimination against non-residents, restrictions on financial services and products that can be offered, and differences in regulatory supervision that can pose significant market entry barriers.

Though financial intermediaries are considered critical for economic growth and development, one of the most important questions in financial history is the circumstances under which integrated capital markets have developed. How did an integrated capital market emerge in the US and EU? What impact has capital mobility had in changing patterns of economic behavior of banks and other financial intermediaries? And what are the consequences of financial market liberalization for economic governance and state authority?

Although capital controls are shaped by the specific institutional structure of the financial system and reflect different political choices about economic governance, restrictions can take a variety of forms and are often the result of complex administrative or regulatory practices that serve both political and economic rationales. Issues of capital movements and fiscal coordination have special political significance for states (Lindberg, 1993). Struggles over the regulation and supervision of financial services and intermediaries have resulted in particular forms of state–finance–industry relations, with distinctive consequences for long-term financial investment and economic

119

performance (Hall, 1986; Zysman, 1983; Fioretes, 2011; Howarth and Quaglia, 2013; Story and Walter, 1997; cf. Deeg and Perez, 2000: 138). An important feature of the financial sector in the US and EU is the high degree of government intervention across different levels of government. To ensure fiscal stability, governments have played a major role in shaping bank loan and deposit markets, determining the type of financial services offered and providing a variety of related support systems (Bisignano, 1992: 155). In the US, states and municipalities competed for capital investment, fostering regulatory competition across jurisdictions by adjusting regulatory burdens and creating investment incentives to retain tax revenues and avoid capital relocation. In a multilevel system such as Europe, similar mechanisms to interstate competition come into play so different levels of government need to coordinate their policies to avoid duplicative regulations, or avoid a competitive race to the bottom as banks or financial intermediaries will choose to be chartered or regulated by the least restrictive government. Governing capital is a contentious process involving struggles over the distribution of authority between different levels of government, and the nature of that governance—especially in the banking sector—is sensitive to regulation and oversight by governments (see especially, McNamara, 2001a; Haber, 2003; Howarth and Quaglia, 2013; Schelkle, 2009a). However, this does not mean that the policies and practices converged in their respective markets, as there were variations in capital requirements for banks generating differential effects in terms of banking stability, and the different structure of banking and financial systems also impacted the performance of banking systems especially during periods of economic recession, when the variable impact of the crisis in terms of losses, speculative attacks, and the availability of credit, generated variation in government intervention to support banks—in terms of capital injections, loans, and debt write-offs (Jabko and Massoc, 2012; Wallis, Sylla, and Legler, 1994; Wallis, 2005).

Much scholarship on capital markets focuses on efficiency gains arising from capital liberalization, or the effects of the technological and communication revolution in integrating geographically distant markets (O'Rourke and Williamson, 1999). Yet of particular interest are their common efforts to control budget deficits and "regulate governments rather than markets" (Schelkle, 2009c: 831). In both the US and EU cases, liberalization of capital movements and financial services is not simply about negative integration or removal of barriers to market access to ease cross-border financial activity, but also the construction of governance mechanisms for positive integration, ensuring the viability of market transactions through the coordination, integration, or approximation of monetary and fiscal policies, and strengthening fiscal surveillance mechanisms, contributing to the regulatory state-building model (see Schelkle, 2009c: 831; see also Lindberg, 1993; Posner and Véron,

2010). Political leaders understood that market integration would have to bind states together, while still protecting local interests and sensitivities. While constitutional or legal provisions provide the foundation for pursuing such goals, they do not suffice to create a common enterprise. Governance mechanisms were shaped, in large part, by the specific ideas regarding institutional design, the role of political competition, and the competitive pressures and dynamics for an increasingly integrated economy. When taken together, the policies of both periods were characterized by dual regulatory regimes that created policies of harmonization, mutual recognition, and regulatory competition. Two important implications emerge from this analysis. First, as capital flows and financial markets became increasingly mobile across borders, they generated different policy preferences and lobbying activities among domestic interests. Second, while formal and informal institutions played a role in shaping regulatory outcomes, both polities have shifted from one where financial institutions, especially banks, were under strict government control, to one where liberalization, innovation, and capital mobility promoted structural reforms, competition, and new financial instruments. This was then followed by constitutional reforms, and hence changes in economic governance, with real effects on government policy.

This chapter first traces the American experience, focusing on the growth of interregional fiscal transfers and barriers to capital mobility. Section two discusses American efforts to address barriers hindering capital movements in both the antebellum and postbellum period, including legal developments pivotal to overcoming those constraints. Section three examines the European experience in fostering capital mobility, focusing on efforts within the EU to overcome barriers to interstate trade and investment. It considers early efforts to reduce capital controls, along with later developments in the context of the single market program. The section concludes by evaluating the impact of capital market integration and the creation of a single market in financial services on market structure and patterns of economic behavior. The chapter ends with a comparison of methods used to integrate the two capital markets. It concludes by noting that both polities confronted legal and political impediments through strategies of regulatory harmonization and regulatory competition.

Both the US and EU have sought to facilitate fiscal mobility by explicitly promoting financial services. Providing a legal and regulatory framework has enabled governments to assert their legitimacy in regulating the money supply and spurred the integration of financial markets. The impact of law on public and private sector investment is crucial to understand the operation of financial institutions, and the adaptations that markets and firms have made to deal with increased legal obligations and regulatory oversight to protect savings, prevent crises and banking failures, and ensure sound market practices. Yet the incongruity between national supervision and international markets has become increasingly apparent. With the eurozone economies experiencing severe fiscal pressures and real risk of default, the corresponding efforts to shore up the struggling economies has drawn parallels with the state defaults in the mid 1860s in the US. However, the creation of an emergency fund to support member states highlights a key difference with the US where the lack of a common debt instrument within the European currency union means that the banks remained highly vulnerable to the exposed debt of the sovereign state making the prospect of bank runs a continual risk, forcing them to restrict credit. While the US is a banking union, which provides more shock-absorbing capacity for states under duress, through providing federal insurance guarantees, the euro area has partially followed suit and now has adopted a common system for handling bank crises. Both aim at enhancing regulatory capacity to deal with investment risks, although as Hallerberg concludes, there remain important structural differences between the US and the EU (Hallerberg, 2014: 100).

American Interregional Finances

The development of a national capital market created important questions regarding the respective authorities of states and the federal government. The financial connection between the federal government and the states was a critical matter in the founding and early operation of the American republic (Trescott, 1955; Garson, 2001). The Constitution gave the federal government the power to create and regulate the supply of money. States were denied the right to issue currency directly, though they could grant that right to charter banks. There are no specific legal provisions for a single currency or central bank, although Congress interpreted the Constitutional provisions to mean they had the right to coin money and regulate its value as an act of sovereign control (Hurst, 1973: 33).

National money and capital markets emerged gradually in the US, closely following the integration of local and regional markets (Davis, 1963; Sylla, 1969; James, 1978). While most capital investment in the nineteenth century was used for domestic economic development, interregional transfers of capital and credit had to overcome considerable impediments to capital mobility in the nineteenth century. The literature on capital market integration offers a number of explanations to account for the development and growth of fiscal flows. While determining the factors that account for domestic integration of the American financial system is the focus of this chapter, foreign capital markets were also extremely important for railroads, and occasionally federal bonds, in linking American and European markets and financial centers

(Sbragia, 1996). Although the size of foreign direct investment is not large in aggregate terms, the infusion of financial capital at specific points in American economic and industrial development was crucial (Davis and Cull, 2000). In the period between 1830 and 1838, the states borrowed $150 million, which coincided with the rapid development of interstate transportation. Between 1860 and 1869, state borrowing had risen to $500 million, coinciding with the Civil War and Reconstruction (Davis and Cull, 2000: 738). As Davis and Cull note, this reached unprecedented proportions. Domestic capital markets were relatively underdeveloped, and so foreign capital provided substantial funds for state governments to expand their commercial banking and transportation sectors and promote land-related investment (see Davis and Cull, 2000: 738).

However, the general shift in output from agriculture to industry, migration and change in the composition of the labor force, and shifts in demands for funds from the industrialized East to the Western frontier and Midwest in the nineteenth century, all marked significant changes in the structure of the American economy (James, 1978: 5). The growth of accumulated capital in the US as a result of increased rates of investment and savings was estimated at 4 percent per annum between 1800 and 1840 and 6 percent between 1840 and 1860 (Gallman as cited by Bodenhorn 2000: 5). Bank-issued money provided the lubricant of the economy and acted as the predominant medium of domestic exchange and transactions (Bodenhorn, 2000: 16). Temin estimates that this amounted to about $40 million in 1820, with half in circulation and half held as bank reserves (Temin, as cited in Bodenhorn, 2000).

Although the older sectors and regions of the country had access to capital, the growing frontiers faced more difficulty in meeting their financial needs. Even with the prospect of commercial development in the West, it was considered difficult to exploit such opportunities without sufficient information about investments. A system of financial intermediaries did not yet exist, and the scarcity of capital in the West was hampered by the fact that it was geographically distant from most holdings of accumulated savings (Bruchey, 1990: 177; Odell, 1989: 297). By the end of the nineteenth century, improvements in transportation and communications along with increased legal certainty and uniformity governing private transactions reduced the barriers to interstate trade and economic development. The resulting interregional and intersectoral investment generated two patterns of capital flows. Vertical flows stemmed from the major urban centers of the manufacturing belt to the peripheral South and West, and from major financial centers such as Chicago and New York to regional cities such as Albany, Buffalo, and Detroit (Bensel, 2000: 70). Horizontal flows stemmed from stagnant industries to new emerging industries and commercial enterprises, particularly in the postbellum period with the expansion of railroads and other corporate debt and equity needs. Capital needs for rapidly expanding industries and agricultural production were met by a variety of financial institutions. Long-term capital investment was provided by private banks, mutual savings banks, building and loan associations, and life insurance companies. Short-term capital investment needs were met by commercial banks, which also provided the means of payment in the form of bank notes or deposits (James, 1978: 7). While it is generally assumed that banks were legally constrained in the nineteenth century, a dense network of financial intermediaries emerged that circumvented those restrictions, forming long-distance relationships that promoted geographic mobility of capital.

Banking and monetary policy was the subject of public debate throughout the nineteenth century. Beginning with the Jacksonian fight over the power of the Bank of the United States and the refusal to renew its charter, the national banking system was widely criticized as unresponsive and unstable. While the banking system as a whole was susceptible to panics, and criticized for hoarding specie when currency became scarce, the news and rumors that banks could no longer redeem their notes into currency often led to long queues and bank failures (Sheridan, 1996: 1148). Coupled with criticism leveled at the existence of banking monopolies, the high level of rural interest rates and the lack of control over the issuance and value of bank notes raised social tension (James, 1978: 7). Such struggles raised problems of the legitimacy of the market, and social-class tensions about the boundaries of state and federal authority in relation to local and national markets (Freyer, 1994: 20).

Barriers to Trade

The development of a national capital market in the US has generated a lively debate among financial historians about the restrictions on capital mobility and the degree to which legal and regulatory barriers were circumvented in practice. Most studies of American financial markets distinguish between the antebellum and postbellum periods in describing changes in the economic landscape, especially with regard to the consolidation of banking and capital markets and the creation of a single currency. This is helpful in understanding the political watershed created by the Civil War, bringing the currency under federal control and allowing Congress to increase government borrowing, requiring all national banks to invest capital in government bonds, and creating a uniform national bank note currency (Sylla, 1969).

The Antebellum Period

The antebellum period was one in which states enjoyed substantial authority over fiscal policies. With no uniform and reliable single currency, states were able to authorize their own paper currency with no uniform redeemable value through chartered banks. Separate currencies presented obstacles to economic integration, particularly given considerable state variation in bills of exchange. In the antebellum period, bank notes were the most common form of payment. Banks issued promissory notes that a given states' amount of coin dollars would be given to the bearer on demand (Sheridan, 1996: 1144). The lack of uniform exchange rates, however, meant a huge variation in state bank notes, with discounted notes reflecting differences in the soundness of the issuing banks (Hurst, 1973: 37). Although bank notes served as the main medium of money in circulation, the rules surrounding their circulation were set by their individual charters of incorporation.

The federal government had chartered two national banks, the First and Second Banks of the United States in 1791 and 1817, respectively. The First Bank received a charter for twenty years to become a depository for public money, issue bank notes, and act as the fiscal agent of the Treasury. When its charter expired in 1811, state and private commercial banks filled the void. The renewal of the bank charter in 1817 subsequently led to "the bank wars" with Andrew Jackson who opposed the privileged position of the Bank. Although a depository for public funds, the Second Bank could use these funds for its own purposes without paying interest and did not have any directly competing financial institution. However, federal bank notes did not enjoy a monopoly, as state banks continued to issue notes. As proponents sought to recharter the Second Bank four years early in 1832, Jackson exercised his historic veto, arguing that the Bank of the United States was subversive of the rights of states (Remini, 1967). With the changed status of the Bank and the withdrawal of federal funds, the surplus funds after paying off war debts, were distributed among the states.[4] With the loss of its charter and impending demise, federal bank notes disappeared from circulation, and left the banking system without a lender of last resort (Haber, 2003: 15).

Although there had been efforts to centralize banking in the early American Republic, a legacy of Alexander Hamilton, the demise of the national bank left the financial field open to banks chartered by states. After 1836, the number of state banks increased rapidly, rising from 634 in 1837 to 901 in 1840. With these changes due to the demise of the federal bank, state banks proliferated, often with lax standards, enabling banks to issue more notes than they could redeem, so the wildcat certificates proved to be worthless. Despite their growing unpopularity, demands for a return to the old national banking system were not met. All banks of issue and deposit were established by states, and the resulting lack of uniformity in terms of central supervision caused considerable problems in fostering capital mobility. While state bank notes were widely accepted in the state or locality of issue, even when banks suspended payments of bank notes into specie during runs and panics, bank failures were still common. The effects of lack of uniformity meant that capital could be transferred across states only at considerable discount. The farther away from the bank at issue the less the currency was worth. Uncertainty about creditors in distant states meant that "financial intermediaries often returned bank notes to test the commitment of the bank to maintain their value" (Sheridan, 1996: 1145). Because information about the solvency of banks in distant states was imperfect, transaction costs were higher across state lines. The lack of a nationwide clearing house meant that banks relied on financial intermediaries that bought notes at discount or premium depending on the safety and reputation of the issuing bank.

Discounted bank notes meant that there was effectively a system of exchange rates in place among currencies. The rates and fluctuations depended on bank lending policies, balance of payments, state fiscal health, and other factors. While some states such as Louisiana adopted strict policies that ensured that their bank notes were repurchased at face value, oftentimes requiring capital reserves, other states such as Illinois had more liberal policies. Though a reputation for "sound money" enabled some states to preserve the value of their currency against speculative attacks, reduce their note issue, and increase their local interest rates, other states ignored banking regulations, pursued "unsound policies" and continued to issue bank notes even in the face of reduced demand generating a depreciation of value for that bank's currency (Sheridan, 1996: 1146; Million, 1894). In these circumstances, state legislatures could suspend payment, often leading to economic depression and monetary contraction. Though the US possessed a common "outside" dollar (specie—gold and coins), each state possessed its own "inside" money, bank note dollars which originate within the banking and financial system. Bank notes were the principal form of paper money in circulation in the antebellum period, although their value was not fixed but rather a flexible exchange rate system (Sheridan, 1996: 1144–6). While exchange rate instability meant that some states suffered balance-of-payments difficulties, currency shortages often led states to circumvent the problem through new bank charters, reduced bank supervision, or an increase of bank note issues.

The lack of federal oversight and consistent rules and regulations created a dispersed and disintegrated system. Davis argues that barriers to mobility were significant and distorted patterns of growth in the nineteenth century (Davis, 1963). The prohibition of interstate banking meant that small and unconnected institutions with different currencies were not able to take advantage of a single market. Private banks were also hampered by the monopolistic or oligopolistic position of state chartered banks. Many states passed restraining acts in the antebellum era that prohibited the activities of private bankers and limited their role as financial intermediaries (Bodenhorn, 1997). Among the most stringent laws adopted was in New York (1818), which prohibited any institution without explicit legislative charter from issuing notes, accepting deposits, and loaning money (Bodenhorn, 1997: 516). Since private banks were unincorporated, such restrictions clearly affected commerce and the scope and volume of financial transactions by private intermediaries. Yet private banking expanded rapidly between 1840 and 1850, with estimates of 460 in 1854 rising to 920 by 1860 (*Bankers Magazine* as cited by Bodenhorn, 1997: 516). Since many uncharted banks were already in existence—especially in the Western states—the state prohibitions on private banking were often unenforceable.

As more liberal attitudes towards banking emerged in the late 1830s, strict state chartering requirements were replaced by the free banking era (1837–63) where banks no longer had to be approved and chartered by the legislature (Temin, 1968). In part driven by growing capital needs, the introduction of free banking in Michigan, New York, and elsewhere eased the conditions for obtaining a bank charter. While some states liberalized regulations such as capital and reserve requirements, which lowered entry barriers still further, the system of granting exclusive charter privileges had fallen into disfavor because it invited charges of abuse and favoritism. Free banking reduced political barriers to entry and ensured that the chartering of banks was no longer a state legislative function (Sylla, 1969: 483). The shift in strategy also meant that more banks could be established even in small towns, undercutting the monopoly powers of state banks, and providing greater public acceptance of private banking (Bodenhorn, 1992, 2000; James, 1978: 232–3).

Even so, private banks were still reluctant to obtain a corporate charter, and with it the right to issue bank notes, since free banking laws were not deregu- latory. Corporate charters entailed substantial regulatory costs in terms of minimum capital adequacy standards and the proportion of capital that was required to be invested in state bonds (Bodenhorn, 1997: 518). Some bankers therefore eschewed such regulatory requirements and continued to operate unregulated branch networks, which would have been prohibited under most free branch statutes. Circumventing state laws allowed private banks to finance mercantile and manufacturing activity in the antebellum period, by some estimates holding one-quarter of investments and one-third of deposits (Sylla, 1969). This led many chartered banks to lobby for restraining acts to protect their monopolies and prevent further competition by restricting the entry of private banks (Bodenhorn, 1997: 541). Virtually all of the banks, except those in the South, were single branch banks, in part to protect rural banks from competition.

Denied the ability to cross state lines and faced with increased competition from private banking, state chartered banks were forced to develop ties with other banks so they could participate in domestic interregional financial dealings (Bodenhorn, 1997: 192). State banks were able to overcome legal constraints on the prohibition of branch banking with a correspondent banking system. Though much of the literature has focused on the reduction of interest rate differentials to determine when capital market integration took place, it has overlooked the role of financial activities in consolidating those markets at the regional level (Odell, 1989). Regional banks acted as financial intermediaries for distant lenders in the northeast, and acted as a focal point to mobilize funds within and across regions, lessened financial isolation for economies of newer regions, and served as agents for other banks in clearing checks (Odell, 1989).

The circumvention of constraints through inter-bank lending, direct interregional investment, and investment in bank stock transformed the view that banks were local or regional enterprises (Bodenhorn, 1997: 186). Stretching out regionally, many banks took on a more national character as they engaged in the commercial paper and exchange markets. While northeastern banks provided short-term interregional capital transfers, based on the real bills or commercial loan doctrine where a short-term, self-liquidating loan is expected to be quickly repayable, rural Western banks were most likely to utilize the paper and commercial market to forge the foundations for a national capital market (Odell, 1989; Bodenhorn, 1997: 186). Although the antebellum market was not as sophisticated as the commercial paper market that developed after the Civil War, it did link state chartered banks, exchange brokers, and private bankers across the country, and enabled them to circumvent legal constraints on their activities (see James, 1978; Bodenhorn, 1997; Lamoreaux, 1994).

Throughout this period, a degree of informal coordination emerged among New England banks. The so-called "Suffolk Bank system" emerged in which the Suffolk Bank of New England redeemed and collected for all New England banks, which meant that bank notes in the region circulated on the same par as the Suffolk Bank, which acted as a clearing house for small and distant banks. The Suffolk Bank applied a discount rate to assess the quality of bank notes, which was critical as there were literally thousands of different bank notes in circulation (see Lamoureaux, 1994). This was the only region that was successful in controlling the quantity of its bank note by restraining the issuance of bank notes (Atack and Passell, 1994: 177). Some states, including New York, and later on Philadelphia and Boston, established deposit insurance funds that in the long run were not very successful. However, it did point to continued effort at promoting uniformity or harmonized standards to improve the stability and security of the monetary supply. But political competition among states made it difficult to create a single federally chartered banking system in the US (Rockoff, 2000; Sylla, 1976, 1969). Institutional substitutes did emerge to circumvent the restrictions placed on interstate banking in response to the growing demands placed on the financial sector (Sylla, 1976: 186).

Integration through Law: Developments in the Antebellum Period

Scholars of commercial law have argued that state variations in the legal certainty of sale, purchase, and collection of bills of exchange adversely impacted interstate trade and financial transactions (Freyer, 1976: 436). Legal decisions at the federal level are considered crucial in establishing the foundation for a more integrated financial market by clearly delineating the rights and obligations of debtors and creditors engaged in interstate trade (Bodenhorn, 2000: 200). Because the legal standing of creditors was uncertain due to differing state doctrines and practices, the resolution of this issue is considered pivotal in improving the functioning of the exchange market and promoting an integrated capital market. In fact, state courts and legislatures frequently changed the rules to create uncertainty among investors.

States generated laws that discriminated against out-of-state business and especially out-of -state creditors, creating a major barrier to economic development (Freyer, 1994: 20). The rights for in-state debtors were strengthened through a variety of practices such as depreciation of legal tender for debts, and extension of time frames for debtors to meet their obligations. Because debtor–creditor laws were used to protect local debtors against out-of-state creditors, such state-based rivalry undermined efforts to increase interstate credit (See Freyer, 1994, 1979). Most state insolvency and bankruptcy laws favored debtors, usually favoring small traders rather than mercantile competitors from out of state (Freyer, 1994: 25). The effect was to protect the weakest participants in the market. Though rhetoric oftentimes lauded specie over credit, the reality was that the government as well as commercial enterprises relied on credit, especially bank credit. This did little to stop state protectionism with regard to creditor–debtor relations. Local credit was further protected by the demise of the First and Second National Banks, since state banks had a competitive advantage within local economies, given their often monopoly status.

To break into this protected market, creditors had to overcome the "rivalry of state legislatures and the unsettled conditions of local law" that were detrimental to the free movement of capital (Freyer, 1976: 476). The disincentive in investing in distant markets was further stymied by the action of courts at the local and federal level. Initially, federal and state courts affirmed the broad authority of states, allowing them to regulate their local economy and affirming a duty to follow local law when it applied. This put outside creditors at the mercy of locally elected judicial officials and spread the costs of defaulting throughout society. Even where a case of rights of distant creditors was heard at the federal level, the Supreme Court in *Riddle* v. *Mandeville* (1803) concluded that federal courts should apply the rules of the state, and it was not their purview to establish a nationally uniform commercial law.[5] This judgment placed non-resident creditors at a disadvantage when a debtor defaulted on a promissory note. Such restrictions and inconsistencies meant that the law surrounding promissory notes hindered their use and value.

A series of legal decisions between the 1820s and 1840s was pivotal in providing the groundwork for a more integrated financial market. The law concerning commercial exchanges altered course as more cases came before federal courts with the expansion of interregional trade. Since the free banking era was also the era of wildcat banking and wildcat bank notes, resulting in large numbers of bank failures and defaults, the Court needed to step in and increase the confidence between states with regard to credit and bills of exchange (Bodenhorn, 2000: 203ff). *Bank of Augusta* v. *Earle* (1839) was a key case for both banks and businesses. Refusing to pay bills of exchange at maturity, Earle argued that out-of-state banks had purchased his debts—which violated the state constitutional prohibition on banks operating without a specific charter from the Alabama Legislature. The implications for interstate trade were clear, if states did not exercise comity—or recognition of the sovereign laws of another state, then it would hamper a well-functioning market for commerce and exchange (Bodenhorn, 2000: 206).

Despite the shift towards a more pro-credit environment in *Bronson* v. *Kinzie* in 1843, lawmakers regularly enacted private or specialized bills that benefited particular debtors (Freyer, 1994: 89). In *Swift* v. *Tyson* (1842), the Supreme Court advocated uniform commercial law, while accepting that federal courts had a duty to follow local law when it applied (Freyer, 1994: 233; Hurst, 1973). The first nationally successful uniform act sponsored by the Commissioners on State Laws, was in response to market pressures from urban creditors for uniformity of commercial instruments and practices, which came on the heels of legal decisions that had strengthened the rights of creditors. This resulted in the Negotiable Instruments Law, which created obligations and claims for deposit-checks, and was later reinforced by the Uniform Commercial Code (Hurst, 1973: 38). The result is a single law in effect that is national in scope without being federal in form, thereby preserving state prerogatives vis-à-vis the federal government and avoiding the need for federal action (Nugent, 2009: 79–84; Nugent, 1999).

While promoting interstate credit markets, the Court allowed state laws to determine the nature of those market relations. Although the federal court was willing to accept the rights of non-resident creditors, eliminating the uncertainty and risk surrounding the movement of funds, the authority and preferences of state legislatures and courts were not displaced (Freyer, 1994: 91–8). Though states' rights and policies undermined efforts at harmonization, reflecting the triumph of localism in the antebellum era, "developments in the law were an important factor in the creation of a national credit market" (Bodenhorn, 1992: 598). Subsequent efforts continued in the postbellum period, with the convergence of regional interest rates in the late nineteenth century providing good indicators of the development of a national capital market (James, 1978; Sylla, 1969; Davis, 1963).

The supply of capital also benefited from legal innovations that changed the structure of business (Davis and Gallman, 1978: 62). When states eased incorporation laws for companies, the number of corporations grew rapidly. From the 1840s onwards, this allowed for more investment to be channeled into corporate bonds. The experience especially with government debt instruments during the Civil War changed attitudes towards investment, restructuring the way funds were borrowed and loaned in the US (Sbragia, 1996: 106). Capital was invested in corporate bonds, and the growth of the securities market was aided by legal decisions that provided for the rise of a national market in industrials, as a recasting of the legal notion of property bolstered legal security guarantees for corporations (Sklar, 1988: 50ff). The growth of formal capital markets had an important effect on investment, and widened the regional and industrial reach of capital mobility in the US.

The Postbellum Period

Although the period is often termed the national banking era, it was preceded by a significant development during the Civil War that brought currency under federal control. This was not simply a mechanism to enhance economic efficiency but rather to unite the country politically around a common symbol. The Legal Tender Act in 1862 and the National Currency Act of 1863 meant that paper currency was to be issued by a new set of federally chartered banks that came to be known as the national banking system (Sheridan, 1996: 1152). Since neither act prohibited state banks from issuing their own notes, a dual currency was in existence during this time. Amended to become the National Banking Acts of 1863 and 1864, with the express purpose of replacing the antebellum system of numerous state bank notes with national bank notes and greenbacks, the national banking system increased federal intervention. Congress had wanted to increase government borrowing during the war and required all national banks to invest their capital in governmental bonds (Sylla, 1969). This resulted in a monetary union in the US, and asserted the legitimacy of legislating to regulate the money supply by conferring legal status on those incorporated national banks to issue bank notes (Hurst, 1973: 64). Asserting federal control over the money supply, as well as spurring the lagging organization of national banks, the idea was not to create a national free banking system. At the time, already existing state banks were to aid the government in the achievement of its objectives by simply converting to national banks (Sylla, 1969: 650).

However, the banking laws also enacted a number of restrictions that constituted serious barriers to national bank entry in some parts of the country, and inadvertently entrenched a persistent dual pattern of banking (Sylla, 1969). The Banking Acts prohibited branching and provided minimum capital requirements and loan restrictions. This constituted a serious barrier to national bank entry as many banks in rural or agricultural communities could not meet capital adequacy requirements. Non-nationals—which included state and private banks—enjoyed an advantage since the legal capital requirements were either lower or non-existent (Sylla, 1969: 661). Equally important, national banks could not hold real estate as collateral, which impeded their efforts to expand to agricultural areas where land was the prime asset. The prohibition of mortgage loans and real estate lending by national banks revived state banking and generated a host of other institutions such as mortgage and trust companies that provided financial services and long-term capital loans.

While few state banks sought national charters initially, the situation changed when Congress passed an act levying a 10 percent tax on all state bank notes issued after 1866. This prohibitory tax removed the profitability of state bank notes and quickly forced many state banks to convert to national banks. National notes then entirely replaced the circulation of state bank notes, and all national banks were legally required to accept notes of other banks at the same value without transaction costs (Sheridan, 1996: 1153; Hurst, 1973: 64). The Supreme Court upheld both the prohibitory tax on state bank notes and the sole issuance of national bank notes as currency seeing these as reasonable measures and legitimate objectives to regulate money supply (*Veazie Bank* v. *Fenno,* 1869; *Knox* v. *Lee,* 1871).

These federal banking laws did not, however, create a centralized national banking system, but instead reinforced a dual banking system. The patchwork of independent national, state, and private banks that existed had approximately forty-nine separate and distinctive bodies granting bank charters and supervising banking operations (Keehn, 1974: 5, 27). According to Sylla, the restrictions under the National Banking Act enabled local or country banks to maintain their monopoly power, and made the operation of a national bank increasingly unattractive in sparsely populated regions. The resultant popular dissatisfaction with financial services ultimately led to the passage of the Gold Act in 1900. This lowered capital adequacy requirements for national banks, increased competition in rural areas and reduced the monopoly practices of country banks, promoting interest rate convergence. While some regulatory constraints were reduced, allowing for the possibility for a more efficient, functioning, and integrated capital market, restrictions to branching remained in place.

Although business and the public bore the costs of a less-than-optimal banking structure, state banks lobbied hard to maintain legal barriers to branch banking, often invoking images of monopoly, centralization, and populism to bolster their cause. Because state regulators were reluctant to see federal authorities assume more control over the chartering and regulation of banks, the dual banking system was kept in place. States continued to increase the attractiveness of state banking through free banking laws, reduced reserve and loan requirements that increased the benefits of incorporation at the state level, fostering vigorous regulatory competition with the existing national banking structure (White, 1982). James argues that legal and institutional constraints were effectively circumvented in the postbellum period through the emergence of a correspondent banking system in which inter-bank lending, as well as interregional lending and investment, overcame the prohibitions on branch or interstate banking.

These efforts by state banks also undermined the local monopoly power of country banks facilitating interregional flows of funds in spite of national banking restrictions (James, 1978: 240). Davis stresses institutional change and argues that such financial innovations were largely responsible for the increase in domestic capital market integration in the US (Davis, 1965). The convergence of short-term interest rates was due to the development of a national market for commercial paper, and the convergence of long-term interest rates similarly resulted from developments in life insurance, mortgage, and national securities markets. Specialized institutions provided for the flow of funds, and contributed to the rise of investment as mortgage banks made funds available for distant markets, commercial banks and insurance companies accumulated capital, and securities markets enabled debt and equity instruments to be traded across sectors and regions (Davis and Gallman, 1978).

Lessons for Europe from the United States

The development of capital markets and banking practices in the nineteenth century has important implications for European financial and economic developments. Unraveling the web of supply and demand factors that brought about the integration of capital markets has led scholars to suggest a number of crucial legal, political, and economic developments. Certainly federal courts provided an impetus to interregional trade and financial mobility by establishing uniform legal principles for commercial transactions and obligations. The decision to create a national currency to foster a political as well as economic identity, although generating some political opposition from agrarian interests, was backed by a political pledge of government behind every note issued (see Million, 1894). The economic development of complex networks between state banks, private banks, and other financial intermediaries ensured that local capital markets were not completely segregated or isolated. The politics of financial market integration was one of regulatory circumvention, regulatory competition, and regulatory harmonization.

The effect of removing restrictions on bank behavior and allowing free circulation of capital in the US provides an important precedent for the EU. The decentralized polity with strong state authority over fiscal issues and independent banking practices emerging into a national capital market in the twentieth century shares some interesting parallels with the EU. Obviously, significant differences exist in terms of level of economic development, and degree of sovereignty exercised by nation-state versus territorial states that are part of a union. Since important barriers to free movement of capital existed in both polities, however, it is worth considering the American example in reviewing the pattern of integration pursued by the EU, and particularly to look for any noteworthy similarities or differences in trade practices and fiscal strategies that can provide insight into the construction and consolidation of markets.

Europe

Historically, the liberalization of trade has taken precedence over the liberalization of capital movements in the EU (see Chapter 4). While early efforts to promote the liberalization of trade flows and current payments under the auspices of the Organization for European Economic Cooperation promoted economic recovery, barriers to non-trade-related capital flows remained in place. Though the emphasis was on improving the free flows of goods and services, the issue of capital flows was not addressed, in part because external convertibility was not restored until 1958 and the destabilizing effects of currency speculation in the interwar period made European states extremely cautious about capital liberalization.

At the Messina Conference in 1955, the intergovernmental committee that produced the Spaak Report included free movement of capital as part of the common market to allow efficient allocation of savings for investment purposes across member states (Bakker, 1994; cf. Deniau, 1961: 79). The liberalization of capital is the last chapter of the Spaak Report, signifying that any progress in this area was contingent on other factors being met, including coordination of economic policies, and social protective measures to foster employment and regional development (Bakker, 1994: 32). Capital liberalization was so dependent on progress on other measures that precise obligations could not be written into the Treaty.

Despite the espousal of full capital liberalization by the Spaak Committee, national sensitivities and differences of opinion meant that the resulting Treaty of Rome reflected a compromise position. The conditional nature of financial capital market integration meant that the Treaty articles on free movement of capital (Articles 67–73) comprised a number of safeguards and limitations (Pelkmans, 1997). This meant that capital liberalization should only take place "to extent necessary to ensure the proper functioning of the common market" (Article 67). A so-called "safeguard clause" meant that states could, after consultation, be authorized to take protective measures to protect domestic capital markets and avoid balance-of-payments difficulties (Article 73). Under the clause d'urgence, states could take their own measures to remedy any sudden financial difficulties (Article 109), which, in effect, meant that the regulation of capital movements would remain primarily a national domain due to member state sensitivities (Von der Groeben, 1987).[6]

The wide acceptance of Keynesian ideas regarding the role of government in managing the economy, backed by popular expectations about full employment and welfare provisions, meant that states were reluctant to pursue greater capital mobility since they were keen to keep control of fiscal and monetary policies in the postwar period (Tsoukalis, 1997: 6; Milward, 1984; Ruggie, 1982). To create a European financial area, member states needed to liberalize capital movements through the abolition of capital exchange controls and create a single market in financial services, products, and intermediaries. This required the removal of conditionalities and the reduction of national authority over macroeconomic policies, so that member states cannot simply resort to safeguards and exemptions to undermine market integration. Capital movements comprise a very broad range of operations including direct investment, purchase and sale of securities, and deposit and lending operations. As a result, the freedom granted by the Treaty applies to the underlying transaction as well as any capital transfer or payment.

Interregional Fiscal Flows

Different national monetary and fiscal cultures characterize European economies. With nation-states having the right to issue currency and regulate the supply of money, the Treaty of Rome provided for monetary policy coordination but not monetary integration (Bakker, 1994). Although there were no specific legal provisions for a single currency and single bank, the establishment of a central bank and single currency has accompanied economic union in Europe. This distinguishes developments from that of the US, where the establishment of a central bank occurred after the establishment of a single currency and single market (see Sbragia, 2004).

Much attention has been given to the institutional differences on economic performance, and the impact of the organization of financial markets, credit policies, and patterns of corporate control in shaping national policymaking. The emergence of an integrated capital market in Europe was influenced by governmental and monetary authority decisions that resulted in very different financial environments across Europe (see Zysman, 1983; Basch 1965; Story and Walter, 1997). Under the French credit system, the state determined the price and allocation of credit and directed economic activities through planning, industrial policy, and state-owned enterprises (Zysman, 1983; Hall, 1986; Schmidt, 1996). By contrast, the German system of corporate finance was based on the major banks, which supplied long-term credit, and served as a strong influence in promoting industrial adjustment (Egan, 1997; Deeg, 2010). In the British case, neither the banks nor the government played a decisive role. Capital markets in Britain were geared towards international trade rather than domestic industry (Hall, 1986; Schmidt, 2002). In Italy, publicly controlled institutions (special credit institutions) played an important role, and the existence of a large public sector under state ownership played an important role in the operations of financial institutions (Basch, 1965: 6). These strongly embedded traditions of local banking and financial intermediation have continued amidst pressures from international capital markets and regional liberalization (Howarth and Quaglia, 2013; Crespy and Schmidt, 2012).

Initially, European states established fixed exchange rates in the postwar period that encouraged trade and investment by promoting economic stability. The combination of fixed exchange rates and autonomous monetary policy coexisted with low levels of capital mobility during the Bretton Woods period (McNamara, 1999: 459). Intra-European trade had been seriously impacted by the World War II, with overseas investments sold or confiscated to finance the war effort. Commercial and trade policies were similarly based on military and political considerations. While rapid growth in intra-European trade followed after the war, boosted by the dismantling of tariffs and customs duties within the European Community, long and short term capital movements and direct investment also underwent substantial change (Chang, 2009; Eichengreen, 2008).

All member states remained net capital importers in the early postwar period.[7] The surge in capital investment started with a large-scale program of financial assistance financed by the US under the Marshall Plan, amounting to about thirteen billion dollars in aid between 1948 and 1951 (see De Long and Eichengreen, 1991). However, the Marshall Plan, by itself, did not promote European growth and recovery, but provided the environment in which economic liberalization and market-oriented policies gained a foothold (see Milward, 1984; De Long and Eichengreen, 1991). By promoting financial stability and open economies, the Marshall Plan laid the foundation for market mechanisms rather than exclusive reliance on government controls and regulations. In postwar Europe, capital was scarce, budgets were pressured, and prices needed to be controlled otherwise rampant inflation would take hold. Trade liberalization coupled with the promotion of exchange rate stability, and the resumption of capital movements, which took place slowly across

Europe in the 1950s, generated increased economic interdependence (Zacchia, 1976).

The literature on capital market integration has offered a number of explanations to account for the growth of fiscal flows. Short-term capital movements were induced by interest rate differential among countries as well as by expected changes in exchange parities. Speculative attacks with sudden withdrawals of funds in the 1950s and 1960s resulted in a precipitous decline in holdings by non-sterling countries and balance-of-payments difficulties for Britain. Coupled with a deterioration in balance of payments in the US in the 1960s and 1970s, short-term movements of capital to offset the devaluation of the dollar occurred largely through the Eurodollar market (Zacchia, 1976). In essence, the emergence of the Eurodollar and other Euro-currencies as international money markets provided further channels for such short-term capital flows.

Long-term capital movements were marked by some important features that distinguished postwar Europe. While European capital was a long-standing feature of American economic development going back to the nineteenth century, it was directed towards portfolio investment or corporate stocks. By contrast, reciprocal investment into Europe from the US constituted direct investment and the establishment of multinational companies in Europe (see Zacchia, 1976: 587). The surge in American investment increased dramatically—from $4,573 million in 1958 to $24.5 million in 1970. This is often attributed to the booming European economy, as Americans sought to capitalize on the fledging common market through efforts to circumvent common external tariffs and capitalize on the differences in labor costs (Zacchia, 1976: 586). The sharp increase in American capital created tensions between foreign enterprises and host countries, in their desire to protect national enterprises in key sectors, as the complex problem of American multinationals factored into domestic debates. Throughout the early postwar period, the US remained the main provider of capital investment in Western Europe. American banks followed the investments of multinationals, providing short-term credit and foreign exchange to US companies in Europe and became pioneers of multinational banking—in which they opened branches outside of their domestic market to offset domestic constraints on capital transactions (Sylla, 2002; see also Battilossi, 2002b). Yet the financial structure of common market countries differed from that of the US and UK, where life insurance companies, pension and mutual funds were far more important as investors in company securities.

While regulatory constraints on credit and capital continued to operate, there were continued pressures for liberalization. In the 1960s a number of factors—such as reprivatization of financial relationships, increased capital mobility, steep growth of international banking business, and the emergence of an unprecedented wave of financial innovations—began to trigger a complex process of transformation (Battilossi, 2002a; Battilossi, 2002b: 158–63). Although some firms were seeking to break out of the restrictive geographic and functional restrictions placed on them, member states traditionally used state controls and public ownership to control and channel the flow of capital (Vipond, 1995). This practice of public lending at subsidized interest rates increased the cost of capital for unsubsidized borrowers, generating significant distributional effects for capital allocation.

While exchange controls were significant barriers, the different regulatory frameworks and banking laws across member states hampered cross-border provision of financial services, and contributed to the negative effects of capital controls (Tsoukalis, 1997: 118). In fact, actions enforced by monetary authorities to offset the consequences of trade and capital flows on domestic money supply took mainly the form of new regulations imposed on short-term capital movements (Battilossi, 2000a: 157–8; Bakker, 1994). Domestic attempts to manage the money supply were constrained by concerns that capital outflow would result if interest rates were lowered. Though freedom of capital movements would allow for the efficient allocation of investment, and reduce fiscal inequalities by allowing enterprises access to sources of capital on equal terms throughout the region, the integration of capital markets would likely result in a financial center gaining ascendancy (Schmitt, 1968). The prospect that capital would gravitate towards areas of higher growth and profits, attracting both an inflow of savings and an outflow of direct investment as firms sought to expand markets and secure sources of supply, generated concern about the distributive effects of capital market integration (Schmitt, 1968; *The Economist*, 1964). Resistance to greater authority at the Community level was in part due to preserving the autonomy of national monetary policy and the ability to finance public sector deficits, and maintaining control over exchange rates to cope with speculative attacks and balance-of-payments crises. Reluctance to accept the financial leadership of Germany, which would be the primary beneficiary of capital liberalization, was also a factor (Schmitt, 1968; Bakker, 1994). Subsequently, monetary union has strengthened Germany and reinforced its economic hegemony during the euro crisis, as it pushes its partners to bring down structural deficits despite calls for more use of fiscal policy to jumpstart the economy and a more flexible approach on budget deficits. The overexpansion of banking and credit problems led Germany to push for firmer controls over states due to concerns that these are thinly disguised monetary bail-outs of profligate governments (Marsh, 2013; Kaltenthaler, 1998).

The importance of finance in the EU derives from the fact that freedom of capital is one of the basic freedoms of the common market. Realizing free movement of capital requires free movement of financial services. The financial environment is considered crucial for the entire European economy, and although estimated gains are now treated with caution, the liberalization of financial services and the removal of restrictions on capital controls were expected to generate significant macroeconomic benefits for the single market (Cecchini et al., 1988). The Cecchini Report on the costs of non-Europe suggested that one-third of the macroeconomic growth generated by completing the internal market would come from expansion of financial services with estimated gains of 22 billion ECU.[8] It was clear that financial services played a substantial role in other areas as well. While financial intermediaries such as insurance and credit institutions provide capital to other firms, their output is used by other manufacturing and service industries to purchase intermediate goods (Josselin, 1996). Capital mobility and trade are therefore complementary, having a wide-ranging effect on the entire European economy. The current financial crisis has increased financial market disintegration in Europe with substantial differences in interest rates for bank loans across member states as well as restrictive measures aimed at retaining liquidity and assets within national borders.

Barriers to Trade

Capital and exchange controls persist to different degrees within member states. Even supposedly liberal countries employ ingenious methods to protect domestic markets, such as privileging national investors in purchasing public bonds, restricting outward transfers of residential capital without prior approval of national authorities, establishing restrictions on domestic establishment and operations of financial services, and hindering investment flows through restrictions on stock exchange transactions and mutual funds (Pelkmans, 1997: 134; Pelkmans and Winters, 1988: 46). Governments still have control of capital allocation through controls on domestic institutions such as pension funds and different rules on financial reporting and disclosure, tax, and withholding requirements influencing the business decisions and strategies of firms (Vipond, 1995; Lannoo, 2002). This violates the ideal of free movement of capital as the freedom to transfer capital assets across national borders is an independent transaction in its own right, and not a consequence of another transaction involving goods or services (Servais, 1988).

Many of the distinctions used in financial services have broken down, partly under pressures of deregulation, but mainly because market forces have rendered them obsolete (Vipond, 1993: 2). The regulation of financial services has become increasingly complex due to the globalization of finance (Cerny, 1993). Traditional divisions between investment banking, securities, and insurance require European financial unification efforts to encompass a broad interconnected set of policies and regulations. Pressure to change the structure of financial supervision in response to market developments, and promote more integrated financial supervision has encountered difficulties due to the different ways that this is carried out by member states (Lannoo 2002: 2). Generally banks, securities, and insurance had their own supervisory authorities and their degree of independence and authority varies across member states. As Eichengreen notes, this creates "a bias towards less regulation and under capitalization, as regulators seek to attract business from abroad" (Eichengreen, 2012: 2). Promoting an integrated financial market means addressing the different mechanisms that have emerged to govern financial markets, fostering regulatory standards for the EU as a whole and providing an adjustment mechanism to eliminate imbalances between states where capital is mobile.

Although various economic arguments have been used to justify capital controls,[9] efforts to remove these barriers were expected to produce substantial gains in economic welfare due to the exploitation of efficiency gains and increased contestability of markets. While the integration of capital markets is often measured by the degree of interest rate convergence, it is important to also trace the evolution of capital market liberalization from its limited Treaty basis into an increasingly entrenched set of commitments and rules to which governments have acquiesced, and the corresponding impact of that choice in the context of the current debt and banking crisis.

The Early Formative Period: The 1960s to the 1970s

Capital liberalization was distinctive in the Treaty of Rome since there were no comparable restrictions or limitations on the other three freedoms. The drafters' intention reflected the priority given to open trade liberalization for goods and services. While progressive liberalization and non-discrimination were the underlying principles in promoting the goal of free movement of capital, it was subject to certain conditionality requirements that were frequently invoked by member states during periods of recession and monetary instability.

The initial efforts seemed promising with two directives adopted quickly in 1960 and 1962. These provided for the full liberalization of direct investment which would enable companies to operate in other markets through subsidiaries, promoting both cross-border trade and intra-Community production. In addition, the directives provided for cross-border transactions in listed securities or shares, which meant investors could acquire an interest in other companies through official stock exchanges. The two directives largely consolidated the status quo in member states (Bakker, 1994: 104).[10] The legislation did not include short-term movement of capital but rather focused on long-term, intra-Community investment flows, without provisions for capital movements between member states and third countries. Essentially, the wish to maintain control over domestic monetary policy as well as deep-rooted concerns about speculative capital flows forged a powerful constraint on further liberalization efforts.

Though the first directive provided a good foundation for the functioning of the common market, focusing on capital transactions with a clear link with trade and investment, the European Commission was keen to promote further liberalization. However, even among the strongest advocates of capital mobility, restrictions on short-term capital flows remained in place throughout the decade. Mindful of exchange rate tensions and the effect of interest rate differentials, the European Commission found progress difficult to achieve on other areas of financial liberalization. The second directive supplemented the previous legislation by liberalizing service-related transactions, and the lowest common denominator agreement simply reflected the low level of economic integration and monetary coordination in place. The intransigence of member states over specific issues such as tax considerations and foreign credit provisions, reflecting differing monetary philosophies, made further progress difficult. The European Commission continued its efforts to liberalize capital movements by introducing a third directive in 1963. While seeking to liberalize capital transactions to allow the issuance of foreign securities on domestic markets, and investments in foreign shares by domestic institutional investors, the Commission also sought to address a number of administrative and legal restrictions hindering capital movements.

The Commission faced strong opposition to its efforts to tackle what it perceived as domestic regulations that served as hidden barriers to capital mobility. Many of these regulations reflected specific goals such as protection of small investors or industrial development. Since different supervisory authorities within member states were involved in regulating different financial institutions and intermediaries, the effort by the European Commission to undercut their role met strong resistance. No further progress was made on a third directive introduced in 1964. This sought to eliminate discrimination in listing and acquisition of securities by financial institutions and institutional investors from other member states, and opening up domestic capital markets to foreign issues by easing domestic restrictions and controls. However, speculative capital flows through the 1960s and 1970s put paid to any further discussions of capital liberalization.

Notwithstanding member state efforts to liberalize capital controls, there was limited political commitment to further European-wide liberalization. Instead of an integrated European capital market based on common rules and harmonized standards, a Eurodollar and loan market emerged in the 1960s which was subject to minimal regulation. By providing alternative options for larger national firms to borrow capital, and to gain a better return from their capital investment, these markets expanded rapidly outside of the Community framework.

However, strains in the international monetary system with large balance of payments deficits and speculative flows out of the US dollar led to increased capital controls in Europe. The abrupt shift towards the regulation of capital flows resulted in a 1972 directive that moved away from the earlier drive towards liberalization. Aimed at curbing undesirable capital inflows, member states could limit non-resident market transactions by introducing discriminatory regulations. Imposing capital controls also had fewer political costs than the alternative of currency devaluation, which was less politically palatable (Bakker, 1994). The resulting situation, which followed upon the oil crisis and 1973 collapse of the Bretton Woods system, marked the introduction of floating exchange rates. Member states undertook a variety of policy responses, with some seeking to restrict capital inflows, and others placing restrictions on capital outflows. The coordination of economic policies was limited and any effort to move towards closer economic integration was put on hold. With new member states also having extensive exchange control systems, at the end of the 1970s financial markets were less integrated than during the previous decade (Bakker, 1994: 141).

There were several uncoordinated efforts at liberalization from Germany and Britain again in the late 1970s, based on domestic considerations. For Germany, the image of drifting policies sent the wrong signal in their effort to promote domestic price stability and strict economic and monetary policies (Bakker, 1994: 142). For Britain, the shift towards a more liberal, market-oriented approach through the abolition of exchange controls in 1979 signaled a shift in economic strategy that brought new impetus towards the liberalization of capital movements, and an effort to increase the competitiveness of European financial services (Moran, 1991). Germany, Holland, and Luxembourg followed suit and removed controls on capital in the late 1970s and early 1980s.

With the shift towards market-oriented policies and the erosion of regulatory authority in maintaining capital controls, two other developments further solidified the move towards capital liberalization. First, the establishment of the European Monetary System in 1979 provided for a zone of monetary stability (see Heisenberg, 1999). Diverging economic policies resulted in exchange rate instability. Since exchange rate uncertainty inhibited capital movements, efforts to coordinate exchange rates and promote monetary coordination implied a reorientation away from the shielding of domestic markets. However, there was no reference in the European Monetary System to financial integration and capital liberalization, which had been pushed into the background. Domestic efforts to liberalize controls and the monetary system provided a new foundation for reintroducing the idea of capital liberalization in the 1980s. Second, adoption of a Banking Directive in 1977 (77/780/EEC) laid down the framework for liberalization of banking activities by promoting the idea that responsibility for prudential control and supervision of banking practices by both domestic and foreign branches rests with the home country (Tsoukalis, 1997). While promoting an integrated banking market through the rights of establishment had resulted in legislative action in 1973,[11] the supply of cross-border financial services was still limited. The Banking Directive provided a legal framework to protect investors and consumers through harmonization of licensing requirements and prudential supervision. Despite this general framework for further regulation at the European level, limited progress was made in reaching agreement on many harmonization measures. Far from being fully integrated, European banking markets remained hampered by restrictions on capital flows, supervision by host countries, and requirements for branches to have substantial endowment capital that often made it difficult for smaller banks to meet these market entry requirements (Baltensperger and Dermine, 1990).

The 1980s: The Renewed Momentum of the Single Market Program

The capacity of member states to reach agreement on collective political action for financial services and capital liberalization shifted in the mid 1980s as a result of a number of factors. Following the lead taken by Britain and Germany domestically to reduce capital controls, France shifted its position in the beginning of the 1980s in response to massive speculative capital movements that resulted from negative reactions to its expansionary policies and nationalization of financial institutions (see Hall, 1986; Moravcsik, 1998; Jones, 2003). France chose to align with German objectives of domestic monetary stability and support the European Monetary System, and to refocus its industrial and financial strategy away from internal controls towards market-oriented policies. This included the liberalization of financial services and strengthened the drive towards further European integration. The European Commission again put capital liberalization back on the agenda. This time the Commission sought to tackle the safeguard clause in the Treaty of Rome that continued to impede their efforts at full-scale liberalization (Bakker, 1994: 154). As Bakker concludes, the Commission perceived that strengthening the exchange rate mechanism and closer economic convergence would facilitate the removal of capital controls (Bakker, 1994: 154). While anxious to promote exchange rate stability, the Commission could not promote a European capital market in anything but an open and non-discriminatory manner. Any effort to promote internal capital liberalization would be negatively perceived by the financial sector, and by those states that had liberalized and opened up their own capital markets.

The European Commission gave new impetus to the creation of a single market in financial services and the promotion of an integrated capital market with the plans drawn up to complete the internal market by 1992. The White Paper published in June 1985 framed the issue of capital liberalization as a key component of market integration. According to the European Commission, an integrated capital market would not only promote economic growth and the efficient allocation of savings, but it would complement the free movement of goods, services, and people. Moreover, the free movement of capital was linked to efforts to reinforce the European Monetary System, since greater financial mobility would also lead to greater discipline on domestic economic policies which were crucial for the proper functioning of the internal market (European Commission, 1985: 27). The White Paper indicated that this would consist of a two-part strategy: the removal of restrictions on capital movements and the coordination of minimal rules to allow financial intermediaries to offer services across borders without a local presence or subsidiary. This meant harmonization of fundamental rules to provide equivalent safeguards for investors and consumers, which then became the basis for allowing financial intermediaries to operate under the principle of mutual recognition and single passport in the banking, securities, and insurance sectors.

To realize their objectives, the European Commission proposed that the Treaty reforms under the ensuing Single European Act (SEA) in 1986 encompass the free movement of capital. However, the SEA provided for a declaration of intent rather than a concrete commitment to full liberalization. The SEA did provide for two changes to the decision-making process that would enable the European Commission to move forward with its integrationist agenda. The shift to qualified majority voting and the principle of mutual recognition changed negotiating dynamics. No longer able to exercise a veto, member states had to build strategic alliances to promote or thwart legislative proposals linked to single market issues including capital liberalization. Furthermore, the principle of mutual recognition provided more regulatory flexibility. Harmonization was limited to broad regulatory guidelines for financial services, allowing national authorities to continue to play a supervisory role, while promoting competition among different regulatory systems (Sun and Pelkmans, 1995).

After a hiatus of almost two decades, the European Commission began making progress in their effort to achieve full capital liberalization, first by fully enforcing early directives of 1960 and 1962, before enlarging the obligations of capital liberalization to include securities and commercial credits. This was followed by lifting capital exchange controls to ensure that the obligations would extend to short-term capital flows such as financial loans, money markets, and other deposit accounts (Bakker, 1994: 168). The adoption of a

1986 directive in the face of growing ineffectiveness of capital controls was a small victory for the Commission in promoting a more liberalized regime.

More importantly, the EU adopted a landmark piece of legislation in 1988—the so-called Capital Movement Directive (88/361/EEC) which abolished restrictions (see Article 1). It presents a rare example of removing restrictions on firms without imposing other restrictions to replace them (Vipond, 1995). However, the directive did not rule out the safeguards that states had continuously invoked. Provisions for derogations continued for small or new member states addressing balance-of-payments crises, and for all member states imposing short-term capital controls to address monetary and exchange rate instability (Article 3). A number of issues remained on the table including national controls on financial institutions such as pension funds, as well as different accounting and tax rules that affect capital mobility (Mogg, 2002). Coordination remained difficult due to distinct national supervisory frameworks and differences in the socioeconomic content of prudential rules that reflected legal and ideological conflicts over market supervision. In practice, free movement of capital implies not only the abolition of exchange controls, but is closely tied to two other related measures on banking and securities that have helped create a single market in financial services.

The Second Banking Directive agreed in 1989 (89/646/EEC) formed the basis for coordinating and regulating the banking sector. This innovative regulatory framework provided for a single banking license allowing banks to operate across borders without further authorization. This "one-stop shopping" model enabled banks to offer any financial product or service, through the home country control principle, where the home country provided the primary supervisory responsibility for banks.

Although host country authorities could still impose controls for purposes of national monetary authority, the overall effect was to liberalize market entry barriers and create the legal conditions for an integrated banking sector (Tsoukalis, 1997: 125). For mutual recognition to work properly, the Second Banking Directive required a minimum set of harmonized standards. Two additional directives included provisions on capital adequacy, providing for minimum capital requirements and what is to count as capital, to ensure financial soundness (Vipond, 1995: 13).[12] While securities were partly addressed in the Second Banking Directive, additional directives established regulatory provisions for how the industry should be supervised. Designed to make it easier to buy and sell shares in different capital markets, as well as raise funds in different national capital markets, the directives provided guidelines on stock market listings, and listings of new securities for sale to the public. While market access was enhanced, the widely different national systems persisted and the integration of financial markets and capital liberalization did not lead to a unitary market, but rather a system in which national regulatory systems are accommodated within a European framework through mutual recognition (Vipond, 1995: 14).

Between 1985 and 1992, twenty-five directives that dealt with financial services and capital flows were adopted (Josselin, 1996). Beyond the Second Banking Directive, these included the UCITS Directive on stock market rules and supporting measures that established minimal standards and harmonized regulatory requirements across member states covering capital adequacy requirements, accounting requirements, guarantee schemes, and the exchange of information among supervisory authorities. Other legislative efforts that were not included in the White Paper became necessary including directives on money laundering (91/308/EEC) and insider trading or market abuse (2003/6/EC) (recently amended in 2014).

The single market program and the 1992 Maastricht Treaty with its provisions on economic and monetary union were pivotal in providing the political impetus to remove capital restrictions and foster an integrated financial area; some restrictions or transaction costs still served to discourage cross border financial flows. The high costs of cross-border payments, something that the American states experienced when local bank notes were traded across borders, suggest parallels between the system of floating exchange rates and multiple currency transactions of the European exchange rate system and early American antebellum economy (Sheridan, 1996). Yet while the advent of a single currency in Europe increased the transparency of such commercial transactions and eliminated such transaction costs, cross-border capital mobility was still hampered by differences in financial reporting and taxation, which affects the ease with which firms can operate within a single financial market (Mogg, 2002).

The need to further lower barriers to trade led to a series of new initiatives under the Financial Services Action Plan in 1999 (Buch and Heinrich, 2002) which set out an ambitious schedule for the adoption of forty-two directives by 2005 to achieve an integrated financial market (see also Lannoo, 2002; Mogg, 2002; Quaglia, 2010). Among the proposals that emerged from those engaged in financial supervision was the creation of a two-tier structure along the lines of the American model with state and federally chartered banks (Lannoo, 2002). The goal was to create a single EU-wide financial market, eliminate capital market fragmentation, promote closer coordination among supervisory authorities and respond to new regulatory challenges with regard to wholesale and retail financial transactions (see Quarles, 2002). Despite efforts to create a single market in financial services, open up retail markets while also making them more secure, and strengthen prudential supervision, under the Investment Services Directive and the Financial Services Action Plan in the 1990s and early 2000s, there continued to be a need for greater convergence of oversight and improvement of the supervisory system due to the continued disjointed supervisory cultures.

As the EU attempted to make the raising of cross-border capital as easy as raising domestic capital, it also became a more prominent player in international financial services regulation (Posner, 2006). Yet for many firms, problems are compounded by continued uncertainty over basic concepts such as the freedom to provide services (*European Report*, 1995). Local rules remained in place, often justified as being in the "general good." For banking and insurance companies, adapting policies and products to fit these different rules presented a serious obstacle, imposing local rules of conduct in addition to those enforced by the home country. The wide variety of definitions and practices creates regulatory challenges for the EU to ensure consistent application of rules governing financial markets (Bolkestein, 2002).

Efforts to allow industry access to liquid markets for investment capital have continued apace, as a means to enhance productivity and growth by allowing borrowers access to capital best suited to promote investment. As Jones concludes, "released from the tight confines of national capital markets, firms and other private actors have sought to whittle down the remaining restrictions on capital flows" (Jones, 2003: 201; Frieden, 1991). Leading European banks and financiers mobilized by forming the European Round Table of Financial Services (*Financial Times*, 2001b). Modeled on the European Round Table (ERT) that played a key role in pushing the single market project, this group was initially led by the same chairman and chief executive that created the ERT. Their goal of a single set of harmonized regulations to bring about a single financial market was driven by the fact that the investment horizons of funds and private investors had become more European, and the existing differences in national legislation across the EU placed them at a comparative disadvantage against less regulated states which could trigger regulatory arbitrage (Pauget, 2009).

While the financial sector is important as a retail industry in its own right, lobbying for liberalization and greater freedom of capital, it is also the supplier of capital to other firms (Vipond, 1993; Heinemann and Jopp, 2002). Institutional investors are increasingly engaged in cross-border transactions in financial markets. The increasing sophistication of financial intermediaries as well as the growing role of innovative financial instruments served to blur the boundaries between short- and long-term capital movements, leading to further market pressures to promote integration and liberalization (see Josselin, 1996). In particular, the boom in the bond market enabled firms to seek new financing options. The growth of an equity culture notably with the expansion of corporate bond markets and venture capital placed pressure on banks, challenging their dominance in European finance (Pozen, 2001). Yet European corporate bond markets remained less than a third of the size of the US market (Quarles, 2002). The advent of the euro also shifted capital from bank deposits and government bonds to mutual funds and stocks, highlighting the problems created by national restrictions regarding foreign corporate take-overs, mutual funds, and pension funds in particular.

By providing a common framework, both manufacturing and service firms could benefit from listing their securities on different markets and gaining access to the various financial instruments available in some capital markets (Vipond, 1993). Supervising such markets is forcing regulators to rethink their traditional methods of regulation, especially given changes in electronic trading practices, with pressure for higher levels of collateral to make markets safer as well as increased transparency for non-equity instruments, such as bonds and derivatives (Posner and Véron, 2010). However, market integration in securities lags behind other financial areas (Quaglia, 2010). Not surprisingly efforts to revise rules on investment services have been politically contentious, as it has the biggest overall impact on the market because it defines the basic parameters of financial regulation (*European Voice*, 2002; *Financial Times*, 2001b). The Lamfalussy Report in November 2000 was the first effort to match developments in the market through the creation of a European Securities Committee and the possibility of "fast track" decision-making. This drew considerable criticism from the European Parliament, which feared being bypassed in its legislative oversight role (*Financial Times*, 2001c; Lannoo, 2002). The report addressed the need for swifter adjustment to a rapidly changing market environment, and greater consultation with investors, financial intermediaries, and issuers throughout the legislative process. Yet the regulatory and supervisory framework also faced considerable difficulties due to different national frameworks, the configuration of their national financial systems and different national vested interests (Quaglia, 2010). In particular, those efforts in the securities area, covered by the Lamfalussy process, namely the Prospectus Directive (2003), the Market Abuse Directive (2003), the Transparency Directive (2004) and the Markets in Financial Instruments Directive (2004) have been as contentious as earlier efforts at financial market integration.

Other issues are equally politically controversial. The poor record of tax coordination in Europe became increasingly salient since the liberalization of capital flows allowed states to offer special tax regimes to attract capital investment (Radaelli, 1999a). Concerns about the effects of such tax competition, as well as differences in corporate taxation in terms of investment tax credits, depreciation allowances, and capital gains remain one of the key outstanding issues for a well-functioning single market. While proposals for tax coordination have been made since the 1960s (see Radaelli, 1999a, 1999b), it has lagged behind all other areas of the single market. Corporate tax harmonization has also moved onto the agenda, since capital liberalization and monetary union brings to the fore tax differences across member states. Although attention focused on the need for positive action to avoid the undesirable consequences of harmful tax competition (Radaelli, 1999a), the resulting voluntary codes of conduct and the withholding tax proposal indicate the difficulties of getting member states to accept large-scale tax harmonization in future. Cross-border tax obstacles continue to plague companies, especially the problems encountered with double taxation, and tax barriers continue to undermine the European financial area (*Financial Times*, 2001a; Radaelli and Kraemer, 2009).

The literature offers different explanations for the driving factors in financial market integration. Jabko considers the Commission as the key driving force (Jabko, 2006). Quaglia argues that private interests and transnational actors shaped policy developments (Quaglia, 2010), whereas Story and Walter point to the dominance of specific member states seeking to promote their own domestic regulatory approach through intensive intergovernmental bargaining (Story and Walter, 1997). Different regulatory cultures have made collective action difficult with Britain keen to promote financial innovation through private sector governance, whereas France and Germany and other states have focused on rule-based regulation which privileges financial stability and consumer protection (Quaglia, 2010). This is triggered in part by concerns about the home country principle and fears of a race to the bottom given the freedom to choose among member states for regulatory approval (Quaglia, 2010, 2008). However, as financial regulation became more complex, European efforts to include new financial instruments and investment services reflected differences between those with larger financial sectors against those with more highly protected sectors, especially in terms of investment banking and stock exchanges (Howarth and Quaglia, 2013). Yet renewed competition with the US along with international financial coordination also moved financial market integration forward (Posner, 2006). In this environment, the market-making, competition-focused approach was viewed more positively as the best model for the EU (Posner and Véron, 2010). The recent financial crisis, however, shifted perceptions about the regulation of financial services, generating a host of new regulatory measures, and fostering a move towards greater investor protection and a rule-based approach. This reflects a more interventionist approach towards regulating credit agencies, who were blamed for exacerbating the crisis due to their slow response to deteriorating market conditions. This spilt over on to hedge funds, who despite themselves being adversely affected by the crisis, were subject to more regulatory oversight to protect depositors and control moral hazard through the adoption of the Alternative Investment Fund Managers Directive (Quaglia, 2010). The crisis demonstrated the need for recognition of the systemic risk in financial markets at the European level, although there was no explicit mention of sovereign default as a result of a bank stress test for fear that it would be self-fulfilling. However, the adoption of the "supervisory package" was one of the key milestones on the path of consolidated financial regulation in Europe. The creation of European Supervisory Authorities for banks (EBA), insurance and occupational pensions (EIOPA) and securities markets (ESMA) was central to deal with cross-border risks and contribute to the creation of the Single Rulebook for financial regulation in Europe (Countryman, Scholes, and Sakhonchik, 2014: 5).

Yet the single market in financial services is far from complete although the single rulebook is designed to provide a unified regulatory framework applicable to all financial institutions in the single market.[13] The goal is to improve depositor protection and maintain the confidence of depositors in the financial safety net through the Deposit Guarantee Schemes, and maintain minimum capital adequacy through the Capital Requirements Directive IV (CRD IV) and the Capital Requirements Regulation (CRR), and Directive on Bank Recovery and Resolution (BRRD) (Countryman, Scholes, and Sakhonchik, 2014). There are also efforts to regulate derivatives, considered a major channel of contagion, as the risks in the over-the-counter market, especially in terms of credit default swaps are now subject to the European Market Infrastructure Regulation (EMIR), increasing market transparency, and creating a central clearing system (CCPs). The Market and Financial Instruments Directive (2004) also aims at enhancing transparency for derivatives, requiring them to be traded in regulated venues, rather than over-the-counter between various parties. The directive on 'Undertakings for the Collective Investment of Transferable Securities' (UCITS) was also revised to increase confidence in money markets, as investor protection for transferable securities was viewed as critical for sustained economic growth.

Pressures for further regulatory reform and coordination have also been influenced by judicial decisions as well as financial crises. The increasing role of the European Court of Justice in deciding financial cases and pushing the member states to eliminate fiscal disparities, suggests that case law has played a role in shaping capital markets and fiscal policies and deserves further consideration. Although monetary integration sets broad guidelines for fiscal behavior, and did not appear to restrict states' behavior in the area of taxation or public expenditure, it did by definition shape public finance, and hence the actions of states (Hallerberg, 2014). Though institutionalizing mechanisms to facilitate fiscal responsibility appears in the current financial crisis to have fostered economic stability, the ongoing effort to stabilize the eurozone through the "Six Pack," the "Two Pack," and "Fiscal Compact" has increased European regulatory capacity and increased pressure for transfer of more state competences to the European level (Hallerberg, 2014). Part of the contractual agreement for the constitutional retrenchment of public finances means that the Court will play a greater market surveillance role in fiscal and welfare issues in member states.

Integration through Law: Capital Markets and Judicial Action

Although legal decisions have played a key role in shaping the capital market environment, the wording of Treaty articles has shaped the European Court of Justice's approach to this area. Since the Treaty lacks a specific definition of what constitutes capital movements, the Court has stepped into the breach, defining and limiting the scope of liberalization in this area. Several cases are crucial in determining the intent of the Treaty framers, and thus establishing the boundaries of encroachment on state sovereignty over fiscal policy. In the landmark *Casati* case of 1982 (Case 203/80), the safeguard clause allowed member states to take protective measures when short-term capital movements came under scrutiny, since this seriously disrupts the conduct of monetary policy. The Court gave a restrictive interpretation of capital liberalization by arguing that capital differed from the other three freedoms, since complete freedom could undermine the economy of a member state and impair the functioning of the common market (see also Bakker, 1994: 47).

The Court opted for caution with regard to capital liberalization, playing a more circumspect role than it has done in the area of goods. Although reserving the right to review the *actions* taken in accordance with treaty obligations, as in the *Luisi and Carbone* case (Case 286/82 and 26/83), the Court tried to define capital movements in broader terms. Two years later, in the *Brugnoni* case (Case 157/85), the Court determined that discriminatory national regulations concerning capital transactions should be eliminated. Recognizing the imbalances that capital liberalization might impose on some member state economies, the Court was extremely cautious in its efforts to remove impediments to capital. Unlike goods, the Court did not play the same independent activist role, preferring to follow the political agreements reached (Bakker, 1994: 47). However, changes in the provisions introduced by the Treaty on European Union regarding capital movements resulted in a growing body of case law testing the boundaries of national controls and prohibitions (Craig and De Búrca, 2003). Increasingly measures which restrict residents from obtaining loans or investing in other member states have been held to constitute an unnecessary restriction on capital (*Sandoz* Case C-439/97). The ECJ draws on its jurisprudence in the other freedoms especially free movement of goods in determining restrictions on free movement of capital and payments (see Snell, 2011). Measures must not constitute arbitrary restrictions or disguised restrictions, and those national measures that are justified on grounds of public policy and security (Article 58 of the Treaty on European Union) must be proportionate to the objective and justified by the member state. This jurisprudence is similar to that of goods in the previous chapter, and indicates a more active role for the Court in determining whether any restrictions on capital are permissible. However, as Schmidt notes, legal texts are incomplete contracts subject to judicial interpretation, so recent efforts to address the financial crisis with new mechanisms that threaten the no bail-out clause of the treaty, through financial aid packages (EFSF and EFSM) generated a German constitutional challenge (Schmidt, 2013). The strengthening of non-majoritarian institutions in response to deepening of market integration is not uncontested, and has become especially salient with increased fiscal consolidation in Europe.

The Effects of Integration on Banking Behavior and Market Structure in US and EU

Although the late nineteenth century saw large-scale capital flows that are mirrored by those of the late twentieth century, they do not tell us about how well integrated capital markets have become. It is the cost of doing business across national frontiers that actually matters, and this can be gauged by other measures of integration (O'Rourke and Williamson, 1999: 208). Assessing banking behavior and market structure may provide some indications about the impact of capital market integration and the effects of regulatory choices upon the strategy and operation of firms.

Forging an integrated capital market has been a painstakingly slow process, encountering substantial obstacles to free movement. Legal and market entry barriers have restricted capital mobility and served to segment markets, limit competition, and protect local practices and providers of financial services. Efforts to overcome such discriminatory practices in Europe and the US encroached on the controls of national or subnational authorities, and increased competition for financial institutions that were formerly protected by local monopolistic practices.

Two dynamics are in evidence in the development of integrated capital markets in the US and EU. Both polities have experienced pressures for harmonization and regulatory competition in their transformation from a loose system of connected markets to a more unified economic entity. Capital rules in the US and EU have certain similarities, stressing the need for framework laws to regulate market activities. The statutory framework of the US and EU in the financial area both emphasize the protection of financial intermediaries against insolvency by using capital adequacy mechanisms and deposit guarantee schemes. However, they differ in operation since the EU has focused on assigning market and credit risk factors to various financial services, whereas the US regulatory strategy separated banking and securities activities (Gerkens, 1996).

In the US, the statutes enacted in the twentieth century built on the foundation established in the nineteenth century. The McFadden Act prohibited interstate banking, the Glass-Steagall Act separated commercial from investment banking, and the Bank Holding Act provided certain restrictions on corporate-banking ownership. Yet important changes in the US financial system mirror that of the EU. Restrictions on interstate banking have been eased and reciprocity provisions are allowing cross-border banking. The removal of restrictions to regional banking can be viewed as analogous to the creation of a single market in Europe "as in both cases, banks have been allowed to expand their activities across borders" (Buch and Heinrich, 2002: 6). At the same time, there is a significant difference in the two systems. Though financial markets were highly interdependent in Europe, supervision remained national but monetary powers have been transferred to the federal level, although the crisis has generated new levels of European intervention (Buch and Heinrich, 2002; Lannoo, 2002; Schelkle, 2009b, 2009c). The advent of the sovereign debt crisis has impacted capital markets as states have been faced with liquidity crises and bank runs, pushing them to reintroduce capital controls, and formalize the fragmentation of capital markets within the eurozone. States have restricted inter-bank lending, and have sought to keep capital and liquidity within their home country to safeguard their domestic financial system from the risk of contagion (Gros, 2012).

Both the US and Europe have experienced balance-of-payments concerns, and the fear of speculative attacks has resulted in regulation to prevent market failure. Concerns about liquidity and panics have led to efforts to protect the stability of the financial system as a whole. Regulatory interventions have resulted in important safeguards and efforts at coordination or harmonization, such as clearing house systems, solvency ratios, or insider trading rules. At the same time, regulatory competition has generated pressure on state regulations to maintain their advantage through domestic change in Europe in the reform of a supervisory framework and creation of a central financial agency. In the US, the reorganization of state banking charters, free banking laws, and single banking licenses all placed pressures on those states with higher or more restrictive regulations to adapt.

The anticipated effects of market integration generated changes in the overall banking structure and behavior as consolidation through mergers and acquisitions have characterized developments in Europe. Restructuring of banks in some member states such as Spain and Italy, where there is considerable room for rationalization, is in evidence, along with many consolidations of banking and other financial intermediaries typically within the confines of nation-states (see Della Salla, 2004). Yet mergers and acquisitions have been influenced by the presence of nationalized state-owned banks, particularly in France and Italy. In addition, smaller or regional banks in Spain (*cajas*), along with cooperative banks in France (*credit mutual*) and specialized regional state banks in Germany have resisted increased competition, promoting their local knowledge and specialization to their advantage and seeking special exemptions from community laws (Smith, 2005). In the US, market integration resulted in the proliferation of state, private, and federal banks. Quite possibly the equivalent of mergers and acquisition activity in the US was a substantial amount of cross-border activity and interactions through correspondent networks and limited branch networks that tied together different local and state markets.

Although scholars of financial and capital market integration assert that there is a hegemonic or core economy that reaps the benefits of such coordination, financial and monetary leadership has evolved differently. From the turn of the century, the dominance of New York and the East Coast generally in the US has been uncontested, reflecting their strong ties to international capital markets, their relatively debt-free position, and the substantial revenues received from federal securities, whereas the potential candidate in Europe—Germany—has been a reluctant hegemon. The early political fears of German financial leadership in the Community, with the Mark becoming the basis for wider integration of capital markets in Europe, generated strong resistance from the French (Jabko, 2006). The intent of preserving national sovereignty as a countervailing measure against German economic and financial hegemony stunted further progress towards capital integration in Europe (Schmitt, 1968). Rather than rely on the German financial core, the movement for financial integration and later on a common currency stems from efforts to control German capability, with economic and monetary union being pushed by France in compensation for support for German unification (cf. Heisenberg, 1999).

Market Matters: The Politics of Capital Movements

Both the US and the EU faced strong resistance from states unwilling to give up their sovereign control over fiscal and monetary issues. What has emerged in both polities is an area of shared responsibility, where jurisdictions may overlap, come into conflict, or require coordination. Within this complex regulatory environment, both the US and the EU have sought to integrate capital markets and financial services to create a common economic identity that would bolster efforts to foster a political identity (for similar views with respect to monetary union, see McNamara, 2001a; Risse, 2003).

In each case, debates about the roles and jurisdiction of different levels of government are tied to prevailing ideologies. In the US, fierce battles about states' rights and the tensions generated about monetary integration and regulation of capital markets have their counterpart in the pivotal role played by Keynesian demand management and dirigisme, where states sought to retain control over their tools of economic policy including capital and fiscal policy. Although capital markets require a regulatory framework to provide legal certainty, economic stability, and political order to operate effectively, the political development of a centralized capital market has been extremely contentious as sovereign states have asserted their right to regulate some aspects of financial instruments, so that the politics among governments is an important consideration in understanding the institutional design and regulatory regime that has emerged. In both cases, intergovernmental politics is a central feature in shaping regulatory outcomes, and the structure of financial markets is a product of statutes and laws, not simply market forces, with increased attention to enforcement and supervision by national regulators.

Trends in financial developments were punctuated by financial crises that affected the economy as a whole, and created long-term changes in the structure of financial regulations (Rockoff, 2000: 665). Private parties have also mobilized to shape and influence the processes of financial services regulation, often creating transnational networks to overcome institutional barriers.

Conclusion

Although barriers to capital movement existed in both the US and the EU, capital markets have developed gradually. The US has a single currency but did not achieve a single banking market. While American financial institutions can move vast sums of money globally, they still face restrictions in operating across state lines. Pressure to reform what many have argued are obsolete barriers preventing banks, securities, and insurance firms from affiliating focuses on Depression era laws, rather than the nineteenth-century provisions on which the current financial system is based. The development of financial ties and thus financial integration was a long-term process shaped by developments and actions taken in the antebellum and postbellum period. Notwithstanding the legal restrictions and constraints under which banks operated, they were overcome through circumvention and adaptation. The need for interregional and inter-industry funds resulted in the growth of a variety of financial intermediaries and mechanisms to foster capital mobility.

In the American case, the evolution and integration of financial markets is tied up with economic growth and development. Coupled with territorial expansion and changes in the organization of business, the mobility of capital is an important part of the consolidation of the American single market.

Scholars have argued that financial integration was affected by a variety of factors including: legal restrictions on banks, lack of uniform commercial law, the probability of banking failures, and availability of adequate credit and risk information. While banks played a crucial role in developing credit channels that encouraged investment in new regions and new industries, and helped integrate a number of distinct regional markets into a more unified national market, restrictions remained (Bodenhorn, 2003: 225). Efforts at promoting capital mobility generated a degree of regulatory harmonization with respect to minimal capital adequacy rules and deposit insurance guarantees, as well as competition among different regulatory systems, as state and federal authorities competed to regulate banks, leading to pressures on regulatory requirements for market entry.

Although the EU moved towards a single currency much more rapidly than the US, financial integration has lagged far behind. The EU was attempting to achieve what the US was initially unable to do, by allowing the freedom of establishment of branch banking in all member states, and permitting them to offer a variety of banking and financial services. Initially, the different banking systems across Europe were accepted as part of the strategy used to integrate financial markets. By not choosing one particular type of banking model over another, the EU appeared to differ from the US.

Perhaps the most important distinction was the role of the US government in establishing financial markets and a national currency. Despite the introduction of the euro, fully integrated financial markets were not achieved, as there has been growing renationalization of credit and lending in the current crisis. Some states have taken prudential measures aimed at retaining liquidity, dividends, and other bank assets within their national borders so that the increasing fragmentation of financial markets has created different lending conditions across Europe. This parallels the situation in the US in the nineteenth century. The recent banking union, which covers the largest banks in the eurozone, provides for a broadly harmonized framework for larger banks, but leaves the regional banks under national supervisory control allowing for mutual recognition of differences in practice. This still provides for surveillance and enforcement by the home country although with harmonized rules and standards within the banking union. The debate over banking union mirrored earlier ones in which the French sought support mechanisms to promote growth while the Germans reinforced fiscal policy commitments, as their preferences derived from the configuration of their domestic banking and financial systems (Howarth and Quaglia, 2013). As Europe tries to stabilize the single market, strengthen banks, and enhance regulatory capacity, with stronger oversight of banks, their capital and liquidity, and risk management, the relevance of credibly committing a government in a precarious fiscal situation through strong procedural safeguards for issuing debt had the desired effect in nineteenth-century America.

Both polities have sought to integrate their capital markets by liberalizing transactions while also fostering regulatory frameworks to provide predictable sets of rules in response to changes in financial instruments and practices. The trade strategies of the US and EU in promoting cross-country or cross-regional financial integration have some broad similarities. Both have engaged in policies of harmonization and regulatory competition. Specifying the dynamics under which capital markets have been constructed allows us to link the theoretical insights generated in the integration literature across the two cases. While this differs from traditional economic assessments that have focused on transaction costs and interest rate convergence, the political and legal factors shaping the development of capital markets are crucial in under-standing the different regulatory and institutional regimes that have emerged. Until the provisions were revised under the Treaties, the role of law appeared to be much more critical in the American case than in that of the EU in terms of shaping capital markets. The role of business in mobilizing for an integrated financial market has played a strong role in the EU case, and in a similar fashion networks of banks and other financial intermediaries have played an integrative role in the US. The allocation of power between constituent units and infringe-ment on monetary and fiscal sovereignty has not been uncontested; and both polities have struggled to determine the regulatory regime that is most appro-priate to market developments. This is clearly salient: the struggles to create a banking union in Europe touch on underlying political sensitivities about sovereign authority as efforts are made to create a single banking authority that is a long way from the US with its federal debt issuance and joint deposit protection scheme (Gros, 2012). While the US emerged as a fiscal state as part of a broader project of state-building, the slower and incomplete pace in Europe was due in part to a lack of central state capacity in Europe making it closer to the antebellum experience, whereas the current hard budgetary constraints fit closer to the post-Civil War experience and constitutional commitments.

Notes

1. Though the money-supply functions of banks are important, their role as financial intermediaries and credit-generating institutions is the principal concern of this chapter.
2. The growth of credit markets faces both political and economic constraints such as monetary instability, insecure property rights, unequal access to loans, or barriers to market entry, and informational asymmetries.

3. This chapter deals with financial services and capital controls. Other service sectors are dealt with in Chapter 6.
4. Nicolas Biddle had the Second National Bank incorporated at the state level as the Pennsylvania Bank of the US, which subsequently folded in 1840.
5. This section draws on Bodenhorn 2003 pp. 202ff.
6. Under current treaty provisions (amended) Articles 56 to 60 of the EC Treaty provide for the freedom of capital movements and payments, not only between member states, but also with respect to operations carried out by third countries. Temporary safeguards are permitted under Article 59, where capital movements, in exceptional cases, threaten or disrupt the operation of EMU, while Article 60 enables the imposition of financial sanctions on a third country or countries where such action is foreseen under the Common Foreign and Security Policy (Source: EU Europa website www.europa.eu).
7. Between 1958 and 1962, the only exception was Germany in 1962.
8. The ECU (1985) was the unit of account of the European Community until the euro was introduced.
9. This includes exchange rate stability to stem speculative attacks and balance-of-payments crises, enhancing maneuverability of domestic monetary authorities to promote domestic objectives, targeting savings and investment flows to promote national industrial development, and enhancing the ability to tax fiscal transactions and avoid the erosion of the tax base through tax circumvention and arbitrage.
10. This section draws heavily on Bakker, 1994.
11. A Directive on rights of establishment had been adopted in 1973 to ensure non-discrimination with regard to entry into domestic markets and equal treatment of conditions under which firms operated (see Directive 73/183 Official Journal L 194/1).
12. Own Funds Directive 89/229/EEC and Solvency Ratio Directive (89/647/EEC).
13. According to the European Commission about 8,300 banks will be subject to requirements imposed by the European Single Rulebook. The goal is also to aim for uniform application of Basel III global commitments in the financial arena.

6

Free Movement of Services

Transportation and Economic Services

Services constitute a wide and diverse category of economic activities including commercial services such as banking and insurance, industrial services such as transportation, professional services such as legal, health, engineering, and architectural activities, and government services.[1] Although services account for the largest and most rapidly growing sector in many advanced economies, negotiations for expanding market access for internationally traded services is a relatively recent development.[2] As services have moved more prominently onto the trade agenda, attention has focused on domestic regulations that affect the openness of markets to global competition. Since states have legitimate concerns as to the character and quality of services that firms may provide on their territory, measures governing the production and sale of services were traditionally considered a domestic policy matter (Feketekuty, 1988). Services were often defined as being produced where they were consumed. Limited attention was given to the economic benefits that could be derived from cross-border trade in services. Typically, cross-border movement of services took place with the movement of a service provider to another jurisdiction. This was initially considered movement of a factor of production rather than trade (Feketekuty, 1988). Yet the increased capacity to process and transmit information through new technologies, and the associated tradability of services, has led to the globalization of production in both goods and services (Feketekuty, 1988; Nicolaïdis and Trachtman, 2000). Despite the dynamism of trade in services prior to the onset of the global economic crisis, less is known about the effects of regulatory policies on trade in services (Kox and Lejour, 2005; OECD, 1996). Though services have assumed greater significance in the global economy, key sectors such as telecommunications, transportation, procurement, communication, and distribution services face heterogeneous national market regulations, as well as restrictions on foreign direct investment that serve as barriers to trade (Kox and Lejour, 2005).

The liberalization of service markets is rather different from that of product markets (cf. Maduro, 1998: 61). The cross-border provision of services is more complex than that of goods due to the intangible and invisible characteristics of many services (Edward, 2002). Government intervention is more prevalent in the provision of services than in manufacturing. The rationale for such intervention is that of consumer protection since the intangible nature of services makes it more difficult to assess quality than is the case with products. In fact "it is impossible to do so prior to consumption" (Pelkmans, 1997: 117). In other cases, the rationale is that many services enjoy some degree of market power and all economic activities related to the provision of services that contain a monopoly component have to be regulated to protect the consumer interest.

The focus of this chapter is on the free movement of transport services—more specifically, the right to provide services and the principle of freedom of establishment to provide services.[3] Since services comprise so many sectors, the chapter will examine the efforts to remove barriers to inland transport markets with an emphasis mainly on railroads and waterways in the US with brief reference to other modes of transport in the EU case.[4] This chapter is presented as follows: the first section discusses the broader economic role of services. Section two traces the American experience, focusing on the growth of the service economy and the barriers affecting the growth of transportation networks. In section three, the chapter discusses American efforts to address barriers that hinder cross-border services, including legal and policy developments. Section four examines the European experience in promoting a common transport policy, both the early developments to promote liberalization and the subsequent efforts in the context of the single market program. The section concludes by evaluating the development and impact of integrated transport markets in both cases.

Although transport markets do vary, all modes of transport have been subject to extensive government regulation, not least because transport policy in Europe and the US has been critical for both market- and state-building (O'Reilly and Stone Sweet, 1998; Berk, 1994). Many modes of transport have enjoyed widespread state intervention and control, but large as these investments were, they have been coupled with major debts and crises. Part of this can be attributed to both the decreasing importance of certain forms of transport as well as the various forms of protectionism and restrictions on commercial services and access. This chapter will examine the efforts to open up transport markets, which are linked to broader issues of regional development, industrial policy, and social policy in Europe and the US.

The potential of the transport sector for economic growth in terms of increased trade and investment is hampered by the structure of the market, the ownership of major firms, and the operational restrictions (Mustelli and

Pelkmans, 2013b: 14). While in the formative period of economic development, the state played a strong role in the growth of the transport sector in both Europe and the US, there have been subsequent efforts in both Europe and the US to curb state intervention through deregulation and privatization. Though many transport sectors were viewed as public goods and were either overseen as state monopolies or subject to strict government controls, the management of many public enterprises has often been considered inefficient in the nineteenth and twentieth century. Yet in both the EU and US cases efforts to tackle economic and regulatory problems have faced a political backlash against the perceived threats to social values and entrenched interests brought about by the pressures of increased competition. As a result, trade-offs between efficiency and equity in Europe or between regulation and confiscation in the US have played an important role in shaping the evolution and operation of transport services (see Berk, 1994; Héritier et al., 2001; Héritier and Schmidt, 2000).

Since the type and level of barriers can differ across service sectors, there is a need to deal with the various ways that services are traded.[5] An integrated services market means a) the abolition of restrictions on freedom of movement and establishment, b) the principle of non-discrimination is practiced, and c) barriers to entry and market access are reduced or eliminated to promote competition and reduce monopolistic behavior. An integrated market in services is expected to generate both static and dynamic welfare gains, especially in terms of increasing competition and promoting economies of scale (Kox et al., 2004). Yet economic and political factors drive each other in unexpected ways, and efforts to liberalize, coordinate, or integrate in these areas are shaped by public and private interest preferences, as well as the regulatory behavior of states (Héritier et al., 2001). Though the particular forms of regulation that emerged are well entrenched, it has been recognized that new technologies and growth have put pressure on traditionally non-competitive markets (Snell, 2002: 21). Sectors that were traditionally thought of as natural monopolies have been challenged by new market entrants, as competition has become more viable in infrastructure services, leading to a redefinition of the role of the state (Dyrhauge, 2013: 53). In the US in the nineteenth century, as different modes of transport evolved, the advent of new technologies revolutionized the processes of transportation, distribution, and production and ushered in an era of intense competition (Taylor, 1951; Taylor and Neu, 1956; Goodrich, 1956). In Europe, the globalization of production has created pressures on governments to shift towards market-oriented reforms as increased competition, in addition to technological and organizational change, has shortened product cycles and increased demands for intermediate services. As a result, new technology has greatly increased the capacity of service providers to supply cross-border services without the need to relocate. Service providers in the telecommunications, financial, professional, and other sectors have also engaged in cross-border acquisitions or other means of establishment with increasing frequency (Nicolaïdis and Trachtman, 2000).

The transport sector is economically one of the most important service sectors (Eeckhout, 1994: 85). Historically, all modes of transport have generated massive government regulation and promotion, although policy changes and business strategies have evolved in response to changes in economic ideas (Dobbin, 1995: 281–2; Berk, 1990; Bensel, 1990; cf. North, 1966: 66–7). How have Europe and the US intervened in different transport modes and what are the corresponding effects of different types of state intervention? How effective have been efforts to promote integrated transport networks? How have they addressed discrimination and distortions of competition? And what degree of success has been achieved in promoting fair competition under conditions which do not impose unnecessary barriers or restrictions to cross-border service provision?

Research on service markets has primarily focused on the welfare gains from liberalization. Economic theory is much less developed in services as there was little attention given to international specialization in the production of services (see Kox et al., 2004). Though the nature of competition in service markets varies, liberalization is expected to increase the number of products available, promote increased efficiency and economies of scale. Though concentration is high in some sectors, inefficiencies in highly protected domestic service industries are considered barriers to economic growth and investment. The services market exemplifies both the phenomenal growth and the problems created by changing market practices that have challenged traditional modes of regulating markets. Despite the prodigious growth of services, there are substantial divergences in public regulation preferences as well as private sector interests that reflect different organizational and regulatory approaches to governance. For some, services are heavily regulated for reasons of financial protection and consumer protection, but also for specific commitments such as quality and universal service requirements. While many professional, industrial, and business services have characteristics conducive to competitive markets, concerns about asymmetric information and negative externalities have led to continual and sometimes heated discussion in the US and EU about the goals of regulation. Yet liberalization of service markets in the US and EU is not simply about removing impediments to trade and market access. Frank Dobbin points out: "once institutionalized public policies tend to persist because they become integrated with wider economic institutions and ways of thinking" (Dobbin, 1995: 280). The policies of both periods were characterized by government promotion, with a strong role for public authorities in the operation and management of such services, often with wide-ranging monopoly privileges within restricted markets (O'Reilly and Stone Sweet, 1998: 448; Hartz, 1955; Scheiber, 1980b; Smith, 2005). Pressed by interest groups to provide access, and obliged to balance different economic and social goals, the governance mechanisms were shaped, in large part, by different ideas regarding the organization and structure of the transportation industry, the different strategies and logics of economic interests, and the conflicts occasioned by the scope and nature of the market (see also Berk, 1994).

American Interregional Development

The development of a national economy in the US owes much to the transportation revolution, although this generated fierce rivalries with interregional rather than inter-firm competition (Taylor, 1951; Dobbin, 1995: 282).[6] Each new method of transportation had to establish itself after a bitter struggle that affected economic growth and development as each new route integrated regional markets into a national market (Berk, 1994: 6; Taylor, 1951).[7] Measures to promote the construction of the means of transport—river improvements, canal-building, and railroad construction—were undertaken by governments at various levels through a variety of relationships between government and private enterprise (Hartz, 1955; Scheiber, 1972; Goodrich, 1956). Yet in spite of a comprehensive national plan, the federal role turned out to be a relatively minor one, as almost every state, as well as cities and local governments, provided substantial amounts of investment.[8] Though the formal and enumerated powers for the federal government in the Constitution include the power to regulate commerce, to grant corporate charters, and to dispose of public lands, initial capital investment came from states and localities, as the Constitution imposed few limits on state economic matters. Though there are no specific provisions regarding internal transportation, the constitutional provisions have been used for both promotional and regulative purposes, playing a crucial but indirect role in promoting state and local, as well as federal economic regulation (Pisani, 1987: 740–1).

A transportation network emerged in the nineteenth century, as the steamboat followed by canals, turnpikes, and railroads reached inland markets.[9] Transport decisions were left almost entirely to the states, leaving them to provide the foundation for the socioeconomic infrastructure through public works, corporate charters, public land policies, eminent domain, and mixed enterprises (Scheiber, 1980b). No longer able to protect domestic markets through tariffs or other discriminatory legislation, states found new ways to compete in attracting labor, capital, and business (Pisani, 1987; Scheiber, 1975). Interstate competition for canals and railroads began in the antebellum era, reflecting intense efforts to enhance or replace existing trade patterns and comparative advantages. Driven in part by ambitious cities as much as state governments, the competition for construction began initially in the East and continued just as fiercely in the West throughout the nineteenth century as good transportation links became critical for economic growth, as those bypassed feared economic stagnation (Sbragia 1996: 46–7; Dobbin, 1995).

In the East, Maryland, South Carolina, and Pennsylvania were the pioneers in railroad-building, each driven by pressures to enlarge their market to the West and each without important waterway connections (Taylor, 1951: 77–9). By contrast, New York with the great success of its canal system chose to restrict construction in the belief that railroads could not compete with existing waterways. Within a decade, railroad construction advanced rapidly in all the Atlantic states, aided by liberal charter provisions granting sweeping privileges of eminent domain in many instances. Despite the public suspicion towards monopolies, a number of states granted exclusive rights to railroads, exemptions from taxation, and other appreciable subsidies. Some states, aware that private capital was insufficient, built and owned railroads. Other states and local governments provided tremendous financial aid to private railroad companies, particularly in the West. This reflected concerns that the West was hampered in terms of its expansion by a number of factors; most important among these was inadequate transportation (Hays, 1995: 151). Eastern agriculture had long enjoyed readily available water routes, as the development of the railroad supplemented existing transportation patterns. The West, however, with almost no navigable rivers, depended solely on railroads for its economic development. Since private investors were reluctant to finance construction of Western railroads, the region required the federal government to subsidize development through land grants so that private railroad corporations could either sell or use land as collateral to raise capital (Hays, 1995: 152; Sbragia, 1996: Gates, 1936). The South also experienced lagging railroad construction prior to the Civil War in part due to the presence of inland waterways. Industrial development required investor confidence, which surged after the end of Reconstruction. However, the rail network needed to overcome significant physical barriers to construction, as well as technological convergence and standardization over rail gauges to integrate the Southern network into the national economy (see Taylor, 1951; Hays, 1995). Equally importantly, the railroads did not simply provide similar services as other modes of transport. They provided more direct routes, reduced costs, and greater speed, as well as increased certainty in shipping and delivery, although there is some debate among historians about whether it was railroads or government intervention that was the significant factor in fostering economic growth (Goodrich, 1970). What the transportation system achieved was remarkable economies of scale enabling the market system to operate more efficiently and made possible similar advances in other industries by unifying a huge domestic market (Berk, 1994).

Yet transportation policy was the subject of substantial public discussions throughout the nineteenth century. Economic growth was a disruptive process, and fluctuations in stocks, bonds, and dividends were both unavoidable and unpredictable (Higgs, 1971: 125). The problems incurred by government intervention through heavy state borrowing and investment in railroads and canals on the one hand, were matched by agitation towards railroads for both high rates and monopoly practices. Railroads, in particular, were at the center of debates about strategies to cope with the economic and social changes wrought by internal economic development. Though regulation was initially directed at the protection of public funds rather than corporate behavior, the continued association of government and enterprises, and the considerable state struggle to maintain control throughout the nineteenth century, suggests that government support for business development was subject to conflicting pressures between the protection of the public interest and role of government in advancing corporate liberalism (Lively, 1955; Sklar, 1988). Not only did railroads figure prominently in this struggle over the competing goals of public policy, but as Berk writes, railroads found themselves at the center of a struggle over the form and place of the modern corporation in the American polity (Berk, 1994: 13). The transportation revolution brought to the fore disagreements about the institutional organization of the economy, and conflicts among interests occasioned by such efforts to regulate and control these emerging corporate structures (Berk, 1994; Shonfield, 1965).

Barriers to Trade

The role of transportation in the creation of a national market has generated a spirited debate among historians about the role of railroads in economic growth, and the corresponding role of public authorities in promoting and regulating such large-scale industrial corporations (Fogel, 1964, 1965; Goodrich, 1970; Berk, 1994; cf. North, 1966). Development often required overcoming localism or even the obstruction of transportation facilities, as those adversely affected by such events often resorted to the courts to protect property rights (Freyer, 1981: 1264). As a consequence, the patterns of regional trade and economic diversification that emerged from national market integration initially needed to address "public use" requirements for the construction of transportation facilities.[10] Subsequent attention turned to market restrictions stemming on the one hand from collusion and anticompetitive practices, and on the other hand from the diversity of equipment, gauges, and interchange rules that required standardization (See Taylor and Neu, 1956; Bensel, 2000). Most studies of transportation often distinguish between the antebellum and postbellum period, especially with regards to changes in construction, technology, and financing (cf. Dobbin, 1995). This is helpful in understanding the impact of the competitive struggles among different modes of transportation as well as the rivalries among states and localities that invested resources in order to gain comparative advantages from improved transportation. Since the transportation system continued to expand throughout the nineteenth century, the developments in both periods are examined since these internal improvements, as some have claimed, provided the conditions for domestic commerce to flourish by lowering costs and facilitating the cross-border movement of goods and persons in the American economy.

The Antebellum Period

"In no other period has government been so active in promoting, owning and controlling turnpikes, bridges, canals and railroads" (Taylor, 1951: 383). State governments chartered corporations and served as entrepreneurs on a large scale, either independently or with private interests (Shonfield, 1965: 302; Hartz, 1948). This meant that "railroads, canals and banks were treated as proper spheres for public enterprise," based on the notion that the legislative grant of privilege would empower corporations to further the public good (Shonfield, 1965: 302; Licht 1995: 90). Between 1820 and 1860 most railroads and canals were chartered under special legislation. To aid, encourage, and stimulate internal improvements, states and localities raised substantial capital, largely through legislation establishing canal and railroad corporations, selling stocks and bonds to both domestic and foreign investors. Starting with a canal-building boom in the 1820s and 1830s that linked communities from the Ohio River to Lake Erie, followed by the boom in railroad construction that began in the 1840s, the entire continent was effectively connected by the transcontinental railway by 1890, thereby allowing an integrated market economy to emerge (Licht, 1995: 82–3).

States and local governments had underwritten much of the costs of construction. Although the total amount of aid given by states and localities cannot be definitely determined, Goodrich estimated that in the antebellum period, localities committed more than $125 million to internal improvements compared to $300 million from state governments (Goodrich as quoted in Sbragia, 1996: 51). During this time, Pennsylvania issued $100 million shares, and Missouri had authorized the purchase of $23 million shares of its chartered railroads and canals (Licht, 1995: 86). Local government activism, according to Sbragia, involved the borrowing of money to assist railroad companies to build terminals or branch lines (see also Goodrich, 1951). Cities invested to serve local needs whereas states invested, propelled by the inadequacy of private investment, in order to shape a regional market and help portions of the state territory achieve economic growth (Sbragia, 1996: 51ff).

Borrowing increased dramatically between 1840 and 1880, although during the antebellum period state indebtedness was primarily in the Eastern region. The vast amounts of capital needed for construction came from either domestic savings or foreign lenders, based on the faith of the state to repay debts and loans. However, states exhausted their credit, particularly during the depression of the 1830s and 1840s when the expected returns on investment in railroads and banks would not materialize (Taylor, 1951: 374). The inability of some states to pay loans caused concern in the financial community, as several states including Pennsylvania, Maryland, and Indiana defaulted on their debts (Taylor, 1951: 375; Goodrich 1950: 154). A number of states struggled for over a decade to recover financial solvency, and many were forced to take a number of drastic measures to meet their obligations. Some introduced general property taxes, others imposed taxes on banks and occupational licenses, while still others were forced to divest themselves of their business interests and sell off public enterprises (Taylor, 1951: 378, 382). Although a number of states did continue to engage in railroad construction, amassing new debts, a significant portion of states affected by the financial crises of the thirties imposed debt restrictions through constitutional amendments (Taylor, 1951; Sbragia, 1996; Wallis, 2005). In curbing the promotional role of states, the process was a gradual one that reflected changing economic conditions rather than outright opposition to the use of public agencies for economic development (Goodrich, 1951; Sbragia, 1996; Pisani, 1987: 746).

Yet the introduction of debt limits on states provided the opportunity for the federal government to play a major role in capital investment (Sbragia, 1996; Shonfield, 1965). Although unwilling to assume state debts, the federal government provided an important role in railroad-building through grants of public lands. Tremendous sections of the public domain were used to aid railroad construction, which spurred on the commodification of the natural resources in the Plains and West (Bensel, 2000: 293). According to Taylor, over eighteen million acres were given in the antebellum period to ten states, benefiting forty-five different railroad companies (Taylor, 1951: 96). Bensel (2000)[11] suggests that the cyclical short booms of the antebellum period disposed of about forty-five million acres. Eminent domain, the right of the government to take private property for public use was central, although its delegation to private enterprises, though controversial, was an essential element in the construction of canals and railroads (Freyer, 1981: 1263). Without the right to acquire land, railroads would have faced serious challenges by property owners in building networks. These delegated powers of legal compulsion assisted growth of a transportation industry which was based on the premise of fulfilling a public purpose but in fact also contributed to a massive concentration of power among corporations in the late nineteenth century as states shifted from aiding industry to regulating prices, leading to cartels and cooperative market behavior (Dobbin, 1995; Shonfield, 1965).

Throughout this period, intense interstate rivalry and competition drove states to engage in the strategic allocation of resources, the assignment of special privileges and immunities, and the granting of specific subsidies to favored enterprises (Scheiber, 1980b). Faced with the prospect that loss in the transport race would diminish regional supremacy, or at worst inflict dramatic economic stagnation and decline, states were engaged in such "rivalistic state mercantilism" that it affected their choice of technology (Scheiber, 1981: 131; Scheiber, 1975; Sbragia 1996: 34). Across the various railroads, there was great diversity in track widths leading to the so-called "war of the gauges."[12] In New England, "standard" gauges of four foot eight-and-half inches were generally used, while the South commonly chose five-foot gauges. The Erie Railroad deliberately chose six-foot gauges, in order to prevent traffic diversion from other lines. Over the long run, this proved self-defeating and forced them to change over to standard gauges. By contrast Pennsylvania and Ohio had railroads representing seven different track widths, with publicly and privately owned railroads operating on different gauges. Progress towards a uniform track width was slow before the Civil War with at least eleven different gauges in the North, and no universal gauge in the South. Thus, the railroad network on the eve of the Civil War was not a really integrated system despite the rapid pace of construction and new mileage. There were over three hundred independent lines, a variety of gauges that hindered mobility across different lines, and links connecting the Northern railroads and Southern railroads were lacking (Taylor, 1951: 86). Sectional politics and alliances continued to play out in antebellum politics and commerce. Political opposition to the federal government taking a direct part in the railroad business, plus effective lobbying by competing railroad lines prevented the rationalization of the railroads which continued to be "built and capitalized well beyond their renumerative capacity" in the continuing decades after the Civil War (Berk, 1994: 25).

Yet in spite of the debts and defaults created by railroad construction, Bensel concludes that "everywhere the railroad network went, the local economy was transformed in one way or another" (Bensel, 2000: 303). The transportation system revolutionized the processes of distribution and production, and generated increased specialization among regions based on their comparative advantage in specific goods and commodities (Bensel, 2000; McCurdy, 1978). However, the notion that states had founded corporations to promote the public good had vanished, as the problems surrounding canal and railroad developments including corruption and management problems lent support to what has been described as the "revulsion against internal improvements" (see Goodrich, 1951: 413). Transportation symbolized the economic volatility and political cleavages created by industrialization, as local elites saw "public capitalization of industry as critical" (Berk, 1994: 283) with local governments stepping in using local finances to promote economic development that continued the interstate rivalry that had begun at the state level (Sbragia, 1996: 46ff).

While the early and mid nineteenth century reflected the priorities of states upheld by courts, with railroads thrust into the center of the politics of industrialization, the reappraisal of judicial behavior and constitutional doctrine in the postbellum period symbolized the increasing dissatisfaction with how markets were constituted (Scheiber, 1980b: 1171; McCurdy, 1979). The pressure for corporate administration and reform meant that the privileged relationship between government and business, the combined promotional and regulatory role of governments, and the actual effect in distributing the burdens and benefits of industrial development in nineteenth-century America became increasingly contested (see Freyer, 1981).

The Postbellum Period

Yet the railroads set the pace for industrialism in the postbellum period. The railroads created new demands that stimulated mass production and distribution, altered the forms of business practices and methods, and affected the scope and scale of commercial farming and manufacturing production. State government intervention continued in the 1850s and 1860s repeating to some degree the experience in the earlier period, as aid to transcontinental lines west of the Mississippi was considered essential for frontier development (Goodrich, 1950). Subsequently, during Reconstruction, railway aid became a key aspect of economic development for the South. Yet Southern debt increased dramatically, and in much the same way as in the antebellum era, half of the railroads in the South defaulted at the onset of depression and panic in 1873 (Sbragia, 1996: 38; Berk, 1994). Again state debt limits were introduced through constitutional amendment in many Southern states. As Hurst points out, states continued to exercise an important influence on economic development, even after the popular agitation in the late nineteenth century forced states to divest themselves of their business interests. Instead, governments lent their power to private corporations, most notably through the right of eminent domain that meant that they could compulsorily acquire any land for their operations, and also through general incorporation laws that further promoted the corporate form of business. The federal government granted federal lands from the public domain for the transcontinental railroad, as well as for land grant colleges and homesteads.[13] By far the largest land grant program was for the construction of railroads, under state supervision in the East and under direct federal supervision in the West after

1862 (Elazar, 1964). During the last boom in railroad construction, the number of acres sold or given to the private economy exceeded sixteen million a year from 1883 to 1887 (Bensel, 2000: 283). By 1869, the Pacific had been reached; and by 1875 with 74,000 miles of track in operation, the overland transportation network system had been constructed (Chandler, 1978: 87). The joining of the Union and Central Pacific railways symbolized the beginning of a national economy (Hays, 1995: 69). As the *New York Times* reported, "the long looked for moment had arrived...the inhabitants of the Atlantic seaboard and the dwellers on the Pacific slopes are henceforth emphatically one people" (*New York Times*, 1869).

As the national network expanded and consolidated, a corresponding standardization effort occurred. A collaboration among competing railroads to adopt a uniform width for track occurred when the Southern lines agreed to change over to the Northern standard gauge, with thousands of miles of track bounded by the Ohio River, Gulf of Mexico, and Mississippi River converted in 1886 (Taylor and Neu, 1956: 78–81). In addition, the establishment of national time zones in 1883 allowed for the coordination of rail traffic, often between different companies. Prior to standardization, some trains in North East left a particular station on Boston time while others left according to New York time schedules (Bensel, 2000: 299) Individual rail companies had created some seventy-five different time zones throughout the American continent (Bensel, 2000: 299).

The advantages accorded to railroads generated increased conflict in the postbellum era. The boom and bust cycles resulted in massive consolidation in the late nineteenth century as smaller railroad lines were absorbed into larger networks. Driven by attempts to control rate competition and the relentless pressure on transportation costs, the railroad network curtailed competition through a series of cooperative agreements. Such pooling arrangements among railroads—later through organization of trusts in manufacturing and marketing enterprises—and other trade associations were intended to regulate market conditions. The numerous bankruptcies, coordination problems, and frequent collapse of many collusive arrangements shifted attention to alternative arrangements. Railroad consolidation, which had followed as the wave of mergers and takeovers generated considerable concentrations of power in the industry, led to the creation of trusts. Once again, the federal government could not prosecute such regulated competition as states held incorporation rights that had encouraged the formation of corporations and promoted later corporate actions such as holding companies and trusts (Licht, 1995: 157). With competition amongst states to entice business, there were tremendous pressures to enact permissive legislation and increase corporate privileges. Having turned public power into private ends, popular agitation for railroad regulation which began in the Midwest generated the Granger Laws—which sought to create regulatory commissions to enforce rates that granted parity to interregional trade (Berk, 1994: 77). Regionalism and sectionalism often coincided on the railroad issues as the effect of railroad rates upon regional growth were subject to increased scrutiny (Sanders, 1999). On the one hand, it reflected concerns about industrial consolidation, but it also reflected on the other hand, localism and regionalism, as the integration of regional markets into the national economy broke down many local monopolistic and administered arrangements (Bensel, 2000: 320).

Under mounting public opposition, the eventual prohibition on cartels and similar collusive practices did in fact promote a dense regulatory structure with state railroad commissions first, followed by a federal regulatory commission and a corresponding body of state and national laws and judicial decisions (Keller, 1990: 43). Though seeking to assert a necessary degree of public control over the economy, a system of federal agencies emerged in a belated effort to assert public interest in the management and financial operations of railroads (Shonfield, 1965). But ironically as the adoption of antitrust law occurred, states liberalized corporate laws in the post-Civil War period with the goal of attracting firms to incorporate in their state, creating a "race to the bottom" effect. States competed to become incorporation havens. They adopted measures permitting corporations to own stock of other companies, granted favorable tax treatment, and thus prompted capital concentration as the formation of trusts accelerated under this liberalization trend.

The problem of trusts necessitated a response at the federal level. Since many companies purchased stocks outside and within their home state, the federal government sought to regulate any restraint on trade on the basis of federal jurisdiction on interstate commerce. Although the efforts to regulate markets through the Interstate Commerce Act of 1887 and the Sherman Antitrust Act of 1890 were modest exercises of sovereign national authority they anticipated the regulatory state in the twentieth century (Kelly et al., 1991: 373). Behind the failure of state and federal regulation was the judiciary, which struck down many laws as transgressing property rights or encroaching on interstate commerce (Bensel, 2000: 312). The Court had specific views about "who would be the final arbiter in the realm of railroad regulation" (Keller, 1990: 45) As such it determined the relationship between corporations and the state, seeking to deal with the implications of the emergence of large-scale enterprise "by extending more reliable legal institutions to investors and producers who operated within a national market" (Gillman, 2002: 512–13). Some such as Kolko viewed the Court as successfully breaking down the railroad cartels that ran afoul of federal regulations, whereas others saw such efforts as simply having a negligible effect on railroad collusion as they engaged in business combinations, trusts, and other forms of organization, and thus legal rulings did not dramatically alter business conduct (Kolko, 1965). Since the Supreme Court also assured that railroads needed to earn a fair return to value in *Smyth* v. *Ames* (1898), the initial efforts to regulate railroads through the ICC were marred by the difficulties of comparing and assessing railroad rates.

Railroads were viewed as providing important innovations in terms of the organizational transformation of American business in the late nineteenth century. As transportation and communications networks grew in geographic range, companies responded by seeking to reduce transaction costs and promote economies of scale. The massive restructuring of firms that saw rapid changes in production and distribution in response to the emergence of a national market evolved into the modern corporation. Railroads, at the forefront of this transformation, expanded and extended their operations through a set of innovative financial structures including "income bonds, preferred stocks and voting trusts" (Tufano, 1997: 2). However, by the end of the nineteenth century, railroads were in financial distress with pressures for liquidation and bankruptcy, driven by overcapacity, excessive competition, and high fixed costs. Railroads became subject to a variety of regulatory strategies, initially challenging the constitutional validity of government regulation, and then seeking relief from the courts to protect their interests to enable them to reorganize distressed firms and to resolve disputes arising from financial failures (Tufano, 1997: 8, 12; Berk, 1994). In fashioning such rules to restructure a critical sector of the American economy, the courts argued that their strategic importance necessitated their continued development as an integrated transportation system (Tufano, 1997: 3–4; Berk, 1994: 45–72).

Integration through Law

Constitutional litigation has played a crucial role in the railroad sector throughout the nineteenth century, generating an array of rulings that have fostered financial and legal innovations, and supported a vast national system that served as a model for other industries in fostering national market integration (Berk, 1994). In both the antebellum and postbellum period, government promotion and regulation were closely linked to judicial decisions (Sbragia, 1996: 99). The thrust of what governments could permit or allow themselves to do was often determined by jurisprudence that had to rule on the notion of public purpose, and thereby determine the relationship between business and government through the balance between legitimate public regulation and the protection of private property (McCurdy, 1975).

The Court sought to promote economic progress, and in doing so fostered competition through preventing existing companies from holding vested rights, privileges, and exclusive monopolies in the *Charles River Bridge* Case

(1837). The Court concluded that the corporation was not a privileged state entity, and as such, the concerns that turnpikes through their privileged charters would impede progress on railroad construction, led to a divided decision in which the original clauses of contracts could be altered to allow for other forms of business organization. The result was that the contract clause, the principal source of protection in the antebellum period, became gradually less important, even if these were charters for public works and internal improvements. The shift from vested rights to substantive rights occurred in context of the rise of the business corporation, and meant that the courts sought to strike a balance between the claims of individual rights—including corporations—under the Fourteenth Amendments and the claims of state governments under their police powers. The general effect of broadening the former and narrowing the latter—affected the ability of states to act on behalf of general welfare (Sbragia, 1996 quoting Fine: 97).

This tension came to the fore in *Munn* v. *Illinois* in 1877 where conflict over the rights of states to regulate business emerged. Grangers actively lobbied for railroad regulation to determine fair rates and prices. The Court concluded that states had the license to regulate "any business affected with a public interest." Although Munn was not a railroad case, the conflict over the term "public purpose" was central to judicial determination over what is permissible, and the Court upheld the validity of government regulation of any business affected with a public interest. *Munn* v. *Illinois* introduced a short era in which US public utilities were subject to increased scrutiny. The state had the right to constitutionally intervene where the public interest was affected by private monopoly to ensure reasonable rates (Hoogenboom and Hoogenboom, 1976: 6–8). However, this was overturned by *Wabash* in 1886, which effectively forbade the states from regulating interstate railroad rates. The economic regulations of states had become increasingly invalid as they encroached on interstate commerce, which was the jurisdiction of the federal government. The Supreme Court struck down many laws regulating private business after the Civil War as a new doctrine—the Fourteenth Amendment—generated an entirely new meaning to protect private business from public regulation (Hays, 1995: 180). At this point, after Wabash, effective regulation would have to be at the federal level. In the pursuit of constitutional protection of their property interests during the period between the Civil War and the end of the nineteenth century, litigation by American railroads resulted in broadening the interpretation of constitutional limitations on governmental power and enhancing power of the federal judiciary to enforce those limitations on the ground that the policies encroached upon fundamental aspects of life, liberty, or property and were consequently invalid under the "substantive due process" clause.

Many of the subsequent cases related to government defaults and debt collection concerning railway bonds and securities in the postbellum era. The fiscal problems incurred by both state and local governments were linked to broader questions about how far government should intervene in the economy (Sbragia, 1996: 91). As a result, the judiciary—not market forces—determined the values of railroad securities, debt repayment, and other contractual issues, providing for judicial intervention and legal innovation in financial markets (Tufano, 1997: 2). This meant that courts played a key role in making sure railroads continued to operate, preventing their wholesale liquidation by allowing them to restructure their finances through equity receivership, and in doing so changed the terms of contracts and property rights. In dealing with failed railroads, it was the courts—and not market forces—that used public interest concerns to keep the railroads running at the expense of fulfilling prior debt obligations. This enabled the development of the nation's railroads as a nationally integrated system by solving their immediate financial needs through innovative capital market practices (Berk, 1994; Tufano, 1997).

Lessons for Europe from the US

The construction and operation of transportation markets in the nineteenth century assumed a central part in the pace of industrialization and change in America. While demographic, market, and technological forces pushed forward the expansion of the transportation and communication system in the US, there are a number of developments that provide important precedents for the EU. The competition among different modes of transport is important, as economic development was deeply contested among states, and vested interests sought to maintain their comparative advantage through particular forms of restrictive practices. State-subsidized corporate development accorded railroads a dominant status in industrialization, although there were tensions between public interest regulation and private interests in such promotional policies. Yet the American political and legal system encouraged the use of the corporate form of enterprise for public purposes: state governments had great leeway to provide important privileges. The resulting indebtedness and inefficiencies of many public enterprises redefined not only the relationship between public and private enterprises, but also the promotional and regulatory role of governments as efforts to build administrative capacity to control corporate activities and behavior generated conflict over the market power of corporations. The change in industrial structure propelled by a decentralized and competitive economic structure allowed railroads to achieve remarkable economies of scale and develop new administrative practices and legal forms (see Chandler and Salsbury, 1968). Such corporate concentrations which generated popular opposition, led to federal intervention on the basis of interstate commerce. The need to assert a necessary degree of public control over economic resources became centralized in the aftermath of judicial decisions which confirmed that transportation and communication across state lines were forms of interstate commerce (Kelly et al., 1991; Bensel, 2000). Tensions about levels of regulatory governance, the relationship between corporate power and public goods, and jurisdictional competition led to contentious debates about institutional control of such large-scale industries. In addition, technological advances were affecting market conditions, production processes and generating both expanding productive capacities and stagnating consumption levels initiating significant economic turbulence.

The politics of transportation markets was one of intense competition and coordination, which resulted in a wide array of experiments in governance that reflected different conceptions about the railroad corporation and other modes of transport, and their legal, political, and economic relationship to the state. The various attempts to manage the economy led different interest groups to mobilize against what was perceived as ruinous competition. These groups then utilized governments to further entrench their position by seeking government regulations on enterprises such as railroads that provided basic services, (Licht, 1995: 194) as well as price support measures for farmers, work and employment rules and other securities, standards of practice for professionals (see Chapter 7), all of which have the same goals of shielding economic competition and institutionalizing entitlements which provides important parallels with the EU.[14] Thus, direct government regulation in the US was aimed at meeting two goals. First, an assessment of reasonable rates for public services in much the same vein as the emphasis on public services and equality of access and provision factors in certain European member states. Second, information on corporate financial affairs, given the separation of ownership and control, led to greater attention on financial reporting and governance structures, so that creditors could assess risk and equity owners could assess surpluses for dividends, thus providing information on revenues, expenses, and profits across different railroad lines within states.

The European Experience

Historically, the liberalization of services lagged behind other freedoms (see Chapter 4). Tariffs and quotas are not significant issues in the service sector since it is difficult to erect barriers to services at the border (Pelkmans, 1997: 74). However, the limited share of tradable services, along with the inherent difficulty of providing many services in jurisdictions with different legal, administrative, and regulatory requirements, meant that the economic significance of cross-border services was initially relatively small. While there was general consensus that the freedom to provide services and freedom of establishment were among the indispensable components of the common market, the severe restrictions on trade that affected European economies in the preceding decades shaped the attitudes of business towards foreign markets (Gehrels and Johnson, 1955). In contrast to the scale of American foreign direct investment, the low stock of direct investment between European states provided few incentives for business to provide cross-border services (Pelkmans 1997: 106).

The original Treaty articles on services contrast markedly with those for product markets. Services are considered a residual category, defined as not being covered by those Treaty rules dealing with free movement of goods, capital, and labor (Snell, 2002: 6). This meant that the Treaty articles covering services (Articles 59–66) are relevant if other treaty articles do not apply. The conditional nature of services is implied by the fact that the free movement of services may involve movement of a person or business, so that services are related to the free movement of labor and rights of establishment provisions in the Treaty as these provisions also envisage the mobility of legal entities or persons.

Although the negotiators at the Messina Conference wanted to introduce competition into highly oligopolistic markets, the service provisions were not generally applicable across all sectors in large part due to national objections to specific market proposals. Since there was reluctance to include "public service" monopolies, the initial proposals for services suffered from some serious limitations. The most important economic service sectors—financial, telecommunications, postal, and transport—were given special treatment which hampered efforts at market liberalization. Since financial services liberalization was conditional upon the progressive liberalization of capital, the adoption of a single currency, and coordination of fiscal and accounting practices, progress in this area was slow (see Chapter 4). Transport issues, were also held back from the general provision on services. Inland transport, in terms of invested capital, represented one of the few service sectors recognized as being of economic significance for cross-border transactions among European states (European Conference of Ministers of Transport, 1954).[15] Yet it was included in a separate "transport title" of the Treaty, pursuing what is called a "common transport policy." The widely varying national transport policies, substantial differences between different modes of transport, and widely differing public and private transport interests meant that the end result was one of compromise.

Transport services were to be governed by specific efforts at avoiding discrimination and distortions of competition (Articles 76–82). However, a common transport policy was not mandatory as in the case of the common market and Common Agricultural Policy (Von der Groeben, 1987: 78; Deniau, 1961: 73). Similarly, postal and telecommunications services were not included in the service sector. With state intervention and ownership to ensure universal service obligations, member states used these sectors as a means to accomplish regional, industrial, and employment goals. Such state-owned monopolies did not generate EC interference despite the fact that Treaty rules forbid member states from maintaining measures contrary to the Treaty with respect to "public undertakings" and enterprises to which member states give "special and exclusive rights." As a result, "there was a general lack of positive guidance given in the Treaty to help members formulate a common policy, and a great deal of disagreement over how such a policy would be constructed" given that there were few references to regulated industries in the Treaty (Aspinwall, 1995: 480; also Abbati, 1987; Despicht, 1964). Moreover, Article 84(2) made clear that the highly international activities of air and sea transport were to be treated separately from the inland modes of road, rail, and inland waterways as the latter were more critical for a customs union (Aspinwall, 1995; Whitelegg, 1988). The Treaty did empower the Council to add maritime shipping and aviation if unanimously agreed, although these industries were highly protected sectors in which governments set conditions for market entry, and provided incentives for investment, and were also governed by long-standing international agreements that determined registration, rate regulation, and routes (Staniland, 2008). Liberalizing these sectors would require addressing national protectionism resulting from bilateral or preferential trade agreements, cabotage rules, and foreign ownership restrictions which distorted competition, as well as avoiding discriminatory transport charges at borders which could easily undermine the reduction of customs duties that had been agreed upon.

In all cases, both inland and intermodal transportation proved to be remarkably resistant to a common transport scheme resulting in a considerable impasse due to entrenched vested interests, national intervention, and different juridical traditions. Although protectionism has been progressively chipped away by the expansion of Community interest to include aviation and maritime modes by new member states, commercial pressures through deregulation, and legal judgments have forced changes upon national regulatory regimes in the context of increased liberalization and competition (see Schmidt, 2000: 39; Aspinwall, 1995, 1999). Yet challenges remain due to different regulatory objectives, divergent standards, and technological developments, high fixed sunk costs and limited intermodal competition. Moreover, the railways, as distinct from other modes of transport have been tied to state-building, and as such, represent one of the most entrenched sectors of state monopoly and control. As a public sector enterprise, it remains markedly inward looking, and thus differs from the American case where interstate competition was prevalent. Yet like the US, the railroad industries were subject to high maintenance costs and huge amounts of public subsidies, with continued pressure to induce more producer competition, improved productivity, and lower prices. Thus, European transport policy has sought to deregulate and liberalize highly regulated road haulage markets and privatize state railroad monopolies to increase efficiency, foster competition, and change the industrial and regulatory structure while also addressing the public welfare implications of service provision.

Interregional Trade Flows and Barriers to Trade

Transportation services in the EU employ more than 9.2 million people. Transportation services are the second most important in value terms for the EU, accounting for 25 percent of total services transactions. Yet there is no consensus on the best way to measure the impact of regulations on trade costs for services as this involves both home and host countries since service firms must adapt and comply with policies in destination countries as well as changes in working practices or fixed costs in the home country. Consequently, the differences in regulation between the exporting and importing country are also important barriers for bilateral trade as regulatory heterogeneity can be a significant barrier to market entry (Kox and Lejour, 2005; Lejour, 2010). In addition, the tradability of transport services depends on international regimes, particularly in the case of shipping and aviation, where international rules and policies have impacted the level of competition in the industry. In the case of airlines, the international framework was based on international security and sovereignty over airspace under the Chicago Convention, while shipping as a highly internationalized industry, operating under a freedom of the seas principle, has also been subject to international rules originating from the International Maritime Organization, UNCTAD, and OECD. In the case of airlines, this agreement over jurisdiction meant that states could bilaterally negotiate air traffic rights and stipulate conditions for commercial air traffic, allowing for limited competition (Staniland, 2008: 18–19). Numerous bilateral agreements between EU member states effectively segment the internal airline services market along national lines. Similarly, the maritime industry is a highly protected cartel, in which national governments set conditions for registry or ownership and provide incentives for investment (Aspinwall, 1995). In the case of transportation, a range of administrative, technical, and legal barriers in road, rail, and air transport services includes legal entry conditions, open skies, regional air agreements, quotas, licenses, and permits (see Kox, Lejour, and Verweij, 2009). In addition prob-lems of interoperability, such as track gauges and signaling systems, hinder the operation of a single transport market. There is no single-track gauge across Europe, as Britain, France, and Germany adopted the standard gauge, Spain and Portugal chose a broader gauge for the Iberian peninsula, Russia a third option that encompassed the former Soviet Republics, with Ireland alone choosing a different width. Not only do the width and height for transported rolling stock vary due to choices made earlier by state-owned rail networks, but even the British do not monopolize driving on the left side of the road. Trains pass in Britain and Belgium on the left, while in France most trains pass on the left, but in Alsace, which was under German control in the rail-building era, French trains pass on the right.

In the case of road transport, competition is restricted by specific tariff controls, licenses and permits, and general prohibition on cabotage in which non-residents are restricted in collecting and delivering goods within the boundaries of other member states (Emerson 1988: 113). Sea transport services are also restricted due to cabotage, although inland waterway trans-portation has long been liberalized due to prior conventions and commissions fostering mutual recognition and freedom of access, with cabotage less of an issue on inland waterways than other modes of transport (Stevens, 2004: 116–17). In the case of railroads, the deeply entrenched regulatory practices made it difficult for railroads to compete with road freight due to specific pricing policies and freight charges. As a result these nationalized industries were subject to licensing practices, and direct subsidies and cross subsidies tended to enhance their competitiveness over longer distances or heavier loads (Stevens, 2004; Dyrhauge, 2013). Such efforts to protect railroads from competition from road transport prevented progressive liberalization of transportation in the single market, both for freight and passenger services. Given that numerous domestic railway organizations evolved, national con-siderations were more prevalent than international concerns in terms of administrative and technical regulations. Thus, even if markets were liberalized, railway infrastructure is not compatible which serves to reinforce national monopolies (Stevens, 2004: 92; Monti, 2010). The European rail network is fragmented, partly through the lack at the European level of infrastructure links, which has promoted the development of Trans-European networks. However, the integration of national rail systems encounters problems of dif-ferent technical and safety standards giving rise to interoperability, causing rail operators to change wagons and crews at borders due to both labor rules as well as operational differences stemming from national variations in standards. Seeking to transform state monopolies into commercially viable businesses, the EU has sought to address differing national regulations of service provision that create significant barriers. Like the US, railroads found themselves heavily in debt, with substantial cumulative losses, resulting in significant state aids and subsidies (Mause and Schreeb, 2011). Over the past two decades, 40 percent of state aid has been directed towards railway industries in the face of constantly declining market share for both freight and passenger transport relative to other modes of transportation. The goal of a single market in railway services is aimed at promoting competition, encouraging a modal shift towards rail freight, and preventing cross subsidies to this historically indebted sector.

Although road haulage is characterized by a high degree of state intervention in order to protect small and medium enterprises due to low market-entry costs, the industry is more fragmented (Héritier et al., 2001: 17). The inland transport system of the EU has seen a rapid shift from public to private transport and from rail and inland waterway use to road use for both freight and passenger services over the past three decades, accounting for more than 70 percent of market share (European Environmental Agency, 2010).[16] Yet transportation costs are considerably higher than if the market was liberalized with estimated costs of some 20 percent due to regulatory restrictions such as cabotage, taxes, and permits as diverse national regulatory regimes create barriers to market entry (Emerson, 1988: 114). Not only is the mode of transport shifting to road haulage but changes in production—through "just-in-time" delivery systems—new technologies, increased competition, and supplementary services have intensified the benefits of market liberalization for road haulage at the expense of railroads, which as public sector enterprises, with social goals and monopoly control, have not faced the same pressures of competition and market developments (see also Aspinwall, 1999).

The Early Formative Period: The 1960s to the 1970s

Although the European Commission promoted a common transport policy in the 1960s, it faced substantial member state opposition due to its emphasis on liberalization (Stevens, 2004; Erdmenger, 1983; Abbati, 1987). The first initial effort, the so-called "Schaus Memorandum" in 1961, attempted to provide guidelines for Community-wide action based on integrating transport markets that would not differentiate between modes of transport (Whitelegg, 1988; Stevens, 2004: 47). However, a comprehensive approach met with opposition from member states, and so action was shelved. To link transport policy with other fields, such as regional and social policy, the Commission sought to promote an intermodal network in which different transport modes would play complementary roles to align national policies rather than replace them with a single European policy (Erdmenger, 1983). However, European transport markets were characterized by distinct national markets with divergent interests. Railroads of the six founding members were nationalized and subject to licensing regimes to protect them from competition from road haulage. Rail concerns were prioritized at the national level given their public sector status, as well as the strength of the rail unions who could often bring services to a halt with strike action, generating significant disruption. With international regimes regulating different aspects of interstate transportation, there was limited pressure to integrate national transport markets at the European level. Unable to harmonize national transportation regulations, the non-compulsory nature of transportation provisions made progress elusive throughout the 1960s and 1970s. Though tariffs could no longer be discriminatory in terms of the transport of bulk goods, and hence railroads were forced to put all member states on equal terms in the customs union, transport was further protected from greater European intervention by being exempt from competition rules that prohibited state aids. Due to public service obligations, most commonly applied to railroads, state aid was disbursed to cover not only public service obligations but also infrastructure and operating losses, providing no incentive for states to change their policies. Railroads were viewed as natural monopolies with high sunk costs for infrastructure and rolling stock that needed government protection and such support shaped government policies. Railroads were often organized as single publicly owned firms, managing both rail services and infrastructure, whereas the management and ownership structure evolved differently in the US. Instead of being managed as commercial enterprises, they came under public service provisions, resulting in different approaches to the supply of transport across member states. Creating a coordinated network at the European level remained hampered by differences in terms of gauges, signaling, and interoperability of networks, although some of these idiosyncrasies are being overcome through investment in high-speed rail networks. For the Baltic states, the switch from dependence on Russian infrastructure to a new railway service using a continental standard gauge, would also offer a sense of security by connecting them directly with the rest of Europe.

Like rail, road haulage markets were also subject to liberalization pressures as the Commission sought to open up markets to competition and have non-resident road haulers operate in other member state markets (Camerra-Rowe, 1994). Like other modes of transport, the creation of a single market for road haulage did not produce much legislative activity in the 1960s and 1970s. In 1962, a small range of specialized services, including local frontier traffic were liberalized. This was followed by the creation of limited Community quotas, which set the groundwork for subsequent liberalization and the abolition of quotas in the late 1980s. However, states regulated demand and supply by controlling market entry and capacity through licensing and tariff rates for road transport services to dampen competition. Since border-crossing was governed by bilateral agreements among member states, this reduced the incentive for coordinating their different national policies. While the EU wanted to streamline the market and abolish the cumbersome and anticompetitive system of bilateral agreements, regulatory fragmentation did not prevent cross-border movement of haulage carriers (Kerwer and Teutsch, 2000: 134). Yet with different rates, taxes, and licensing requirements governing domestic road haulage markets, European efforts had little immediate concrete effect, although subsequently progressive liberalization moved more quickly for road haulage than railroads due to domestic pressures for greater liberalization in some member states.

The Single Market and Beyond: Liberalization and Contestation in the 1980s

With numerous regulatory, technical, and administrative barriers preventing the creation of a common transport policy, progress had been minimal toward a common transport market. However, the transportation sector has undergone massive change as privatization and liberalization have affected almost all European countries, cutting into areas that hitherto had not been subject to competition (Eberlein and Grande, 2005; Smith, 2005; Schmidt, 2005). Across Europe, the state acted as a direct provider of infrastructure services through public ownership in railways, or public authorities have supervised and regulated the private provision of services in road haulage. However, with increasing fiscal indebtedness and unprofitable services, as well as technological changes, states were shifting towards market-oriented solutions, following domestic developments in the US and Britain. Eberlein and Grande conclude that European regulation has also increased in importance in terms of monitoring market processes as a result of internal market legislation—taking a more informal form than expected to provide de facto coordination and operational rules within specific sectors (Eberlein and Grande, 2005: 101–3).

Although harmonization had originally been considered essential for liberalization, the European Commission had shifted its strategy towards one of mutual recognition and minimal harmonization as it provided for a level playing field while accepting national regulatory diversity (Schmidt, 2002). As the single market program pressed for the liberalization of network-based services, the Commission's view changed that these markets were not natural monopolies but contestable markets with potential for new entrants and hence could not be regulated "at will" through restrictive market-entry and pricing arrangements (Schmidt, 2005: 160). Political differences about the means and ends of transport policy have made agreement difficult in the past, reflecting different views about the organization of these markets. While these sectors were considered public services, with general access and provision rights for all citizens, they underwent massive changes as these monopolies were privatized or liberalized to allow private service providers to operate (Smith, 2005; Schmidt, 2005, Héritier et al., 2001). Because network industry products and services were used as inputs for the production of traded goods, different levels of subsidization began to be seen as violations of the level playing field in the single European market.

Domestic reform efforts also laid the foundation for EU action, facilitating change as different member states pushed for liberalization in different transport sectors. However, the Commission initiated more than a dozen different directives and regulations liberalizing different modes of transport in the aftermath of the 1992 program, promoting market access, infrastructure development, and harmonization of social and technical standards. Since the mid 1980s a key goal of the Common transport policy has been the creation of a single market for road haulage services regardless of nationality, dismantling fixed prices and controls on market access to provide for intra-European competition (Héritier, 2001; Camerra-Rowe, 1994). The EU finally adopted a number of directives that enhance access to the road haulage market, including (96/26/EC) on admission and practice of road transport operators, regulation (881/92/EEC) on access to the market in the carriage of goods by road within the Community, and regulation (3118/93/EEC) on cabotage which provides for liberalized market access. However, member states were deeply divided about the single market for road haulage (Schmidt, 2005: 162). Various proposals were shelved as Germany and France feared that their national markets would attract operators from countries with low wage costs, such as Spain, Greece, and Portugal, and the subsequent accession of Central and East European states. Cabotage was particularly contentious, requiring significant negotiation as six member states were initially opposed, and road haulage associations mobilized in Germany against the proposed liberalization due to concerns about "ruinous competition" that would undermine smaller operators and promote concentration in the industry (Héritier, 1997a: 540).

Several member states, including Germany and Italy, regulated road haulage in order to protect their railways. Liberalization would make their domestic hauliers less competitive since they were subject to substantial taxes due to the countervailing efforts to protect the railways. Since cabotage allows member states to retain the domestic rules of the host country, not home country, under mutual recognition, Germany proposed a road toll for trucks from other states so they could improve the competitiveness of domestic hauliers through vehicle and fuel tax cuts, while maintaining their commitment to protect the railway and the environment. The proposal failed due to judicial action that viewed the toll as illegal since it discriminated against non-nationals (Schmidt, 2000: 54). Although EU action has led to a degree of formal liberalization in road transportation, generating increased competition and lower prices, cabotage remains low in terms of total transport levels, suggesting that the single market was more marginal than anticipated as markets still remain national (Schmidt, 2001). Too many lorries still travel empty across the EU. Cabotage represents barely 1 percent of road transport activities in the EU, despite accounting for 70 percent of all land transport activities (*Agence Europe,* 2014). Since states could still maintain quantitative restrictions and price controls, European efforts had little direct impact on transnational trade, as liberalization did not create more competition from foreign providers but, rather, spurred domestic reform efforts. As a result, national rules are allowed to stand under mutual recognition if valid, such as social regulations, as the main concerns in the road haulage sector are not competition among rules but rather the presence or absence of toll roads to offset user costs of infrastructure and road usage (see Pelkmans, 2003, for further discussion).

In the railroad sector, the European Commission applied the principles of the internal market to rail services in the 1990s. According to Lehmkuhl, "the idea that incumbent and possibly newly emerging railway companies may provide transport services by rail was derived from the same logic line as the Commission's efforts to realize the Single Market Program in the area of public utilities such as telecommunication and electricity" (Lehmkuhl, 2002: 4). The core goal has been to open up both freight and passenger markets to competition, and to separate infrastructure from operations to allow for the gradual opening up of the market for new operators which led the Commission to propose rules for allocation of slots and for infrastructure use to ensure non-discrimination for new operators. Hoping to encourage intermodal competition, the pressure for market reform has meant both changes in regulatory structure, including the creation of independent regulatory agencies, and the adoption of a legal framework for the opening up of network access. This provides principles for the allocation of routes for domestic and international freight services, and usage charges for infrastructure, balancing public service obligations with the introduction of competition to access the network (Stevens, 2004: 98; Laperrouza and Finger, 2009: 4). Since road also paid infrastructure charges, through tolls, taxes or licenses, this was designed to make rail compete on an equal basis. However, these measures adopted in the early 1990s to promote commercial practices in rail services left substantial discretion to member states. Britain and the Netherlands were unconditional supporters of liberalization, whereas France and Italy were much more skeptical and sought to minimally comply with Community obligations (Héritier, 2001; Stevens, 2004: 98; Lehmkuhl, 2002).

However, the efforts to open up rail services continued as the Commission called for the full liberalization of international rail transport in both the passenger and freight sectors. Rail had assumed greater importance, as the European Commission pushed for the liberalization of both freight and passenger services to stem the continuing loss of market share due to the widely acknowledged problems in the rail sector (Stevens, 2004: 99; European Commission, 2001). Proposing an ambitious opening to all rail freight operations, including cabotage services, as well as international passenger services, it took almost five years for the first package of rail freight liberalization measures to be adopted in 2001 (Abbati, 1987). The "first railway package" consisted of three directives (2001/12/EC, 2001/13/EC, and 2001/14/EC) that sought to open the market for rail freight by 2007 and for international passenger services by 2010. Since rail transport was still largely in the hands of national state monopolies and confined to their domestic markets, the Commission pushed for the separation of infrastructure from rail transport leading to different national variations from full privatization to holding companies, mirroring some of the debates about governance structure that occurred earlier in the US. This was followed by a second package in 2004 and a third package in 2007 as there was no immediate discernible effect on rail freight access (Dyrhauge, 2013). The deregulation of rail, like in other sectors, was accompanied by regulatory efforts to ensure the functioning of the single market. Though primarily focused on the introduction of market forces, the subsequent packages aimed at building an integrated European railway area, creating a European Railway Safety Agency, and addressing the more sensitive area of passenger services, including exposing incumbent operators to competition in provision of local and regional services.

While several member states, including Britain, the Netherlands, Germany, and Sweden, had already engaged in domestic reform prior to EU action, and thus supported the strategy, a significant group of states including France, Belgium, and Luxembourg were strongly opposed (Knill and Lehmkuhl, 2002; Dyrhauge, 2013). However, despite efforts at infrastructure charging, licensing rail operators, and unbundling services and network access, numerous challenges remain. Tensions remain over the governance of the railway market as the introduction of market forces has not led the railways to play a leading role in economic integration: the European network is still fragmented along financial, technical, and organizational lines. Although historically train services and tracks were owned by incumbent rail operators, new operators continue to face market entry barriers as low levels of competition continue, often the result of continued discriminatory practices in member states, such as limited track and terminal access, and conditions of use. Friction over the effects of unbundling railway systems has led to concerns that changes in the organization of rail infrastructure will lead to greater fragmentation or reduced investment on local lines, as heightened concerns about the effects on highly protected public sector jobs has generated intermittent strike action and mobilization against further competition (see European Commission, 2001; Dyrhauge, 2013). Recurrent delays in implementing EU legislation illustrate the still-contested views about the market-led framework among member states. There was and remains marked "resistance to any Community attempt to intervene in domestic railway policy . . . due to the (perceived) incompatibility of European and national arrangements" (Knill and Lehmkuhl, 2002: 266, 272). The European railway market is not yet a reality despite efforts over the past twenty years to restructure the railway market and promote the growth of the rail market (Stehmann and Zenger, 2011: 12). But Europe faces some of the same issues that plagued transportation in the US due to interoperable networks that result in "differences in track width, electricity systems, gauges, signals, and the types of cars" that operate in different member states (Stehmann and Zenger, 2011: 17). Member states are still experimenting with railway governance systems, and progress towards liberalization has varied enormously across countries.

In part this reflects different models of capitalism as transport policy often strives to balance different objectives and economic models. The EU has sought to liberalize transport services across modes and national borders, promote the structural and development objectives of investment in transportation infrastructure, and balance the needs for public service provision with emphasis on commercial access. While for some states, this means that the state plays a major role in transportation development, for others, the state should regulate through economic instruments such as pricing and taxation to ensure the efficient provision of services. But railways, as the last and most reluctant mode of transport to embrace the single market, still require substantial effort to address the barriers created by interoperable infrastructures. The different bridge and tunnel sizes in Britain, and the different electrification systems in Britain and France, also bear testimony to the difficulties that still remain in creating Trans-European networks. Yet it is clear that the network industries, which had traditionally been shielded from competition and were run within national boundaries, have been dramatically transformed in response to market integration (Héritier, 2001; Lehmkuhl, 2002; Schmidt, 2005). This change—which in some countries resulted from European legislation—and in other cases was preceded by domestic market liberalization—triggered a backlash about the provision of public services after liberalization, with well-entrenched interests in some states mobilizing against EU action while other proponents advocated for more liberalization to match their domestic reform efforts (Jabko, 2006; Smith, 2005).

Although there has been resistance to opening up the rail market, especially in France and Germany, few of the new private operators that had been expected to challenge the state-owned incumbents have survived. With the publication of the Transport White Paper in 2011, the Commission has again called for further market opening in all forms of transport. Proposals for a "fourth rail package" aimed at the opening of the domestic passenger market and the unbundling of infrastructure from transport operations has generated widespread protest. Transport workers have focused on the impact in terms of employment and quality of services, especially given the relative decline in employment, and concerns about the universality and accessibility of services when rail companies invest in the most profitable tracks. As market liberalization and fiercer competition emerges in the rail sector now that rail operators can cross borders and offer passenger services, heavily indebted countries like Greece and Spain are selling rights to operate passenger and freight routes on the network, as they sell government assets to meet public borrowing requirements. While some $200bn of European transport remains in state hands, privatization of the rail sector to slash public debts has also led to concerns about the impact of shifting domestic monopolies onto the European level as France and Germany engage in acquisitions or alliances with competitors, leading to a consolidation of rail operators in much the same way that airlines have done over the past two decades.

Integration through Law

Legal decisions were critical in pushing for the liberalization of transportation services and fostering competition among different modes of transportation. Faced with a clear majority of member states opposed to liberalization, the catalyst for addressing restrictions on competition came from key cases addressed by the European Court of Justice. In two pivotal cases, the Court ruled that both sea transport and airlines could not be excluded from the general rules of the Treaty unless specific action was taken (Aspinwall, 1995). In 1974, in the so-called "French seaman case" (Case 167/73), France had maintained rules that discriminated against non-French nationals arguing that Article 84 (2) allowed for discriminatory rules concerning the free movement of seafarers. In the subsequent *Nouvelles Frontières* case (Case 209–213/ 84), air transport, which had also been excluded from the common transport policy, was also found to be subject to competition rules and that the airline industry could not continue its anticompetitive pricing and revenue-pooling arrangements. Such views, also confirmed by the *Reyners* case (Case 2/74) meant that the general rules of the treaty on state aids and competition, as well as freedom of establishment applied to transport, despite specific exemptions from the freedom to provide services under Article 61.

However, it was the European Parliament, frustrated by the slow progress towards a common transport policy, that further shaped developments in the sector by taking the Council to the European Court of Justice for failure to act. Some forty Commission proposals were blocked by Council (Abbati, 1987: 54). Arguing that the Council had infringed the Treaty by failing to meet its obligations to establish a common transport policy, Case 13/83 found that the Council had not guaranteed the freedom to provide international transportation services within the member states, nor had it provided the foundation for non-resident transport services to operate within any member states, thus curtailing freedom of services and rights of establishment. The cumulative effect of such judgments was to provide the impetus for an irreversible liberalization process for intra-European transport (Stevens, 2004: 55ff). But the "inactivity verdict" strengthened the hands of those that wanted more far-reaching liberalization (Young, 1995; Héritier, 1997a). The cost of no agreement would be more judicial intervention so those states that were already pursuing public sector reform and privatization were able to push for more coordination and liberalization of inland transport policies (Héritier, 1997a; Knill and Lehmkuhl, 2002).

Because network industry products and services were used for the production of traded goods, their substantial subsidies were viewed as contrary to the single market and it seemed until the 1980s that public utilities were not part of market integration (Ugur, 2007: 2). While the Court had begun to identify many exemptions and exclusive rights as incompatible with Treaty obligations, states actively sought to protect domestic transport interests, especially monopolies, using provisions aimed at providing state aids and cross subsidies for services of a general interest. In the absence of European legislation, case law became an important tool against enterprises granted exclusive rights under Article 90 (Schmidt, 2000). In the *Corbeau* case in 1993, the Court places the burden of proof to maintain the legal monopoly onto member states by assessing whether the Belgian utility company would be able to meet its public service commitments without the legal monopoly. While the Court has acknowledged that general interest concerns can prevail over competition under certain conditions,[17] the Court raised the possibility of whether lesser restrictive, pro-competitive options were possible. The Court noted that Article 90 can apply if the new market entrant can offer viable services distinct from that of general public service provisions (Pelkmans, 2006; Mustelli and Pelkmans, 2013b; Schmidt, 2005). The issue has become increasingly sensitive in member states, as the Court has expanded competition rules to previously exempted public monopolies such as transport and energy, and in doing so continually determines the balance between public service obligations and market integration and so defines the role that the state plays in the market economy (Smith, 2005: 68–9). However, the Treaty of Lisbon continues to make a distinction between modes of transport by including rail, road, and inland waterway in Treaty provisions, but allowing sea and air transport to be specifically included in transport policies if agreed to by the Parliament and Council, illustrating the reticence of member states to relinquish their authority fully in all aspects of transportation sector (Article 80 TFEU).

Effects of Integration on Corporate Behavior and Market Structures in US and EU

The transportation sector has evolved dramatically in both Europe and the US. Railroads were the first American big business that fostered organizational changes in the structure and operation of firms resulting in the vertical integration of firms (Chandler and Salsbury, 1968: 234ff; Chandler, 1962). Railroads were the hub of the new transportation system that stimulated mass production and distribution, and significantly altered the structure of American agriculture (Chandler, Bruchey, and Galambos, 1968: 202). In addition, modern financing and accounting emerged with railroads pioneering the creation of managerial capitalism. Competition created by a national marketplace induced corporations to grow (Licht, 1995: 163). As transport and communication networks grew in geographic extent, so did the intensity of corporate integration (Hays, 1995: 69). With intense competition firms were forced to act in new ways through vertical and horizontal integration, as extended transportation and communication induced companies to focus on management, supply, and distribution of goods to a wider market (Licht, 1995: 164).

Yet a long period of speculative stock market excesses occurred in the nineteenth century around the railroads as the emerging new technology led to excessive debt, state defaults, and subsequent consolidation into trusts. But investment in railroads also generated new financial instruments, generating high levels of capital investment with new profit opportunities as well as greater elements of risk as credit standards shifted and generated much speculation. As Europe now tackles high sovereign debt levels by cutting public budgets and introducing austerity measures that include privatization of railroads, competition in domestic freight and passenger services and network access, they might recognize the relevance of economic conditions in nineteenth-century US. As transportation and communication costs were lowered, the collapse of geographic barriers and the integration of domestic markets resulted in overextension of credit, massive overbuilding, and subsequent rate wars in the US. While the expansion and contraction of the American economy is thus tied to American railroad development (Fishlow, 1964), it also means that it generated opponents and supporters depending on the social costs involved (Freyer, 1981: 1284) in much the same way that efforts to change entrenched practices in European transport markets have brought to the fore divergent interests and preferences.

While railroads have long been the tools of the state in Europe, sustained legal efforts to promote a consolidated market have faced different transport policies and national philosophies. Beyond this, different gauges, safety standards, operating systems, not to mention rules protecting favored operators

189

make for a patchwork of divergent regulatory systems. In Europe, over the last two decades, the industrial landscape and regulatory structures of the network industries such as telecommunications, energy, and rail transport have undergone a massive transformation. Liberalization has fragmented the former natural monopoly sectors, and new players have emerged in the road and rail sector. In assessing the competitive effects of liberalization in Europe, the regulated industries have been impacted differently. In the case of domestic road haulage markets, these national markets have not been transformed into a European one (Schmidt, 2002: 942). The rail sector is still fragmented, but there is a convergence of effort to make the railways competitive with other modes of transport, following a pattern developed initially in fostering the liberalization of airlines (Dyrhauge, 2013).

Conclusion

In the US, the promotional impulse did not disappear but regulation became a more visible expression of governance in the post-Civil War era (Pisani, 1987). The railroad was the culmination of the nation-state expanding its role in the US as various land grants had been used first to support American railroads and canals and subsequently to support interstate highways. In Europe, the state also played a key role in infrastructure development, as large railway companies were established as state-owned enterprises. Road haulage was strictly regulated in the postwar period to protect railways from intermodal competition. In both cases, regulation over the ownership and operation of transportation networks has generated significant debate (Chandler, 1978; Chandler and Salsbury, 1968; Goodrich, 1956; Dobbin, 1994).

What began in the antebellum era as a local project for internal improvements, with states responsible for promoting and regulating the American transportation system, was shifted to federal level as a result of intense state rivalries. The development of the railroad system brought political conflict among different interest groups over a range of issues from rate-setting to corporate management to state regulation. While states had been actively promoting administrative and economic development, providing services and goods, it also produced conflict among states as well as differential levels of investment, regulations, rates, and local access to routes. State governments could intervene and force corporate reorganization, provide land through eminent domain, and manage markets through a range of regulatory and business practices. However, the delegation of authority to states reached its limits generating the centralization of American rail-planning and control in the post-Civil War era, and thus consolidating central state administration by linking different regions, increasing state dependency on federal aid, and changing patterns of railroad development towards commercial centers rather than providing local rail connections. Various groups sought aid from public agencies in their attempts to solve their problems, and many used the courts to assist in fashioning or responding to the change in government action towards rail construction in the US (Hays, 1995: 232).

Like the US, there are multiple actors and contradictory interests involved in the rail sector and road sector in Europe. While the European Round Table of Industrialists lobbied for investment in infrastructure in the context of the single market, the establishment of Trans-European networks had the explicit aim of using public aid to integrate markets. While some of the main benefi-ciaries are former communist countries in Central and Eastern Europe to tie them through capital investment to the West, these funds have predomin-antly been invested in constructing highways rather than rail networks. How-ever, the sovereign debt crisis is impacting efforts across Europe to maintain their transportation assets. Even as Europe invests in large transportation networks to promote growth, what has emerged is a patchwork of road and rail projects. While road continues to dominate, further efforts to promote reorganization in the rail sector in Europe are meeting strong resistance. Vested interests have fought strongly against the mandatory separation of the management and operation of tracks, which often deters competitors in the rail freight market. Both Germany and France have strongly opposed such action, and British rail companies do not support a Europe-wide unbundling. The proposed plans for further changes under the fourth liberalization pack-age has generated political conflict in the rail sector, with a backlash over further cuts in pensions, status, and employment contracts across Europe as well as opposition from those anxious to avoid further fragmentation of markets.

Both the US and the EU sought to deal with the distortions of competition in the transport sector, addressing both infrastructure and operating condi-tions, in which tariff rates, standardization issues, and selective incentives and subsidies affected different modes of transport. Transportation politics brought to the fore the relationship between public and private forms of governance, the impact of changing technology on markets, and the role of the state in promoting economic development (Berk, 1994; Dobbin, 1994). The regulated monopoly in both contexts ultimately led the railroads to decline relative to other modes of transport. High fixed costs, rate discrimin-ation, and social agitation characterized the US market, while efforts to pro-mote competition between different suppliers on the same infrastructure, thus shifting from the notion of railroads as natural monopolies to allowing market competition, has generated a significant backlash among various pub-lic services in Europe. Both the US and Europe aimed to introduce new management techniques, to reformulate the relationship between state and railroads, as well as to introduce new rules for market access, which were deeply contested in the states, the courts, and the federal institutions (Lehmkuhl, 2002).

Obviously, there are a number of factors that have shaped their respective developments, including the dynamics of federalism, judicial action, class conflict and labor unrest, technological developments and organizational innovations. Clearly the pre-existing state governance systems have shaped the development of transportation systems. Member states view their transportation networks as public monopolies, but have been subject to liberalization pressures and legal action, to introduce competition and non-discrimination for new competitors. In the US, standardization of rates in the nineteenth century was designed to ensure fair access and non-discrimination, but this has changed as the US railroad sector allows differential pricing, less open access and does not have a universal service obligation, standing in stark contrast to the deep-rooted philosophies of many European states. However, the history of eminent domain in the US suggests a much closer parallel to European notions of public services obliged as they were to serve as common carriers, since the expropriation of private property for "public purposes" held sway for part of the nineteenth century as courts balanced public goods against private rights. While nationalization was the dominant mode of governance in Europe in the initial postwar period, encompassing a range of services from utilities to transportation, those private entities that were beneficiaries of government largesse through eminent domain and tax-backed stock subscriptions were also subject to state constraints and regulatory intervention as businesses "affected by a public interest" (see Scheiber, 1971). Competing doctrines between vested rights and public interest in the US provide yet again a more nuanced view of nineteenth-century political development in which the law provides an important role in facilitating, shaping, and enabling the exercise of state power. The resulting shift towards economic centralization through the growth of bureaucratic agencies to regulate markets while also recognizing the need to address industrialism with conservation efforts could as easily apply to contemporary European efforts in the transportation sector. At present, however, the full potential of the service economy remains hampered in Europe (see Mustelli and Pelkmans, 2013b; Lejour, 2010), but applying different concepts of market behavior and state intervention across a long time period has, according to Dobbin, led to different conceptions of planning and finance, technical coordination, and competition that can reinforce divergent state practices (Dobbin, 1994, 2001) and makes coordination of transport markets extremely difficult in Europe. While in the US, Dobbin argues, new policy shifts—and state action— occurred in response to democratic concerns about corporate power and changing conceptions of economic efficiency over time, European resistance stems from concerns about the reconfiguration of state power and the proposed economic policy prescriptions for enhancing increased competition (Dobbin, 1994).

Notes

1. Inland transport was chosen as a case study since regulation of transport activities is one of the most important segments of the internal market program in Europe and inland transport—particularly canals and railroad networks—were critical components in promoting national integration and the extension of the American national market. The primary emphasis in the chapter will be placed on railroads with reference to other modes of transport as well.
2. The Uruguay Round of Multilateral Trade Negotiations included the General Agreement on Trade in Services.
3. An initial difficulty might appear to be the unusual distinction between freedom of establishment and freedom to supply services, which is used in the European context. Such a distinction is rare in international practice (see Maestripieri, 1971).
4. In the Treaty of Rome, air transport and maritime transport were excluded from provisions covering common transport policies. Civil aviation played a small role in cross-border European transport in the 1950s and freight traffic was negligible at the time.
5. There are four modes of service transaction: mobile users in country A consume services produced by immobile providers in country b; mobile consumers in country A consume services in country b; mobile providers from A provide services in b and providers from A establish a branch or subsidiary or produce service locally in country b.
6. It is important to note that in early American history, infrastructure for transportation did not constitute a service but an essential tool of economic development.
7. The development of different modes of transportation can be categorized into four stages: turnpikes, canals, steamboats, and railroads.
8. Albert Gallatin Secretary of the Treasury submitted a comprehensive plan on roads and canals, March 1807.
9. After the transportation revolution, the communication revolution paralleled the rail network in the mid nineteenth century. However, the spread of the telegraph system was primarily a private enterprise achievement.
10. This results from eminent domain statutes.
11. Bensel (2000: 293–294) notes the scale of land redistribution was self consciously state driven.
12. This draws extensively on the seminal work of Taylor, 1951 pp. 82ff and Taylor and Neu, 1956.
13. The Homestead Act of 1862 provided land for settlers in designated areas of the West and the Morrill Land Grant Act of 1862 provided federal lands to states for building colleges for agriculture and mechanical education.

14. The work of Licht, 1995 and Hays, 1995 have shaped my argument in this paragraph.
15. The focus in this chapter is on inland transportation, principally rail and road haulage with a brief mention of other modes of transportation.
16. Road transport has grown much more rapidly (3.7% per year on average between 1970 and 1994) and 4.5% between 1985 and 1990. Between 1970 and 1994, the railways lost 22.3% of the freight market, losing out to road transport with similar structural changes also seen in CEE. For statistics see Laperrouza and Finger (2009); Dyrhauge (2013). One consultancy company, Bain and Company, noted losses of €5 billion from rail freight from main state-owned operators for the period 2007 to 2011, as cited in *European Railway Review*, 1, February 2013.
17. On the concept of services of general economic interest in EC law, see the Communications of the Commission on services of general interest, COM (1996) 443 and COM (2000) 580, OJ 1996, C 281 and OJ 2001, C 17/4.

7

Labor Mobility and the Free Movement of Professionals

The full potential of labor can be utilized only if there is mobility in labor. If there was to be a new Europe, there not only had to be a common market, but also greater mobility in labor.

Paul G. Hoffman, Economic Cooperation Administration, 1948–1950[1]

The presence of large numbers of foreign workers has long been a politically sensitive issue in both Europe and the United States. Political campaigns against immigrants reflect the shifts in attitudes towards mass migration in receiving states. These political pressures for restrictions and controls on labor mobility have focused on non-national immigrants, with measures of exclusion including quotas, asylum, and other immigration policy restrictions, as well as controversial efforts to impose conditional rights of access in the civil, social, and political sphere (Menz and Caviedes, 2010; Geddes, 2000; Klebaner, 1958; Lee, 2002). Notwithstanding the political salience of immigration control, there is also a corresponding effort for liberalization of certain kinds of labor movements related to the free movement of services (Lavenex, 2002; Nicolaïdis, 2005; OECD, 1996; Richardson, 2000: 8–9; Schmidt, 2009; Bertola and Mola, 2009). The specific configuration of the service sector pushes for the liberalization of certain immigration provisions,[2] and the inclusion of labor mobility in the framework of the international trade regime has placed issues of national labor market regulations into the framework of multilateral liberalization efforts. Multilateral efforts to promote wide applicability of the relevant economic freedoms would certainly induce significant economic effects. These developments have implications that reach beyond the area of immigration policy to include social and labor market policy, as well as fiscal and trade policy. However, it has been difficult to disaggregate the provision of services from movement of labor, as barriers to the movement of people are considered barriers to trade.

In contrast to the attention given to financial and product market integration, the emergence of an integrated labor market has received much less attention in Europe and the United States (for exceptions, see Rosenbloom, 1990; Rosenbloom, 2002; Reder and Ulman, 1993; Zimmerman, 2009). While some observers argue that improvements in the efficiency of labor markets are an important feature of economic growth, others argue that greater competition will undermine labor standards and working conditions. While most efforts to measure labor market integration have focused on geographic wage differentials (Molle and Van Mourik, 1989) as well as variation in rates of labor demand on labor mobility (Rosenbloom, 1990, 1996), it is also important to focus on the effects of organizational responses to intensified labor market competition, as well as the regulatory policies that shape market conditions (Menz and Caviedes, 2010). Not unlike goods and services, a number of measures have to be adopted before the regulatory framework is sufficient for labor market integration. While the goal is the free flow of factors of production, there are often concerns about avoiding competitive devaluation of social standards in member states due to disparities in wages and working conditions (Scharpf, 1999a; cf. Barnard, 2000: 57). Since mobility rates and regional labor market performance are related, it underscores the importance of different regional welfare effects such as variation in income, unemployment, cost of living, and the availability of public goods upon labor mobility (Zimmerman, 2009).

An integrated labor market means that workers at every location are aware of employment opportunities elsewhere and through migration can offer their services to employers without restrictions (Rosenbloom, 1990). Free movement means the right to accept offers of employment and to move freely for this purpose to another location, and to reside there and take advantage of those employment conditions. While migrants must bear the costs of acquiring information about the risks and opportunities of employment, they often face specific regulatory or legal provisions that make market entry more difficult or costly.[3] Laws on collective bargaining and wages, occupational and licensing differences, professional membership and qualifications, and a host of other requirements—that differ across territorial boundaries—can have a discouraging effect on cross-border labor mobility (Bertola and Mola, 2009; Lovecy, 1993). It is not only the simultaneous effects of supply-and-demand factors such as relative scarcity of high skilled labor in determining labor mobility, it is also the transaction costs of mobility and restrictive or protectionist regulations. Cross-border labor flows can also be limited due to the availability of other market mechanisms to cope with labor shortages including outward direct investment or relocation.

Given the connection outlined above between trade in services and labor market mobility, the focus of this chapter is on the free movement of professional workers, including the right to provide services and the principle of freedom of establishment to provide services.[4] Rather than focus on immigration controls which impact third-country nationals, our focus here is primarily on internal barriers to mobility for legal residents in professional services, although cross-state discrimination occurs in a variety of regulated occupations.[5] Clearly the threat of unleashing competitive market forces in this economic sector usually generates far less public attention than changes in immigration policies. However, service liberalization has become a lightning rod in Europe as the cause célèbre of the Polish plumber symbolizes fears of cheaper migrant workers taking advantage of labor mobility in an enlarging European polity (Nicolaïdis, 2007). Since both the United States and Europe have a long and varied history of regulating professions, efforts to liberalize trade in professional services involves measures to remove restrictions to labor mobility as well as cross-border operation and provision of professional services on both a temporary or permanent basis. Although these cross-border labor flows may seem residual, the labor market experience of regulated professions in the US and EU provides a comparative assessment of the integration or segmentation of labor markets.[6]

Section one of this chapter traces the American experience, focusing on the rise of the professions and the barriers affecting professional mobility. Section two discusses American efforts to address barriers that hinder cross-border labor mobility for regulated professions. Section three examines the European experience in promoting professional mobility in the single market, first focusing on early developments to promote harmonization, along with later efforts in the context of the single market program to promote liberalization. The chapter concludes with a comparison of US and EU liberalization efforts in regulated professions, and the remaining restrictions to cross-border mobility as both struggle to deal with current regulatory structures that segment markets, and the pressures emerging from changing business practices in a global economy.

Few markets in the modern economy operate under such restrictive limitations on interstate commerce as those covering professional and occupational services. Yet the continued regulatory role is attributed to the desire to improve the market for such professional services as increased specialization and knowledge makes it necessary to set quality standards and reduce information asymmetries. Typically, the activities of the liberal professions (legal, medical, technical, and accountancy professions) have legitimized their need for exemption from competition on the basis of the societal role liberal professions assume. Such efforts include discrimination against non-residents, preferential treatment for domestic or local service providers, and restrictions on professional services that can be offered. Other less overt discriminatory practices can include requirements for specific residency, training, or professional qualifications to practice in the host state or mandatory membership

Table 7.1. Barriers to professional licensing and mobility

Barriers	Types of oversight	Rationale for regulation
Restrictions on fees and contracts	Government regulation (state or local)	Market failure (asymmetry of information)
Restrictions on organizational forms (number of providers, specific titles to practice)	Self-regulation	Private interest (rent-seeking)
Restrictions on conduct and procedures (advertising, marketing)	Regulation by third party (boards, commissions)	Public interest
Lack of recognition of licensing, certification, and accreditation requirements	Self-regulation, regulation by third parties	
Nationality, age, and residency requirements		Private interest (rent-seeking)

Source: Author

in a professional association (see Table 7.1). Whether it is public regulation or private self-regulation, the effects of such anticompetitive practices are similar (Jenny, 2001). For individuals, the principle of equal treatment or non-discrimination is not always sufficient to ensure that professionals can practice their trade or profession in another state. Substantial practical obstacles such as linguistic barriers, differences in welfare benefits, and restrictive tax and pension regulations also present barriers (Green, Hartley, and Usher, 1991: 156; OECD, 1996). Since those engaged in the conduct of a profession are usually licensed or authorized by the state or a self-governing professional body acting with authority delegated by the state, they can encounter marked differences in entry requirements even across seemingly similar specialties (Nicolaïdis, 1997). Critics argue that many of these restrictions constitute unreasonable barriers to trade by restricting market entry into the field rather than ensuring professional competence (Snell, 2002: 19; Heremans, 2012). Supporters argue that occupational licensing provides quality control by ensuring that only the best operators enter the market (Friedman and Kuznets, 1945).

Specific professions are generally exempted from long-standing competition and restrictive business practice laws so they are able to structure their markets in ways not permitted in other areas of economic activity (OECD, 1996: 40; Heremans, 2012: 1). These include restrictions on advertising, permissibility of contingency fees, and fixed rates for specific services, all of which limit market competition. Such long-standing statutes sheltering professions in Europe and the United States have come under intense scrutiny as they adversely affect competitive conditions, and critics claim many licensing requirements target those in low-paid professions (Lovecy, 1999; OECD, 1996). Although acknowledging the right to protect consumers, many argue that these restrictions have hindered productivity and growth, and often lack substantial justification in terms of consumer welfare. Such practices should also be viewed in terms of their corresponding costs (Rollo and Winters, 1999). To what degree do legal and regulatory restrictions hinder the right of professions to offer cross-border services? What efforts have been undertaken to remove barriers to labor mobility? Does the elimination of restrictions lead to convergence in the terms and conditions of employment?

American Professions and Democracy

Nineteenth-century patterns of local economic regulation have persisted with regard to the professions. In the United States, states retain the right to regulate the access to professions. State governments engaged initially in licensing medical and legal professions, with occupational licensing on a broader scale for other labor market activities occurring in the late nineteenth century. The state regulation of professional practices has not followed the same kind of economic restructuring that characterized other sectors, where the national regulation of production, capital, and consumption sustained the growth and consolidation of the American internal market. Constitutional history and Congressional silence have contributed to the maintenance of state control (Hazard, 1997). Since the power to regulate professional commerce under the interstate commerce clause of the Constitution has not been exercised by Congress, the vast majority of rules governing professional practices have been state legislative measures, usually through regulatory commissions, public bodies, or courts.

In fact, the US Constitution does not provide any express provisions concerning freedom to provide interstate services and the related right of establishment (Goebel, 2002: 425). Nor does the Constitution provide explicit provisions regarding free movement of persons. This has meant that several constitutional clauses with relevance to freedom of movement have often been invoked. The Articles of Confederation were much more explicit in stating that the rights of trade and commerce for people of one state should be similar to those from any other state (Article IV, Articles of Confederation). Subsequently when the Constitution was adopted, the Privileges and Immunities Clause supplemented with the Fourteenth Amendment is believed to have covered such rights. State regulations are thus subject to constitutionally imposed limits to protect the interstate provision of business and commercial services. However, since the political realm has not actively intervened to mitigate state power, it has been left to the judiciary to curb state infringements that undermine interstate commerce. The result is that professional mobility in the American constitutional system is much less precise and more difficult to promote than in the EU (Goebel, 2002).

Questions about the relationship between professionalism and democracy had been the subject of substantial public discussion and debate throughout the nineteenth century. From the unpopularity of lawyers who defended English Tories against state confiscation laws in the early Republic, to strident attacks on established elites in politics, law, and medicine with the rise of Jacksonian democracy, the professions have generated tensions based on their claims for autonomy and control (Hatch, 1988: 3–4). While the professions as a whole struggled for status and security, they encountered deep hostility to imposing special qualifications potentially leading to a monopoly over the exercise of their work through licensure and certification. This raised considerable social tensions about the role of expertise and monopoly, and the relationship between professional self-government and state control in an era of economic growth and burgeoning societal demands (Numbers, 1988; Friedman, 1965).

Barriers to Trade

Most studies of the development of professional services in the United States usually focus on specific occupations, describing efforts at regulatory reform with special regard to professional education and training. Amid changes in the status of professions throughout the nineteenth century, a common development was the emergence of various associations and societies to accommodate and represent the interests of distinctive professions. Though less dramatic than other economic developments, the increasing formation of specific interest groups enabled professions to cement their positions with a variety of occupational licensing laws in the later part of the nineteenth century as the unsettling effects of mass industrialization led them to seek protection through numerous occupational licensing laws and ordinances. While government control of occupations was, in general, weak and diffuse throughout much of the nineteenth century, the effect of such fragmentation is crucial to understanding the continued barriers to mobility in professional services, and attempts to circumvent or reduce their impact.

The Antebellum Period

During the early founding and operation of the American Republic, the states established courts and an embryonic legal profession that ensured that the regulation of lawyers remained with the states as a matter of tradition (Hazard, 1997: 1177). Although the early federal government sought to establish the authority of the federal judiciary over the state court system, in general it did not intrude on the rights of states to regulate specific professions. At the beginning of the nineteenth century, fourteen out of the nineteen states or organized territories prescribed a definite period of legal training, but require-ments for admission to the bar were not uniform. There was considerable variation in terms of the role of courts in licensing lawyers. In Massachusetts, the high court controlled all admissions; in Rhode Island, Delaware, and Connecticut each county court admitted its own attorneys whereas in South Carolina local courts admitted lawyers who had reciprocal access to practice in all states (Friedman, 1965: 276). In Alabama, trial court judges licensed lawyers to practice (Pruitt, 1997). In the Western states, requirements for admission to the bar were considerably more lax. While many lawyers displayed all the diversity in social background, education, and training generally found on the frontier, the often low standard of legal education in the face of complex questions of land titles, contract law, and bankruptcies contributed to wide-spread fear of public disorder.

Despite a national trend of founding law schools to improve legal training, along with efforts to promote county bar associations in the late eighteenth to mid nineteenth century, the system lacked any sense of professional cohesion (Shryock, 1967; Friedman, 1965). County bar associations raised entry barriers by requiring long periods of education and training, and eliminating untrained lawyers from the practice of law (Gawalt, 1973: 34; Gawalt, 1979). In many states, lawyers created a system that required apprenticeship as a means of regulating and restricting membership of the profession, as well as ensuring a profitable monopoly for an exclusive few by establishing minimum fees and restricting the opportunities for laymen to use irregular "practi-tioners" or serve as their own attorney (Gawalt, 1973: 33–6). On the East Coast, the apprenticeship system provided an inexpensive source of labor as well as income, which also presented the rationale for excluding lawyers trained in other states (Gawalt, 1973: 33). Bar associations often required practical experience before State Supreme Courts or Courts of Common Pleas, before the granting of full practice rights. Many commentators argue this made it virtually impossible for out-of-state lawyers to gain full admission (Abel, 1981). Others point to the minimal restrictions on who could provide legal services along with the absence of formal educational requirements in most states as evidence of the lack of formal entry barriers (see Kritzer, 1991).

The exclusive nature of the legal profession generated strong hostility dur-ing the antebellum period (Gawalt, 1979). After numerous attempts to put an end to the power of bar associations, opposition reached its height during the period of Jacksonian democracy when restrictive professional institutions and requirements came under sharp attack, with special hostility generated towards lawyers (Gawalt, 1979). The intensification of public antipathy resulted in widespread legislative action curtailing their activities and fees, along with restrictions on the rights of bar associations to control the admission and practice of law (Kommers 1966; Gawalt, 1979). State laws made entrance into the legal profession easier and broke down restrictive barriers. Scaling down admission requirements to the bar or eliminating them altogether in New Hampshire and Wisconsin, for example, reflected how local bar associations were viewed as political pressure groups impairing economic competition (Bloomfield, 1968: 306). Often the targets of deep mistrust, the effort to bring the administration of law under popular control in the 1830s and 1840s made it more difficult for lawyers to exercise market control. Yet throughout the nineteenth century, they continued their efforts to limit competition within the profession as well as seeking to exclude outsiders from areas considered the domain of legal practitioners (Friedman, 1965). In this regard, the transformation of the American economy changed the functions of the legal profession. Competition from companies that had not existed prior to the Civil War began to encroach upon the staples of legal practice such as debt collection and title searches, forcing the legal profession to continue to seek limitations to entry into their field (Friedman, 1965: 549ff). Even so, the profession was larger in 1860 than in 1800, as large private law firms emerged along with company legal departments and in-house counsel, as the financial interests of corporations, trusts, and holding companies made corporate law increasingly important (Friedman, 1965: 549ff). According to Friedman, such corporate legal positions were highly desirable (Friedman, 1965). This unique professional role has subsequently emerged as a separate organizational power and influence in the legal field through the creation of their own professional organization and identity, producing changes in the structure and norms of the legal professions through mobilization on issues of multidisciplinary practice, professional regulation, and legal education.

The medical profession faced a parallel crisis in the nineteenth century. It fought vigorously to protect professional boundaries and limit competition from other groups. In this respect, the medical and legal professions were similar, reflecting the difficulties of limiting entry into the field and raising standards. Like the legal profession, the first efforts to organize practitioners preceded efforts to establish medical schools. Local societies emerged along the same lines as the early bar associations (Shryock 1967: 13). State licensing requirements first materialized in the mid eighteenth century in New York. Following this, New Jersey adopted a licensing system after pressure by provincial medical societies concerned with raising standards and incomes of practitioners (Shryock, 1967). However, continued efforts by local professional societies to reassert professional control through licensure generated opposition against such monopolies. While not suffering the same degree of criticism and public distrust as lawyers, states began to set standards for medical education. By 1830, state medical societies existed in nearly all the states of the Union with only three states—North Carolina, Virginia, and Pennsylvania—lacking statutes (Shryock, 1967: 23).

State regulations varied widely in terms of the bodies responsible for testing and licensing. In some states, medical societies were responsible for determining admission requirements, whereas in others examining boards were created, creating a diversity of requirements that impeded cross-border mobility (Shryock, 1967). Similar to the legal profession, medical oversight was difficult as states struggled to deal with the vested interests of those already engaged in practice, and with deciding whether to outlaw or exempt practices that were often the staple of many laymen such as home remedies, root medicine, or other quackery. The medical profession thus faced the same tensions between apprenticeship and university education that had arisen in the legal profession.

The medical profession gradually faced a considerable loss of status. Medical licensing deteriorated in the antebellum era. State laws that had accepted medical degrees as equivalent to a license by an approved medical body encouraged the creation of medical schools, which increased competition. This led schools to lower admission standards and pushed medicine towards becoming a trade rather than a profession (Numbers, 1988: 52). The medical profession was further undermined by the establishment of competing colleges specializing in botany, homeopathic, and eclectic medicine (Numbers, 1988; Shryock, 1967). The acrimonious debates among the various groups raised suspicion about monopolies and privileges. Swayed by such sentiments, states revoked licensing laws and reduced the privileged status of physicians in the 1830s and 1840s (Numbers, 1988: 55). Indicative of the low public esteem for the medical profession, states west of Appalachia enacted no licensing laws, and many others revoked them in a pattern that echoed the legal field. Both professions suffered from the anti-monopolistic, populist sentiments of Jacksonian democracy.

It was in reaction to these circumstances that professional leaders sought to protect their own interests through mobilization. Medical reformers sought self-regulation in view of the indifference of the federal and state governments to medical affairs. The establishment of the American Medical Association (AMA) in 1847—preceding that of the American Bar Association (ABA)—provided a concerted effort to raise educational and licensing standards. Yet the proliferation of sub-standard schools continued, in part due to the limited impact of the AMA, which remained weak and divided for much of the nineteenth century.

Postbellum Period

The period following the Civil War was one of profound change for the professions, as their monopolistic efforts bore fruit, through curtailing and subordinating other allied professionals, enacting stricter licensing laws, and raising educational standards. Efforts were made to lobby states to reverse the trend towards educational requirements and make them more stringent.

A number of professions slowly began to organize into professional associations and to revise the moribund groups then in existence (Brockman, 1966). Among the most universal motives for professional associations was the need for recognition of their expertise and the need to control the supply of practitioners. This was established in the medical profession by state or self-regulation, outlawing the undesirables or quacks, overseeing midwives and nurses, and distinguishing licensed medical practitioners from related professions by licensing barbers, nurses, and midwives. It would, however, be some time before the professional associations would mature into effective organizations able to promote regulatory reform (Brockman, 1966).

The legal profession founded the American Bar Association (ABA) in 1878 to restrict access to the bar and prevent competitors from encroaching on their profession (Bloomfield, 1976, 1968). Pursuing a strategy of consolidation and autonomy, lawyers sought to define their services broadly in order to secure large areas of commercial and financial law under their monopoly control. Although the ABA purported to speak for the legal profession, their efforts to secure and maintain market control did not mean that the profession was unified. A short-lived rival organization, the National Bar Association, also emerged in 1887, to serve the interests of local and state associations.

Considerable differentiation emerged within the legal profession along the lines of clientele and expertise, with legal services for large corporate clients distinguishing themselves from legal services for individuals and small businesses. Yet the main cause of dissatisfaction was not the emergence of different types of lawyers but rather the limited control exercised by courts for admission to the bar and the varied standards of admission (Friedman, 1965). After 1890, more states required stringent educational preparation in response to pressure from the ABA, and state laws remained vigorous in terms of regulating and licensing professions. Though legal challenges removed some of the vestiges of discrimination against specific social groups,[7] state laws remained crucial for rules of admissions and the right to practice. They often contain discretionary reciprocity provisions that permit the licensing authority, which is usually the highest court of the state in question, to allow either foreign lawyers to carry on the practice of law or to allow members of the bar in another state to have a reasonable and practical opportunity to provide cross-border services.

Like the legal profession, the medical profession in the postbellum era sought a counteroffensive to protect their profession against unqualified practitioners crowding the field and depressing their overall status and income (Numbers, 1988). General reform was achieved sooner in the medical profession as pressure for educational reform came from the states themselves. Every state passed some form of medical licensing act in the last quarter of the nineteenth century. Some revived earlier controls, although others resisted efforts at regulation (Shryock, 1967). Many states required candidates to pass an examination. In addition, states defined the very practice of medicine, by allowing exemptions for dentists, nurses, midwives, and other healers to engage in public health provision. Other states provided for licensing of professions such as midwives and pharmacists. Physicians were unable to establish a monopoly over their work since many unorthodox practitioners continued to be licensed. Their efforts to control allied health professionals also met with resistance.

As the number of trained nurses increased in the aftermath of the Civil War, physicians sought to limit their role in providing medical services, and also sought to limit the role of pharmacists in diagnosing and providing remedies and treatments. The medical profession enjoyed much less success in monopolizing the practice of medicine by controlling what they regarded as their rightful domain. Judges and legislators repeatedly sided with their opponents including homeopaths, midwives, and optometrists, as they sought legal recognition to remain independent of the medical profession. Although many of these related health professionals organized, they faced much the same problem. Cumulative efforts to improve licensing did not result in national uniform standards as, for example, the unevenness of state medical standards inevitably created problems for the nursing profession (Roberts, 1954: 50). One of the unintended consequences of state registration was that it drove unqualified nurses out of state to practice where legal barriers had not yet been established (Roberts, 1954: 75). However, as state licensing evolved across the various medical professions, the advent of state boards and examinations created barriers to mobility. By the end of the nineteenth century, certain boards with strict requirements refused to approve medical professionals licensed in another state. This trend resulted in efforts to grant reciprocity among licensing boards. Mutual recognition of professional licensing standards emerged slowly and the bulk of this reciprocity occurred among states west of Appalachia (Shryock, 1967: 59). Both in the medical and legal sphere, the social and political realities of local situations proved an important factor in the different patterns of professional regulation that emerged across the country. The increase in specialization and urbanization played an important role in licensing regulations as individuals became less knowledgeable about goods and services in the market, reflecting the need to address the issues of dependence, anonymity, and the complexity of markets (Law and Kim, 2010).

Integration through Law

Although state regulation of professions is subject to constitutionally imposed limits, scholars have long argued that interstate practice rights are not well established in spite of the growth of a national economy (Goebel, 2002: 427; Goebel, 2000: 307; Law and Kim, 2010). Exercising varying degrees of control of the professions over time, state courts and legislatures have restricted both the rights of establishment and maintained political authority over licensing and certification matters. While the substance of these regulations varies across states, as well as from profession to profession, in general they set standards on rights to practice. In some instances, state laws make it illegal to practice without meeting specific standards for their profession. State regulations of professional practices were, however, subject to constitutionally imposed limits.

The legitimacy of state laws to regulate professions came under scrutiny in a leading nineteenth-century case, *Dent* v. *West Virginia* (1888). The US Supreme Court affirmed the right of states to regulate professions, by allowing states to require a license to practice medicine if it served the public interest. Occupational licensing was thus a legitimate function of the inherent police powers reserved to the states. Because it became increasingly apparent that licensing served a public function in an era of charlatans, quacks, and itinerant practitioners, state laws could regulate professional practices. However, the Court concluded that states must do so in a manner which is based on reasonable educational qualifications assessed in a non-arbitrary and non-discriminatory manner (Goebel, 2002: 427). Although constitutional provisions have enabled state courts to exercise authority over professional regulation, such authority is still subject to federal constitutional and statutory law.

Lessons for Europe from the United States

Although labor market regulation takes many different forms within and across European labor markets, it is generally acknowledged that European labor markets are more heavily regulated than American ones (Bertola and Mola, 2009). Yet the US regulates an estimated eight hundred or more different professions (see Table 7.2). Nearly 30 percent of the labor force requires some form of occupational license from federal, state, or local government to practice their profession (see Kleiner and Krueger, 2010). Not all of them are regulated by each state, so there can be variation in both the nature and degree of rules across states for occupational regulations, as well as differences in levels of regulation.

In the US, states can ease restrictions through mutual reciprocity that allows for mutual recognition of qualifications, but these are often limited regionally, and those wishing to pursue professional activities in another state often seek membership in a professional association, or seek licensing and certification requirements in several jurisdictions. States may accept specific professional

Table 7.2. Number of licensed job categories by state

Number of licensed job categories	State	Number of licensed job categories	State
32	Washington	129	Georgia
49	South Carolina	130	Oklahoma
55	Idaho	134	Vermont
58	Mississippi	137	Missouri
69	Texas	143	North Dakota
76	Virginia	147	South Dakota
79	West Virginia	149	Nevada
84	Indiana	149	New Jersey
85	Arizona	150	New Hampshire
85	Kansas	154	New York
85	Utah	154	North Carolina
87	Ohio	155	Rhode Island
88	Colorado	158	Nebraska
92	Wyoming	162	Minnesota
98	Maryland	164	New Mexico
103	Alabama	187	Kentucky
103	Delaware	190	Oregon
109	Montana	190	Tennessee
110	Hawaii	198	Wisconsin
110	Pennsylvania	221	Connecticut
113	Louisiana	228	Maine
117	Alaska	233	Michigan
117	Florida	252	Arkansas
124	Iowa	254	Illinois
127	Massachusetts	285	California

Source: Byron Schlomach, Goldwater Institute Policy Report No. 247, July 2012, data from CareerOneStop Licensed Occupations tool (http://goldwaterinstitute.org/sites/default/files/Policy%20Report%20247%20Licensing.pdf)

equivalence but the host state can impose additional considerations for market access and rights of establishment. Unlike Europe, the prohibitions on providing temporary cross-border services for many regulated professions in the US means that some professions have to use local service providers, seek additional licensing in the host state, or offer multi-state practices. In many areas, an interstate compact between two or more states for the purposes of remedying a particular problem of multi-state concern is used to promote partial mutual recognition of professional qualifications (Zimmerman and Wendell, 1976; Zimmerman, 2002). The mutual recognition model of nurse licensure is the most comprehensive, applying to twenty-three states.

Although reciprocity restrictions can limit intrastate mobility, there are differences among liberal professions, as doctors face far fewer restrictions on reciprocity than dentists or lawyers in the US (Pashigian, 1977). The US has pursued partial reciprocity in some professions, through mutual recognition of professional qualifications, such as bar and medical examinations in select states, as well as conditional rights to practice, but this does not constitute full liberalization nor does it reflect the economic reality of a national economy. Despite constitutional provisions for interstate commerce, the rules governing interstate practice rights and establishment are still subject to substantial risks and restraints that hinder the creation of a single market for professions (Goebel, 2002). As interstate practice rights are much less precise than in the EU, the US has not seen professional and commercial mobility across the entire market area, or the coordination of qualifications, certification, and licensure. Just like Europe, there are restrictions on the type of services and activities that specific professions can offer. State restrictions on nurses and paramedics prevent them from engaging in the practice of medicine independently of a physician. And there are restrictions on the multiple offering of services, so that lawyers cannot enter multidisciplinary practices with accountants and business consultants, and as a result professional rules have continued to segment markets both professionally and geographically in the US.

The service sector—which is the focus of many licensing laws—has also seen a significant increase in occupational licensing and enforcement. Consequently, glass installers, or glaziers, are only licensed in Connecticut, while Colorado regulates hunting guides. Florida requires licensing and training for interior designers, while New Jersey, along with forty-six other states, requires no credentials to practice. Alabama has perhaps the strictest licensing requirements in the nation for hairdressing, while barbers in California require a year-long course of study. Landscape designers have substantial fees and training in North Carolina but not in neighboring South Carolina. And more recently, "cat groomers, tattoo artists, tree trimmers and about a dozen other specialists across the country" are clamoring for more occupational licensing rules (Simon, 2011; Klein, 2012). The increase in occupational licensing may also reflect the emergence of a successful labor market institution in response to declining unionization in the US (Kleiner and Krueger, 2010).

Through such actions, states can discriminate against out-of-state companies, restrict certain professions from the right to provide services on a temporary basis, prevent specific advertising, marketing, and ownership practices, and require citizenship or age requirements. Such actions have generated concerns about anticompetitive practices from anti-trust officials at the Federal Trade Commission and the Department of Justice. However, these agencies have increasingly addressed anticompetitive practices over the past three decades, focusing on price-fixing, commercial practices, or contractual obligations, across a range of professions through increased scrutiny of state occupational licensing laws and related business practice regulations (Cox and Foster, 1990). However, there is no comparable set of federal rules for guaranteeing access for temporary practice of regulated professions across states, interstate practice rights, or automatic rights of permanent establishment in the US. The problem has become more serious given globalization, and the multi-state locations for many companies, so that interstate compacts and federal–state compacts can offer advantages in dealing with both the licensing and the standards problem in the US. Such options are difficult as compact implementation may be delayed or prevented if one or more of the concerned states make participation contingent upon specified other states enacting the compact. While the Supreme Court has upheld both the constitutionality of compacts, not requiring Congressional consent to operate (*Virginia* v. *Tennessee, 1893*), it has opined that Congressional consent does make a compact subject to both federal and state law. Consequently, economic interest groups wishing to discourage Congressional exercise of its preemption powers, are primarily responsible for the establishment of regulatory compacts, and are pushing for intra-state action to avoid national regulation.

The European Experience

The free movement of persons is one of the fundamental principles of European integration, and an integral part of the market-economy concept. Yet efforts to increase labor mobility in Europe have not been solely due to the provisions of the common market. Earlier agreements to promote cross-border labor mobility, by providing equal pay and conditions for work for non-nationals, and easing restrictions on work permits and entry requirements, were promoted by the OEEC in 1953 through the International Clearance of Vacancies Scheme, as well as within the Benelux and Scandinavian states (Lewin, 1965). The issue was pushed by the Italian government, who saw labor mobility as a means of exporting their surplus labor. The aim of the European Community was to build on these efforts at facilitating employment mobility through additional measures including social funds, vocational training, and social security provisions. But the initial steps taken towards labor mobility in the European Coal and Steel Community had little impact on labor flows, in part due to the emphasis on skilled workers, when in reality those ready to migrate were for the most part unskilled and unable to show specific sectoral qualifications (Feldstein, 1967: 28).

During the subsequent negotiations for the Treaty of Rome, the Spaak Committee proposed expanding the rights of workers, since the undistorted rights of mobility formed an integral part of the market integration process (Maas, 2005: 1011–19). Although the Treaty contained new employment provisions, the Community did not gain competence in all areas of labor and employment issues. However, the resulting compromise was that free movement of labor was to be achieved at the same time as that of industrial and agricultural goods, although states maintained restrictions on the immigration of non-national workers. Any progress on meeting the conditions of the Treaty would require the coordination of social and economic development policies to alter the existing constraints on labor mobility. Despite the postwar expansion that was creating conditions of almost full employment and a rising demand for foreign workers, the Treaty of Rome still contained conditional requirements in that area. The provisions for the free movement of labor (Articles 48 et seq.) and separate Treaty provisions for the self-employed and the professions (Articles 52–66) did result in a number of safeguards and limitations being put in place (Woolridge, 1977). This meant that "offers of employment" must actually be made. The liberalization of restrictions agreed early in the Treaty negotiations did give priority to the national labor market and allowed for the suspension of labor mobility in cases of manpower surplus, gave priority to domestic intra-Community labor over non-Community labor, and provided for conditional work permits for professional or occupational mobility (see Regulation 38/64/EEC 1964). States could invoke these so-called safeguard clauses to remedy sudden labor difficulties. The sustained opposition among employers with regard to work councils and extension of labor representation to non-nationals also demonstrated the gaps between the specific goals of free movement and the vaguer social and employment objectives inherent in the Treaty. Though the economic orientation of the policy was to abolish unemployment and promote a balance between labor supply and demand, it has progressively widened in scope to include other issues such as investment policy, regional policy, and vocational training policy (see Barzanti, 1965).

The impact of labor mobility was intended to apply to the entire Community. Its effect was much less clear, since internal labor flows within the Community did not increase significantly. Intra-EC labor flows represented 60 percent of total flows in the early 1960s; the corresponding figure was only 20 percent a decade later (Straubhaar, 1988). Though designed to deal with a particular problem, in terms of movement of workers from low-income to high-income regions, in reality, it is the influx of non-community labor that has increased significantly. Immigration from outside the EU has a larger impact on labor markets in European countries than migration within the EU, which remains low. For intra-European labor, the initial focus on the "migration of necessity" has shifted, as the type of labor movement has become one of "voluntary migration" in keeping with the concept of freedom of movement. Instead of mass labor movements among the member states, different kinds of mobility have extended the right of free movement to other European citizens including students, pensioners, and professionals (Romero, 1990; Fligstein, 2008).

Although the Treaty contains separate sets of rules, the right for professions to provide services has much in common with that of workers seeking cross-border employment.[8] The treaty provisions concerning the free movement of services are residual, in that they apply when the other freedoms do not, but it is often hard to separate the issues concerning service providers and labor mobility. Unlike workers, professionals face additional obstacles in offering services on either a temporary or permanent basis across multiple jurisdictions. Though the Treaty provides for the right of establishment and the right to provide services by commercial, industrial, and professional persons, whether they are self-employed or part of professional group or firm,[9] they have to overcome the problem of lack of recognition of professional qualifications. While Treaty articles provide for the right of national treatment so that foreign professionals receive the same rights as those of domestic professionals (Article 60), and provide for the abolition of discrimination based on nationality, this does not deal with national regulations which regulate access to a profession (Capelli, 1993: 437). Because of the varying national rules on the establishment of business and occupations, the initial idea was to promote the freedom of movement through the abolition of discrimination based on nationality, and then promote harmonization of legislation and mutual recognition of qualifications (Von der Groeben, 1987: 69).[10] It is not simply a matter of removing barriers to cross-frontier trade, but also creating the conditions for mobility, access, and entry in areas where the structure, organization, and operating methods of professions reflects different societal assumptions and approaches to regulation (Edward, 2002: viii).

Interregional Flows and National Controls

National regulations of the professions and other services are deeply rooted in the history and traditions of each country in Europe (Ascher, 2004). Different professions even in the same sector have often resulted in differences in national requirements, as well as different characteristics with respect to the form and organization of the professions (Paterson, Fink, and Ogus, 2003: 19). For example, notaries are appointed by the state and hold public office, having exclusive rights to perform certain services. While the Dutch have partially liberalized the notary profession, with no cap on the number of notaries, the French have defended their civil law system that caps their number, requires the purchase of a notary business from a prior notary, and even then must be approved by senior notaries in regional and national votes before being admitted to practice (Vinocur and Thomas, July 5, 2013). For liberalization of practice rights, the Treaty calls for the elimination of restrictions on freedom of establishment and freedom to provide services in member states for those engaged in liberal professions. While regulated professions represent about 9 percent of EU GDP, and are often viewed as a subset of business services, the overall competitiveness of the sector is restricted by significant barriers imposed on the access to and exercise of professional activities (*Agence*

Europe, 2013). Although regulation of the professions affects employment mobility, it also contributes to the size and concomitant specialized business and industry structure. Thus, the overall gains are affected by such factors as market concentration, demand for services, and diversity of services offered across the member states.

Barriers to Trade

Professional services are a major and rapidly growing component of invisible trade. Impediments to trade often take the form of unnecessary or arduous conditions for establishment and operation, which raise the cost of market entry (Pelkmans and Winters, 1988: 45; Mustelli and Pelkmans, 2013a). An important feature of the service sector is the high degree of government intervention on the grounds of consumer protection. However, it is difficult to avoid characterizing some of the restrictions as protectionist. For many types of professional services, the critical issue is whether the firms or individuals from one country or another can establish themselves without facing problems that stem from domestic regulations.

Promoting an integrated market means ensuring that conditions allow for professionals to pursue cross-border service activities, and have rights and treatment guaranteed to be the same as for nationals. Such barriers can include lack of recognition of professional qualifications, as well as lack of authorization to practice within another member state. Educational requirements, licensing, certification and accreditation systems, and the actual training and practice undertaken by professionals differ both within and across member states (see OECD, 1995; Orzack, 1980). With variations in the scope of public control, the authority or institution providing education and training, and the range of skills, training, and competency-testing across different professions within member states, seemingly similar specialties have evolved somewhat differently across Europe. Institutional variation in the organization, structure, and governance of various professions necessitates efforts to reduce local barriers to access along with changes in domestic regulatory environments. While the removal of restrictions is expected to enhance competition, this has not reduced the importance or need for the harmonization of legislation. This involves mutual recognition of qualifications and coordination of regulations concerning access to and pursuit of self-employed occupations.

While European legislation and case law have focused on the rights of practice of individual professionals, it is no longer possible to ignore the importance of appropriate coverage of the extent of rights of business firms and service providers to carry out activities in other member states (Goebel, 1992). States often impose a variety of restrictions on access to economic activities including financial restrictions, specific guarantees or rights of security, restrictions on legal entities, as well as different treatment in terms of administrative concessions or licenses, and the purchase, sale, and use of assets (Cath, 1993). International or cross-border practices of many services are often carried out by firms rather than by individual practitioners; although individual practitioners have often joined with local practices or companies to provide services in another jurisdiction. While in some professions, networks of branch offices in leading commercial centers outside their home country, or joint venture or affiliated relations with firms in other countries have emerged, making the right of establishment pivotal. In other instances, the rules of free movement apply more traditionally to individuals. However, in evaluating the course of progress in Europe toward cross-border Community-wide practice rights, it is necessary to consider those rules that are desirable not only for individual professionals but also for firms (Goebel, 1992). The mobility of corporate service providers, so essential for the liberalization of that sector of the economy, also depends on other factors including the coordination of company law in terms of standards of protection and certain specified legal rights. Harmonization of these provisions will help ensure equal conditions of competition, and will further progress towards attaining a certain degree of legal protection for commercial agents in carrying out business and professional services. Professional mobility requires both the removal of market entry barriers, as well as the removal of conditional barriers on the right to practice. An unfettered right to seek employment means removing restrictive and unjustified rules, but also coordinating policies through the recognition of professional qualifications and rights to practice.

The Early Formative Period: The 1960s to the 1970s

Although freedom of movement for employed workers resulted in some early agreements that abolished restrictions on movement and residence, progress towards the integration of labor markets for various professions has lagged behind.[11] The Community was expected to abolish existing restrictions on the rights of establishment and freedom to provide services during the initial transition period, so the general conditions for professional mobility would be achieved in conjunction with other similar deadlines for achieving the common market. The two general programs on services adopted in 1961 laid out the priorities for liberalization in terms of production and trade, identified the major restrictions that needed to be abolished, and sought to promote mutual recognition of formal qualifications relevant to the provision of services and the exercise of professions (Lasok, 1986: 34).[12] The initial efforts were clearly directed at restrictions applied by member states, not with the actions of private parties (Snell, 2002: 140). The focus was initially on the principle of non-discrimination on the grounds of nationality, which seemed to be the key approach towards promoting the mobility of workers and their establishment. The emphasis on equal treatment meant that efforts focused on removing restrictive national regulations, but did not address some of the underlying problems in addressing other impediments to professional mobility.

Part of the problem was the different interpretations and practical applications of the Treaty provisions (Lasok, 1986). This reflected different perspectives about the degree to which home or host country would exercise control with regard to compliance with regulations for professional mobility. The intransigence of member states in ceding authority over legislative and administrative provisions meant that many proposals encountered significant delays. While addressing such problems, the European Commission also sought to promote the right to supply services without restriction for specific trades and professions through a variety of legislative measures. This included standstill measures aimed at preventing member states from introducing new legislation that would undermine efforts at liberalization, along with the removal of restrictions identified in the general program. Yet this would not ensure the effective application of the right of freedom of establishment and the freedom to provide services (Von der Groeben, 1987: 194). So the European Commission has sought to address such problems through legislative measures aimed at harmonization, which is often necessary before it is possible to mutually recognize qualifications as required by Article 57 (1) of the Treaty. Because such efforts have encountered strong resistance, particularly in some sectors where professional associations are opposed to any changes in their professional status, the European Commission has promoted transitional measures as a stop-gap measure. This allows host states to determine the rights of access based on specific professional or technical knowledge equivalent to that required of nationals (Wendt, 2012; Barnard and Scott, 2002). Since different supervisory authorities or professional associations within member states regulate different professions, there continued to be discrimination against a whole range of liberal professions, as national commercial knowledge, language competency, or educational qualifications proved to be a serious obstacle (Pelkmans, 1984: 180).

Throughout the 1960s and 1970s, the European Commission adopted a sectoral approach, focusing on particular professions. The European Commission encountered substantial legislative delays, and progress was slower than anticipated in many sectors, despite the fact that the single market for professions was supposed to be operational by 1970. By this time, only thirty-two directives had been adopted dealing with the right of establishment, and the majority covered the elimination of restrictions on a variety of self-employed activities in the commerce, craft, and industry sectors. The problem of applying the principle to technical, medical, and liberal professions remained, however, because of the deep disagreements among member states about the

differing qualifications required to practice. For architects, proposals introduced in 1967 were stalled due to the lack of uniform definition of the
activities of an architect valid in all member states. For lawyers, proposals
introduced in 1969 for mutual recognition of diplomas were blocked, in part
due to the bar associations in Germany and Luxembourg which have been
tenacious about defining their rights of admission. While efforts have been
made to ease procedures for lawyers to appear in the courts of member states
other than their own, the problem still remains that access to the profession
depends on the possession of qualifications prescribed at the national level,
and this hinders lawyers being able to appear in criminal and civil courts of
other member states (European Council, 1976; 77/249/EEC). For accountants,
proposals for mutual recognition have encountered widespread problems due
to differences in accounting and auditing functions among member states
that hinder reciprocal rights to practice, not to mention differences in company law with respect to public and private companies, financial environments, and corporate structures.

After being pressed to report on the current status of implementing the
treaty provisions on services, after the deadline for the common market had
passed, the European Commission acknowledged that the situation was
unsatisfactory (*Agence Europe*, 1970). The problems were due to the failure to
reach agreement on proposals for the mutual recognition of diplomas, with
constant pressure from member states to include specific training requirements, detailed courses of academic study and other educational provisions
(European Commission, 1973). The European Commission sought to promote a more flexible strategy and stressed instead an approach based on
comparability with regard to training as a means of avoiding the problems
inherent in the detailed harmonization of legislation (European Council,
1974 OJ C 98/1). The coordination of educational policies would be promoted
by advisory committees assessing mutual equivalence and comparable standards of training (European Commission, 1976). This would draw upon the
breakthrough that had been achieved with the adoption of two directives on
the right of establishment and provisions of services and the mutual recognition of qualifications for doctors (75/362/EEC and 75/363/EEC). Throughout
this period, many directives were introduced for particular professions, but the
European Commission was unable to capitalize on this framework for liberalization outside of the medical professions, in part due to the strenuous objections from other professions about professional competence and training that
resulted in slow and laborious negotiations in many fields.[13]

In spite of limited progress at the European level, the promotion of the
liberalization of professional services spurred action by certain member states.
Regulators in Spain, Denmark, and Britain eased certain restrictions and promoted reform of professional bodies (Monti, 2003). However, many regulatory

restrictions remained in place, which coupled with restrictions on professional mobility affected the supply and demand of professional services, and continued to reinforce market activities along national lines (see Table 7.3). The progress expected on free establishment and freedom to supply services failed to materialize. In some cases, harmonization of administrative and regulatory requirements to ensure the principle of free movement for professionals suffered from serious setbacks and delays in implementation. In other areas agreement was difficult as professions enjoy a considerable degree of autonomy over their own affairs, yielding the lesson that liberalization depends not only on national laws and administrative regulations, but also in addressing the deeply entrenched and highly institutionalized rules and practices within the professions themselves (Lasok, 1986: 112).

In the case of lawyers, the directive adopted reflected the right to provide cross-border services only on a temporary basis (77/249/EEC; Goebel, 1992). The issues of mutual recognition of educational qualifications, and the right of establishment were avoided due to the variations in national legal systems and the exclusive prerogatives of several types of lawyers that were steadfastly defended in certain member states. Although this directive imposed conditions on the rights to practice, these were subsequently constrained by legal judgments that liberally interpreted Treaty provisions on the rights to offer interstate professional services (Goebel, 2002; *Van Binsbergen* (Case 33/74) and *Gebhard* (Case 55/94). Yet the imbalance between stated economic goals and Treaty objectives and internal movement should not imply lack of interest. On the contrary, intense concerns about harmonization negotiations attracted widespread participation in virtually all professional fields (Orzack, 1980; Hurwitz, 1990). Many of these interest groups argued that regulation is necessary for the overriding protection of public interests, and have sought to retain autonomy and control over the rights to regulate their own professions. Professional groups struck back, forming transnational alliances to develop common positions, and lobbying at both the member state and community level.

Each proposal entailed extensive negotiations among national professional bodies, regulatory bodies, and community institutions, in several instances for more than a decade (Orzack, 1991). The directives adopted in the early period of the common market in the 1960s and 1970s shared a key feature: they usually focused primarily on regulatory convergence to the determinant of regulatory competition (Messerlin 2001: 141).[14] This was in large part because the principle of mutual recognition was either undermined by detailed specific directives or was ignored by member states in practice (Pelkmans, 2007; European Commission, COM (1999) 299 final; European Council, 1999 OJ C141). The negotiating process made efforts to create a single market dependent on regulatory harmonization without addressing the underlying problems of market access, such as the conditional entry requirements and restrictive regulations that remained in place.

Single Market: Promoting Competition through Liberalization and Reciprocity

Although the European Commission desired substantive results, the harmonization of rules governing specific professions floundered due to the reluctance of many professional associations to give up privileged positions that provided restrictions on market entry (Lasok, 1986: 166; Nicolaïdis, 1997). The process of harmonization for each profession, first of educational and training standards and then the requirements for professional status, was thus replaced by a different strategy that provided a general framework for the mutual recognition of educational qualifications (Peixoto, 2001: 36; Orzack, 1991).

New impetus to promoting the liberalization of professional services was generated by the European Commission in its White Paper on Completing the Single Market. This laid out the view that barriers to trade in services were considered analogous to that of goods; and stressed that the provision of cross-border services should be on an equal footing with other freedoms. For professions, there was limited attention given to restrictive provisions on rights of establishment. Much of the emphasis was given to easing restrictions on professional mobility, which had lagged behind due to the complexity of harmonizing professional qualifications (European Commission, 1985: 27).

Thus, the Commission proposed a general approach where each member state would recognize the diploma of another member state as equivalent (89/48/EEC).[15] Those regulated professions not covered by the existing sectoral directives would fall under the General System for Mutual Recognition of Professional Qualifications.[16] The General System is founded on the presumption that an individual qualified in one member state to exercise a specific profession should be regarded in principle as qualified to exercise that same profession in another member state.[17] This rejects the principle of harmonization and instead requires mutual trust in the credibility of profession training across member states (see Orzack, 1991). Although promoting the right to practice, government regulators and professional bodies expressed their concerns that mutual recognition may lead to a lowering of professional standards (Nicolaïdis, 1993; Orzack, 1991). None of the existing or proposed directives gave EU professionals an unfettered right to operate throughout the EU on the basis of qualifications in a single jurisdiction. EU professionals wishing to establish in another member state are still required to apply for recognition in that member state and may be subject to compensatory measures in the form of an adaptation period or an aptitude test where requirements of the two member states differ (Goebel, 1992; Lonbay 1988a, 1988b).[18]

The single market program pushed efforts to expand market opportunities for a variety of professions through altering the existing operation of regulatory systems across Europe. The Commission had shifted towards liberalization rather than discrimination in an effort to secure mobility (Craig and De Búrca, 2003: 768). However, it did not receive unqualified approval from professional bodies. Sectoral approaches continued to complement the broad horizontal approach to professional mobility, based in part on the need for greater specificity. For doctors (93/16/EEC), nurses (77/452/EEC and 77/453/EEC), dental practitioners (78/686/EEC and 78/687/EEC), veterinary surgeons (78/1026/EEC and 78/1027/EEC), midwives (80/154/EEC and 80/155/EEC), pharmacists (85/432/EEC and 85/433/EEC), and architects (85/384/EEC) minimum training requirements have been harmonized at the Community level. For other regulated professions, recognition is based on acceptance of professional skills and experience. In the legal field, the situation was further clarified with the adoption of legislation that specified rights of establishment, allowing cross-border rights to law firms in addition to lawyers, as well as allowing individual lawyers and law firms to practice throughout Europe under their home title. This was a controversial issue considering the variation and differences in the scope of activities permissible or allowed across national systems (98/5/EC).[19]

Yet the measures taken were still partial. The multiple jurisdictions with distinct and sometimes incompatible regulatory systems continue to create barriers to the right of free movement. Recognizing that service activities have been important for EU growth for many years, the Commission launched a review of the economic impact of regulation in the field of the liberal professions (Paterson, Fink, and Ogus, 2003). On the basis of this stocktaking exercise, the Commission sought to address the anticompetitive effects of professional rules, as legal judgments were allowing for individual exemptions based on the necessity and reasonableness of professional rules, undermining multijurisdictional partnerships. The resulting legislation on professions consolidated and simplified the mutual recognition of professions and replaced the existing regime for professional recognition, including the sectoral directives adopted over a twenty-year period in the 1970s and 1980s (2005/36/EC). The Commission also adopted the Services Directive, which establishes a horizontal legal framework facilitating conditions for establishment and cross-border service provision. In an effort to further promote professional mobility, the European Commission proposed further changes to 2005/36/EC on the recognition of professional qualifications by promoting the automatic recognition of doctors, dentists, pharmacists, nurses, midwives, veterinary surgeons, and architects through a professional skills card (European Commission, COM (2011) 883). Despite all the attention given to the Services Directive, the potential for professional services, commercial services that

Table 7.3. Regulated professions per EU member state

Country	Number of professions regulated*
Austria	214
Belgium	140
Bulgaria	116
Croatia	50
Cyprus	112
Czech Republic	399
Denmark	154
Estonia	47
Finland	120
France	150
Germany	153
Greece	168
Hungary	130
Ireland	115
Italy	155
Latvia	61
Lithuania	69
Luxembourg	107
Malta	136
Netherlands	135
Poland	368
Portugal	148
Romania	95
Slovakia	181
Slovenia	247
Spain	174
Sweden	85
United Kingdom	220

Source: Calculated from European Commission data covered by Directive 2003/36/EC

require occupational licensing, as well as cross-border temporary provision of services, requires a combination of harmonization, mutual recognition, and competition policy to realize a single market. While there have been a number of reforms at the national level related to business structures that impact the organization and practices of law firms, the legal forms or requirements in specific sectors still limit multidisciplinary activities and partnerships. In a further effort to encourage cross-mobility of professionals, the Directive on the Mutual Recognition of Professionals, one of the priorities of the Single Market Act has been updated (2013/55/EU) to include mutual evaluation of professions, as well as a European professional card. As some states preserve their markets and reserve certain business activities for specific professions, the financial crisis has placed increased pressure to liberalize their professions as part of the bail-out packages. While Greece has been forced to liberalize notaries and a host of other professions under the conditions of the bail-out, as part of a broader structural reform of their labor market, corresponding Italian efforts to liberalize a host of professional groups from pharmacists and journalists to notaries and taxi drivers has stalled. As the liberal professions dictate who may offer what sort of service, the charges allowed for professionals, and how they may advertise, reform is difficult. However, the application of competition law to the liberal professions, and whether they should continue to enjoy special or exclusive rights, has shifted the debate towards conceptualizing these professions as service providers subject to the general norms of regulatory competition (Wendt, 2012).

Integration through Law

Notwithstanding their importance and impact on the European economy, professional services have not received the same amount of attention as goods.[20] There are few references to the legal decisions that fostered service liberalization, despite the fact that many key decisions pointed the way to resolving the conflict between the imperatives of the single market, the right of free movement and other imperatives of the Treaty (Edward, 2002). Six years before *Cassis*, two cases were crucial in promoting liberalization when the legislative process had ground to a halt. Since the absence of legislation to remove obstacles to the freedom of establishment and freedom to provide services meant that member states could continue to impose restrictions, the European Court of Justice affirmed in *Reyners* (Case 2/74) that the imposition of restrictions based on nationality could not be upheld in the case of professionals who wished to take advantage of their right of establishment. Similarly, in *Van Binsbergen* (Case 33/74), the Court affirmed the right to provide services without specific residency requirements, thereby affirming the freedom of movement of people and services, to be directly applicable once the transition period had ended.[21] Although this implied the removal of protectionist regulations, which even if not directly discriminatory limited the practice of professional activities, there still remained barriers arising from different educational systems and from specific requirements to meet professional qualifications of a member state in order to exercise a profession (Capelli, 1993: 441).

Though the Treaty had advocated the mutual recognition of diplomas (Article 57), slow progress on this front led the Court to step in and provide guidelines on the issue of equivalence. While case law has been instrumental in promoting market liberalization, there have also been certain limits on what constitutes restrictions to trade.[22] Part of the problem was that the general program on services only dealt with restrictions by member states, not the actions of private parties. Although the Commission initially believed that Article 49 (ex 59) was not applicable to private practices, the Court upheld this view and did not question the actions of private parties, only those of member states (*Walgrave and Koch* (Case 36/74) 1974; Snell, 2002). In the *Thieffry* case (Case 71/76), the Court affirmed that acceptance of equivalent qualifications by a host state was sufficient to engage in professional activities without further restrictions and conditions even in the absence of Community legislation.[23] The Court argued that these bodies had specific positive obligations to secure the free movement of workers and rights of establishment, even in the absence of European legislation providing for equivalence and recognition of qualifications (Craig and De Búrca, 2003: 775). This did not undermine the right of professional associations to set their own professional rules, provided that their practices were in accordance with Treaty objectives.

Yet the level of regulation of professions in general, and lawyers in particular, varied widely in terms of market entry and the regulation of conduct (see Paterson, Fink, and Ogus, 2003). Efforts to stimulate competition and increase mobility through application of competition rules have not been upheld by the law. Unexpectedly, the Court did not include private associations under the purview of competition rules, viewing them as bodies entrusted with regulatory powers by the state (De Vries, 2006). In two seminal cases, *Wouters* (Case C-309/99) and *Arduino* (Case 35-99), the application of competition rules to the professions was clarified. In *Arduino*, the Court made clear that member states have the right to regulate a profession. Member states may delegate this responsibility to professional associations, provided that they retain some mechanisms of oversight and control. However, in *Wouters*, the Court recognized that some rules and regulations are crucial for public interest reasons, and that there is a margin of discretion for professional associations to set rules in member states.[24] Although these rules cannot in principle be caught by the prohibition of anticompetitive agreements, decisions, and practices, those that are restrictive are open to challenge. In the absence of European harmonization, each member state is free to regulate professions within their own territory, which means that professional rules may vary across member states (CCBE, 2006). Traditionally their regulatory schemes have been legitimized on the basis of the societal role liberal professions assume, undercutting competition law as a means of addressing restrictions in professional services markets. Similar to the case law in goods, there have been judicially created exceptions that allow for certain national rules that could be justified on grounds of specific societal or public interests if they are not directly or indirectly discriminatory. In *Gebhard* (Case C 55/94), the Court referred to imperative requirements, so that specific exemptions have to be deemed proportionate, with professional regulatory practices still subject to judicial scrutiny. In 2011, the Court, in a much-awaited decision, ruled against seven member states that the conditions of access to the notary profession were discriminatory. The Court ruled that member states may not impose a nationality requirement in order to practice (Cases C-47/08, C-50/08, C-51/08,

C-53/08, C-54/08, C-61/08, and C-52/08).[25] These states had contended that notaries in their exercise of authority were not subject to EU rules regarding freedom of establishment.

More recently, in Cases C-58/13 and C-59/13, *Angelo Alberto Torresi and Pierfrancesco Torresi* v. *Consiglio dell'Ordine degli Avvocati di Macerata*, the Court reaffirmed that states cannot impose restrictions on rights of establishment for lawyers, from one member state establishing themselves in another member state under their home title without integrating themselves in the local profession. If nationals seek out the most favorable jurisdiction in which to acquire their professional qualifications, and then choose the member state in which they want to practice, the right to exercise such mobility is the purpose of a single market, even if educational training, access to legal practice, and range of activities reserved for lawyers varies across member states.

Despite sustained legal efforts to remove unjustified restrictions in regulated sectors and professions, the financial crisis has slowed down or generated opposition to labor market reform in many professional and occupational sectors. Competition has put enormous pressure on vested interests to change their business practices. Notaries continue to defend their centuries-old system as fulfilling a critical state function (European Commission, 2013; Devaux, 2013) as they calculate state taxes and legal charges for commercial transactions. To them the institutional architecture was built for specific reasons that have been legally challenged: "Notaries are important gatekeepers in many economies, in particular when it comes to establishing property rights—the bedrock of markets" (*The Economist*, 2012).

Impacts of Integration on Professional Mobility and Services in US and EU

Forging an integrated market for professions proved a difficult process for both the US and EU. They faced strong resistance from states unwilling to give up their sovereign control over setting the rules for rights of establishment and rights to practice. In both cases, the structure of professional labor markets is a product of statutes and laws as well as market forces. In the EU, the right to practice is constitutionally required because of Treaty provisions guaranteeing freedom of mobility which requires the removal of discriminatory legislation, as well as the coordination of accreditation and licensing to ensure the mutual recognition of qualifications. The cross-border practice laws that apply to European professionals are "significantly more liberal than the multi-jurisdictional provisions found in many U.S. states" (Terry, 2001; Goebel, 2002). Legally, within Europe, there is a recognition of professional qualifications in relation to the provision of professional services on a temporary and occasional basis, and a right of establishment for professional persons of one member state in a host member state. By contrast, free movement is the subject of explicitly vested legislative power and not constitutional rights in the United States.

In the US, vested interests have sought to define their professions through control of licensing and accreditation, as well as retaining exclusive jurisdiction over specific professional activities. Many decisions have built on the foundations established in the nineteenth century. Legal decisions have upheld the importance of the public interest in regulating professions, with efforts to distinguish between reasonable and restrictive regulations. Yet in spite of the fragmentation inherent in the American market, there have also been recommendations for interstate compacts in various professions that would ease mobility through mutual recognition agreements. Interstate practice rights would require the removal of restrictive practices as well as some degree of mutual recognition or uniformity of law, perhaps along the lines prevailing in the EU to achieve a "full faith and credit" model that fits the commercial realities of an internal market.

In both cases, the ability to practice across jurisdictional lines is impacted by structural rigidities entrenched at the national and subnational level. In Europe, the anticipated effects of market integration have generated some changes in specific professional activities. Many American and British firms have taken advantage of the single market through expansion of law practices in Europe, and have engaged in mergers and acquisitions. This was facilitated by their leading role as financial centers, the new fields of practice in the area of business and transactional law, and their view that law was a tradable activity. This has resulted in defensive strategies by many smaller continental law firms through transnational alliances and lobbying as economic interest groups (see Flood and Sosa, 2008). For some, the influence of coordinated capitalism and the civil law tradition are poorly equipped to adjust rapidly to the economic pressures of the business world.

By contrast, efforts to increase competition by offering integrated professional services among accountants, lawyers, and business consultants across multiple jurisdictions also depends on existing national prohibitions and practices. While such multidisciplinary practices are under increasing scrutiny in the wake of financial scandals, so are anticompetitive practices, based on exclusive jurisdictions (Lovecy, 1995). Barriers to professional rights of establishment with restrictions on service provision are not uncommon. Opposition to greater liberalization is complicated by the significant cross-national as well as cross-professional institutional arrangements and legitimizing norms. Concerns about variation in medical training, and different competences and skills of healthcare professionals, in Europe led to opposition towards temporary work rules allowing medical professionals to circumvent requirements for registration, and has led to alert mechanisms to prevent the unauthorized practice of medicine. In the US, concerns about the unauthorized practice of the law also exist in every state. Those within the legal profession have opposed allowing accounting firms, management consulting firms, insurance agencies, investment banks, and other entities to offer legal services, and the prohibition against ownership of law firms by non-lawyers continues in the US. For some, state laws prohibiting alternative legal structures to allow non-lawyers owning a stake in law firms restrict interstate commerce. Yet such intra- and inter-professional struggles, based on historically embedded institutions and norms, are being challenged by new organizational practices and market opportunities for different professions (Lovecy, 1995; Terry, 2001).

Conclusion

Although the focus of this chapter is on the free movement of professionals in particular, labor mobility is considered one of the most important impediments to achieving an integrated market in Europe. Despite provisions to ease the transfer of benefits and educational qualifications, the reality is starkly different. This is partly due to cultural and linguistic differences, but it is also the result of legal and administrative barriers, which prevent or discourage workers from other member states from seeking employment within another territory. Yet more labor mobility is considered crucial in addressing some of Europe's striking labor market imbalances, in which there are regions of high unemployment and regions with skills shortages. While seeking to remove internal restrictions to mobility for European nationals, the EU is also liberalizing entry requirements for third-country nationals, by offering a work permit scheme for skilled labor that does not provide the same mobility rights within the single market, as that provided under the Treaty for EU nationals.

Although Europe has undergone tremendous economic integration as indicated by increased trade and capital flows, labor market integration lags behind. Intra-European capital mobility has substituted for intra-European labor mobility (Koslowski, 1994; Straubhaar, 1988). The relative paucity of intra-European labor mobility is notable in comparison with the US where massive internal migration flows in the nineteenth century provide historical evidence of significantly higher levels of labor mobility that continue today. Despite substantial free movement guarantees for European citizens in the Treaty of Rome, there continue to be low levels of geographic and occupational mobility. While some two hundred thousand citizens have been seeking recognition of their professional qualifications, the internal market for professional services is still rather restricted (Mustelli and Pelkmans, 2013a: 47).

While the wide range of variability across jurisdictions with regard to fiscal, social, and educational policies impact incentives for labor mobility, internal labor flows within the EU remain comparatively slow despite efforts to ease restrictions.

Undoubtedly states have retained their power to regulate most professions. Despite specific efforts to improve competitive conditions for professional services, there remain a number of regulatory restrictions hindering freedom of movement. Regulation of professions also remains one area where market segmentation continues to exist in the US, which has maintained restrictions on occupational mobility that make it harder for professions to offer cross-border services without additional licensing and accreditation. Each profession has its activities under various kinds of jurisdiction at the state level, so that local markets remain segmented both geographically and functionally in spite of the existence of a national market in other areas. In the US, the service sector—which is the focus of many licensing laws—has seen a significant increase in occupational licensing and enforcement coupled with a corresponding decline in labor mobility in recent decades.

Despite the fact that differences in substantive laws and procedural rules are far greater among the member states of the EU than the states of the US, the liberalization of professional mobility has progressed more rapidly over the past forty years in the European case (Goebel, 2002). The EU has pursued strategies to improve the conditions of competition for professional services within its market, and sought to remove restrictions to market entry and mobility for both individuals and companies. Recognizing that regulatory restrictions increase the costs of entry and exit into different markets, the EU has sought to promote both the removal of impediments to cross-border activities, and to coordinate policies to ease labor mobility. This means that restrictive practices come under the purview of competition rules, as national competition authorities will have a more prominent role in assessing the legality of rules and regulations in the professions (see Monti, 2003).

Recognizing that there are a number of factors that affect the costs of entry and exit into different labor markets, neither the US nor the EU has created the conditions for an integrated market in professional services. Both have faced pushback from entrenched vested interests. Neither has created the unfettered right to provide services based on a single qualification that is valid across all jurisdictions. Both have sought reciprocity of qualifications, although mutual recognition is not an aim in itself but rather the means by which the US and EU have sought to ease the special conditions and restrictions that hamper the ability to offer professional services. Here the EU has arguably been more effective in structuring the regulatory environment. The EU has sought full reciprocity among the member states through the mutual recognition of educational qualifications, whereas the US has opted for partial reciprocity, with mutual recognition in some professions based on geographic proximity. Legal redress has been much more fruitful in Europe, where treaty obligations provide a sounder basis for achieving an integrated market for professions than that of the US where the rights are more difficult to discern from the Constitution (Goebel, 2002: 426). Ironically, as the development of a more unified market for professional services continues in the EU, it can be held up as an example for the US with its multiple regulatory jurisdictions (Ascher, 2004). However it is still extremely difficult to come up with appropriate counts or measurements of the remaining barriers in the internal market for professional services and the actual economic impact of such barriers. As pharmacists strike over unpaid medical reimbursements from debt-ridden governments, taxi drivers halt service and block roads to airports, and notaries, one of the most privileged professions in Europe, protest about efforts to reduce their quotas, fees, and long-established privileges, efforts to promote free movement of services without disproportionate or discriminatory state regulations, and allow for the liberalization of regulated professions continues to be watered down (*The Economist*, 2012). Professions have thus been insulated against market competition as states conferred specific authority on them, which legitimated their regulatory arrangements, and made it harder to promote regulatory reform due to their privileged position in relation to both markets and states. Despite pressure for liberalization and efforts to promote mutual recognition, restrictive regulations are widespread in professional services as well as skilled trades and crafts, although this varies by sector and state in both the US and Europe.

Notes

1. Oral History Interview, October 25, 1964, New York, Harry S. Truman Library.
2. Known as GATS "mode 4 supply of services" which is on the negotiating table in the multilateral services trade negotiations. Mode 4 parallels the traditional concept of service provision in EU law. This is the temporary movement of persons to provide services abroad but is limited in scope. The GATS Agreement (1994) covers cross-border movement of services including the cross-border movement of labor for the purposes of supplying services.
3. Complete integration is prevented by imperfect information about employment opportunities.
4. Although similarities between establishment and services are evident, the "right of professionals to practice occasionally in other states is founded on the right of freedom to provide services, while the right of professionals to practice while residing in another state is founded on the right of establishment" (Goebel 1992).

5. Professional services as defined in the GATS include among others, legal services, accounting, auditing and bookkeeping services, taxation services, architectural services, engineering services, integrated engineering services, urban planning and landscape architectural services, medical and dental services, veterinary services, services provided by midwives, nurses, physiotherapists, and para-medical personnel.

6. This suggests caution when making inferences about the overall integration of labor markets, given the role and impact of migration, economic circumstances, and institutional conditions, for example, on the labor market experience.

7. State bar admissions traditionally required citizenship to practice law. This meant that foreign lawyers were excluded from practicing until 1973 when the US Supreme Court struck down this requirement. The original intent of the restrictions was to prevent immigrants, mainly from Southern or Eastern Europe, from pursuing a legal profession.

8. The free movement of services may involve movement of persons as either the provider or recipient of services moves to another member state—so there is an interrelationship between the various freedoms, and neither is mutually exclusive (see Snell, 2002).

9. Article 52 outlines three different aspects of the right of establishment: (1) the right to set up "agencies, branches or subsidiaries"; (2) "the right to take up and pursue activities as self-employed persons"; and (3) the right to "set up and manage undertakings, in particular companies or firms."

10. Article 54 directed the Council of Ministers to set up a general program "for the abolition of existing restrictions freedom of establishment" (which thus was intended to achieve freedom of professional establishment as well as commercial or financial establishment) and then to implement this program by directives.

11. See Regulation NO 15 *Official Gazette of the EC*, 1961; Regulation 38/64 *Official Gazette of the EC*, 1964 and Directive 64/240 EC, 1964.

12. General Programme for the abolition of restrictions on freedom to provide services of December 18, 1961, OJ No. 2 of January 15, 1962 and General Programme for the abolition of restrictions on freedom of establishment of December 18, 1961, OJ No. 2 of January 15, 1962.

13. Following on from the model framework for doctors, agreement was reached on dentists, midwives, nurses, and veterinary medicine.

14. The Sectoral Directives adopted deal with specific regulated professions (physicians and specialists, general nurses, dentists, midwives, veterinarians, pharmacists, and architects).

15. Unlike the Lawyers Services Directive 77/249, which applies to the temporary provision of legal services in another member state, the Diplomas Directive was intended to cover permanent establishment.

16. This is operated by Directive 89/48/EEC (known as the First Diplomas Directive) and Directive 92/51/EEC (known as the Second Diplomas Directive).

17. This broad-based equivalence is based on the notion of proportionality so that it is premised on broad-scale equivalence with local adaptation.

18. This was supplemented by directive 92/51 which covered education and training other than requirements set out in the earlier directive including diplomas and certificates. A third general directive 99/42 replaced earlier directives in a range of professional and industrial sectors based on mutual recognition of skills and experience not just formal educational qualifications.
19. This right is confirmed again and highlighted in a separate proposed Directive of March 2002.
20. In Case 55/94 the ECJ argued that the treaty provisions on goods, services, and workers should be similarly interpreted.
21. The ECJ was alluding to direct applicability of Articles 52 and 59.
22. The notion of imperative requirements originated with the Van Binsbergen case. It is similar to the Cassis rule of reason exceptions.
23. See also Case 340/89 *Vlassopolou* v. *Ministerium für Justiz* 1991.
24. Rules can be maintained to uphold professional ethics (deontology). It considered that there was no breach of Article 81 EC because any restriction on competition was in the public interest, and that there was no breach of Article 82 EC because the Bar did not constitute an undertaking or a group of undertakings.
25. Infringements against member states for non-compliance: *European Commission* v. *Kingdom of Belgium*; *European Commission* v. *French Republic*; *European Commission* v. *Grand Duchy of Luxembourg*; *European Commission* v. *Federal Republic of Germany*; *European Commission* v. *Hellenic Republic*, and *European Commission* v. *Portugal*; *European Commission* v. *Republic of Austria*.

8

Conclusion

Single Markets has focused on the creation of an integrated economy in which the US and EU experienced different ideas shaping their respective market economies, conflict over the allocation of institutional authority, and pressure from interests over the role and consequences of increased competition. In both cases, the previous chapters illustrate that the challenges of managing production, distribution, and social conflict that followed from the shift from local markets to national markets to international markets required crucial policy choices by government institutions. As important as economic imperatives are, market integration is also the product of politics, and most notably the tensions between sovereignty and effective governance (Cameron, 1998; Schelkle, 2010). With pressures to regulate market relations and promote economic redistribution, both polities faced new social demands that competed with notions of market competition, to encompass political and social claims of fairness, equity, and inclusion. Such debates about market formation lead us to think about the conditions under which government plays an important, even dominant role in shaping transactions and exchanges, linking market integration within its larger institutional and political framework.

Single Markets seeks to explain how states collectively knit together their economies so that markets are constituted into broader territorial units. Although the focus is on the transformation of market forces by largely internal rather than external stimuli, that process of market-making cannot be separated from constitutional rights, functional and sectional interests, and the dynamics of regulation and redistribution. Though it appears that the EU has created a continental market without a centralized state, the dynamics of market-building in the American case also point to the disaggregated nature of state capacity across different policy domains (Fabbrini, 2004). The American state became a functional—and legitimate—entity, institutionalizing policy commitments towards free trade and dealing with problems of anonymity, complexity, dependency, and concentrations of power emerging from changes in industrial organization, finance, and governance. Similarly,

European states have also dealt with the challenges of creating a single market in which there were divergent political ideas, incongruities, and dissonance about the relationship between social democracy, economic liberalism, and market governance (Hooghe and Marks, 1997; Fioretes, 2011).

What emerged in both cases was a style of capitalism that was initially characterized by increased rates of growth, modernization of economies, and state interventionism in economic policy (Shonfield, 1965; Evans, 1995). The implied commitment to a free market economy, stressing the virtues of competition and greater efficiencies, was balanced by a widespread acceptance of dirigisme and intervention. Scholars of American Political Development (APD) have focused on different conceptions of state power in nineteenth-century economic development, and in doing so have highlighted the different organizational manifestations of the American state as decentralized, regulatory, coercive, or interventionist in explaining how a national market evolved in the midst of sectional rivalries, territorial expansion, and evolving and contested institutions. They stress how institutional change may be generated by "incurrence" between multiple political orders and traditions, or driven by interactions with other institutions in a way that resonates with efforts to understand the balancing between functional and territorial interests in the European polity (see Orren and Skowronek, 2004: 17; Fabbrini, 2004, 2005). Just as the US struggled to create a single market against the centrifugal forces of American states, so the EU has also sought to address the effects of divergent rules and jurisdictions, moving beyond a purely economic arrangement to reconstitute and transform public authority. While the EU is not a nation-state, it has forged a market in which institutions and practices have resulted in a multiplicity of laws, rules, and administration across multiple jurisdictions, constituting both a *jural* state as well as a regulatory state (Novak, 2008: 767). The legal changes and constitutional transformation created a new kind of jurisprudence with cross-jurisdictional competence over economic rights and privileges (see Novak, 2008, 2009, No Date)[1]. This book tries to understand that process by highlighting the role of institutions in shaping bargaining dynamics and creating rules to govern the process of policymaking. This requires arbitrating interests with different concerns and expectations about the restructuring of economies in terms of the distribution of costs and benefits. In other words, there are disparate ideas about how to stabilize and regulate markets, conflict and bargaining over institutional power and authority, and continual pressure from interests to shape the evolving political economies.

The concluding chapter addresses the dynamics of market consolidation on either side of the Atlantic, highlighting some of the main themes addressed in this volume. The chapter is structured as follows: the first section highlights some general themes involving the European and American experiences in market integration. The second section provides some summary conclusions from the case studies that highlight aspects of their experience that were important for successful market integration. The third section is concerned with differences in their relative experiences. The fourth section focuses on the importance of popular support and legitimacy. The chapter concludes with some ideas about what may be relevant in terms of the economic successes of the EU and US for broader efforts elsewhere.

Markets, Politics, and State-Building

While there are important differences in the political, economic, and social histories of the American and European experience, this book provides some general comparisons of their respective experiences of market consolidation. And yet when we think about the US and EU experiences, the former is tied to state-building which implies the internal consolidation of power (McNamara, 2003: 6, 2005: 21), whereas the latter is tied to post-national democracy with a different pattern and organization of power and institutions.[2] Once we think about them as political systems characterized by compromises and bargains based on deeply rooted territorial cleavages, we begin to understand the critical importance of their efforts to balance their goals of a centralized economic order while preserving regional and local diversity (Sbragia, 2004: 94ff). Since governments have institutional self-interests that they try to defend vis-à-vis other governments, the ways in which the US and EU have resolved conflict between central and local units of government provide important lessons to other regional integration efforts regarding the importance of the institutional dynamics in which market integration takes place.

Both cases demonstrate a strong relationship between economic and political developments, as "the single market and its ancillary policies require political support and legitimacy on the one hand, and institutional capabilities and effectiveness on the other."[3] This argument, which draws on literature in political and economic development, along with the more familiar integration literature, is premised on the assumption that an effective political and legal framework for market integration was responsive to the fundamental necessities of economic development. Market economies face a complex set of rules and regulations that shape their structure and operation. Even though markets are politically and socially constructed entities, subject to intense ideological debates about their operation and organization, markets do not receive the same kind of attention as traditional political institutions such as parties, legislatures, courts, and bureaucracies. Despite the linkages between governments and markets, the main emphasis in recent scholarship has been on freeing markets, which involves removing government barriers to private exchange through deregulation and privatization with much less attention given to facilitating markets which involves creating or permitting a particular market through specific interventions (Egan, 2001; Patashnik, 2000). What is clear is that despite the prevailing discourse about liberalism, property rights, and economic freedoms, with scholars often invoking Louis Hartz, Alexis De Tocqueville, Béla Balassa, or Friedrich Hayek, as Mark Gilbert points out, such analyses often highlight very positive narratives and progressive outcomes that shape historians' accounts of the integration process (Gilbert, 2008, see also Rasmussen, 2013). We should historicize their analysis, understanding they were writing in a specific context, and compare the different forms and action of state power not simply because the conditions for functioning markets were laid out by the state(s), but because the pattern of governance that emerged was premised on a legal–regulatory framework that was an indispensable and inseparable part of the creation of a market economy in different eras. And arguably what has evolved is not simply about achieving rationalization and efficiency but also about forging new ideas about sovereignty, law, administration, and ultimately about how to govern markets (Garson, 2001; McNamara, 2001a; Scharpf, 1999b; cf. Weingast, 1995).

Summary of Cases

Each of the case studies in this book illustrates the channels through which both polities promoted market integration. Neither the US nor the EU followed a single trajectory, oscillating between different legal doctrines, market pressures, and political ideas and ideologies. While the integration process has been uneven, it has reinforced the centralizing tendencies of both polities across a range of issue areas. Economic and political integration is now assured in the American context, though some gaps remain in the US market (e.g. state professional certification and licensing is required for different occupational groups to practice in different geographic markets) (see Hoffman, 2011). Economic market integration has proceeded quickly in the EU, one could argue at a more rapid and coherent pace than in the US, but political integration has lagged behind and its future remains uncertain.[4] Here it is important to recognize that lessons from the US experience are instructive as the US began with a plurality of identities and sought to create a polity constituted by distinct but not fully sovereign territorial units, but this cannot be directly applied to the European polity (Deudney, 1995: 215–16; Fabbrini, 2004; McNamara, 2005: 7). The "United States of America" only shifted from being understood in the plural to the singular after the Civil War, and the building of the single market was closely tied to its political identity and development whereas the EU has distinct national identities with a burgeoning European identity built upon the interplay of European and national institutional governance (see especially McNamara, 2005: 5, 9; Fligstein, 2008). In the EU case, regional market integration represented the way forward following the catastrophic political failures of sovereign nation-states, and economic developments have often led those at the political level. These differences are important and acknowledged in the introduction.

On the other hand, there is much in common with the US where there is often debate as to how power is shared between constituent elements of the federal system. Though the US constitutional design calls for functions to be divided between the national government and the states, just how is left open to political and judicial disputes (Derthick, 1996, 2001). The powers granted to states were often vague and unlimited, delineating the powers given to the federal government, while providing residual powers to states. While it may be argued that the basic institutional design of US federalism is well established, with the most significant domestic activities as necessary responsibilities of the federal government, many of these functions were settled in the nineteenth and early twentieth century in the aftermath of the US Civil War and other contentious political and judicial conflicts. From this perspective, this sort of tension across multiple levels of governance, with the institutional framework evolving over time, has much in common with the EU. Chapters 2 and 3 provide a basis for the comparison, drawing on the abilities of the US and EU political systems to adapt to changing circumstances. In both cases, we see the interplay between different levels of government in determining distributive outcomes, the evolution of a legal framework for the market, and the development of new regulatory strategies to deal with changing economic realities.

Economic and Welfare Goals

The emergence of interlocking commerce and investment across borders compelled the US and EU to create new powers within their borders—powers to intervene in market forces to soften the economic crises and restore economic growth and prosperity. The need to assure an acceptable distribution of benefits among states and classes has led both polities to consider the social impact of their respective economic development.[5] Economic integration has created pressures to modify market outcomes to correct market failures and carry out various forms of redistribution. In the US and EU, this has resulted in flanking measures, in order to mitigate the effects of increased competition, and respond to demands for regulation beyond the confines of the economic sphere to include important areas of social and environmental regulation. Fearful that excessive competition would increase social conflict, proponents of regulated capitalism proposed a variety of inclusive mechanisms to generate broad-based support for the single market (Hooghe and Marks, 1997). In the US, the effort to serve communal values or societal interests through public trust in the area of eminent domain and police powers were indicative of the effort to promote the "public good" in a society undergoing rapid social and economic change (Novak, 1996; Scheiber, 1984). In the EU, the effort to pursue social citizenship through an expanded welfare state occurred primarily at the national level. While there were, however, EU efforts to promote social harmony and cohesion, through the Common Agricultural Policy and Structural and Cohesion funds, as well as efforts to prevent reductions in social standards induced by the competitive pressures of the single market, Conant however perceives the expansion of EU social rights, addressing the rights of individuals, not only in terms of "market citizenship" through employment rights, working conditions, and pay equity, but also through new social rights for third-country nationals through family reunification, social protection, and assistance schemes, as critical for socioeconomic legitimacy (Conant, 2008).

While economic integration has spilled over into other areas, the ensuing growth in social safety nets in the American progressive era in the late nineteenth and early twentieth century and the postwar period in Europe provide important legitimizing effects for market integration. However, the welfare state in terms of labor protection, unionization, and bargaining was initially contested, and viewed as inimical to the American common market, whereas the welfare state and the postwar settlement between labor and capital were not considered contrary to European market integration (Sbragia, 2005; Moses, 2011).

Law and Markets

The creative and constitutive role of law is crucial in understanding the consolidation of markets in Europe and the US. Market integration involves a substantive legal project that shapes public and private policies (Novak, 1996). In the US case, federal constitutional law gradually displaced local common law in the post-Civil War era (Novak, No Date: 21). Local and state law came under the purview of the US Supreme Court, which sought to establish boundaries between public and private rights and federal and state authority. Likewise, the European Court of Justice also placed state and local laws under its purview, and also determined the economic relationship between public intervention and the market, and the political relationship between member states and the union (Maduro, 1998). The expropriation of legal authority in both cases has altered patterns of legal rule and played a crucial role in creating and regulating the conditions for the growth of an integrated economy. Since legal decisions have rendered important support for market processes by resolving conflict between central and local units of government, law has been crucial in both the creation of a national state and economy in the US and a regional state and economy in Europe. In both cases, this was not uncontested as patterns of acceptance of federal authority—and the supremacy of law—did encounter state resistance (Alter, 2001, 2010; Goldstein, 2001).

However, law opened up opportunities by reducing much of the cost of innovation and entrepreneurship by shifting the focus towards creating the context for open markets and competition (Hurst, 1956). This legal transformation was a central feature in the creation of a single market, and reflected "bold juridical innovation" in which courts introduced new doctrines to expedite economic development through addressing trade barriers, negating preferential treatment, and challenging vested rights—sometimes with unintended consequences for different regions, industries, classes, or groups (Scheiber, 1975: 63; Novak, No Date, 2008; Horwitz, 1977). What emerges from this positive "Hurstian" comparison is the creative and constitutive role of law in balancing market liberalism and social welfare, individual rights against collective public goods, and promoting national and international commerce through regulating the conditions for economic growth, competitiveness, and development (Egan, 2013: 1253). Thus as Scheiber notes, "law was far-ranging and deep in the shaping of the economic marketplace, economic and business institutions, and the dynamics of material growth and innovation" (Scheiber 1980b: 1159), it was also not benign in its effect. Law also marginalized and excluded certain groups from participating in the market. Equally relevant, APD scholars have focused on the structural weakness of other institutions—namely legislative and executive—to understand why other actors and institutions assert or assent to such legal activism (Whittington, 2007). Such a position also accords with Weiler's seminal argument that portrays "integration through law" as a rational response to a changing political environment in Europe in which the Court pursued a "quiet revolution" by steadily enhancing the scope of Community law (Weiler, 1991).

Regulation and Governance

Government intervention in the economy has grown, in part due to the need to establish economic security and stability, reduce transaction costs, and respond to increased societal pressures and demands. The challenges of managing production, distribution, and social conflict that followed from the shift from local markets to national and international markets fostered the growth and expansion of market regulatory policies. The operation of the market was not left unfettered. The market needed protection not only against private transactions that threatened the fair operation of market processes but also against the abuse of public power with regard to resource allocation, monopolies, and protectionism (Carstensen, No Date). While the ability of governments to provide welfare benefits may be diminishing, their role in creating and sustaining rules for a functioning market economy has not eroded or diminished (Sbragia, 2000). A mere reliance on the removal of constraints is not sufficient. The integration of divergent economies requires the constraint of at least some domestic policy instruments, combined with the irrevocable transfer of one or more instruments to the central level (Majone as quoted in Egan, 2001).

In both the US and EU, central institutions enlarged the scope of their regulatory activities, so as to include new areas, that were initially either exempt or regulated at the state level, thus expanding their regulatory reach incrementally often without formal, constitutional changes (Majone, 2009). In the midst of such socioeconomic transformations of the late nineteenth century—when "class distinctions and public burdens were clearly accelerating"—the actual power and policies of the American "regulatory" state expanded and increased (Novak, No Date: 5; Novak, 1996; Lowi, 1984; McCraw, 1984; Keller, 1977). In the EU, the regulatory remit focused initially on market regulation, with the privatization of public enterprises and creation of regulatory agencies, the actual power and policies of the European "regulatory state" also expanded and increased in various formal and informal institutional formats (Majone, 1996a; Lodge, 2008; Eberlein and Grande, 2005). Market expansion, technological change, and corporate pressures placed strains on efforts to regulate capital, goods, and services in ways that protected and served state economic and constituent interests. Scrambling to compete with other states, there was tremendous pressure in the US and EU to adopt policies that moved beyond protectionism and mercantilism. And at the same time, regulations to protect and insulate markets were struck down by courts, which reinforced the centralizing tendencies of both polities across a range of issue areas. While often overcoming state and local preferences, in order to reduce transaction costs and uncertainty, there were also legal and political efforts to insulate state regulations and rules. In terms of governance, states still continued to play a significant role in shaping the conditions for economic growth, with courts often involved in "balancing standards" between local preferences and central rules.

The durability of states, and the important role that they played in nineteenth-century regulation and economic development, often exceeded that of the federal government in the US. While there was a centralization and expansion of federal power in wartime, including centralizing banking functions, growth of armed forces, and paper currency for example, states also exerted their regulatory power in numerous social and economic activities (Gerstle, 2009: 71), resulting in a network of federal, state, and local activities. In response to industrialism there was also the growth of well-organized groups for professional, business, and functional interests, aimed at shaping government regulation and promoting the "gospel of efficiency" (Hays, 1999).

In the EU, state preferences remain critical, as interstate bargaining and inter-governmental policy coordination continue to shape many economic areas, although delegation to supranational institutions is designed to enhance credible commitments (Moravcsik, 1998b). Yet the EU has also experienced the growth of multilevel networks, the mobilization of interests, and the growth of technocratic governance much like the emerging role of reformers, experts, and interest groups in the US in response to the need for new policy instruments to manage changes in the economy (Johnson, 2009: 96). In both cases, as the federal government gained new functions in an expanding range of policy areas, there was a corresponding increase in intergovernmental collaboration as enforcement and implementation were often decentralized in both the US and the EU (Scheiber, 1975; Elazar, 1964; Hooghe, 1998). Yet the persistence of the powers of states is a central feature in European and American governance (Lindberg and Campbell, 1991; King and Lieberman, 2009; cf. Hooghe and Marks, 2010).

Single Markets illustrates three important factors about market consolidation in the US and EU. First, the fact that governments can—and do—strongly influence how markets work is crucially important in understanding eco-nomic developments in the US and EU. Government responses come in a variety of forms, not only does it tax, transfer income, and regulate private firms, it also carries out many of the activities that a private firm does. Government intervention comes in many forms: market-correcting, market-regulating, and market-enhancing. Government intervention in the economy has grown, in part in response to the need to establish economic security and stability, reduce transaction costs, and also respond to increased societal pressures and demands. In light of both ideological pressures for liberalization and increased pressure to reduce public intervention in markets, the emphasis on public authorities in this book is to highlight the critical role that govern-ments play in constructing and maintaining markets. The notion that the capacity of the state to provide collective goods is constrained by the pressures of globalization is influenced by the view that the primary function of the state is the provider of benefits (Sbragia, 2000: 245). While the politics of retrenchment suggests that the role of public authorities are increasingly constrained by markets, the state does not only provide benefits (and deter-mine exclusions), it also builds and regulates markets (Egan, 2001; Polanyi, 1944; Sbragia, 2000; Lodge, 2008). A single market contributes to the admin-istrative and bureaucratic expansion of the state, although the balance between local authority and national control in the regulatory arena evolves and changes over time.

Second, markets need to be differentiated as the specific characteristics of each factor market can yield different degrees of integration. On the one hand, commodity trade flows and capital movements are prominent features of both

US and EU market integration. Both experienced rapid advances in trade and commercial transaction—and rapid increases in domestic capital market formation as well as foreign direct investment. Labor mobility, on the other hand, has been radically different since historical flows of mass migration in the nineteenth century to the US have not been matched in postwar Europe. The US experienced a massive influx of both forced and voluntary migration, with high levels of geographic mobility within the US often through chain migration (Rosenbloom, 2002). Waves of immigration were tied to domestic economic activity, and the labor force grew more rapidly than the population (Margo, 2000). Postwar levels of migration are nowhere near the scale relative to the size of the population that characterized nineteenth-century mass migration. Both have experienced a backlash against immigration, with organized groups mobilizing to impose restrictions on foreign employment amid concerns of cheaper labor, with resentment flaring as soon as the pressures of crises emerged. Yet in both the US and the EU, labor mobility has been impeded by a variety of state enforced legal and regulatory practices, as professional and functional groups mobilized to create and defend market entry barriers with new forms of professional identity and rules (Johnson, 2009: 96; Hoffman, 2011). Furthermore, advances in transportation and communication technology in nineteenth-century America were important factors in the rapid pace of economic integration with profound effects on the structure of the economy (Bruchey, 1990). By contrast, liberalization in transportation has made slow progress in the EU, and markets have been highly segmented due to public ownership, protectionism and monopolies. However, pressures for European regulation, as well as technological and economic developments have weakened national market boundaries.

Third, attention needs to be given to the tremendous social problems created—or at least partially compensated—by market integration. Social rights were not universal in either the US or EU political economy. Market rights—or market citizenship—were in both cases exclusive, with restrictions imposed on specific groups through differentiated integration, border controls, restrictive property rights, and residency laws (Novak, 1996; Egan, 2013). The calculus of consent or full market freedoms were not conferred upon all residents. To enhance political support for market integration, governments sought to compensate specific sectors and groups through distributive and compensatory policies. But this does not mean that market integration unfolded without social discontent. The political backlash against rising competitive pressures did foster certain protectionist inclinations in both the US and EU through the imposition of tariffs and non-tariff barriers on agricultural and industrial products, immigration restrictions, and other measures to protect domestic markets and particularistic interests. And the current economic crisis in Europe with high unemployment, credit contraction, bankruptcies, and other visible forms of market failure match the propensity for similar economic recurrences and panics in the US, where pressure for economic modernization brought about painful changes, in which farmers, workers, and reformers sought relief, often resorting to social disruption, as the elements of innovation and change, created painful dislocations (Larson, 2010). The consequences of the early market revolution in the US shaped a host of policies from banking to bankruptcy, from democracy to the expansion of slavery, in ways reminiscent of the current fiscal and economic crisis where flashpoints erupted over the insecurities and uncertainties wrought by market actions. The impact of economic distress created the foundation for new institutions to deal with destructive competition in the US that finds a similar response in Europe where more permanent stability mechanisms have evolved to deal with fiscal crisis and debate rages over the liabilities and responsibilities for public debt.

From Uncommon Markets to Dissimilar Markets

By using a comparative approach, the book brings together two closely related but largely unacquainted bodies of scholarship in the US and EU and seeks to contribute to our understanding of the policies required and political support necessary to build and sustain a single market. There has been significant debate about the origins, content, and development of the single market in Europe which has been routinely cited in the field of integration studies.[6] These parallel many of the same interpretations and scholarly debates generated by American legal and business historians to explain and determine the conditions for economic growth and integration in the US. European accounts of the relationship between the role of law and institutions in shaping the market, the entrepreneurial energy and effort to enhance the productive power of the economy, and the mobilization of interests in shaping economic development and integration are reminiscent of the many and varied interpretations of the American experience. The parallel to the US is not surprising since early advocates often referred to the economic success of the US as evidence of the advantages of a large integrated economy (Dell, 1959). Yet the experience of the US, though on a much smaller scale than that of the EU, has become a useful analogy, as McNamara concludes, in terms of its concurrent political units, its plurality of territorial identities, and its fragmented form of governance, which has largely conditioned its political and economic development (McNamara, 2003, 2005, 2011).

Despite its title, *Single Markets* deals, much less prominently, with different trajectories of development as well as commonalities. Although the EU in its institutional structure and policymaking bears a strong resemblance to the US, the US is not the only federal model to which the EU is often compared (Sbragia, 1992a; Schmidt, 2004; Börzel and Hosli, 2003). However, it is the one that has generated substantial comparisons across numerous policy areas. As Fabbrini suggests in his historical comparison, both polities have confronted the need to legitimate their exercise of political authority, but the political problems faced by each polity and their complex resolutions have resulted in historically different solutions (Fabbrini, 2002). While the pattern of state growth in the US differed from its European counterparts, the resulting institutional arrangements have subsequently converged as the EU—as distinct from its member states—has resulted in a system of overlapping jurisdictions with elements of shared power that resembles the American "compound polity" (Fabbrini, 2002, 2004). But if, as Moravcsik (2001) has pointed out, different historical periods operate within an institutional context that shapes policies and outcomes, the pattern of economic integration may also be highly contingent on prevailing political and economic circumstances. Influenced by this argument, this section highlights the specific contingent factors that have resulted in different modes of economic governance.

Building on the discussion in Chapter 1, the economic and technological structures, the size and nature of domestic and international commerce, and the organization of production and work are in many ways unique. This section explores this line of argument by focusing on some distinctive political economy patterns that shaped their respective markets.

As regards scale, the US was a small country when it chose its democratic institutions, constructed its system of governance, and consolidated its market. What emerged in the nineteenth century in the US was a shift in the *colonial* orientation of the economy towards a national economy. What propelled this process was government promotion of railroads and canals, along with public intervention in corporate law, taxation, and subsidies (Taylor, 1951; Scheiber, 1984; Hurst, 1982). In the US, the "transportation revolution" was not simply a series of technological innovations, but an integral part of industrialization and the process of economic integration. Coupled with rapid urbanization, the changes in the American economy meant that the dependence on foreign trade and European markets was declining. On the eve of the Civil War, domestic sources of capital increased, despite the continued influx of foreign capital. With the diversification of agriculture and industry, there was an expansion of domestic trade and consumption. Other factors that played a critical role in American industrialization include abundant resources and cheap land. These unique resources provided enormous advantages to the US in the late nineteenth century in terms of their contribution to exports and economic growth. In addition, the legal status of labor, and the sociological problems in response to the changing organization of work, and the recruitment and discipline of industrial workers were markedly different from the

European context where unionization, social democracy and welfare gains were part of the postwar settlement.

The most striking characteristics of postwar Europe were the ambitious welfare services and the deliberate pursuit of full employment and incomes policy. In the European context, the interwar economy shifted from cata-strophic failure into postwar economic prosperity. What propelled high rates of growth and rapid increases in production was—like the US—the significant rise in domestic investment. Coupled with improved techniques in manufac-turing and agriculture, manufacturing trade—then services trade—replaced primary trade as a proportion of international trade. Yet free trade is well known to lead to significant distributional consequences. Some industries gain, others lose and the existence of such losers often prevents steps towards further liberalization. One unexpected consequence from the European experience was that there were initially very few losers. Partly this was due to buoyant growth, but more importantly it was also due to the unforeseen very rapid development of intra-industry trade.[7] This greatly mitigated any unfavorable effects on import-competing sectors since resources, instead of being forced to move to other sectors, could still very often be used within the same branches producing somewhat different varieties of similar goods. Since intra-industry trade is very much a postwar development, this is substantially different from the historic norm.

In the late nineteenth century, the internal pressures of industrialism promoted the expansion of national administrative capacities to regulate the economy and "thrust America irrevocably onto the international scene to preserve their material interests" (Fabbrini, 2002: 16; Skowronek, 1982; Katznelson and Shefter, 2002). The nationalization of the economy chal-lenged prevailing institutional patterns, fostering the growth of national administrative agencies that became new and important instruments of action. Europe differed in its choice of institutional structures to manage and correct markets although arguably it has extended its material interests through market power (Damro, 2011). Nationalization was the functional equivalent in Europe to American-style regulation, with nothing analogous to the specialized administrative agencies that emerged in late nineteenth-century America (Egan, 2001; Majone, 1996a). American regulation emerged in response to market failure. Since it was based on the ideology of efficiency, corrective policies were designed to generate efficient solutions. By contrast, the regulatory responses of European governments are explicable by reference to the more general aims of an interventionist system. This intervention, along with the expansion of the welfare state, assisted the process of European integration as governments were able to compensate and adjust for increased competition and openness of national economies. During the last two dec-ades, however, the need to enhance state capacity in order to make markets work right has generated new public sector reforms, including the establishment of independent agencies that have replaced nationalization as the preferred mode of governance.

There are a few other important areas where the development of the European political economy departs from the American experience. These include: the scope of market integration, the importance of social policies to maintain political support for market integration, and the heterogeneous currency union. Thus, a crucial difference is the "asymmetrical character" of market integration in both polities (Elazar, 2001: 38). In the US, federal power does not apply equally to all states, as vast swathes of public land in the West are subject to federal ownership. The federal government imposed different constituent units with different conceptions of statehood, rights, and governance, not as a means of recognizing the ethnic or territorial diversity of states, but to meet federal objectives (Tarr, 2008: 15ff). In Europe, key areas are the subject of special exemptions and transition periods, as well as provisions for opting out of particular policies, notably monetary and defense issues and social welfare, and labor mobility in the case of Central and East European states (see Grabbe, 2005; Dyson and Sepos, 2010). While many US states have retained authority over specific issues, the core elements of a common market—including a national currency—are applicable to all constituent units unlike the euro. In Europe, the institutional design of EMU provided for no central budget for counter-cyclical demand management and was established without fiscal capacity. Monetary union has historically been accompanied by fiscal union (Bordo et al., 2011; McNamara, 2011). The sovereign debt crisis has signaled concerns about European economic governance and generated changes in macro-fiscal arrangements leading to a new framework for fiscal coordination (Schelkle, 2009b; Hallerberg, 2014). Finally, there is a lack of EU-wide transfer programs with the EU focused on labor market activation policies through soft law mechanisms. While social welfare and labor protection is primarily provided by national governments, and is generally viewed as part of the postwar settlement between labor and capital, the issue of social protection and wealth redistribution was struck down by the courts as contrary to market integration in the US. The Lochner era was based on the tenets of a commercial republic in which government intervention could not favor special interests, even social efforts to promote minimum wages, since such market adjustment benefited a specific group or faction rather than served a broader public purpose (Gillman, 1993). The US did not fully extend social protection to compensate for changing economic circumstances to mitigate rising class conflict in the early twentieth century in marked difference to the postwar European response to the interwar period of class conflict (Luebbert, 1984).

Legitimacy and Market Integration

The recent surge of interest in comparing the US and EU has generated a wealth of academic and political commentary driven in part by the parallel but distinctive developments in each of their polities (Fabbrini, 2003; Howse and Nicolaïdis, 2001; Parsons and Roberts, 2003; Glencross, 2007). Interest in the development of American federalism has increased among European scholars, in part due to economic, political, and institutional developments in the EU that have shifted "attention from the market-building logic of federalism" to discussions about citizenship, rights, and democracy (Parsons, 2003: 3; Frost et al., 2002; Moravcsik, 2002a; Schmidt, 2004; Howse and Nicolaïdis, 2001; Egan, 2013). The general consensus is that the democratic legitimacy of the EU differs radically from the US.[8] As Moravcsik notes, the main concerns have focused primarily on the weakness of political representation (Schmitter, 2000; Scharpf, 1999a), the absence of strong centralized parties (Hix and Lord, 1997), the ambivalent nature of public support, and the delegation of authority to expert non-majoritarian institutions (Majone, 1994a). By contrast, Weiler stresses that democracy may never have been part of the original vision of the EU, but in the current exercise of public power, there is "weak political accountability" and limited representation where voter preference shapes European governance (Weiler, 2012b: 252ff). These concerns are based in large measure upon the rapid expansion of EU competencies vested in institutions and processes that have drawn criticism for their lack of transparency and accountability. The backlash against European integration had led to increased contestation around both polity and market generating a "constraining dissensus" (Hooghe and Marks, 1997, 2009).[9] As European policies and institutions have become more contested, the loss of access to counter-cyclical monetary and fiscal policies in Europe and the tensions between structural reform, fiscal consolidation, and local models of social protection have generated deep concerns about the constitutional asymmetry in Europe (Scharpf, 2002, 1999a; Alber, 2006; Moses, 2011; cf. Caporaso and Tarrow, 2009).

While the legitimacy of the European polity has assumed particular prominence in the EU, if we compare the situation with the US, the criticism leveled at the European Union needs to be qualified" (Moravcsik, 2002b: 605; cf. Majone, 2009). The fact is that the contemporary American political system is one in which there are some striking resemblances in terms of decreasing public participation and involvement, weakness of centralized parties, and increasing delegation to non-majoritarian institutions (see Moravcsik, 2002b). Even given such limitations, it is still possible to make an argument that the collective outcomes of inter-branch processes in a separation-of-powers system are democratically legitimate. If one sees the original federal design as the solution to the problem of representation, then it seems remarkably similar to current European concerns about legitimacy and democracy. However, such an argument would be that the system has a defensible balance between electorally responsive institutions and other institutions designed to provide checks on power (Beer, 1978). The *Federalist Papers* also make frequent observations along these lines about the American system.

Thus, the history of the US provides an important starting point in terms of the relationship between democracy and legitimacy in sustaining integration. If we are interested in political support for market integration, we will need an assessment of its significance in early America. In this instance, industrial change had a profound effect on modes of governance. These initiatives included electoral innovations and changes to the party system, in order to enhance direct democracy and undermine machine politics. Direct primaries, direct senatorial elections and initiatives, referendums and recalls all emerged as a response to pressures for reform and the demand for a looser system allowing grassroots impulses to have a voice through elected government representatives. Consumers mobilized against the rising cost of living which they attributed to the growing number of corporate monopolies, while farmers joined with urban reformers against the urban immigrant working class which they felt was responsible for the problems stemming from industrial society (Hays, 1995).

These proposals were aimed at making the political system more responsive to the complexities of industrial change, calling for new instruments including more direct democracy, more partisan politics, and more technocratic and efficiency-based economic management. Such pressures stimulated a wide variety of specialized demands rather than developing any capability of reconciling them; interest groups spoke for segments of the private economy that were well organized; and the promotion of efficient and systematic administration sought to shift power and control to experts (Hays, 1995: 199; Wiebe, 1967). Like the debates on the "democratic deficit" in the EU, the various proposals were often distinct and in conflict in addressing the need for political reform to manage the effects of economic change (for the EU debate, see Follesdal and Hix, 2006; Majone, 2009; Moravcsik, 2002a, 2002b).

At the very least, discussions about the legitimacy of market consolidation in the US, are in large measure constituted by the explicit distinction between legitimate social protection and illegitimate class preference (see Gillman, 1999, 1993).[10] The legitimacy of democratic capitalism was maintained through the explicit compromise between markets and social protection (Polanyi, 1944).[11] When antebellum Americans confronted the problems of industrialization and growth, the dominant perspective was of unfettered participation in the market economy as consistent with Republican independence and individual autonomy, but that fails to account for significant illiberal prescriptions surrounding market practices and specific identities or "legal doctrines that were used to constrain or confine development" (Scheiber, 1981: 106; Smith, 1993).[12] So long as public power was not used to impose special burdens or benefits on specific groups or classes then there was broad consensus on supporting market consolidation (Gillman, 1999). In the US, the social consensus on the capacity of open markets to generate socially accept-able outcomes had, by the late nineteenth century, broken down, largely in the face of the emergence of concentrations of private power. As demand for action increased, much of that pressure for change went through the legal system. While courts often conferred a legal advantage on specific businesses relative to competitors, or viewed corporations as individuals with specific rights, labor did not fare as well in protective statutes and expanded rights (Gillman, 1999). Thus, American market integration generated broad resist-ance from elements of society that benefited only marginally or that actually seemed to lose from the advent of rapid industrialization and change. Like the EU, the US faced widespread demands for social and political reform to address the impact of increased market competition. Though they may have taken different forms, concerns about addressing socio-modernization have been an important element in shaping the development and success of market inte-gration, and in both cases there has been a growing contestation around the relationship between polity and market, and the structure of contemporary capitalism.

Globalization and Integration

By analyzing their respective experiences, this book may also help us under-stand the complexities facing transatlantic and other regional integration efforts. The process of integration, it is argued, is becoming an increasingly global phenomenon. Although scholars continue to argue about the depth and reach of globalization, they stress the "increasing interconnectedness and interdependence which is driven by capital flows, technology, investment patterns, growing linkages between societies and more rapid dissemination of ideas" (Laffan, 1998: 235). But while many studies of globalization have suggested that we are moving towards greater levels of economic integration, they have paid much less attention to recognizing that market integration is part of a larger project of institutional development. In other parts of the world, economic integration is proceeding, but political integration is either not desired or so limited that many debates about territoriality, sovereignty, and governance have not yet been addressed (Sbragia, 2004: 93, 2005). The political processes and institutions that evolve—or not—in support of the growth of a single market play an equally important role in the economic successes of the EU and US.

With insights gained from the literature on American Political Development and European integration, it is possible to suggest some fundamental features that affect how, why, and under what circumstances market integration is likely to be successful. Once we begin thinking about possible lessons, we have to be careful about using historical antecedents. But in order to enrich our understanding of the policies and public support required to build and sustain integrated markets, it is possible to discuss some implications of the US and EU experience for regional and global integration. Both cases are examples of regional integration in which the scope and depth of market integration, as well as the level of institutionalization have been marked by "institutional creativity" that allows for "many options for the organization of political authority" (Elazar as quoted in Sbragia, 1992: 261).

With the benefit of the cases in the previous chapters, we can suggest some generic market characteristics that may help us understand why and how they achieved closer economic integration. At this level, however, we are not accounting for sector-specific or country-specific features. Nonetheless, at the level of overall patterns, three features associated with market-building stand out: political mobilization and representation, compliance and enforcement, and distributional and welfare implications.

Political Mobilization and Representation

The issue of political mobilization and representation is a crucial factor in determining acceptance of and support for integration. In the US, nation and democracy reinforced each other, long before the consolidation of a federal state and a modern economy (Fabbrini, 2002: 15, 2004). While (limited) electoral democracy developed in the nineteenth century in the US, thus deepening the democratic shape of the national identity, the EU has long developed without much direct involvement from European citizens. This has resulted in a so-called "democratic deficit," as the integration process has largely been technocratic and elite driven, thereby suffering from a lack of collective European identity. Thus "representative democracy is viewed as more robust at the national level, so that the EU is viewed as undemocratic in comparison with its constituent member states" (Sbragia, 2004, 2003). The increasing lack of legitimacy among the populace of the EU is also of great importance to the member states as issues of integration have become a significant factor in the evaluation of national governments as well (Laffan, 1998: 247 passim). Yet in the nineteenth century, intensified sectional divisions, increases in urbanization and immigration, and repeated cycles of economic boom and bust helped to fuel an anxious desire for political reform.

The process of market-building clearly has implications for domestic politics and national sovereignty as it redefines relationships between ideologically- and territorially-based interests. In both the US and the EU, the scope of participation has widened as a variety of interest groups have mobilized to use their influence to provide benefits to strategic constituencies. The influence of civil society on decision-making is an important factor in explaining the momentum of the single market (Cowles, 1995; Young and Wallace, 2000). Some groups redefined their goals in response to the changing economic circumstances, whereas others were slow to mobilize and exert their influence on the political process. The organization of collective action—social classes, the organization and mobilization of labor and capital, and other forms of interest articulation—are crucial means by which groups can obtain collective benefits that may result in their acquiescence, support, or cooperation with the state in implementing and steering policy change.

In both the US and the EU, the political realities of a strong territorially-based identity led both polities to seek parity between different territorial interests. In both cases no one state had a preponderance of power in the system, which meant that no one state could impose its preference. The issue of the respective power of small and large states is undoubtedly a key factor in understanding the efforts to address concerns about the political and economic power that large states wield as a matter of course in their respective polities (see also Sbragia, 2005: 94–5, 2003). As a result, the process of integration is a compromise between market integration and territorial autonomy, in which the representation of territory plays a crucial role in the relationship between democratic accountability, governance, and markets in the US and EU. Since market integration affects the internal consolidation of political power, by shaping patterns of political mobilization and institutional development, issues of cleavage management may well be key factors in how states can succeed in creating broadly supported integrated markets (see Bensel 1990, 1984, 2000). The nineteenth century was a period of rapid transition. Intensified sectional divisions, increases in urbanization and immigration, and repeated cycles of economic boom and bust helped to fuel an anxious desire for political reforms, caused Americans to confront interlocking narratives of "prosperity and progress" on the one hand, and "counter-narratives of loss, frustration, and dependence," on the other (Larson, 2010: 98). Like contemporary events in Europe, the impact of economic distress created the foundation for new institutions to deal with destructive competition.

Enforcement and Compliance

Both single markets are highly regulated economic and social systems. Since regulations constitute and define the market, they have elicited a great deal of attention in terms of their costs and benefits. Yet their effectiveness also requires attention to issues of implementation and enforcement so that the benefits of market consolidation can be realized. This has meant that market management issues are salient ones, and efforts to make the single market work effectively have to be squarely placed on the political agenda. In the US and EU case, there are well-defined legal and judicial mechanisms that serve to establish contractual obligations on states to meet specific requirements. Yet concerns about the effectiveness of governmental performance raise important considerations about both the need to distribute functions efficiently between different governments while responding to the imperatives of representation and diversity. The effects of interstate rivalry in the US and EU can generate pressure to reduce social and economic legislation to the lowest common denominator. To be sure, positive guarantees of minimal common standards may demand uniformity to ensure a level playing field. But there are strong pressures in each case towards diffused governmental power to encourage diversity of ideas and innovation. Leadership by several states in certain policy areas such as environmental policy, tax policy, and welfare policy often leads to policy learning and policy transfer among the constituent elements of a federal system that can provide substantial impact upon the system as a whole (Walker, 1969). Both polities have struggled with the challenges created by the pressures for convergence, and the idiosyncratic and distinctive features of their respective national or subnational political economies. In the US and EU respectively the uniform state movement and in the EU harmonization both promoted the simultaneous adoption of laws, but were time-consuming and not able to achieve substantial results (Nugent, 1999; Egan, 2001; Johnson, 2009: 92).

However, the successes and failures of such regulatory strategies led to alternative modes of governance including reciprocity, mutual recognition, and policy diffusion, as well as soft law mechanisms such as voluntary coordination, informal networks, and intergovernmental collaboration (Egan, 2012b). Thus, in both cases, the US and EU have adopted market surveillance mechanisms to deal with the pressures of interstate competition through a mixture of judicial and non-judicial remedies to improve the functioning and operation of the single market (Kelemen, 2011). As both opted for the institutionalization of new forms of governance to regulate markets, from state commissions to labor bureaus, and anti-trust authorities to health and environment inspectorates, the variety of legislative acts and regulatory commissions aimed at regulating economic and social activities has focused attention on the centrality of enforcement and compliance. However, this institution-alized expansion of state activity did not mean that the "laws passed were always effectively enforced" (Gerstle, 2009: 70).

Distributional Preferences and Welfare Gains

While economic regionalism privileges trade and competition, the distribu-tional stakes and outcomes are key factors in explaining the continued com-mitment to economic policy coordination (see Pastor, 2001). The progressive expansion of activities brings into sharp focus the costs and benefits of eco-nomic liberalization across states and societies. A key factor in generating political support and legitimacy for economic integration is the pursuit of an acceptable distribution of tangible benefits. While the US and EU have responded with a number of social policy initiatives, they have also struck down features that are deemed incompatible with the development of the single market.[13] The process of economic integration has affected and shaped social policies, as the responses of social actors to market developments as well as the cumulative effect of judicial intervention have emerged as part of the process of market-building itself. As Scharpf (2002) and subsequently Moses (2011) have argued, the decoupling of social protection and market integra-tion in Europe, made more visible by recent legal cases,[14] suggests that secur-ing state-based redistributive and social protection in an integrated market is difficult due to the trade-offs between economic growth and social protection, and the pressures of regulatory competition and freedom of establishment and freedom of movement. But the perceived economic effects and concerns about the implications of market liberalization and market competition have also created a patchwork of benefits tied to market citizenship, resulting in disparate welfare benefits, categorical forms of assistance, and durable inequalities, that makes a common social policy hard to deliver. In this respect, the relationship between economic rights and social rights needs to be considered since viable and sustainable integration is likely to be more successful if economic growth is fairly distributed (Maduro, 2000; Jones, 2006).

This has come to the fore in the current climate where the past five years have forced the EU to confront many challenges about the nature of integra-tion in terms of its identity, solidarity, and direction. There is genuine concern about the economic situation in Europe, focusing mainly on the sovereign debt crisis and the efforts to tackle burgeoning public deficits through growth and austerity measures. But the result is a steady fall in labor income as a proportion of national income; differing wage trends have led to greater inequality, and labor market reforms have fostered part-time or temporary work which has further depressed wages (Tilford, 2010, 2011, 2012). Internally, the region is experiencing market fatigue, with the period of unprecedented investment and trade that accompanied the 1992 project being replaced by a situation where the benefits are less apparent. And while monetary integration built upon the single market to maximize access to international liquidity and stabilize exchange rates, the subsequent crisis beginning in 2008 and 2009 led to tightened lending conditions, reduced liquidity, increased unemployment and a slowdown in output growth. For many, the single market is all but forgotten. The virtual disappearance of discourse on the single market from the politics of many member states suggests that it simply left the public's radar screen.[15] Still the EU has become the target of lightening criticism, blamed for the downturn in the economy, as public opinion tends to sour on trade when economies contract, and opposition has also emerged against further market liberalization. The real problem is that governance did not keep pace with the integration process. The member states did not provide mechanisms for dealing with or alleviating the macroeconomic crisis, with the EU initially stumbling badly, as several countries stood on the precipice of bankruptcy. Though the lack of capacity in terms of the remit of the European Central Bank initially led to criticism within the financial markets, there are fears of losing mutual gains from a broader European market and a concern about the impact on wider economic policies (Jones, 2012).

Without doubt, the crippling debt woes in Europe have generated significant attention, both within Europe and globally. Drawing on the experience of the US, we should not be surprised by European developments. Although historians disagree about whether wage gaps became a source of labor unrest in the US, contributing to the rise of third parties such as populists and progressives, the recent growth of diverse radical right-wing parties in Europe has some parallels. Not only was there voter disaffection towards governing parties, but the US also saw a backlash against foreign immigration in the nineteenth century when the surplus of unskilled labor put downward pressure on wages and labor markets (Atack et al., 2004; Margo, 2000). And debt problems also forced US states to create credible long-term commitments that provided stronger safeguards through constitutional amendments (Dove, 2012). By 1865, interest-bearing public debt stood at $2.2 billion, although by the end of the century the government's financial situation had improved, and the union had been preserved.

As Europe addresses the current crisis, with sharp divergences in performance, uneven growth and productivity, and contradictory preferences, there are deep concerns about the solidarity, legitimacy, and outcome of European integration (Jones, 2012). While addressing the problems of economic governance through similar procedural safeguards, the roles and responsibilities of different levels of government are in flux and new institutions are evolving. It is interesting that the US in the nineteenth century also sought to strengthen institutions and enact constitutional constraints to ensure that mistakes made by states would not be repeated. Whether integration occurs by stealth or design, state capacity (in various guises) is important in removing constraints on mobility and market access while also resolving fiscal and monetary coordination problems across multiple jurisdictions to create a durable single market. Many of these governance issues that are ongoing within the EU, and resolved within the US, will be examined anew by other efforts at regional integration. There is arguably a richness and depth of experience in these two cases in which efforts at market integration are rooted in the reconfiguration of state power in response to changing economic conditions, buttressed by the role of law in providing foundations, tools, and frameworks for economic regulation, and the mobilization of interests across regions, industries, and social groups to shape social and economic outcomes.

Notes

1. The term "jural state" is used in the US context by William Novak, and applied to the EU case.
2. The EU has been variously described as a regional state (Schmidt, 2004), consociational state (Bogaards and Crepaz, 2003), regulatory state (Majone, 1996, 1997), post-modern state (Caporaso, 1996), and federal state (Sbragia, 1992a).
3. I am grateful for the roundtable discussions as part of the IIE/Syracuse project "Lessons for a Globalizing World: European and US Experiences at Market Integration," organized by Ellen Frost, David Richardson, Craig Parsons, and Michael Schneider. The quote is from their non-published original memo. See also Parsons and Roberts (2003).
4. However, many barriers to a single market remain as the chapters in this book illustrate. Examples include consumer insurance, taxation, and financial services.
5. See the account in Karl Polanyi's *Great Transformation* about the re-embedding of the market system.
6. Among the best scholarship is Moravcsik (1998); Milward (1984, 1992). See also Sandholtz and Zysman (1989) and Young and Wallace (2000).
7. I am grateful to one of the reviewers from Oxford University Press for these comments.
8. For a challenge to this perspective, see the excellent work of Moravcsik, 2002a. This paragraph draws extensively on his analysis and comparison but see also the response from Follesdal and Hix (2006) and recent commentary by Weiler (2012b).
9. One could argue a similar development in the US in the post-Civil War period largely as a response to the forces of industrialization that generated the dramatic upheavals and protest over the distribution of resources and the terms and conditions under which market forces operated.

10. Gillman is highlighting the importance of general welfare rather than particularistic interests or individual rights, and the irony that the expansion of modern state power led to increased judicial responsibility about which freedoms where to be preferred—so called balancing—came in response to changes in market practices and concerns for specific protection.
11. Polanyi's "double movement" in *The Great Transformation*.
12. Hurst's "release of energy" is relevant here.
13. Cases *Lochner* v. *New York*, Case C-341/05, 1905; *Laval un Partneri Ltd*, ECR 2007, I-11767; Case C-346/06, *Rüffert*, ECR 2008, I-1989; Case C-438/05, *Viking*, ECR 2007, I-10779.
14. C-341/05 *Laval un Partneri*, ECR 2007 I-11767; C-346/06 Rüffert, ECR 2008 I-1989 and C-438/05 The International Transport Workers' Federation and The Finnish Seamen's Union, ECR 2007 I-10779.
15. The January 2013 speech by David Cameron is quite notable for its emphasis on the centrality of the single market as a rationale for membership.

Appendix

Much of the discussion in this book is based on the original treaty articles, given that the project spans from the foundation of the EC to the present EU.

APPENDIX 1

General Treaty of Rome Provisions and their Subsequent Treaty of Lisbon Counterparts

Article 2 The Treaty of Rome, officially the Treaty establishing the European Economic Community (TEEC)

The Community shall have as its task, by establishing a common market and progressively approximating the economic policies of Member States, to promote throughout the Community a harmonious development of economic activities, a continuous and balanced expansion, an increase in stability, an accelerated raising of the standard of living and closer relations between the States belonging to it.

Article 3 (TEEC)

For the purposes set out in Article 2, the activities of the Community shall include, as provided in this Treaty and in accordance with the timetable set out therein:

(a) the elimination, as between Member States, of customs duties and of quantitative restrictions on the import and export of goods, and of all other measures having equivalent effect;

(b) the establishment of a common customs tariff and of a common commercial policy towards third countries;

(c) the abolition, as between Member States, of obstacles to freedom of movement for persons, services and capital;

(d) the adoption of a common policy in the sphere of agriculture;

(e) the adoption of a common policy in the sphere of transport;

    (f) the institution of a system ensuring that competition in the common market is not distorted;

    (g) the application of procedures by which the economic policies of Member States can be coordinated and disequilibria in their balances of payments remedied;

    (h) the approximation of the laws of Member States to the extent required for the proper functioning of the common market;

    (i) the creation of a European Social Fund in order to improve employment opportunities for workers and to contribute to the raising of their standard of living;

    (j) the establishment of a European Investment Bank to facilitate the economic expansion of the Community by opening up fresh resources;

    (k) the association of the overseas countries and territories in order to increase trade and to promote jointly economic and social development.

Article 3 Treaty on European Union (TEU)

The new catalogue of aims contained in Article 3 TEU simply states: "the Union shall establish an internal market" and does not make reference to competition policy provisions on distorted competition; however, despite its exclusion from Article 3 and its placement in a TFEU Protocol (No 27) on the internal market and competition, the Court has ruled that TFEU Protocol (No 27) on the internal market and competition, and Article 3 are relevant to ensure competition is not distorted in internal market.

APPENDIX 2

Changes in the Treaty of Lisbon (TFEU) and Renumbering of Internal Market Policies: Comparison with *Existing* Treaty on European Community (TEC) and Treaty on European Union (TEU)

Title I: Internal Market

Article 26 (22a): In substance the same as Article 14 TEC. New reference to the aim of ensuring the functioning of the internal market.

Article 27 (22b): In substance the same as Article 15 TEC.

Title II: Free Movement of Goods

Article 28 (23): In substance the same as Article 23 TEC.
Article 29 (24): Unchanged from Article 24 TEC.

Chapter 3: Prohibition of Quantitative Restrictions between Member States
Article 34 (28): Unchanged from Article 28 TEC.
Article 35 (29): Unchanged from Article 29 TEC.
Article 36 (30): Unchanged from Article 30 TEC.
Article 37 (31): Unchanged from Article 31 TEC.

Title IV: Free Movement of Persons, Services, and Capital

Chapter 1: Workers
Article 45 (39): Unchanged from Article 39 TEC.

Article 46 (40): In substance, the same as Article 40 TEC.

Article 47 (41): Unchanged from Article 41 TEC.

Article 48 (42): Draws on Article 42 TEC. Adds clarification regarding application to both employed and self-employed, moves decision-making to QMV, and introduces an emergency brake procedure.

Chapter 2: Rights of Establishment
Article 49 (43): Unchanged from Article 43 TEC.

Article 50 (44): In substance the same as Article 44 TEC.

Article 51 (45): Draws on Article 45 TEC. QMV already applies, decision-making moves to co-decision.

Article 52 (46): In substance the same as Article 46 TEC.

Article 53 (47): Draws on Article 47 TEC. Certain elements are moved to QMV.

Article 54 (48): Unchanged from Article 48 TEC.

Article 55 (48a): In substance the same as Article 294 TEC.

Chapter 3: Services
Article 56 (49): Draws on Article 49 TEC. QMV already applies, decision-making moves to co-decision regarding extension to third-country nationals.

Article 57 (50): In substance the same as Article 50 TEC.

Article 58 (51): Unchanged from Article 51 TEC.

Article 59 (52): Draws on Article 52 TEC. QMV already applies, decision-making moves to co-decision.

Article 60 (53): In substance, the same as Article 53 TEC.

Article 61 (54): Unchanged from Article 54 TEC.

Article 62 (55): Unchanged from Article 55 TEC.

Chapter 4: Capital and Payments

Article 63 (56): Unchanged from Article 56 TEC.

Article 64 (57): Draws on Article 57 TEC. Paragraph 2 QMV already applies, decision-making moves to co-decision, but paragraph 3 makes clear that the EP will only be consulted on specified measures that require unanimity in the Council.

Article 65 (58): Paragraphs 1 to 3 unchanged from Article 58 TEC. Paragraph 4, on authorization by unanimity of restrictive tax measures towards third countries, is new.

Article 66 (59): Unchanged from Article 59 TEC.

Title VI: Transport

Article 90 (70): In substance the same as Article 70 TEC.

Article 91 (71): Draws on Article 71 TEC. Co-decision applied to paragraph 2.

Article 92 (72): In substance the same as Article 72 TEC.

Article 93 (73): In substance the same as Article 73 TEC.

Article 94 (73): In substance the same as Article 74 TEC.

Article 95 (75): In substance the same as Article 75 TEC, with a new requirement to consult the EP.

Article 96 (76): Unchanged from Article 76 TEC.

Article 97 (77): Unchanged from Article 77 TEC.

Article 98 (78): In substance the same as Article 78 TEC, with a new power for the Council, by QMV, to repeal this provision.

Article 99 (79): In substance the same as Article 79 TEC.

Article 100 (80): Draws on Article 80 TEC. QMV already applies, co-decision applied to paragraph 2.

Compiled by Robertus Anders based on the Foreign and Commonwealth Office's "A Comparative Table of the Current EC and EU Treaties as Amended by the Treaty of Lisbon," London: 2008.

Bibliography

Abbati, C. D. 1987. *Transport and European Integration*. Luxembourg: Office for Official Publications for the European Communities.

Abbott, A. 1988. *The System of Professions: An Essay on the Division of Expert Labor*. Chicago: University of Chicago Press.

Abel, A. S. 1947a. "Commerce Regulation before Gibbons v. Ogden: Interstate Transportation Facilities." *North Carolina Law Review* 25 (2): 121–71.

Abel, A. S. 1947b. "Commerce Regulation before Gibbons v. Ogden: Trade and Traffic Part I." *Brooklyn Law Review* 14 (1): 38–77.

Abel, A. S. 1948. "Commerce Regulation before Gibbons v. Ogden: Trade and Traffic Part II." *Brooklyn Law Review* 14 (2): 215–43.

Abel, R. L. 1981. "Toward a Political Economy of Lawyers." *Wisconsin Law Review* 1981 (5): 1117–87.

Advancing Regulatory Reform in Europe: A joint statement of the Irish, Dutch, Luxembourg, UK, Austrian, and Finnish Presidencies of the European Union, December 7, 2007. Available at <http://www.betterregulation.dk/graphics/EU/Jointstatement7December.doc> accessed December 29, 2013.

Agence Europe. 1970. February 13, Brussels.

Agence Europe. 2013. September 28, Brussels.

Agence Europe. 2014. April 15, Brussels.

Alber, J. 2006. "The European Social Model and the United States." *European Union Politics* 7 (3): 393–419.

Allen, D. 2000. "Cohesion and Structural Funds: Transfers and Trade-offs." In *Policymaking in the European Union*, 4th edn., ed. H. Wallace and W. Wallace. Oxford: Oxford University Press.

Alter, K. J. 1998. "'Who Are the 'Masters of the Treaty'?: European Governments and the European Court of Justice." *International Organization* 52: 121–48.

Alter, K. J. 2001. *Establishing the Supremacy of European Law: The Making of an International Rule of Law in Europe*. Oxford: Oxford University Press.

Alter, K. J. 2009. "Jurist Advocacy Movements in Europe: The Role of Euro-law Associations in European Integration (1953–1975)." In *The European Court's Political Power: Selected Essays*, ed. K. J. Alter. New York: Oxford University Press.

Alter, K. J. 2010. *The European Court's Political Power: Selected Essays*. Oxford: Oxford University Press.

Alter, K. J., and S. Meneuir-Aitsahalia. 1994. "Judicial Politics in the European Community: European Integration and the Pathbreaking Cassis de Dijon Decision." *Comparative Political Studies* 26 (4): 535–61.

Amato, G., and L. L. Laudati (eds) 2001. *The Anticompetitive Impact of Regulation.* Cheltenham, UK: Edward Elgar.

Anderson, G. (ed.) 2012. *Internal Markets and Multi-level Governance: The Experience of the European Union, Australia, Canada, Switzerland, and the United States.* Oxford: Oxford University Press.

Ansell, C. K., and G. Di Palma. 2004. *Restructuring Territoriality: Europe and the United States Compared.* Cambridge, UK: Cambridge University Press.

Apeldoorn Van B. 2000. "Transnational Class Agency and European Governance: The Case of the European Round Table of Industrialists." *New Political Economy* 5 (2): 157–81.

Armstrong, K. A. 1993. "Regulatory Regimes within the Single Market." Paper presented at the annual EUSA conference, May 27–29, Washington, DC. Available at <http://aei.pitt.edu/7102/> accessed December 28, 2013.

Armstrong, K. A., and S. Bulmer. 1998. *The Governance of the Single European Market.* Manchester: Manchester University Press.

Ascher, B. 2004. "Toward a Borderless Market for Professional Services." American Antitrust Institute. <www.antitrustinstitute.org/node/10415> accessed December 26, 2013.

Aspinwall, M. 1995. "International Integration or Internal Politics: Anatomy of a Single Market Measure." *Journal of Common Market Studies* 33 (4): 475–99.

Aspinwall, M. 1999. "Planes, Trains and Automobiles: Transport Governance in the European Union." In *The Transformation of Governance in the European Union*, ed. Beate Kohler-Koch and Rainer Eising. London: Routledge.

Atack, J., F. Bateman, and R. A. Margo. 2004. "Skill Intensity and Rising Wage Dispersion in Nineteenth-century American Manufacturing." *Journal of Economic History* 64 (1): 172–92.

Atack, J., F. Bateman, and W. N. Parker. 2000. "Northern Agriculture and the Westward Movement." In *The Cambridge Economic History of the United States,* ii: *The Long Nineteenth Century*, ed. S. L. Engerman and R. E. Gallman. Cambridge, UK: Cambridge University Press.

Atack, J., and P. Passell. 1994. *A New Economic View of American History: From Colonial Times to 1940*, 2nd edn. New York: W. W. Norton.

Baker, S. L. 1984. "Physician Licensure Laws in the United States, 1865–1915." *Journal of the History of Medicine and Allied Sciences* 39 (2): 173–97.

Bakker, A. F. P. 1994. *The Liberalization of Capital Movements in Europe: The Monetary Committee and Financial Integration 1958–1994.* Dordrecht and Boston: Kluwer Academic.

Balla, S. J. 2001. "Interstate Professional Associations and the Diffusion of Policy Innovations." *American Politics Research* 29 (3): 221–45.

Balleisen, E. J. 2009. "Private Cops on the Fraud Beat: The Limits of American Business Self-regulation, 1895–1932." *Business History Review* 83: 113–60.

Balogh, B. 2009. *A Government out of Sight: The Mystery of National Authority in Nineteenth-century America.* Cambridge, UK: Cambridge University Press.

Balta, N. and J. Delgado. 2009. "Home Bias and Market Integration in the EU." *CESifo Economic Studies* 55 (1): 110–44.

Baltensperger, E., and J. Dermine. 1990. "European Banking: Prudential and Regulatory Issues." In *European Banking in the 1990s*, ed. J. Dermine. Oxford: Blackwell.

Barnard, C. C. 2000. "Social Dumping Revisited: Lessons from Delaware." *European Law Review* 25: 57–78.

Barnard, C. C. 2004. *The Substantive Law of the EU: The Four Freedoms*. Oxford: Oxford University Press.

Barnard, C., and J. Scott. 2002. *The Law of the European Market: Unpacking the Premises*. Oxford and Portland, OR: Hart Publishing.

Bartolini, S. 1993. "On Time and Comparative Research." *Journal of Theoretical Politics* 5 (2): 131–67.

Barzanti, S. 1965. *The Underdeveloped Areas within the Common Market*. Princeton, NJ: Princeton University Press.

Basch, A. 1965. *Capital Markets of the European Economic Community: Problems of Integration*. Ann Arbor, MI: Bureau of Business Research, Graduate School of Business Administration, University of Michigan.

Bateman, F., and T. Weiss. 1975. "Comparative Regional Development in Antebellum Manufacturing." *Journal of Economic History* 35 (1): 182–208.

Battilossi, S. 2000a. "Financial Innovation and the Golden Ages of International Banking: 1890–1931 and 1958–81." *Financial History Review* 7: 141–75.

Battilossi S. 2000b. "Workshop Report: Central Banking and Economic Interdependence in the 1960s. A Workshop at the European University Institute." *Bulletin: Newsletter from the EABH* 1: 28–30.

Battilossi, S. 2002a. "Banking with Multinationals: British Clearing Banks and the Euromarkets' Challenge, 1958–1976." in S. Battilossi and Y. Cassis eds. *European Banks and the American Challenge: Competition and Cooperation in International Banking under Bretton Woods*. Oxford: Oxford University Press.

Battilossi, S. 2002b. "International Banking and the American Challenge in Historical Perspective" in S. Battilossi and Y. Cassis eds. *European Banks and the American Challenge: Competition and Cooperation in International Banking under Bretton Woods*. Oxford: Oxford University Press.

Beard, C. A. 1935 [1913]. *An Economic Interpretation of the Constitution of the United States*. New York: Macmillan.

Beard, C. A., and M. R. Beard. 1927. *The Rise of American Civilization*. New York: Macmillan.

Beer, S. H. 1965. British Politics in the Collectivist Age. New York: Alfred A. Knopf.

Beer, S. H. 1978. "Federalism, Nationalism, and Democracy in America." *The American Political Science Review* 72 (1): 9–21.

Bell, D. S., and C. Lord. 1998. *Transnational Parties in the European Union*. London: Ashgate.

Bensel, R. F. 1984. *Sectionalism and American Political Development, 1880–1980*. Madison, WI: University of Wisconsin Press.

Bensel, R. F. 1990. *Yankee Leviathan: The Origins of Central State Authority in America, 1859–1877*. Cambridge, UK: Cambridge University Press.

Bensel, R. F. 2000. *The Political Economy of American Industrialization, 1877–1900*. Cambridge, UK: Cambridge University Press.

Berk, G. 1990. "Constituting Corporations and Markets: Railroads in Gilded Age Politics." *Studies in American Political Development* 4: 130–68.

Berk, G. 1994. *Alternative Tracks The Constitution of American Industrial Order, 1865–1917*. Baltimore, MD: Johns Hopkins University Press.

Berman, G. A. 1994. "Taking Subsidiarity Seriously: Federalism in the European Community and the United States." *Columbia Law Review* 94: 332–455.

Bertola, G., and L. Mola. 2009. "Services Provision and Temporary Mobility: Freedoms and Regulation in the EU." CEPR Discussion Paper DP7350. London: Centre for Economic Policy Research.

Bertrand, R. 1956. "The European Common Market Proposal." *International Organization* 10 (4): 559–74.

Bieber, R. et al., 1988. *1992: One European Market? A Critical Analysis of the Commission's Internal Market Strategy*. Florence: European University Institute.

Bisignano, J. 1992. "Banking in the European Economic Community: Structure, Competition, and Public Policy" in G. G. Kaufmann ed. *Banking Structures in Major Countries*. Netherlands: Kluwer Academic.

Bloomfield, M. 1968. "Law vs. Politics: The Self-image of the American Bar (1830–1860)." *American Journal of Legal History* 12 (4): 306–23.

Bloomfield, M. 1976. "Law vs. Politics: The Self-Image of the American Bar (1830–1860)." In *Essays in Nineteenth-Century American Legal History*, ed. Wythe Holt. Westport, CT: Greenwood Press.

Bodenhorn, H. 1992. "Capital Mobility and Financial Integration in Antebellum America." *Journal of Economic History* 52 (3): 585–610.

Bodenhorn, H. 1997. "Private Banking in Antebellum Virginia: Thomas Branch and Sons of Petersburg." *Business* 71 (4): 513–42.

Bodenhorn, H. 2000. *A History of Banking in Antebellum America: Financial Markets and Economic Development in an Era of National-building*. New York: Cambridge University Press.

Bodenhorn, H. 2003. *State Banking in Early America: A New Economic History*. New York: Oxford University Press.

Boerger-De Smedt, A. 2012. "Negotiating the Foundations of European Law, 1950–57: The Legal History of the Treaties of Rome and Paris." *Contemporary European History* 21 (3): 339–56.

Bogaards, M., and M. M. L. Crepaz. 2002. "Consociational Interpretations of the European Union." *European Union Politics* 3 (3): 357–81.

Bolkestein, R. 2002. "Integration in the EU Financial Market and Beyond." Speech American Enterprise Institute Washington DC, May.

Bolitho, A. 1982. *The European Economy: Growth and Crisis*. Oxford: Oxford University Press.

Bordo, M. D., A. Markiewicz, and L. Jonung. 2011. "A Fiscal Union for the Euro: Some Lessons from History." National Bureau of Economic Research Working Paper 17380. Rochester, NY: National Bureau of Economic Research.

Börzel, T. A., and M. O. Hosli. 2003. "Brussels Between Bern and Berlin: Comparative Federalism Meets the European Union." *Governance* 16 (2): 179–202.

Börzel, T. A. and T. Risse, 2010. "Governance without a State: Can it Work?" *Regulation and Governance* 4 (2): 113–34.

Brazier, M., J. Lovecy, and M. Moran. 1993. *Professional Regulation and the Single European Market: A Study of the Regulation of Doctors and Lawyers in England and France.* Manchester: University of Manchester, [mimeo].

Bright, C. C. 1984. "The State in the United States during the Nineteenth Century." In *Statemaking and Social Movements: Essays in History and Theory,* ed. C. C. Bright and S. Harding. Ann Arbor, MI: University of Michigan Press.

Brock, W. R. 1984. *Investigation and Responsibility: Public Responsibility in the United States, 1865–1900.* Cambridge, UK: Cambridge University Press.

Brockman, N. 1966. "The National Bar Association, 1888–1893: The Failure of Early Bar Federation." *American Journal of Legal History* 10 (2): 122–7.

Bruchey, S. 1990. *Enterprise: The Dynamic Economy of a Free People.* Cambridge, MA: Harvard University Press.

Brusse, W. A. 1997. *Tariffs, Trade, and European Integration, 1947–1957: From Study Group to Common Market.* New York: St. Martin's Press.

Brusse, W. A., and R. T. Griffiths. 1997. "The Incidence of Manufacturing Cartels in Post-War Europe." In *Cartels and Market Management in the Post-War World,* ed. C. Morelli. Business History Occasional Papers No. 1. London: LSE.

Bryan, W. J. 1896. "Cross of Gold." Speech Democratic Convention Chicago.

Bryant, K. L., Jr., and H. C. Dethloff. 1990. *A History of American Business,* 2nd edn. Engelwood Cliffs, NJ: Prentice-Hall.

Buch, C. M., and R. P. Heinrich. 2002. "European Financial Integration and Corporate Governance." Research Notes Working Paper Series no. 2. Frankfurt: Deutsche Bank. Available at <https://www.econstor.eu/dspace/bitstream/10419/40281/1/356079090.pdf> accessed February 9, 2014.

Buiges, P., F. Ilzkvitz, and J. F. Lebrun. 1990. *The Impact of the Internal Market by Industrial Sector: The Challenge for the Member States.* Brussels: Commission of the European Communities.

Büthe, T., and W. Mattli. 2011. *The New Global Rulers: The Privatization of Regulation in the World Economy.* Princeton, NJ: Princeton University Press.

Calvert, T. H. 1980 [1907]. *Regulation of Commerce under the Federal Constitution.* Littleton, CO: Rothman.

Cameron, D. R. 1998. "Creating Supranational Authority in Monetary and Exchange-rate Policy: The Source and Effects of EMU." In *European Integration and Supranational Governance,* ed. W. Sandholtz and A. Stone Sweet. Oxford: Oxford University Press.

Camerra-Rowe, P. 1994. "New Roads of Political Influence: The Response of German and British Road Haulage Firms to 1992 Single European Market." International Conference of Europeanists, Chicago [unpublished mimeo].

Campbell, B. C. 1992. "Federalism, State Action, and 'Critical Episodes' in the Growth of American Government." *Social Science History* 16 (4): 561–77.

Campbell, J. L., J. R. Hollingsworth, and L. N. Lindberg (eds) 1991. *Governance of the American Economy.* Cambridge, UK: Cambridge University Press.

Camps, M. 1959. *The Free Trade Area Negotiations,* xviii. Center of International Studies, Woodrow Wilson School of Public and International Affairs, Princeton University.

Capelli, F. 1993. "The Free Movement of Professionals in the European Community." In *Free Movement of Persons in Europe: Legal Problems and Experiences*, ed. H. G. Schermers, et al. Dordrecht, the Netherlands: Martinus Nijhoff.

Caporaso, J. A. 1996. "The European Union and Forms of State: Westphalian, Regulatory or Post-Modern?" *JCMS: Journal of Common Market Studies* 34 (1): 29–52.

Caporaso, J. A. 1997. "Does the European Union Represent an N of 1?" *ECSA Review* 10 (3): 1–5.

Caporaso, J. A., and M. Kim. 2009. "The Dual Nature of European Identity: Subjective Awareness and Coherence." *Journal of European Public Policy* 16 (1): 9–42.

Caporaso, J. A., and A. Stone Sweet. 1998. "From Free Trade to Supranational Polity: The European Court and Integration." In *European Integration and Supranational Governance*, ed. W. Sandholtz and A. Stone Sweet. New York: Oxford University Press.

Caporaso, J. A., and S. Tarrow. 2009. "Polanyi in Brussels: Supranational Institutions and the Transnational Embedding of Markets." *International Organization* 63 (4): 593–620.

Cappelletti, M., M. Seccombe, and J. H. H. Weiler (eds) 1986. *Integration through Law: Europe and the American Federal Experience*, i: *Methods, Tools, and Institutions*. Berlin: Walter De Gruyter.

Carlton, D. L. 1990. "The Revolution from Above: The National Market and the Beginnings of Industrialization in North Carolina." *Journal of American History* 77 (2): 445–75.

Carstensen, F. No Date. "Capitalism." University of Connecticut [unpublished mimeo].

Cath, I. G. F. 1993. "Free Movement of Legal Persons" In *Free Movement of Persons in Europe: Legal Problems and Experiences*, ed. H. G. Schermers, et al. Dordrecht, The Netherlands: Martinus Nijhoff.

CCBE. 2006. "CCBE Economic Submission to Commission Progress Report on Competition in Professional Services." Available at <http://www.oa.pt/upl/%7B1ad759e7-dd10-4879-992b-eb6ed4b85ccf%7D.pdf> accessed July 30, 2014.

Cecchini, P., M. Catinat, and A. Jacquemin. 1988. *The European Challenge, 1992: The Benefits of a Single Market*, trans. J. Robinson. Aldershot: Wildwood House.

Cerny, P. G. (ed.) 1993. *Finance and World Politics: Markets, Regimes, and States in the Post-Hegemonic Era*. Aldershot: Edward Elgar.

Chandler, A. D., Jr. 1962. *Strategy and Structure: Chapters in the History of the American Industrial Enterprise*. Cambridge, MA: MIT Press.

Chandler, A. D., Jr. 1978. "The United States: Evolution of Enterprise." In *The Cambridge Economic History of Europe*, vii: *The Industrial Economies: Capital, Labour, and Enterprise. Part 2: The United States, Japan, and Russia*, ed. P. Mathias and M. M. Postan. Cambridge, UK: Cambridge University Press.

Chandler, A. D., Jr., and S. Salsbury. 1968. "The Railroads: Innovators in Modern Business Administration." In *The Changing Economic Order: Readings in American Business and Economic History*, ed. A. D. Chandler, Jr., S. Bruchey, and L. Galambos. New York: Harcourt, Brace and World.

Chandler, A. D., Jr., S. Bruchey, and L. Galambos (eds) 1968. *The Changing Economic Order: Readings in American Business and Economic History*. New York: Harcourt, Brace and World.

Chang, M. 2009. *Monetary Integration in the European Union*. Basingstoke: Palgrave Macmillan.

Chase, K. A. 2005. *Trading Blocs: States, Firms, and Regions in the World Economy*. Ann Arbor, MI: University of Michigan Press.

Childs, W. R. 2001. "State Regulators and Pragmatic Federalism in the United States, 1889–1945." *Business History Review* 75 (1): 701–38.

Christiansen, T. 1997. "Legitimacy Dilemmas of Supranational Governance: The European Commission between Accountability and Independence." EUI Working Paper Series RSC 97/14. Florence, Italy: European University Institute.

Claessens, S. J. F. J. 2008. *Free Movement of Lawyers in the European Union*. Nijmegen, The Netherlands: Wolf Legal Publishers.

Coen, D. 1997. "The Evolution of the Large Firm as a Political Actor in the European Union." *Journal of European Public Policy* 4 (1): 91–108.

Colchester, N., and D. Buchanan. 1990. *Europower: The Essential Guide to Europe's Economic Transformation in 1992*. New York: Random House.

Conant, L. 2007. "Judicial Politics." In *The SAGE Handbook of European Union Politics*, ed. K. E. Jorgensen, M. A. Pollack, and B. Rosamond. London: SAGE Publications.

Conant, L. 2008. "When Courts Decide: Foreigners' Rights and Social Citizenship in Europe and the US." *European Political Science* 7 (1): 43–51.

Conant, M. 1991. *The Constitution and the Economy: Objective Theory and Critical Commentary*. Norman, OK: University of Oklahoma Press.

Cook, C. M. 1981. *The American Codification Movement: A Study of Antebellum Legal Reform*. Westport, CT: Greenwood Press.

Cooke, F. H. 1908. *The Commerce Clause of the Federal Constitution*. New York: Baker, Voorhees, & Co.

Council of the European Communities' General Programme for the abolition of restrictions on freedom of establishment of December 18, 1961 (OJ No. 2 of 15.1.1962).

Council of the European Communities' General Programme for the abolition of restrictions on freedom to provide services of December 18, 1961, (OJ No. 2 of 15.1.1962).

Countryman, C., B. Scholes, and A. Sakhonchik. 2014. "European Financial Regulations and Reforms: A Comparison with Dodd-Frank Act." Unpublished paper, American University [mimeo].

Cowles, M. G. 1995. "Setting the Agenda for a New Europe: The ERT and EC 1992." *JCMS: Journal of Common Market Studies* 33 (4): 501–26.

Cowles, M. G. 1997. "The Changing Architecture of Big Business." In *Collective Action in the European Union: Interests and the New Politics of Associability*, ed. J. Greenwood and M. Aspinwall. London: Routledge.

Cox, C. and S. Foster, 1990. "The Costs and Benefits of Occupational Regulation." *Federal Trade Commission Bureau of Economics Staff Report*, October.

Craig, P., and G. De Búrca (eds) 2003. *EU Law: Text, Cases, and Material*, 3rd edn. Oxford: Oxford University Press.

Crespy, A., and V. A. Schmidt. 2012. "The Clash of Titans/The White Knight and the Iron Lady: France, Germany, and the Simultaneous Double Game of EMU Reform." Paper presented at the ESCA-Canada Biennial Conference, April 27–28,

Ottawa. Available at <http://web.uvic.ca/ecsac/biennial2012/best-papers/crespy-schmidt-paper.pdf> accessed February 13, 2014.

Crosskey, W. 1953. *Politics and the Constitution in the History of the United States*. Chicago: University of Chicago Press.

Croust, A.-H. 1965. *The Rise of the Legal Profession in America*. Norman, OK: University of Oklahoma Press.

Curzon, G., and V. Curzon. 1970. "Hidden Barriers to International Trade." Thames Essay No. 1, Trade Policy Centre London.

Dahlberg, K. A. 1968. "The EEC Commission and the Politics of the Free Movement of Labour." *JCMS: Journal of Common Market Studies* 6 (4): 310–33.

Damro, C. 2006. "Transatlantic Competition Policy: Domestic and International Sources of EU-US Cooperation." *European Journal of International Relations* 12 (2): 171–96.

Damro, C. 2011. "Market Power Europe." Paper presented at the EUSA Biennial Conference, March 3–5, Boston. Available at <http://www.euce.org/eusa/2011/papers/2j_damro.pdf> accessed August 30, 2014.

Dashwood, A. 1983. "Hastening Slowly: The Communities' Path towards Harmonization." In *Policy-making in the European Communities*, 2nd edn., ed. H. Wallace, W. Wallace, and C. Webb. London: John Wiley.

Davies, B. 2012. *Resisting the European Court of Justice: West Germany Confrontation with European Law, 1949–1979*. Cambridge, UK: Cambridge University Press.

Davis, L. E. 1963. "Capital Immobilities and Finance Capitalism: A Study of Economic Evolution in the United States, 1820–1920." *Studies in Entrepreneurial History* 1 (19): 88–105.

Davis, L. E. 1965. "The Investment Market, 1870–1914: The Evolution of a National Market." *Journal of Economic History* 25 (3): 355–99.

Davis, L. E. 1971. "Capital Mobility and American Growth." In *The Reinterpretation of American Economic History*, ed. R. W. Fogel and S. L. Engerman. New York: Harper and Row.

Davis L. E., and R. J. Cull. 2000. "International Capital Movements, Domestic Capital Markets, and American Economic Growth, 1820–1914." In *The Cambridge Economic History of the United States*, ii: *The Long Nineteenth Century*, ed. S. L. Engerman and R. E. Gallman. Cambridge, UK: Cambridge University Press.

Davis, L. E., and R. E. Gallman. 1978. "Capital Formation in the United States during the Nineteenth Century." In *The Cambridge Economic History of Europe*, vii: *The Industrial Economies: Capital, Labour, and Enterprise. Part 2: The United States, Japan, and Russia*, ed. P. Mathias and M. M. Postan. Cambridge, UK: Cambridge University Press.

Davis, L. E., and D. C. North. 1971. *Institutional Change and American Economic Growth*. New York: Cambridge University Press.

De Long, J. B., and B. Eichengreen. 1991. "The Marshall Plan: History's Most Successful Structural Adjustment Program." NBER Working Paper Series No. 3899. Cambridge, MA: National Bureau of Economic Research.

De Tocqueville, A. 1969. *Democracy in America*, trans. G. Lawrence. New York: Anchor Books.

De Vries, S. A. 2006. *Tensions within the Internal Market: The Functioning of the Internal Market and the Development of Horizontal and Flanking Policies*. Groningen: Europa Law Publishing.

Deeg, R. 2010. "Industry and Finance in Germany since Reunification." *German Politics and Society* 28 (2): 116–29.

Deeg, R., and S. Perez. 2000. "International Capital Mobility and Domestic Institutions: Corporate Finance and Governance in Four European Cases." *Governance* 13 (2): 119–53.

Dell, S. 1959. "Economic Integration and the American Example." *The Economic Journal: The Journal of the Royal Economic Society* 69: 39–54.

Della Salla, V. 2004. "The Italian Model of Capitalism: On the Road Between Globalization and Europeanization?" *Journal of European Public Policy* 11 (6): 1041–58.

Deniau, J. F. 1961. *The Common Market*. London: Barrier and Rockcliff.

Department of Trade and Industry. 1988. "DTI—the Department for Enterprise." Government White Paper. London: HMSO.

Derthick, M. 1996. "Crossing Thresholds: Federalism in the 1960s." *Journal of Policy History* 8 (1): 64–80.

Derthick, M. 2001. *Keeping the Compound Republic: Essays on American Federalism*. Washington, DC: Brookings Institution Press.

Despicht, N. S. 1964. *Policies for Transport in the Common Market*. Sidcup, Kent: Lambarde Press.

Deudney, D. H. 1995. "The Philadelphian System: Sovereignty, Arms Control and Balance of Power in the American States-union, Circa 1787–1861." *International Organization* 49 (2): 191–228.

Devaux, A. 2013. "Is the Role of the French Notary in Danger?" *Jurist*, University of Pittsburgh. Available at <http://jurist.org/sidebar/2013/07/angelique-devaux-french-notaire.php> accessed July 29, 2014.

Dinan, D. 1994. *Ever Closer Union: An Introduction to European Integration*. London: Palgrave Macmillan.

Dinan, D. 1999. *Ever Closer Union? An Introduction to the European Community*, 2nd edn. Boulder, CO: Lynne Reiner.

Dobbin, F. 1994. *Forging Industrial Policy: The United States, Britain, and France in the Railway Age*. New York: Cambridge University Press.

Dobbin, F. 1995. "The Origins of Economic Principles: Railroad Entrepreneurs and Public Policy in Nineteenth Century America." In *The Institutional Construction of Organizations* ed. W. R. Scott and S. Christensen. London: Sage.

Dobbin, F. 2001. "Why the Economy Reflects the Polity: Early Rail Policy in Britain, France, and the United States." In *The Sociology of Economic Life*, ed. M. Granovetter and R. Swedberg. Boulder, CO: Westview.

Donahue, J. D., and M. A. Pollack. 2001. "Centralization and its Discontents: The Rhythms of Federalism in the United States and the European Union." In *The Federal Vision: Legitimacy and Levels of Governance in the United States and the European Union*, ed. K. Nicolaïdis and R. Howse. Oxford: Oxford University Press.

Donnelly, S. 2010. "The Regimes of European Integration: Constructing Governance of the Single Market." Paper presented at the State of the European Economic Union, November 5–6, American University.

Dove, J. A. 2012. "Credible Commitments and Constitutional Constraints: State Debt Repudiation and Default in Nineteenth Century America." *Constitutional Political Economy* 23 (1): 66–93.

Drezner, D. W. 2006. *All Politics Is Global: Explaining International Regulatory Regimes.* Princeton, NJ: Princeton University Press.

Duina, F. 2006. *Social Construction of Free Trade: The European Union, NAFTA, and Mercosur.* Princeton, NJ: Princeton University Press.

Dumke, R. H. 1991. "Tariffs and Market Structure: The German Zollverein as a Model for Economic Integration." In *German Industry and German Industrialisation*, ed. W. R. Lee. London: Routledge.

Dyrhauge, H. 2013. *EU Railway Policy-making: On Track?* Basingstoke: Palgrave Macmillan.

Dyson, K, and A. Sepos. 2010. *Which Europe? The Politics of Differentiated Integration.* Basingstoke: Palgrave MacMillan.

Eberlein, B., and E. Grande. 2005. "Beyond Delegation: Transnational Regulatory Regimes and the EU Regulatory State." *Journal of European Public Policy* 12 (1): 89–112.

Edens, D. F., and S. Patijn. 1972. "The Scope of the EEC System of Free Movement of Workers." *Common Market Law Review* 9 (3): 322–8.

Edward, F. 2002. "Introduction." In *Services and Free Movement in EU Law*, ed. M. Andenas and W.-H. Roth. Oxford: Oxford University Press.

Eeckhout, P. 1994. *The European Internal Market and International Trade: A Legal Analysis.* Oxford: Oxford University Press.

Egan, M. 1997. "Modes of Business Governance: European Management Styles and Corporate Cultures." *West European Politics* 20 (2): 1–21.

Egan, M. 2001. *Constructing a European Market: Standards, Regulation, and Governance.* Oxford: Oxford University Press.

Egan, M. (ed.) 2005. *Creating a Transatlantic Marketplace: Government Policies and Business Strategies.* Manchester: Manchester University Press.

Egan, M. 2008. "The Emergence of the US Internal Market." In *The EU Internal Market in Comparative Perspective: Economic, Political, and Legal Perspectives*, ed. J. Pelkmans, D. Hanf, and M.Chang. Brussels: Peter Lang Publishers.

Egan, M. 2012a. "Single Market Governance: Lessons from the European Experience." In *Toward a North American Legal System*, ed. J. T. McHugh. New York: Palgrave Macmillan.

Egan, M. 2012b. "Single Market." In *The Oxford Handbook of the European Union*, ed. E. Jones, A. Menon, and S. Weatherill. Oxford: Oxford University Press.

Egan, M. 2013. "Toward a New History in European Law: New Wine in Old Bottles." *American University International Law Review* 28 (5): 1223–55.

Egan, M., and H. Guimarães. 2012. "Compliance in the Single Market." *Business and Politics* 14 (4): 1–28.

Eichengreen, B. 2008. *The European Economy Since 1945: Coordinated Capitalism and Beyond.* Princeton, NJ: Princeton University Press.

Eichengreen, B. 2012. "Implications of the Euro's Crisis for International Monetary Reform." Available at <http://emlab.berkeley.edu/~eichengr/Implications_Euro_JrnPolModel_2012.pdf> accessed February 17, 2014.

Eichengreen, B. and K. H. O'Rourke. 2010. "A Tale of Two Depressions: What Do the New Data Tell Us?" *VoxEU. Org* 8. Available at <http://www.voxeu.org/article/tale-two-depressions-what-do-new-data-tell-us-february-2010-update> accessed December 29, 2013.

Elazar, D. J. 1964. "Federal-State Collaboration in the Nineteenth-century United States." *Political Science Quarterly* 79 (2): 248–81.

Elazar, D. J. 2001. "The United States and the European Union: Models for Their Epochs." In *The Federal Vision: Legitimacy and Levels of Governance in the United States and the European Union*, ed. K. Nicolaïdis and R. Howse. Oxford: Oxford University Press.

Ellis, J. J. 2000. *Founding Brothers: The Revolutionary Generation*. New York: Alfred A. Knopf.

Emerson, M. 1988. *The Economics of 1992*. European Economy No. 35 Brussels: Commission of European Communities DG for Economic and Financial Affairs.

Engerman, S. L., and K. L. Sokoloff. 2000. "Technology and Industrialization, 1790–1914." In *The Cambridge Economic History of the United States*, ii: *The Long Nineteenth Century*, ed. S. E. Engerman and R. E. Gallman. Cambridge, UK: Cambridge University Press.

English, W. B. 1996. "Understanding the Costs of Sovereign Default: American State Debts in the 1840s." *American Economic Review* 86 (1): 259–75.

Erdmenger, J. 1983. *The European Community Transport Policy: Towards a Common Transport Policy*. Aldershot: Gower.

Ernst and Whinney. 1987. "The 'Cost of Non-Europe': Border Related Controls and Administrative Formalities." In *Research on the Costs of 'Non-Europe' – Basic Findings*, European Commission. Brussels.

European Commission. 1970. "Industrial Policy of the European Community." Colonna Report. Brussels.

European Commission. 1972. "Industrial Policy: Status Report of the Community's Work." Supplement to the EC Bulletin, No. 6. Brussels.

European Commission. 1973. "Sixth general report on the activities of the Communities." Brussels.

European Commission. 1976. Background Note May 28. Brussels.

European Commission. 1985a. "Completing the Internal Market." COM (85) 310 Final. Brussels.

European Commission. 1985b. "Technical Harmonization and Standards: A New Approach." COM (85) 19 Final. Brussels.

European Commission. 1996a. "Communication on Simpler Legislation for the Internal Market (SLIM): A Pilot Project." COM (96) 204 Final. Brussels.

European Commission. 1996b. "Communication on the Impact and Effectiveness of the Single Market." COM (96) 520 Final. Brussels.

European Commission. 1996c. "Communication on the Services of General Interest in Europe." COM (96) 443 Final. Brussels.

European Commission. 1999. "Mutual Recognition in the Context of the Single Market Action Plan." COM (1999) 299 Final. Brussels.

European Commission. 2000. "Communication on the Services of General Interest in Europe." COM (2000) 580 Final. Brussels.

European Commission. 2001. White Paper "European Transport Policy for 2010: Time to Decide" COM (2001) 370 Final. Brussels.

European Commission. 2002a. "Communication on Impact Assessment." COM (2002) 276 Final. Brussels.

European Commission. 2002b. "Economic Reform: On the Functioning of Product and Capital Markets." Cardiff Report. COM (2002) 0743 Final. Brussels.

European Commission. 2002c. "Regulatory Action Plan." COM (2002) 278 Final. Brussels.

European Commission. 2004. "Commission Calls for Abolition of Unjustified Restrictions of Competition in Professional Services." Press release IP/04/185, February 9. Available at <http://europa.eu/rapid/press-release_IP-04-185_en.htm> accessed December 27, 2013.

European Commission. 2005. "Communication on Better Regulation for Growth and Jobs in the European Union." COM (2005) 97 Final. Brussels.

European Commission. 2010. "Commission Sets out Measures to Improve Rail Services." Press release IP/10/1139, September, 17.

European Commission. 2011. Proposal for a Directive of the European Parliament and Council amending Directive 2005/36/EC on the recognition of professional qualifications and Regulation [...] on administrative cooperation through the Internal Market Information System COM (2011) 883.

European Commission. 2012. "Making the Single Market Deliver: Annual Governance Check-up 2011." Commission Staff Working Document SWD (2012) 25 Final. Brussels.

European Commission. 2013. "Final Assessment of the 2013 National Reform and Stability Program for France." Commission Staff Working Document SWD (2013) 360 Final. Brussels.

European Commission Directorate-General for Competition. 2003. "Stocktaking Exercise on Regulation of Professional Services: Overview of Regulation in the EU Member States." Brussels: European Commission Directorate-General for Competition. Available at <http://www.cgil.it/archivio/politiche-economiche/Professionalit%C3%A0OrdiniEAssociazioni/IlQuadroEuropeoEInternazionale/ServiziProfess09.10.03.pdf> accessed December 27, 2013.

European Conference of Ministers of Transport. 1954. "Council of Ministers Resolutions, ii." October 21–22. Available at <http://www.oecd-ilibrary.org/docserver/download/7555023e.pdf?expires=1408377947&id=id&accname=ocid194320&checksum=091AF92CE8EC96C71A29B847A434E03E> accessed August 28, 2014

European Council. 1993. "Conclusions of the Presidency – Copenhagen." June 21–22. Available at <http://www.consilium.europa.eu/ueDocs/cms_Data/docs/pressData/en/ec/72921.pdf> accessed August 27, 2014.

European Council. 2000. "Presidency Conclusions: Lisbon Summit." March 23–24. Available at <http://www.europarl.europa.eu/summits/lis1_en.htm> accessed December 29, 2013.

European Council Resolution of 28 October 1999 on mutual recognition (OJ C 141 of 19.05.2000).

European Council Resolution of 6 June 1974 on the mutual recognition of diplomas, certificates and other evidence of formal qualifications (OJ C 98 of 20.8.1974).

European Environment Agency. 2010. "The European Environment—State and Outlook 2010: Synthesis." State of the Environment Report No. 1. Copenhagen. Available at <http://www.eea.europa.eu/soer/synthesis/synthesis> accessed September 2, 2014.

European Report. 1995. November 11.

European Voice. 2002. "Dehaene: Treaty ideal outcome for Convention." February 28.

European Voice. 2002. "Deadline for Single Market Tight." March 21.

Evans, P. B. 1995. *Embedded Autonomy: States and Industrial Transformation.* Princeton, NJ: Princeton University Press.

Fabbrini, S. 1999. "American Democracy from a European Perspective." *Annual Review of Political Science* 2: 465–91.

Fabbrini, S. 2002. "The Puzzle of the Compound Republic: The EU, US and the Implications of Federalization." RSCAS Working Paper 27/02. Florence, Italy: European University Institute.

Fabbrini, S. 2003. "A Single Western State Model? Differential Development and Constrained Convergence of Public Authority Organization in Europe and America." *Comparative Political Studies* 36 (6): 653–78.

Fabbrini, S. 2004. "Transatlantic Constitutionalism: Comparing the United States and the European Union." *European Journal of Political Research* 43 (4): 547–69.

Fabbrini, S. (ed.) 2005. *Democracy and Federalism in the European Union and the United States: Exploring Post-National Governance.* London and New York: Routledge.

Fabbrini, S. 2007. *Compound Democracies: Why the United States and Europe Are Becoming Similar.* Oxford and New York: Oxford University Press.

Falkner G., O. Treib, M. Hartlapp, and S. Leiber (eds) 2005. *Complying with Europe: EU Harmonisation and Soft Law in the Member States.* Cambridge, UK: Cambridge University Press.

Feketekuty, G. 1988. *International Trade in Services: An Overview and Blueprint for Negotiations.* Cambridge, MA: Ballinger Publishing Company.

Feld, W. J. 1970. *Transnational Business Collaboration among Common Market Countries: Its Implication for Political Integration.* Westport, CT: Praeger.

Feldstein, H. S. 1967. "A Study of Transaction and Political Integration: Transnational Labour Flow within the European Economic Community." *JCMS: Journal of Common Market Studies* 6 (1): 24–55.

Financial Times. 2001a. "Brussels in Retreat over Drive to Harmonise Taxes across the EU." January 24.

Financial Times. 2001b. "Financiers Move to Support Single Market." March 2.

Financial Times. 2001c. "Lamfalussy Set for Battle on Securities Market Regulation." February 15.

Fioretes, O. 2011. *Creative Reconstruction: Multilateralism and European Varieties of Capitalism after 1950.* Ithaca, NY: Cornell University Press.

Fishlow, A. 1964. "Antebellum Interregional Trade Reconsidered" *American Economic Review* 54 (4): 352–64.

Fishlow, A. 1985. "Lessons from the Past: Capital Markets during the 19th Century and the Interwar Period." *International Organization* 39 (3): 383–439.

Flam, H. 1992. "Product Markets and 1992: Full Integration, Large Gains?" *Journal of Economic Perspectives* 6 (4): 7–30.

Fligstein, N. 1990. *The Transformation of Corporate Control.* Cambridge, MA: Harvard University Press.

Fligstein, N. 2001. *The Architecture of Markets: An Economic Sociology of Twenty-first-century Capitalist Societies.* Princeton, NJ: Princeton University Press.

Fligstein, N. 2008. *Euroclash: The EU, European Identity, and the Future of Europe.* Oxford: Oxford University Press.

Fligstein, N, and A. Stone Sweet. 2002. "Constructing Markets and Polities: An Institutionalist Account of European Integration." *American Journal of Sociology* 107 (5): 1206–43.

Flood, J., and F. Sosa. 2008. "Lawyers, Law Firms, and the Stabilization of Transnational Business." *Northwestern Journal of International Law & Business* 28: 489–526.

Fogel, R. W. 1964. *Railroads and American Economic Growth: Essays in Econometric History.* Baltimore, MD: Johns Hopkins University Press.

Fogel, R. W. 1965. "Railroads and the Axiom of Indispensability." In *New Views on American Economic Development: A Selective Anthology of Recent Work,* ed. R. L. Andreano. Cambridge, MA: Schenkman Publishing Co.

Fogel, R. W. 1989. *Without Consent or Contract: The Rise and Fall of American Slavery.* New York: W. W. Norton.

Follesdal, A., and S. Hix. 2006. "Why There Is a Democratic Deficit in the EU: A Response to Majone and Moravcsik." *JCMS: Journal of Common Market Studies* 44 (3): 533–62.

Foner, E. 1988. *Reconstruction: America's Unfinished Revolution, 1863–1877.* New York: Harper & Row.

Fontana, Cipolla C. M. (ed.) 1976. *The Fontana Economic History of Europe: The Twentieth Century,* vol. 5.2. Glasgow: Collins/Fontana.

Foreign and Commonwealth Office. 2008. "A Comparative Table of the Current EC and EU Treaties as Amended by the Treaty of Lisbon." Command Paper Cm 7311. London.

Fowke, V. C. 1956. "National Policy and Western Development in North America." *The Journal of Economic History* 16 (4): 461–79.

Frankel, J. A. 1982. "The 1807–1809 Embargo Against Great Britain." *Journal of Economic History* 42 (2): 291–308.

Frankfurter, F. 1937. *The Commerce Clause under Marshall, Taney, and Waite.* Chapel Hill, NC: University of North Carolina Press.

Frankfurter, F., and J. M. Landis. 1928. *The Business of the Supreme Court: A Study in the Federal Judicial System.* New York: Macmillan.

Franklin, B. 1787. "To Rodolphe-Ferdinand Grand (unpublished)." October 22 [Letter]. Available at <http://franklinpapers.org/franklin/framedVolumes.jsp?vol=45&page=229> accessed August 27, 2014.

Franklin, M. N. 1996. "European Elections and the European Voter." In *European Union: Power and Policy-Making*, ed. J. Richardson. London: Routledge.

Franko, L. G. 1974. "The Origins of Multinational Manufacturing by Continental European Firms." *Business History Review* 48 (3): 277–302.

Franko, L. G. 1976. *The European Multinationals: A Renewed Challenge to American and British Big Business*. Stamford, CT: Greylock Publishers.

Freyer, T. A. 1976. "Negotiable Instruments and the Federal Courts in Antebellum American Business." *Business History Review* 50 (4): 435–55.

Freyer, T. A. 1979. "The Federal Courts, Localism, and the National Economy, 1865–1900." *Business History Review* 53 (3): 343–63.

Freyer, T. A. 1981. "Reassessing the Impact of Eminent Domain in Early American Economic Development." *Wisconsin Law Review* (6): 1263–86.

Freyer, T. A. 1992. "The Paradox of Federal Judicial Power in Antebellum Alabama." *Alabama Law Review* 44 (2): 477–554.

Freyer, T. A. 1994. *Producers versus Capitalists: Constitutional Conflict in Antebellum America*. Charlottesville, VA: University of Virginia Press.

Frieden, J. A. 1991. "Invested Interests: The Politics of National Economic Policies in a World of Global Finance." *International Organization* 45 (4): 425–51.

Friedman, L. M. 1965. "Freedom of Contract and Occupational Licensing 1890–1910: A Legal and Social Study." *California Law Review* 53: 487–534.

Friedman, L. M. 2005. *A History of American Law*, 3rd edn. New York: Simon & Schuster.

Friedman, M., and S. Kuznets. 1945. *Income from Independent Professional Practice*. New York: National Bureau of Economic Research.

Frost, E. L., C. Parsons, J. D. Richardson, and M. Schneider. 2002. "Lessons for a Globalizing World: European and U.S. Experiences in Market Integration." Revised version for the IEE/Syracuse Colloquium, Washington DC [unpublished mimeo].

Gaines, P. 2001. "The 'True Lawyer' in America: Discursive Construction of the Legal Profession in the Nineteenth Century." *The American Journal of Legal History* 45 (2): 132–53.

Galambos, L., and J. Pratt. 1988. *The Rise of the Corporate Commonwealth: United States Business and Public Policy in the 20th Century*. New York: Basic Books.

Gallman, R. E. 2000. "Economic Growth and Structural Change in the Long Nineteenth Century." In *The Cambridge Economic History of the United States*, ii: *The Long Nineteenth Century*, ed. S. L. Engerman and R. E. Gallman. Cambridge, UK: Cambridge University Press.

Garrett, G. 1995. "Capital, Mobility, Trade, and the Domestic Politics of Economic Policy." *International Organization* 49 (4): 657–87.

Garrett, G., R. D. Kelemen, and H. Schulz. 1998. "The European Court of Justice, National Governments, and Legal Integration in the European Union." In *International Law and International Relations*, ed. B. A. Simmons and R. H. Steinberg. Cambridge, UK: Cambridge University Press.

Garson, R. 2001. "Counting Money: The US Dollar and American Nationhood, 1781–1820." *Journal of American Studies* 35 (1): 21–46.

Garzon. I. 2007. *Reforming the Common Agricultural Policy: History of a Paradigm Change*. Basingstoke: Palgrave Macmillan.

Gates, P. W. 1936. "The Homestead Law in an Incongruous Land System." *The American Historical Review* 41 (4): 652–81.

Gawalt, G. W. 1973. "Massachusetts Legal Education in Transition: 1766–1840." *American Journal of Legal History* 17 (1): 27–50.

Gawalt, G. W. 1976. "Sources of Anti-Lawyer Sentiment in Massachusetts, 1740–1840." In *Essays in Nineteenth-Century American Legal History*, ed. W. Holt. Westport, CT: Greenwood Press.

Gawalt. G. W. 1979. *The Promise of Power: The Emergence of the Legal Profession in Massachusetts, 1760–1840.* Westport, CT: Greenwood Press.

Geddes, A. 2000. *Immigration and European Integration: Towards Fortress Europe.* Manchester: Manchester University Press.

Gehrels, F., and B. J. Johnson. 1955. "The Economic Gains from European Integration." *Journal of Political Economy* 63 (4) 275–92.

Genschel, P., and M. Jachtenfuchs. 2011. "How the European Union Constrains the State: Multilevel Governance of Taxation." *European Journal of Political Research* 50 (3): 293–314.

George, A. L. 1979. "Case Studies and Theory Development: The Method of Structured, Focused Comparison." In *Diplomacy: New Approaches in History, Theory and Policy*, ed. P. G. Lauren. New York: The Free Press.

Gerkens, F. W. 1996. "Opportunities for Regulatory Arbitrage Under the European Economic Community's Financial Services Directives and Related United States Regulations." *New York Law School Journal of International and Comparative Law* 16: 455–88.

Germond C. 2013. "Preventing Reform: Farm Interest Groups and the Common Agricultural Policy." In *Societal Actors in European Integration: Polity-Building and Policy-Making 1958–1992*, ed. W. Kaiser and J. H. Meyers. Basingstoke: Palgrave Macmillan.

Gerschenkron, A. 1962. "Economic Backwardness in Historical Perspective. In *Economic Backwardness in Historical Perspective: A Book of Essays.* Cambridge, MA: Harvard University Press.

Gerstle, G. 2009. "The Resilient Power of the States across the Long Nineteenth Century: An Inquiry into a Pattern of American Governance." In *The Unsustainable American State*, ed. L. Jacobs and D. King. Oxford: Oxford University Press.

Gerstle, G. 2010. "AHR Exchange: A State Both Strong and Weak." *The American Historical Review* 115 (3): 779–85.

Gilbert, M. 2008. "Narrating the Process: Questioning the Progressive Story of European Integration." *JCMS: Journal of Common Market Studies* 46 (3): 641–62.

Gillman, H. 1993. *The Constitution Besieged: The Rise and Demise of Lochner Era Police Powers Jurisprudence.* Durham, NC: Duke University Press.

Gillman, H. 1996. "More on the Origins of the Fuller Court's Jurisprudence: Reexamining the Scope of Federal Power over Commerce and Manufacturing in Nineteenth-Century Constitutional Law." *Political Research Quarterly* 49 (2): 415–37.

Gillman, H. 1999. "Reconnecting the Modern Supreme Court to the Historical Evolution of American Capitalism." In *The Supreme Court in American Politics: New Institutionalist Interpretations*, ed. H. Gillman and C. W. Clayton. Lawrence, KS: University Press of Kansas.

Gillman, H. 2002. "How Political Parties Can Use the Courts to Advance Their Agendas: Federal Courts in the United States, 1875–1891." *American Political Science Review* 96: (2) 511–24.

Glencross, A. 2007. *What Makes the EU Viable? European Integration in the Light of the Antebellum US Experience*. Basingstoke: Palgrave Macmillan.

Glickstein, J. A. 2002. *American Exceptionalism, American Anxiety: Wages, Competition, and Degraded Labor in the Antebellum United States*. Charlottesville, VA: University of Virginia Press.

Goebel, R. J. 1992. "Lawyers in the European Community: Progress towards Community-wide Rights of Practice." *Fordham International Law Journal* 15 (3): 556–51.

Goebel, R. J. 2000. "The Liberalization of Interstate Legal Practice in the European Union: Lessons for the United States?" *The International Lawyer* 34 (1): 307–45.

Goebel, R. J. 2002. "The Liberalization of Interstate Legal Practice in the European Union: Lessons for the United States?" In *Services and Free Movement in EU Law*, ed. M. Andenas and W.-H. Roth. Oxford: Oxford University Press.

Goldstein, L. F. 1997. "State Resistance to Authority in Federal Unions: The Early United States (1790–1860) and the European Community (1958–94)." *Studies in American Political Development* 149: 149–89.

Goldstein, L. F. 2001. *Constituting Federal Sovereignty: The European Union in Comparative Context*. Baltimore, MD: Johns Hopkins University Press.

Goodnow, F. J. 1910. "The Power of Congress to Regulate Commerce." *Political Science Quarterly* 25 (2): 220–56.

Goodrich, G. 1950. "The Revulsion Against Internal Improvements." *Journal of Economic History* 10 (2): 145–69.

Goodrich, C. 1951. "Local Government Planning of Internal Improvements." *Political Science Quarterly* 66 (3): 411–45.

Goodrich, C. 1956. "American Development Policy: The Case of Internal Improvements." *The Journal of Economic History* 16 (4): 449–60.

Goodrich, C. 1970. "Internal Improvements Reconsidered." *Journal of Economic History* 30 (2): 289–311.

Gorges, M. 1996. *Euro-Corporatism? Interest Intermediation in the European Community*. Lanham, MD: University Press of America.

Grabbe, H. 2001. "How Does Europeanization Affect CEE Governance?: Conditionality, Diffusion and Diversity." *Journal of European Public Policy* 8 (6): 1013–31.

Grabbe, H. 2005. *The EU's Transformative Power: Europeanization through Conditionality in Central and Eastern Europe*. Basingstoke: Palgrave Macmillan.

Graebner, W. 1977. "Federalism in the Progressive Era: A Structural Interpretation of Reform." *Journal of American History* 64: 331–57.

Grant, J. A. C. 1937. "State Power to Prohibit Interstate Commerce." *California Law Review* 26 (1): 34–75.

Gray, V. 1973. "Innovation in the States: A Diffusion Study." *The American Political Science Review* 67 (4): 1174–85.

Green, N., T. C. Hartley, and J. A. Usher. 1991. *The Legal Foundations of the Single European Market*. Oxford: Oxford University Press.

Greenwood, J. 1997. *Representing Interests in the European Union*. Basingstoke: Macmillan.

Greenwood, J. and M. Aspinwall (eds.) 1998. *Collective Action in the European Union: Interests and the New Politics of Associability*. London: Routledge.

Grieco, J. 1990. *Cooperation among Nations: Europe, America, and Non-tariff Barriers to Trade*. Cornell, NY: Cornell University Press.

Gros, D. 2012. "The Single European Market in Banking in Decline—ECB to the rescue?" *Vox*. Available at <http://www.voxeu.org/article/single-european-market-banking-decline-ecb-rescue> accessed July 29, 2014.

Grubel, H. G., and P. J. Lloyd. 1975. *Intra-industry Trade: The Theory and Measurement of International Trade in Differentiated Products*. London: Macmillan.

Guimarães, H., and M. Egan. 2014. "Tackling Barriers to Trade in the Single Market." Paper presented at the 5th Standing Group on Regulatory Governance (ECPR) Biennial Conference [unpublished mimeo].

Haas, E. B. 1958. *The Uniting of Europe: Political, Social, and Economic Forces, 1950–1957*. Notre Dame, IN: University of Notre Dame Press.

Haber, S. 2003. "Political Institutions and Banking Systems: Lessons from the Economic Histories of Mexico and the United States, 1790–1914." Center for Research on Economic Development and Policy Reform Working Paper 163. Stanford, CA: Stanford University [mimeo].

Hacker, L. M. 1940. *The Triumph of American Capitalism: The Development of Forces in American History to the End of the Nineteenth Century*. New York: Simon & Schuster.

Hackett, C. P. 1994. "Subsidiarity and the Pertinence of the American Federal Experience." Paper presented at the 2nd ECSA-World Conference: Federalism, Subsidiary and Democracy in the European Union, April 4–6. Brussels.

Hager, W. 1982. "Protectionism and Autonomy: How to Preserve Free Trade in Europe." *International Affairs* 58 (3): 413–28.

Halberstam, D. 2001. "Comparative Federalism and the Issue of Commandeering." In *The Federal Vision: Legitimacy and Levels of Governance in the United States and the European Union*, ed. K. Nicolaïdis and R. Howse. Oxford and New York: Oxford University Press.

Halberstam, D. 2009. "Federal Powers and the Principle of Subsidiarity." In *Global Perspectives on Constitutional Law*, ed. V. Amar and M. Tushnet. New York: Oxford University Press.

Hall, P. 1986. *Governing the Economy: The Politics of State Intervention in Britain and France*. New York: Oxford University Press.

Hallerberg, M. 1996. "Tax Competition in Wilhelmine Germany and Its Implications for the European Union." *World Politics* 48 (3): 324–57.

Hallerberg, M. 2014. "Why Is There Fiscal Capacity but Little Regulation in the US, but Regulation and Little Fiscal Capacity in Europe? The Global Financial Crisis as a Test Case." In *Beyond the Regulatory Polity: The European Integration of Core State Powers*, ed. P. Genschel and M. Jachtenfuchs. Oxford: Oxford University Press.

Hamilton, A. 1961 [1788]. "Federalist No. 85." In *The Federalist*, ed. J. E. Cooke. Middletown, CT: Wesleyan University Press.

Hanf, D. 2008. "Legal Concept and Meaning of the Internal Market." In *The EU Internal Market in Comparative Perspective: Economic, Political and Legal Analyses*, ed. J. Pelkmans, D. Hanf, and M. Chang. Brussels: Peter Lang.

Hartz, L. 1948. *Economic Policy and Democratic Thought: Pennsylvania 1776–1860*. Cambridge, MA: Harvard University Press.

Hartz, L. 1955. *The Liberal Tradition in America: An Interpretation of American Political Thought Since the Revolution*. Florida: Harcourt, Brace & Co.

Hatch, N. O. (ed.) 1988. *The Professions in American History*. Notre Dame, IN: University of Notre Dame Press.

Hattam, V. 1993. *Labor Visions and State Power: The Origins of Business Unionism in the United States*. Princeton, NJ: Princeton University Press.

Hays, S. P. 1995. *The Response to Industrialism, 1885–1914*, 2nd edn. Chicago, IL: University of Chicago Press.

Hays, S. P. 1999. *Conservation and the Gospel of Efficiency*, 2nd edn. Pittsburgh, PA: University of Pittsburgh Press.

Hazard, G. C., Jr. 1997. "State Supreme Court Regulatory Authority over the Legal Profession." *The Notre Dame Law Review* 72 (4): 1177–80.

Heinemann, F., and M. Jopp. 2002. "The Benefits of a Working European Retail Market for Financial Services." Report to European Financial Services Round Table.

Heisenberg, D. 1999. *The Mark of the Bundesbank: Germany's Role in European Monetary Cooperation*. Boulder, CO: Lynne Rienner Publishers, 1999.

Heller, T., and J. Pelkmans. 1986. "The Federal Economy: Law and Economic Integration and the Positive State—The USA and Europe Compared in an Economic Perspective." In *Integration Through Law: Europe and the American Federal Experience*, i: *Methods, Tools, and Institutions*, ed. M. Cappelletti, M. Seccombe, and J. H. H. Weiler. Berlin: Walter De Gruyter.

Henderson, W. O. 1981. "The German Zollverein and the European Economic Community." *Zeitschrift für die gesamte Staatswissenschaft/ Journal of Institutional and Theoretical Economics* 137 (3): 491–507.

Henning, C. R., and M. Kessler. 2012. "Fiscal Federalism: US History for Architects of Europe's Fiscal Union." Peterson Institute for International Economics Working Papers No. 2012–1. Washington, DC: Peterson Institute for International Economics.

Heremans, T. 2012. *Professional Services in the EU Internal Market: Quality Regulations and Self-Regulation*. Oxford: Hart Publishing.

Héritier, A. 1997a. "Market-making Policy in Europe: Its Impact on Member State Policies. The Case of Road Haulage in Britain, the Netherlands, Germany and Italy" *Journal of European Public Policy* 4 (4): 539–55.

Héritier, A. 1997b. "Policy-Making by Subterfuge: Interest Accommodation, Innovation and Substitute Democratic Legitimation in Europe—Perspectives from Distinctive Policy Areas." *Journal of European Public Policy* 4 (2): 171–89.

Héritier, A. 2001. "Market Integration and Social Cohesion: The Politics of Public Services in European Integration." *Journal of European Public Policy* 8 (5): 825–52.

Héritier, A., and M. Rhodes (eds) 2011. *New Modes of Governance in Europe: Governing in the Shadow of Hierarchy*. Basingstoke: Palgrave Macmillan.

Héritier, A. and S. K. Schmidt. 2000. "After Liberalization: Public-interest Services and Employment in the Utilities." In *Welfare and Work in the Open Economy*, ii: *Diverse Responses to Common Challenges*, ed. F. W. Scharpf and V. A. Schmidt. Oxford: Oxford University Press.

Héritier, A., D. Kerwer, C. Knill et al. (eds) 2001. *Differential Europe: The European Union Impact on National Policymaking*. Lanham, MD: Rowman & Littlefield.

Higgs, R. 1971. *The Transformation of the American Economy, 1865–1914: An Essay in Interpretation*. New York: Wiley.

Hillman, J. S. 1991. *Technical Barriers to Agricultural Trade*. Boulder, CO: Westview Press.

Hirschman, A. O. 1970. *Exit, Voice, and Loyalty: Responses to Decline in Firms, Organizations and States*. Cambridge, MA: Harvard University Press.

Hix, S. 1994. "The Study of the European Community: The Challenge to Comparative Politics." *West European Politics* 17 (1): 1–30.

Hix, S., and C. Lord. 1997. *Political Parties in the European Union*. Basingstoke: Palgrave Macmillan.

Hodges, M. 1983. "Industrial Policy: Hard Times or Great Expectations?" In *Policy-making in the European Communities*, 2nd edn., ed. H. Wallace, W. Wallace, and C. Webb. Chichester, UK: John Wiley.

Hodson, D. 2012. "EU Regional and Cohesion Policy." In *The Oxford Handbook of the European Union*, ed. E. Jones, A. Menon, and S. Weatherill. Oxford: Oxford University Press.

Hoffman, L. S. B. P. O. 2011. "Land of the Free, Home of the (Un)Regulated: A Look at Market-building and Liberalization in the EU and the US," PhD dissertation, University of Oregon.

Hoffman, P. G. 1964. "Oral History Interview with Paul G. Hoffman." *Harry S. Truman Library*. New York. Available at <http://www.trumanlibrary.org/oralhist/hoffmanp.htm> accessed August 27, 2014.

Hoffman, S. 1966. "Obstinate or Obsolete: The Fate of the Nation-State and the Case of Western Europe." *Daedalus* 95 (3): 862–915.

Hoke, S. C. 1992. "Transcending Conventional Supremacy: A Reconstruction of the Supremacy Clause." *Connecticut Law Review* 24 (3): 829–92.

Hollander, S. C. 1964. "Nineteenth Century Anti-Drummer Legislation in the United States." *Business History Review* 38 (4): 479–500.

Hood, C., C. Scott, O. James, G. Jones, and A. Travers. 1999. *Regulation inside Government: Waste-Watchers, Quality Police, and Sleazebusters*. Oxford: Oxford University Press.

Hoogenboom, A., and O. Hoogenboom. 1976. *A History of the ICC: From Panacea to Palliative*. New York: W. W. Norton.

Hooghe, L. 1998. "EU Cohesion Policy and Competing Models of European Capitalism." *JCMS: Journal of Common Market Studies* 36 (4): 47–477.

Hooghe, L., and G. Marks. 1997. "The Making of a Polity: The Struggle over European Integration." *European Integration Online Papers* 1 (4). Available at <http://eiop.or.at/eiop/texte/1997-004a.htm> accessed December 29, 2013.

Hooghe, L., and G. Marks. 2003. "Unraveling the Central State, But How? Types of Multi-level Governance." *The American Political Science* Review 97 (2): 233–43.

Hooghe, L., and G. Marks. 2004. "Does Identity or Economic Rationality Drive Public Opinion on European Integration?" *Political Science and Politics* 37 (3): 415–20.

Hooghe, L., and G. Marks. 2007. "Sources of Euroscepticism." *Acta Politica* 42 (2): 119–27.

Hooghe, L., and G. Marks. 2009. "A Postfunctionalist Theory of European Integration: From Permissive Consensus to Constraining Dissensus." *British Journal of Political Science* 39 (1): 1–23.

Hooghe, L., and G. Marks. 2010. "Types of Multi-level Governance." In *Handbook on Multi-level Governance*, ed. H. Enderlein, S. Wälti, and M. Zürn. Cheltenham, UK: Edward Elgar.

Horwitz, M. J. 1977. *The Transformation of American Law, 1780–1860*. Cambridge, MA: Harvard University Press.

Hovenkamp, H. 1991. *Enterprise and American Law, 1836–1937*. Cambridge, MA: Harvard University Press.

Hovenkamp, H. 1992a. "Capitalism." In *The Oxford Companion to the Supreme Court of the United States*, ed. K. L. Hall. New York: Oxford University Press.

Hovenkamp, H. 1992b. "The Supreme Court as Constitutional Interpreter: Chronology without History." *Michigan Law Review* 90 (6): 1384–91.

Howarth, D., and L. Quaglia. 2013. "Banking Union as Holy Grail: Rebuilding the Single Market in Financial Services, Stabilizing Europe's Banks, and 'Completing' Economic and Monetary Union." *JCMS: Journal of Common Market Studies* 51 (S1): 103–23.

Howarth, D., and T. Sadeh. 2010. "The Ever Incomplete Single Market: Differentiation and the Evolving Frontier of Integration." *Journal of European Public Policy* 17 (7): 922–35.

Howse, R., and K. Nicolaïdis. 2001. "Introduction: The Federal Vision, Levels of Governance, and Legitimacy." In *The Federal Vision: Legitimacy and Levels of Governance in the United States and the European Union*, ed. K. Nicolaïdis and R. Howse. Oxford and New York: Oxford University Press.

Hurst, J. W. 1956. *Law and the Conditions of Freedom: In the Nineteenth-century United States*. Madison, WI: University of Wisconsin Press.

Hurst, J. W. 1964. *Law and Economic Growth: The Legal History of the Lumber Industry in Wisconsin, 1836–1915*. Cambridge, MA: The Belknap Press of Harvard University Press.

Hurst, J. W. 1971. "Legal Elements in United States History." In *Law in American History*, ed. D. Fleming and B. Bailyn. Boston, MA: Little, Brown and Company.

Hurst, J. W. 1973. *A Legal History of Money in the United States, 1774–1970*. Lincoln, NE: University of Nebraska Press.

Hurst, J. W. 1977. *Law and Social Order in the United States*. Ithaca, NY: Cornell University Press.

Hurst, J. W. 1982. *Law and Markets in United States History: Different Modes of Bargaining among Interests*. Madison, WI: University of Wisconsin Press.

Hurwitz, L. 1990. *The Free Circulation of Physicians within the European Community*. Brookfield, VT: Avebury.

Imig, D. R., and S. G. Tarrow. 2001. "Studying Contention in an Emerging Polity." In *Contentious Europeans: Protest and Politics in an Emerging Polity*, i, ed D. R. Imig and S. G. Tarrow. Lanham, MD: Rowman & Littlefield.

Ingebritsen, C. 1998. *The Nordic States and European Unity*. Ithaca, NY: Cornell University Press.

Irwin, D. A. 2001. "Tariffs and Growth in Late Nineteenth Century America." *The World Economy* 24 (1): 15–30.

Jabko, N. 2006. *Playing the Market: A Political Strategy for Uniting Europe, 1985–2005*. Ithaca, NY: Cornell University Press.

Jabko, N., and E. Massoc. 2012. "French Capitalism under Stress: How Nicolas Sarkozy Rescued the Banks." *Review of International Political Economy* 19 (4): 562–85.

Jacobs, F. G. 1977. "The Free Movement of Persons within the EEC." *Current Legal Problems* 30 (1): 123–41.

Jacobs, L., and D. King. 2009. *The Unsustainable American State*. Oxford and New York: Oxford University Press.

Jacobs, M., and J. E. Zelizer. 2003. "The Democratic Experiment: New Directions in American Political History." In *The Democratic Experiment: New Directions in American Political History*, ed. M. Jacobs, W. J. Novak, and J. E. Zelizer. Princeton, NJ: Princeton University Press.

Jacoby, S. M., and M. W. Finkin. 2004. "Labor Mobility in a Federal System: The United States in Comparative Perspective." *International Journal of Comparative Labour Law and Industrial Relations* 20 (3): 313–37.

James, J. A. 1978. *Money and Capital Markets in Postbellum America*. Princeton, NJ: Princeton University Press.

James, J. A. 1984. "Public Debt Management Policy and Nineteenth-century American Economic Growth." *Explorations in Economic History* 21: 192–217.

Jenny, F. 2001. "Regulation, Competition and the Professions." In *The Anticompetitive Impact of Regulation*, ed. G. Amato and L. L. Laudati. Cheltenham, UK: Edward Elgar.

John, R. R. 1995. *Spreading the News: The American Postal System from Franklin to Morse*. Cambridge, MA: Harvard University Press.

John, R. R. 1997. "Governmental Institutions as Agents of Change: Rethinking American Political Development in the Early Republic, 1787–1835," *Studies in American Political Development* 11 (2): 347–80.

John, R. R. 2008. "Rethinking the Early American State Polity." *Polity* 40: 332–9.

Johnsen, J. E. 1940. *Interstate Trade Barriers*. New York: H. W. Wilson Company.

Johnson, K. S. 2009. "The First New Federalism and the Development of the Modern American State: Patchwork, Reconstruction, or Transition?" In *The Unsustainable American State*, ed. L. Jacobs and D. King. Oxford: Oxford University Press.

"Joint Initiative on Regulatory Reform: An Initiative of the Irish, Dutch, Luxembourg, and UK Presidencies of the European Union." January 26, 2004. Available at <http://web.archive.org/web/20051215164523/http://www.hm-treasury.gov.uk/media/47C54/jirf_0104.pdf> accessed December 29, 2013.

Jones, E. 2003. "Liberalized Capital Markets, State Autonomy, and European Monetary Union." *European Journal of Political Research* 42: 197–222.

Jones, E. 2006. "Europe's Market Liberalization Is a Bad Model for a Global Trade Agenda." *Journal of European Public Policy* 13 (6): 943–57.

Jones, E. 2012. "European Crisis, European Solidarity." *JCMS: Journal of Common Market Studies* 50 (S2): 53–67.

Josselin, D. 1996. "Domestic Policy Networks and European Negotiations: Evidence from British and French Financial Services." *Journal of European Public Policy* (3) 3: 297–317.

Jupille, J., and J. A. Caporaso. 1999. "Institutionalism and the European Union: Beyond International Relations and Comparative Politics." *Annual Review of Political Science* 2 (1): 429–44.

Kahler, M. 1985. "European Protectionism in Theory and Practice." *World Politics* 37 (4): 475–502.

Kaiser, W., and J.-H. Henrik. 2013. *Societal Actors in European Integration*, Basingstoke: Palgrave Macmillan.

Kaiser, W., B. Leucht, and M. Gehler (eds) 2010. *Transnational Networks in European Integration: Governing Europe, 1945–83*. Basingstoke: Palgrave Macmillan.

Kaltenthaler, K. 1998. *Germany and the Politics of Europe's Money*. Durham, NC: Duke University Press.

Katznelson, I. 1997. "Structure and Configuration in Comparative Politics." In *Comparative Politics: Rationality, Culture, and Structure*, ed. M. I. Lichbach and A. S. Zuckerman. Cambridge, UK: Cambridge University Press.

Katznelson, I. 2002a. "Flexible Capacity: The Military and Early American Statebuilding." In *Shaped by War and Trade: International Influences on American Political Development*, ed. I. Katznelson and M. Shefter. Princeton, NJ: Princeton University Press.

Katznelson, I. 2002b. "Rewriting the Epic of America." In *Shaped by War and Trade: International Influences on American Political Development*, ed. I. Katznelson and M. Shefter. Princeton, NJ: Princeton University Press.

Katznelson, I., and M. Shefter (eds) 2002. *Shaped by War and Trade: International Influences on American Political Development*. Princeton, NJ: Princeton University Press.

Keating, M. 2010. "The Spatial Dimension." In *Which Europe: The Politics of Differentiated Integration*, ed. K. Dyson and A. Sepos. Basingstoke: Palgrave Macmillan.

Keehn, R. H. 1974. "Federal Bank Policy, Bank Market Structure, and Bank Performance: Wisconsin, 1863–1914." *Business History Review* 48 (1): 1–27.

Kelemen, R. D. 2003. "The Structure and Dynamics of EU Federalism." *Comparative Political Studies*, 36, 1–2: 184–208.

Kelemen, R. D. 2007. "Built to Last? The Durability of EU Federalism." In *Making History: State of the European Union*, viii, ed. S. Meunier and K. McNamara. Oxford: Oxford University Press.

Kelemen, R. D. 2011. *Eurolegalism: The Transformation of Law and Regulation in the European Union*. Cambridge, MA: Harvard University Press.

Kelemen, R. D., and E. C. Sibbitt. 2004. "The Globalization of American Law." *International Organization* 58: 103–36.

Kelemen, R. D., and D. Vogel. 2010. "Trading Places: The Role of the United States and the European Union in International Environmental Politics." *Comparative Political Studies* 43 (4): 427–56.

Keller, M. 1963. *The Life Insurance Enterprise, 1885–1910: A Study in the Limits of Corporate Power.* Cambridge, MA: Harvard University Press.

Keller, M. 1977. *Affairs of State: Public Life in Late Nineteenth Century America.* Cambridge, MA: The Belknap Press of Harvard University Press.

Keller, M. 1979. "Business History and Legal History" *Business History Review* 53 (3): 295–303.

Keller, M. 1981. "The Pluralist State: American Economic Regulation in Comparative Perspective." In *Regulation in Perspective: Historical Essays*, ed. T. K. McCraw. Cambridge, MA: Harvard University Press.

Keller, M. 1990. *Regulating a New Economy: Public Policy and Economic Change in America, 1900–1933.* Cambridge, MA: Harvard University Press.

Keller, M. 1994. *Regulating a New Society: Public Policy and Social Change in America, 1900–1933.* Cambridge, MA: Harvard University Press.

Keller, M. 2007. *America's Three Regimes: A New Political History.* Oxford: Oxford University Press.

Kelly, A. H., W. Harbison, and H. Belz (eds) 1991. *The American Constitution: Its Origins and Development.* New York: W. W. Norton.

Keohane, R. O. 1983. "Associative American Development, 1776–1860: Economic Growth and Political Disintegration." In *The Antinomies of Interdependence: National Welfare and the International Division of Labor*, ed. J. G. Ruggie. New York: Columbia University Press.

Keohane, R. O. 2002. "International Commitments and American Political Institutions in the Nineteenth Century." In *Shaped by War and Trade: International Influences on American Political Development*, ed. I. Katznelson and M. Shefter. Princeton, NJ: Princeton University Press.

Keohane, R. O., J. S. Nye, and S. Hoffman (eds) 1993. *After the Cold War: International Institutions and State Strategies in Europe, 1989–1991.* Cambridge, MA: Harvard University Press.

Kerber, W. 2009. "Mutual Recognition as a Governance Mechanism." Presentation at the Modern Law Review Workshop on the Regulation of Trade in Services: Trust Distrust and Economics Integration, London/Cambridge, June 30–1 July.

Kerber, W., and R. van den Bergh. 2007. "Unmasking Mutual Recognition: Current Inconsistencies and Future Chances." Marburg Papers on Economics, No. 11–2007. Marburg, Germany: Philipps-University Marburg.

Kerwer, D., and M. Teutsch. 2000. "Elusive Europeanization: Liberalising Road Haulage in the European Union." *Journal of European Public Policy* 8 (1): 124–43.

Key, V. O., Jr. 1964. *Politics, Parties and Pressure Groups*, 5th edn. New York: Crowell.

King, D., and D. Rueda. 2008. "Cheap Labor: The New Politics of 'Bread and Roses' in Industrial Democracies." *Perspectives on Politics*, 6(02): 279–97.

King, D., and M. Stears. 2011. "How the U.S. State Works: A Theory of Standardization." *Perspectives on Politics* 9 (3): 505–18.

King, D., and R. C. Lieberman. 2008. "Finding the American State: Transcending the 'Statelessness' Account." *Polity* 40: 368–78.

King, D., and R. C. Lieberman. 2009. "Ironies of State Building: A Comparative Perspective on the American State." *World Politics* 61 (3): 547–88.

Kirkland, E. C. 1956. *Dream and Thought in the Business Community, 1860–1900.* Ithaca, NY: Cornell University Press.

Kitch, E. W., and A. D. Tarlock. 1981. *Regulation, Federalism, and Interstate Commerce.* Cambridge, MA: Oelgeschlager, Gunn and Hain.

Klaassen, L. H., and W. T. M. Molle (eds). 1983. *Industrial Mobility and Migration in the European Community.* Aldershot, UK: Gower, 1983.

Klebaner, B. J. 1958. "State and Local Immigration Regulation in the United States before 1882." *International Review of Social History* 3 (2): 269–95.

Klein, E. 2012. "The Occupational Licensing Racket." wonkbook, *Washington Post* June 13. Available at <http://www.washingtonpost.com/blogs/wonkblog/post/the-occupational-licensing-racket-wonkbook/2012/06/13/gJQAd59dZV_blog.html> accessed July 29, 2014.

Kleiner, M. M. and A. B. Krueger, 2010. "The Prevalence and Effects of Occupational Licensing." *British Journal of Industrial Relations* 48 (4): 676–87.

Knill, C. and D. Lehmkuhl, 2002. "The National Impact of European Union Regulatory Policy: Three Europeanization Mechanisms." *European Journal of Political Research* 41: 255–80.

Kohler-Koch, B. 2003. *Linking EU and National Governance.* Oxford: Oxford University Press.

Kolko, G. 1965. *Railroads and Regulation, 1877–1916.* Princeton, NJ: Princeton University Press.

Kommers, D. P. 1966. "Reflections on Professor Chroust's the Rise of the Legal Profession in America." *American Journal of Legal History* 10: 201–13.

Kommers, D., and M. Waelbroeck. 1985. "Legal Integration and the Free Movement of Goods: The American and European Experience." In *Integration Through Law: Europe and the American Federal Experience,* i, ed. M. Cappelletti, M. Seccombe, and J. H. H. Weiler. Berlin: Walter de Gruyter.

Koslowski, R. 1994. "Intra-EU Migration, Citizenship, and Political Union." *JCMS: Journal of Common Market Studies* 32 (3): 369–402.

Kox, H., and A. Lejour. 2005. "Regulatory Heterogeneity as Obstacle for International Services Trade." CPB Discussion Paper 49, CPB Netherlands Bureau for Economic Policy Analysis.

Kox, H., A. Lejour, and R. Montizaan. 2004. "The Free Movement of Services within the EU." CPB Document 69. The Hague, the Netherlands: CPB Netherlands Bureau for Economic Policy Analysis. Available at <http://ideas.repec.org/p/cpb/docmnt/69.html> accessed February 13, 2014.

Kox, H., A. Lejour, and G. Verweij. 2009. "Regulatory Barriers in Business and Transport Services Trade." Available at <http://www.etsg.org/ETSG2009/papers/lejour.pdf> accessed February 19, 2014.

Krash, A. 1984. "The Legacy of William Crosskey." (Review of W. W. Crosskey and W. Jeffrey, Jr., *Politics and the Constitution in the History of the United States, Volume III: The Political Background of the Federal Convention*). *Yale Law Journal* 93 (5): 959–80.

Kreile, M. 1978. "West Germany: The Dynamics of Expansion." In *Between Power and Plenty: Foreign Economic Policies of Advanced Industrial States*, ed. P. J. Katzenstein. Madison, WI: University of Wisconsin Press.

Kreppel, A. 2006. "Understanding the European Parliament from a Federalist Perspective: The Legislatures of the USA and EU Compared." In *Comparative Federalism: The European Union and the United States*, ed. M. Schain and A. Menon. Oxford: Oxford University Press.

Kritzer, H. M. 1991. "Abel and the Professional Project: The Institutional Analysis of the Legal Profession." *Law and Social Inquiry* 16 (3): 529–52.

Kutler, S. I. (ed.) 1984. *The Supreme Court and the Constitution: Readings in American Constitutional History*, 3rd edn. New York: W. W. Norton.

Laffan, B. 1998. "The European Union: A Distinctive Model of Internationalization." *Journal of European Public Policy* 5 (2): 235–53.

Laffan, B., and M. Shackleton. 2000. "The Budget." In *Policy-making in the European Union*, 4th edn., ed. H. Wallace and W. Wallace. New York: Oxford University Press.

Lamoreaux, N. R. 1994. *Insider Lending: Banks, Personal Connections, and Economic Development in New England*. Cambridge, UK: Cambridge University Press.

Lankowski, C. 1995. "Financing Integration: The European Investment Bank in Transition." *Law and Policy in International Business* 27 (4): 999–1045.

Lannoo, K. 2002."Supervising The European Financial System." CEPS Policy Brief No. 21, Brussels.

Laperrouza, M. and M. Finger. 2009. "Regulating Europe's Single Railway Market: Integrating Performance and Governance." Available at <http://mir.epfl.ch/files/con tent/sites/mir/files/users/181931/public/wp0905.pdf> accessed July 29, 2014.

Laqueur, W. 1992. *Europe in Our Time: A History, 1945–1992*. New York: Viking.

Larson, J. L. 2010. *The Market Revolution in America: Liberty, Ambition and the Eclipse of the Common Good*. Cambridge, UK: Cambridge University Press.

Lasok, D. 1986. *The Professions and Services in the European Economic Community*. Deventer, the Netherlands: Kluwer Law and Taxation Publishers.

Laurent, P. H. 1970. "Paul-Henri Spaak and the Diplomatic Origins of the Common Market, 1955–1956." *Political Science Quarterly* 85 (3): 373–96.

Lavenex, S. 2002. "Labour Mobility in the General Agreement on Trade in Services (GATS) –Background Paper." The Political Economy of Migration in an Integrating Europe. Working Paper 1/2002. PEMINT No publisher.

Law, M. T. and S. Kim. 2010. *The Rise of the American Regulatory State: A View from the Progressive Era*. JPRG Paper No. 6. Jerusalem: Jerusalem Forum on Regulation & Governance.

Lee, E. 2002. "The Chinese Exclusion Example: Race, Immigration, and American Gatekeeping, 1882–1924." *Journal of American Ethnic History* 21 (3): 36–62.

Lehmkuhl, D. 2002. "Harmonisation and Convergence? National Responses to the Common European Transport Policy." *German Policy Studies* 2 (4): 1–26.

Lejour, A. 2008. "Economic Aspects of the Internal Market for Services." In *The EU Internal Market in Comparative Perspective: Economic, Political and Legal Analyses*, ed. J. Pelkmans, D. Hanf, and M. Chang. Brussels: Peter Lang.

Lejour, A. 2010. "The Prospect for the Internal Market in Services after the Great Recession." Paper presented at the American University Conference. November 5–6 [mimeo].

Lewin, K. 1965. "The Free Movement of Workers." *Common Market Law Review* 2 (3): 300–24.

Licht, W. 1995. *Industrializing America: The Nineteenth Century*. Baltimore, MD: Johns Hopkins University Press.

Liddle, R., and F. Lerais. 2007. "Europe's Social Reality." Consultation Paper. Brussels: Bureau of European Policy Advisors.

Lindberg, L. N. 1993. "Financial Deregulation, Monetary Policy Coordination, and Economic and Monetary Union." In *The 1992 Project and the Future of Integration in Europe*, ed. D. L. Smith, and J. L. Ray. Armonk, NY: M. E. Sharpe.

Lindberg, L. N. and J. L. Campbell. 1991. "The State and the Organization of Economic Activity." In *Governance of the American Economy*, ed. J. L. Campbell, J. R. Hollingsworth, and L. N. Lindberg. Cambridge, UK: Cambridge University Press.

Lindsay, S. M. 1910. "Reciprocal Legislation." *Political Science Quarterly* 25 (3): 435–57.

Lindseth, P. L. 2010. *Power and Legitimacy: Reconciling Europe and the Nation-state*. Oxford: Oxford University Press.

Lipsey, R. E. 2000. "U.S. Foreign Trade and the Balance of Payments, 1800–1913." In *The Cambridge Economic History of the United States*, ii: *The Long Nineteenth Century*, ed. S. L. Engerman and R. E. Gallman. Cambridge, UK: Cambridge University Press.

Lipset, S. M. 1996. *American Exceptionalism: A Double-Edged Sword*. New York: W. W. Norton.

Lively, R. A. 1955. "The American System: A Review Article." *The Business History Review* 29 (1): 81–96.

Lodge, M. 2008. "Regulation, the Regulatory State and European Politics." *West European Politics* 31 (1): 280–301.

Lonbay, J. 1988a. "Cross-Frontier Provision of Services by Lawyers." *European Law Review* 13: 347–50.

Lonbay, J. 1988b. "Free Movement for Professionals." *European Law Review* 13: 275–9.

Lonbay, J. 1991. "Picking Over the Bones: Rights of Establishment Reviewed." *European Law Review* 16: 507–20.

Lonbay, J. 2001. "Free Movement of Persons, Recognition of Qualifications, and Working Conditions." *International and Comparative Law Quarterly* 50: 168–75.

Lovecy, J. 1993. "Regulating Professional Services in the Single European Market: The Cases of Legal and Medical Services in France and the United Kingdom." Paper presented at ECSA Third Biennial International Conference, May 27–29. Washington, DC.

Lovecy, J. 1995. "Global Regulatory Competition and the Single Market for Professional Services: The Legal and Medical Professions in France and Britain." *Journal of European Public Policy* 2 (3): 514–34.

Lovecy, J. 1999. "Governance Transformation in the Professional Services Sector: A Case of Market Integration 'by the Back Door'?" In *The Transformation of Governance in the European Union*, ed. B. Kohler-Koch and R. Eising. London: Routledge.

Lowi, T. J. 1979. *The End of Liberalism: The Second Republic of the United States*. New York: W. W. Norton.

Lowi, T. J. 1984. "Why Is There No Socialism in the United States? A Federal Analysis." *International Political Science Review* 5 (4): 369–80.

Lucarelli, B. 1999. *The Origin and Evolution of the Single Market in Europe.* Brookfield, VT: Ashgate.

Luebbert, G. M. 1984. "Social Foundations of Political Order in Interwar Europe." *World Politics* 39 (4): 449–78.

Maas, W. 2005. "The Genesis of European Rights." *JCMS: Journal of Common Market Studies* 43 (5): 1009–25.

Maddison, A. 1976. "Economic Policy and Performance in Europe, 1913–1970." In *The Fontana Economic History of Europe: The Twentieth Century*, v: Part 2, ed. C. M. Cipolla. Glasgow: Collins/Fontana.

Madison, J. 1999 [1788]. "Federalist No. 46: The Influence of the State and Federal Governments Compared." In *The Federalist Papers: Alexander Hamilton, James Madison, John Jay*, ed. C. Rossiter. New York: Mentor.

Maduro, M. P. 1997. "Reforming the Market or the State? Article 30 and the European Constitution: Economic Freedom and Political Rights." *European Law Journal* 3 (1): 55–82.

Maduro, M. P. 1998. *We the Court: The European Court of Justice and the European Economic Constitution: A Critical Reading of Article 30 of the EC Treaty.* Oxford: Hart Publishing.

Maduro, M. P. 2000. "Europe's Social Self: 'The Sickness Unto Death.'" *Webpapers on Constitutionalism & Governance beyond the State* (2): 1–26.

Maduro, M. P. 2010. "The Chameleon State: EU Law and the Blurring of the Private/Public Distinction in the Market." Florence: European University Institute SSRN 157552 accessed February 19, 2014.

Maestripieri, C. 1971. "The Free Movement of Persons and Services in the E.E.C: Notes for Lectures Given at the Course on the Common Market." May 12–15 [typescript].

Mahler, V. A., B. J. Taylor, and J. R. Wozniak. 2000. "Economics and Public Support for the European Union: An Analysis at the National, Regional, and Individual Levels." *Polity* 32 (3): 429–53.

Mahoney, C. 2007. "Lobbying Success in the United States and the European Union." *Journal of Public Policy* 27 (1): 35–56.

Maier, C. S. 1977. "The Politics of Productivity: Foundations of American International Economic Policy after World War II." *International Organization* 31 (4): 607–33.

Majone, G. 1992. "Regulatory Federalism in the European Community." *Government and Policy* 10: 299–316.

Majone, G. 1993. "The European Community Between Social Policy and Social Regulation." *JCMS: Journal of Common Market Studies* 31 (2): 153–70.

Majone, G. 1994a. "Independence vs. Accountability? Non-Majoritarian Institutions and Democratic Government in Europe." EUI Working Paper SPS 94/3. Florence, Italy: European University Institute.

Majone, G. 1994b. "The Rise of the Regulatory State in Europe." *West European Politics* 17 (3): 77–101.

Majone, G. 1995. *The Development of Social Regulation in the European Community: Policy Externalities, Transaction Costs, Motivational Factors.* Florence, Italy: European University Institute.

Majone, G. 1996a. *Regulating Europe*. London and New York: Routledge.

Majone, G. 1996b. "Temporal Consistency and Policy Credibility: Why Democracies Need Non-Majoritarian Institutions." EUI Working Paper RSC No. 96/57. Florence, Italy: European University Institute.

Majone, G. 1997. "From the Positive to the Regulatory State: Causes and Consequences of Changes in the Mode of Governance." *Journal of Public Policy* 17 (2): 139–67.

Majone, G. 1998. "State, Market, and Regulatory Competition in the European Union: Lessons for the Integrating World Economy." In *Centralization or Fragmentation? Europe Facing the Challenges of Deepening, Diversity, and Democracy*, ed. A. Moravcsik. New York: Council on Foreign Relations Press.

Majone, G. 1999. "The Regulatory State and Its Legitimacy Problems." *West European Politics* 22 (1): 1–24.

Majone, G. 2002. "Delegation of Regulatory Powers in a Mixed Polity." *European Law Journal* 8 (3): 319–39.

Majone, G. 2006. "The Common Sense of European Integration." *Journal of European Public Policy* 13 (5): 607–26.

Majone, G. 2009. *Dilemmas of European Integration: The Ambiguities and Pitfalls of Integration by Stealth*. Oxford: Oxford University Press.

Manderlkern Group on Better Regulation. 2001. "Final Report." November. Brussels. Available at <http://ec.europa.eu/smart-regulation/better_regulation/documents/mandelkern_report.pdf> accessed December 29, 2013.

Mansfield, E. D., and H. V. Milner. 1997. *The Political Economy of Economic Regionalism*. New York: Columbia University Press.

Mansfield, E. D., and M. L. Busch. 1995. "The Political Economy of Nontariff Barriers: A Cross-national Analysis." *International Organization* 49 (4): 723–49.

Marcussen, M. 1999. "The Power of EMU-Ideas: Reforming Central Banks in Great Britain, France, and Sweden." Robert Schuman Center for Advanced Studies Working Paper 99/19. Florence: European University Institute.

Margo, R. 2000. "The Labor Force in the Nineteenth Century." In, *The Cambridge Economic History of the United States*, ii: *The Long Nineteenth Century*, ed. S. L. Engerman and R. E. Gallman. Cambridge, UK: Cambridge University Press.

Margo, R. A. 2000. *Wages and Labor Markets in the United States, 1820–1860*, 1st edn. Chicago: University of Chicago.

Marks, G. 1997. "A Third Lens: Comparing European Integration and State Building." In *European Integration in Social and Historical Perspective: 1850 to the Present*, ed. J. Klausen and L. A. Tilly. Lanham, MD: Rowman & Littlefield.

Marsh, D. 2013. *Europe's Deadlock: How the Euro Crisis Could Be Solved—And Why It Won't Happen*. New Haven, CT: Yale University Press.

Marsh, S., and N. Rees. 2012. *The European Union in the Security of Europe: From Cold War to Terror War*. London: Routledge.

Mashaw, J. L. 2006. "Recovering American Administrative Law: Federalist Foundations, 1787–1801." *Yale Law Journal* 115 (6): 1256–344.

Mashaw, J. L. 2007. "Reluctant Nationalists: Federal Administration and Administration Law in the Republican Era, 1801–1829." *Yale Law Journal*, 116 (8): 1636–740.

Mashaw, J. L., and A. Perry. 2009. "Administrative Statutory Interpretation in the Antebellum Republic." *Michigan State Law Review*, 7: 7–49.

Mathias, P., and M. M. Postan (eds) 1978. *The Cambridge Economic History of Europe*, vii: *The Industrial Economies: Capital, Labour, and Enterprise. Part 2: The United States, Japan, and Russia*. Cambridge, UK: Cambridge University Press.

Matson, C. D., and P. S. Onuf. 1990. *A Union of Interests: Political and Economic Thought in Revolutionary America*. Lawrence, KS: University of Kansas Press.

Matthijs, M. M. 2013. "The Euro Crisis and the Erosion of Democratic Legitimacy: Lessons from the Gold Standard." ACES Cases, No. 2013.3. Washington, DC: American Consortium on European Union Studies EU Center of Excellence. Available at <http://transatlantic.sais-jhu.edu/ACES/ACES_Cases/ACES%20Cases%202013.pdf> accessed February 16, 2014.

Mattli, W. 1999. *The Logic of Regional Integration: Europe and Beyond*. Cambridge, UK: Cambridge University Press.

Mause, K., and K. Schreeb. 2011. "On the Political Economy of Railway Subsidies: Evidence from Western Europe, 1994–2008." Paper presented at the 67th Congress of the IPF, August 7–11. Ann Arbor, MI.

Mazey, S. 1996. "The Development of the European Idea: From Sectoral Integration to Political Union." In *European Union: Politics and Policy-making*, ed. J. J. Richardson. London: Routledge.

Mazey, S., and J. Richardson (eds) 1993. *Lobbying in the European Community*. Oxford: Oxford University Press.

McCraw, T. K. 1984. *Prophets of Regulation: Charles Francis Adams, Louis D. Brandeis, James M. Landis, Alfred E. Kahn*. Cambridge, MA: The Belknap Press of Harvard University Press.

McCraw, T. K. (ed.) 1981. *Regulation in Perspective: Historical Essays*. Cambridge, MA: Harvard University Press.

McCurdy, C. W. 1975. "Justice Field and the Jurisprudence of Government–Business Relations." *Journal of American History* 65: 970–1005.

McCurdy, C. W. 1978. "American Law and the Marketing Structure of the Large Corporation, 1875–1890." *Journal of Economic History* 38 (3): 631–49.

McCurdy, C. W. 1979. "The Knight Sugar Decision of 1895 and the Modernization of American Corporation Law, 1869–1903." *Business History Review* 53 (3): 304–42.

McGowan, F. 2000. "Competition Policy: The Limits of the European Regulatory State." In *Policy-making in the European Union*, 4th edn., ed. H. Wallace and W. Wallace. Oxford: Oxford University Press.

McKay, D. H. 1996. *Rush to Union: Understanding the European Federal Bargain*. New York: Oxford University Press.

McKay, D. H. 2001. *Designing Europe: Comparative Lessons from the Federal Experience*. Oxford and New York: Oxford University Press.

McNamara, K. R. 1998. *The Currency of Ideas: Monetary Politics in the European Union*. Ithaca, NY: Cornell University Press.

McNamara, K. R. 1999. "Consensus and Constraint: Ideas and Capital Mobility in European Monetary Integration." *Journal of Common Market Studies* 37 (3): 455–76.

McNamara, K. R. 2001a. "Making Money: Political Development, the Greenback, and the Euro." Presentation at Princeton University, November.

McNamara, K. R. 2001b. "Where Do Rules Come From? The Creation of the European Central Bank." In *The Institutionalization of Europe*, ed. A. Stone Sweet, W. Sandholtz, and N. Fligstein. Oxford: Oxford University Press.

McNamara, K. R. 2003. "Does Money Make the State? Political Development, Greenback, and the Euro." Georgetown University [unpublished mimeo].

McNamara, K. R. 2005. "Making Money: Political Development, the Greenback and the Euro." Paper presented at Yale University, April 28. New Haven, CT: Yale University.

McNamara, K. R. 2011. "Historicizing the Unique: Why the EMU Has no Fiscal Authority and Why It Matters." Georgetown University: Mortara Working Paper 2011–12 September.

McPherson, J. M. 1982. *Ordeal by Fire: The Civil War and Reconstruction*. New York: Alfred A. Knopf.

McPherson, J. M. 1996. *Drawn with the Sword: Reflections on the American Civil War*. Oxford: Oxford University Press.

Menon, A., and M. A. Schain (eds) 2006. *Comparative Federalism: The European Union and the United States in Comparative Perspective*. Oxford: Oxford University Press.

Menz, G., and A. Caviedes (eds) 2010. *Labour Migration in Europe*. Basingstoke: Palgrave Macmillan.

Merkel, P. L. 1984. "The Origins of an Expanded Federal Court Jurisdiction: Railroad Development and the Ascendancy of the Federal Judiciary." *The Business History Review* 58 (3): 336–58.

Messerlin, P. A. 2001. *Measuring the Costs of Protection in Europe: European Commercial Policy in the 2000s*. Washington: Institute for International Economics.

Million, J. W. 1894. "The Debate on the National Bank Act of 1863." *Journal of Political Economy* 2 (2): 251–80.

Milward, A. S. 1984. *The Reconstruction of Western Europe, 1945–51*. Berkeley, CA: University of California Press.

Milward, A. S. 1992. *The Reconstruction of Western Europe: 1945–1951*. London: Routledge.

Mogg, J. 2002. "Regulating Financial Services in Europe: A New Approach." *Fordham International Law Journal* 26 (1): 58–82.

Molle, W., and A. van Mourik (eds) 1989. *Wage Differentials in the European Community: Convergence or Divergence*. Brookfield, VT: Avebury/Gower Publishing.

Monti, M. 2003. "Competition in Professional Services: New Light and New Challenges." Speech at Bundesanwaltskammer, March 21. Berlin.

Monti, M. 2010. "A New Strategy for the Single Market at the Service of Europe's Economy and Society." Report to the President of the European Commission José Manuel Barroso, May 9. Available at <http://ec.europa.eu/bepa/pdf/monti_report_final_10_05_2010_en.pdf> accessed December 29, 2013.

Montinola, G., Y. Qian, and B. R. Weingast. 1995. "Federalism, Chinese Style: The Political Basis for Economic Success in China." *World Politics* 48 (1): 50–81.

Moore, B. 1966. *Social Origins of Dictatorship and Democracy: Lord and Peasant in the Making of the Modern World*. Boston, MA: Beacon Press.

Moore, C. D. 2011. "State Building through Partnership: Delegation, Public-private Partnerships, and the Political Development of American Imperialism, 1898–1916." *Studies in American Political Development* 25 (1): 27–55.

Moran, M. 1991. *The Politics of the Financial Services Revolution: The USA, UK, and Japan.* London: Macmillan.

Moravcsik, A. 1998a *Centralization or Fragmentation? Europe Facing the Challenges of Deepening, Diversity, and Democracy.* New York: Council on Foreign Relations.

Moravcsik, A. 1998b. "De Gaulle and European Integration: Historical Revision and Social Science Theory." Program for the Study of Germany and Europe. Working Paper Series 8.5 Harvard University.

Moravcsik, A. 1998c. *The Choice for Europe: Social Purposes and State Power from Messina to Maastricht.* Cornell, NY: Cornell University Press.

Moravcsik, A. 2001. "Federalism in the European Union: Rhetoric and Reality." In *The Federal Vision: Legitimacy and Levels of Governance in the United States and the European Union*, ed. Kalypso Nicolaïdis and Robert Howse. Oxford: Oxford University Press.

Moravcsik, A. 2002a. "Defending the Democratic Legitimacy of the European Union: European Policy-Making in Light of the American Model." manuscript, presented at the Syracuse University European Union Center Colloquium on Lessons for a Globalizing World? Historical Experiences of Europe and the United States in Market Integration, September 25–26. Washington, DC.

Moravcsik, A. 2002b. "In Defence of the 'Democratic Deficit': Reassessing Legitimacy in the European Union." *JCMS: Journal of Common Market Studies* 40 (4): 603–24.

Moseley, E. A. 1895. "Interstate Commerce." In *1795–1895: One Hundred Years of American Commerce*, ed. C. M. Depew. New York: D. O. Haynes.

Moses, J. W. 2011. "Is Constitutional Symmetry Enough? Social Models and Market Integration in the US and Europe." *JCMS: Journal of Common Market Studies* 49 (4): 823–43.

Murphy, W. F. 1959. "Lower Court Checks on Supreme Court Power." *American Political Science Review* 53: 1017–31.

Mustelli, F., and J. Pelkmans. 2013a. "Access Barriers to Services Markets: Mapping, Tracing, Understanding and Measuring." CEPS Special Report 77. Brussels: Centre for European Policy Studies.

Mustelli, F., and J. Pelkmans. 2013b. "Establishing a Genuine Single Market for Services Could Generate Significant Growth across the EU." LSE European Politics and Policy (EUROPP) blog, January 8. Available at <http://eprints.lse.ac.uk/49298/> accessed December 29, 2013.

Myrdal, G. 1957. *Economic Theory and Under-developed Regions.* London: Gerald Duckworth.

Nettels, C. P. 1962. *The Emergence of a National Economy, 1775–1815.* New York: Holt, Rinehart and Winston.

Neuman, G. L. 1993. "The Lost Century of American Immigration Law, 1776–1885." *Columbia Law Review* 93: 1833–901.

New York Times. 1869. "East and West: Completion of the Great Line Spanning the Continent." May 10.

Nicolaïdis, K. 1993. "Mutual Recognition Among Nations: The European Community and Trade in Services." PhD dissertation, Harvard University.

Nicolaïdis, K. 1997. "Managed Mutual Recognition: The New Approach to the Liberalization of Professional Services." In *Liberalization of Trade in Professional Services*. Paris: Organisation for Economic Co-operation and Development.

Nicolaïdis, K. 2005. "Globalization with Human Faces: Managed Mutual Recognition and the Free Movement of Professionals." In *The Principle of Mutual Recognition in the European Integration Process*, ed. F. Kostoris, and P. Schioppa. Basingstoke: Palgrave Macmillan.

Nicolaïdis, K. 2007. "Trusting the Poles? Constructing Europe through Mutual Recognition." *Journal of European Public Policy* 14 (5): 682–98.

Nicolaïdis, K., and R. Howse (eds) 2001. *The Federal Vision: Legitimacy and Levels of Governance in the United States and the European Union*. Oxford and New York: Oxford University Press.

Nicolaïdis, K., and S. K. Schmidt. 2007. "Mutual Recognition 'on Trial': The Long Road to Services Liberalization." *Journal of European Public Policy* 14 (5): 717–34.

Nicolaïdis, K. and J. Trachtman. 2000. "Liberalization, Regulation, and Recognition for Services Trade." In *Services Trade in the Western Hemisphere: Liberalization, Integration, and Reform*, ed. S. M. Stephenson. Washington, DC: Brookings Institution Press.

Niemi, A. W. 1974. *State and Regional Patterns in American Manufacturing, 1860–1900*. Westport, CT: Greenwood Press.

Noble, Charles. 1985. "Wilson's Choice: The Political Origins of the Modern American State." *Comparative Politics* 17 (3): 313–36.

Norman, P. 2004. "Brussels Pledges Funds Revamp." *ft.com*, December 4. Available at <http://search.proquest.com/docview/228912964?accountid=8285> accessed August 27, 2014.

North, D. C. 1966. *The Economic Growth of the United States, 1790–1860*. New York: W. W. Norton.

North, D. C. 1981. *Structure and Change in Economic History*. New York: W. W. Norton.

North, D. C. 1990. *Institutions, Institutional Change and Economic Performance*. New York: Cambridge University Press.

Notaro, G. 2011. "European Integration and Productivity: Exploring the Early Effects of Completing the Internal Market." *JCMS: Journal of Common Market Studies* 49 (4): 845–69.

Novak, W. J. 1993. "Public Economy and the Well-ordered Market: Law and Economic Regulation in 19th-century America." *Law & Social Inquiry* 18 (1): 1–32.

Novak, W. J. 1994. "Common Regulation: Legal Origins of State Power in America." *Hastings Law Journal* 45 (4): 1061–97.

Novak, W. J. 1996. *The People's Welfare: Law and Regulation in Nineteenth-Century America*. Chapel Hill, NC: University of North Carolina Press.

Novak, W. J. 2003. "The Pluralist State: The Convergence of Public and Private Power in America." In *American Public Life and the Historical Imagination*, ed. W. Gamber, M. Grossberg, and H. Hartog. Notre Dame, IN: University of Notre Dame Press.

Novak, W. J. 2008. "The Myth of the 'Weak' American State." *American History Review* 113 (3): 752–72.

Novak, W. J. 2009. "Public-Private Governance A Historical Introduction." In *Government by Contract: Outsourcing and American Democracy*, ed. J. Freeman and M. Minow. Cambridge, MA: Harvard University Press.

Novak, W. J. 2010. "AHR Exchange: Long Live the Myth of the Weak State? A Response to Adams, Gerstle, and Witt." *The American History Review* 115 (3): 792–800.

Novak, W. J. No Date. "Legal Origins of the Modern American State." Available at <http://www.constitution.org/ad_state/novak.htm> accessed February 17, 2014.

Nugent, J. D. 1999. "National Policymaking the Hard Way: The Uniform State Laws Process in Pre-New Deal America." Paper presented at APSA meeting, September 2–5. Atlanta, GA.

Nugent, J. D. 2009. *Safeguarding Federalism: How States Protect Their Interests in National Policymaking*. Norman, OK: University of Oklahoma Press.

Numbers, R. 1988. "The Fall and Rise of the American Medical Profession." In *The Professions in American History*, ed. N. O. Hatch. Notre Dame, IN: University of Notre Dame Press.

Odell, K. A. 1989. "The Integration of Regional and Interregional Capital Markets: Evidence from the Pacific Coast, 1883–1913." *Journal of Economic History* 49 (2): 297–310.

Oliver, P. 1996. *Free Movement of Goods in the E.E.C.: Under Articles 30 to 36 of the Rome Treaty*, 3rd edn. London: Sweet and Maxwell.

Onuf, P. S. 1990. "American Federalism and the Politics of Expansion." In *German and American Constitutional Thought: Contexts, Interaction, and Historical Realities*, i, ed. H. Wellenreuther. New York: Berg Publishers.

O'Reilly, D., and A. Stone Sweet. 1998. "The Liberalization and Regulation of Air Transport." *Journal of European Public Policy* 5 (3): 447–66.

Organisation for Economic Co-operation and Development. 1995. *Liberalisation of Trade in Professional Services*. Paris: Organization for Economic Co-operation and Development.

Organisation for Economic Co-operation and Development. 1996. *International Trade in Professional Services: Assessing Barriers and Encouraging Reform*. Paris: Organisation for Economic Co-operation and Development.

O'Rourke K. H. and J. G. Williamson. 1999. *Globalization and History: The Evolution of a Nineteenth-Century Atlantic Economy*. Cambridge, MA: MIT Press.

Orren K., and S. Skowronek. 2004. *The Search for American Political Development*. Cambridge, UK: Cambridge University Press.

Orzack, L. H. 1980. "Educators, Practitioners and Politicians in the European Common Market." *Higher Education* 9 (3): 307–23.

Orzack, L. H. 1991. "The General Systems Directive: Education and the Liberal Professions." In *The State of the European Community: Policies, Institutions & Debates in the Transition Years, 1989–90*, ed. L. Hurwitz and C. Lequesnes. Boulder, CO: Lynne Rienner.

Owen, N. 1983. *Economies of Scale, Competitiveness and Trade Patterns within the European Community*. Oxford: Oxford University Press.

Page, S. A. B. 1981. "The Revival of Protectionism and its Consequences for Europe." *JCMS: Journal of Common Market Studies* 20: 17–40.

Parker, G. 2004. "This Time It's Serious, Say Ministers in Renewed Onslaught on Red Tape." *Financial Times*, December 7, p. 4.

Parsons, C. 2003. *A Certain Idea of Europe*. Ithaca, NY: Cornell University Press.

Parsons, C., and A. Roberts (eds) 2003. *Evolving Federalisms: The Intergovernmental Balance of Power in America and Europe*. Syracuse, NY: Campbell Public Affairs Institute, Maxwell School of Syracuse University.

Pashigian, B. P. 1977. "The Market for Lawyers: The Determinants of the Demand for the Supply of Lawyers." *Journal of Law and Economics* 20 (1): 53–85.

Pashigian, B. P. 1979. "Occupational Licensing and the Interstate Mobility of Professionals." *Journal of Law and Economics* 22 (1): 1–25.

Pastor, R. A. 2001. *Toward a North American Community: Lessons from the Old World for the New*. Washington, DC: Peterson Institute for International Economics.

Pastor, R. A. 2011. *The North American Idea: A Vision of a Continental Future*. Oxford: Oxford University Press.

Patashnik, E. 2000. "Political Science and the Study of 'the Market': The Role of Market Forces in American Politics and Government." Paper presented at annual meeting of the American Political Science Association, August 31–September 3. Washington, DC.

Paterson, I., M. Fink, and A. Ogus. 2003. "Economic Impact of Regulation in the Field of Liberal Professions in Different Member States." Research report for the European Commission. Vienna, Austria: Institute for Advanced Studies. Available at <http://ec.europa.eu/competition/sectors/professional_services/studies/executive_en.pdf> accessed December 27, 2013.

Patterson, L. A. 1997. "Agricultural Policy Reform in the European Community: A Three-level Game Analysis." *International Organization* 51 (1): 135–65.

Pauget, G. 2009. "EFR Input for the De Larosière Group." February 10 [Letter]. Available at <http://www.efr.be/documents%5Cpublication%5C55.2009.02.%20EFR%20letter%20to%20de%20Larosiere%2010.02.2009.pdf> accessed August 27, 2014.

Pearce, J. 1983. "The Common Agricultural Policy: The Accumulation of Special Interests." In *Policy-making in the European Communities*, 2nd edn., ed. H. Wallace, W. Wallace, and C. Webb. Chichester, UK: John Wiley.

Pearce, J., J. Sutton, and R. A. Batchelor. 1985. *Protection and Industrial Policy in Europe*. London: Routledge and Keegan Paul.

Peixoto, J. 2001. "Migration and Policies in the European Union: Highly Skilled Mobility, Free Movement of Labour and Recognition of Diplomas." *International Migration*, 39 (1): 33–61.

Pelkmans, J. 1984. *Market Integration in the European Community*. The Hague/ Boston: Martinus Nijhoff.

Pelkmans, J. 1987. "The New Approach to Technical Harmonization and Standardization." *Journal of Common Market Studies* 25 (3): 249–69.

Pelkmans, J. 1997. *European Integration: Methods and Economic Analysis*, 1st edn. Heerlen: Open University of the Netherlands.

Pelkmans, J. 2003. "Mutual Recognition in Goods and Services: An Economic Perspective." ENEPRI Working Paper No. 16. Brussels: European Network of Economic Policy Research Institutes.

Pelkmans, J. 2005. "Subsidiarity between Law and Economics." European Legal Studies—Research Papers in Law No. 1. Brugge: College of Europe.

Pelkmans, J. 2006. *European Integration: Methods and Economic Analysis*, 3rd edn. Harlow: Prentice Hall.

Pelkmans, J. 2007. "Mutual Recognition in Goods: On Promises and Disillusions." *Journal of European Public Policy* 14 (5): 699–716.

Pelkmans, J. 2008. "Economic Concept and Meaning of the Internal Market." In *The EU Internal Market in Comparative Perspective: Economic, Political and Legal Analyses*, ed. J. Pelkmans, D. Hanf, and M. Chang. Brussels: Peter Lang.

Pelkmans, J. 2010. "Single Market Revival." Brussels: Centre for European Policy Studies.

Pelkmans, J. 2012. "Mutual Recognition: Economic and Regulatory Logic in Goods and Services." Bruges European Economic Research Paper No. 24. Brugge: College of Europe.

Pelkmans, J., and A. C. de Brito. 2012. *Enforcement in the EU Single Market*. Brussels: Centre for European Policy Studies. Available at <http://www.ceps.eu/system/files/Enforcement%20in%20the%20EU%20Single%20Market_0.pdf> accessed February 17, 2014.

Pelkmans, J., and P. Robson. 1987. "The Aspirations of the White Paper." *JCMS: Journal of Common Market Studies* 25 (3): 181–92.

Pelkmans, J., and A. Winters. 1988. *Europe's Domestic Market*. London: Routledge.

Pentland, C. C. 2009. "Enlargement: Expanding the Realm of European Governance." In *Innovative Governance in the European Union: The Politics of Multilevel Policymaking*, ed. I. Tömmel and A. Verdun. Boulder, CO: Lynne Reiner Publishers.

Pisani, D. J. 1987. "Promotion and Regulation: Constitutionalism and the American Economy." *Journal of American History* 74: 740–68.

Polanyi, K. 1944. *The Great Transformation: The Political and Economic Origins of Our Time*. Boston, MA: Beacon Press.

Pollack, M. A. 1997. "Representing Diffuse Interests in EC Policy-making." *Journal of European Public Policy* 4 (4): 572–90.

Pollack, S. 2009. *War, Revenue, and State Building: Financing the Development of the American State*. Ithaca, NY; Cornell University Press.

Pomfret, R. 1981. "The Impact of EEC Enlargement on Non-member Mediterranean Countries' Exports to the EEC." *Economic Journal* 91 (September): 726–9.

Pomfret, R. 1986. "The Trade-diverting Bias of Preferential Trading Arrangements." *Journal of Common Market Studies* 25 (2): 109–17.

Pope, C. 2000. "Economic Inequality in the Nineteenth Century." In *The Cambridge Economic History of the United States*, ii: *The Long Nineteenth Century*, ed. S. L. Engerman and R. E. Gallman. Cambridge, UK: Cambridge University Press.

Posner, E. 2006. "Sources of Institutional Change: The Supranational Origins of Europe's New Stock Markets." *World Politics* 58 (1): 1–40.

Posner, E., and N. Véron, 2010. "The EU and Financial Regulation: Power without Purpose?" *Journal of European Public Policy* 17 (3): 400–15.

Pozen, R. C. 2001. "Continental Shift: The Securitization of Europe." *Foreign Affairs* 80 (3): 9–14.

Prentice, E. P., and J. G. Egan. 1898. *The Commerce Clause of the Federal Constitution.* Chicago, IL: Callahan & Co.

Pruitt, P. M., Jr. 1997. "The Life and Times of Legal Education in Alabama, 1819–1897: Bar Admissions, Law Schools, and the Profession." *Alabama Law Review* 49 (1): 281–321.

Pryce, R., ed. 1987. *The Dynamics of European Union.* London: Croom Helm.

Putnam, R., R. Leonardi, and R. Y. Nanetti. 1993. *Making Democracy Work: Civic Traditions in Modern Italy.* Princeton, NJ: Princeton University Press.

Quaglia, L. 2008. "Financial Sector Committee Governance in the European Union." *Journal of European Integration* 30 (4): 563–78.

Quaglia, L. 2010. "Completing the Single Market in Financial Services: The Politics of Competing Advocacy Coalitions." *Journal of European Public Policy* 17 (7): 1007–23.

Quarles, R. 2002. "Congressional Testimony Committee on Financial Services on EU Financial Services Action Plan." Congressional Record V 148 D 265 Daily Record.

Radaelli, C. M. 1999a. "Harmful Tax Competition in the EU." Paper presented at the 40th annual convention of the International Studies Association, February 16–20. Washington, DC.

Radaelli, C. M. 1999b. "Whither Tax Coordination? The Changing Agenda of the European Union." Paper presented at Conference on Globalization at Georgia Tech University, March. Atlanta, GA.

Radaelli, C. M., and U. S. Kraemer. 2009. "Modes of Governance in EU Tax Policy." In *Innovative Governance in the European Union: The Politics of Multilevel Policymaking*, ed. I. Tömmel and A. Verdun. Boulder, CO: Lynne Reiner Publishers.

Raisner, R. 1964. "National Regulation of the Movement of Workers in the European Community." *American Journal of Comparative Law* 13 (3): 360–84.

Rasmussen, M. 2013. "Rewriting the History of European Public Law: The New Contribution of Historians." *American University International Law Review* 28 (5): 1187–221.

Reder, M., and L. Ulman. 1993. "Unionism and Unification." In *Labor and an Integrated Europe*, ed. L. Ulman, B. J. Eichengreen, and W. T. Dickens. Washington, DC: Brookings Institution.

Reilly, D. 2005. "EU's McCreevy Seeks Delay in Trading Rules." *The Wall Street Journal Europe*, January 25, p. M1.

Remini, R. V. 1967. *Andrew Jackson and the Bank War: A Study in the Growth of Presidential Power.* New York: W. W. Norton.

Richardson, J. D. 2000. "The WTO and Market-supportive Regulation: A Way Forward on New Competition, Technological, and Labor Issues." *Federal Reserve Bank of St. Louis Review* 82: 115–26.

Riker, W. H. 1964. *Federalism: Origin, Operation, Significance.* Boston, MA: Little, Brown and Company.

Risse, T. 2003. "The Euro between National and European Identity." *Journal of European Public Policy* 10 (4): 487–505.

Risse, T. 2010. *A Community of Europeans? Transnational Identities and Public Spheres.* Ithaca, NY: Cornell University Press.

Rittberger, B. 2009. "The Historical Origins of the EU's System of Representation." *Journal of European Public Policy* 16 (1): 43–61.

Roberts, M. M. 1954. *American Nursing: History and Interpretation*. New York: Macmillan.

Robertson, D. B. 1989. "The Bias of American Federalism: The Limits of Welfare-state Development in the Progressive Era." *Journal of Policy History* 1 (3): 261–91.

Robertson, D. B. 2000. *Capital, Labor, and State: The Battle for American Labor Markets from the Civil War to the New Deal*. Lanham, MD: Rowman & Littlefield.

Rockoff, H. 2000. "Banking and Finance, 1789–1914." In *The Cambridge Economic History of the United States*, ii: *The Long Nineteenth Century*, ed. S. L. Engerman and R. E. Gallman. Cambridge, UK: Cambridge University Press.

Rohrschneider, R. 2002. "The Democratic Deficit and Mass Support for an EU-wide Government." *American Journal of Political Science* 46 (2): 463–75.

Rollings, N., and M. Moguen-Toursel. 2012. "European Organised Business and European Integration in the Post-Second World War Period." *Jahrbuch für Wirtschaftsgeschichte/ Economic History Yearbook* 53 (1): 9–306.

Rollo, J., and L. A. Winters. 1999. "Domestic Regulation and Trade: Subsidiarity and Governance Challenges for the WTO." Paper presented at the WTO/World Bank Conference on Developing Countries in a Millennium Round, September 20–21. Geneva: WTO Secretariat. Available at <http://www.iatp.org/files/Domestic_Regulation_and_Trade_Subsidiarity_and.htm> accessed December 27, 2013.

Rolnick, A. J., and W. E. Weber. 1982. "Free Banking, Wildcat Banking, and Shinplasters." *Federal Reserve of Minneapolis Quarterly Review* 6: 10–19.

Romero, F. 1990. "Cross-border Population Movements." In *The Dynamics of European Integration*, ed. W. Wallace. London: Pinter/RIIA.

Rosenbloom, J. L. 1990. "One Market or Many? Labor Market Integration in the Late Nineteenth-century United States." *Journal of Economic History* 50 (1): 85–107.

Rosenbloom, J. L. 1994. "Looking for Work, Searching for Workers: U.S. Labor Markets after the Civil War." *Social Science History* 18 (3): 377–403.

Rosenbloom, J. L. 1996. "Was There a National Labor Market at the End of the Nineteenth Century? New Evidence on Earnings in Manufacturing." *Journal of Economic History* 56 (3): 626–56.

Rosenbloom, J. L. 1998. "The Extent of the Labor Market in the United States, 1870–1914." *Social Science History* 22 (3): 287–318.

Rosenbloom, J. L. 2002. *Looking for Work, Searching for Workers: American Labor Markets During Industrialization*. Cambridge, UK: Cambridge University Press.

Rosenbloom, J. L., and W. A. Sundstrom. 2009. "Labor-market Regimes in U.S. Economic History." NBER Working Paper No. 15055. Cambridge, MA: National Bureau of Economic Research.

Ross, W. G. 1994. *A Muted Fury: Populists, Progressives, and Labor Unions Confront the Courts, 1890–1937*. Princeton, NJ: Princeton University Press.

Rossiter, C. (ed.) 1999. *The Federalist Papers: Alexander Hamilton, James Madison, John Jay*. New York: Mentor.

Rothenberg, W. B. 1992. *From Market-places to a Market Economy: The Transformation of Rural Massachusetts, 1750–1850*. Chicago, IL: University of Chicago Press.

Ruggie, J. G. 1982. "International Regimes, Transactions, and Change: Embedded Liberalism in the Postwar Economic Period." *International Organization* 36 (2): 379–415.

Saloutos, T. 1948. "The Agricultural Problem and Nineteenth Century Industrialism." *Agricultural History* 22 (3): 156–74.

Sandalow, T., and E. Stein. 1982. *Courts and Free Markets: Perspectives from the United States and Europe.* Oxford: Clarendon Press.

Sanders, E. 1999. *Roots of Reform: Farmers, Workers and the American State 1877–1917.* Chicago, IL: University of Chicago Press.

Sandholtz, W., and J. Zysman. 1989. "1992: Recasting the European Bargain." *World Politics* 42 (1): 95–128.

Saunders, C. 1975. "From Free Trade to Integration in Western Europe." Chatham House/ PEP European Series No. 22. London: Chatham House, the Royal Institute of International Affairs.

Sbragia, A. M. (ed.) 1992a. *Euro-politics: Institutions and Policymaking in the "New" European Community.* Washington, DC: Brookings Institution Press.

Sbragia, A. M. 1992b. "Thinking about the European Future: The Uses of Comparison." In *Euro-politics: Institutions and Policymaking in the "New" European Community,* ed. A. M. Sbragia. Washington, DC: Brookings Institution.

Sbragia, A. M. 1996. *Debt Wish: Entrepreneurial Cities, U.S. Federalism, and Economic Development.* Pittsburgh, PA: University of Pittsburgh Press.

Sbragia, A. M. 2000. "Governance, the State, and the Market: What is Going On?" *Governance* 13 (2): 243–50.

Sbragia, A. M. 2001. "Territory, Electorates and Markets: The Construction of Democratic Federalism." In *Nation, Federalism and Democracy: The EU, Italy and the American Federal Experience,* ed. S. Fabbrini. Bologna: Editrice Compositori.

Sbragia, A. M. 2002. "Conclusion to Special Issue on the Institutional Balance and the Future of EU Governance: The Treaty of Nice, Institutional Balance, and Uncertainty." *Governance* 15 (3): 393–411.

Sbragia, A. M. 2003. "Post-national Democracy: A Challenge to Political Science?" Paper delivered as the introductory presentation at the *Convegno Nazionale Della Societa Italiana di Scienza Politica,* (SISP) Universita degli Studi di Trento, September 15. Trento, Italy.

Sbragia, A. M. 2004. "Territory, Representation and Policy Outcome: The United States and the European Union Compared." In *Restructuring Territoriality: Europe and America Compared,* ed. C. K. Ansell and G. Di Palma. Cambridge, UK: Cambridge University Press.

Sbragia, A. M. 2005. "Seeing the European Union through American Eyes: The EU as a Reflection of the American Experience." *European Political Science* 4 (2): 179–87.

Schain, M. 2006. "Immigration Policy." In *Comparative Federalism: The European Union and the United States in Comparative Perspective,* ed. A. Menon and M. A. Schain. Oxford: Oxford University Press.

Scharpf, F. W. 1988. "The Joint-decision Trap: Lessons from German Federalism and European Integration." *Public Administration* 66 (3): 239–78.

Scharpf, F. W. 1999a. *Governing in Europe: Effective and Democratic?* Oxford: Oxford University Press.

Scharpf, F. W. 1999b. "The Viability of Advanced Welfare States in the International Economy: Vulnerabilities and Options." MPIfG Working Paper 99/9. Cologne: Max-Planck-Institut für Gesellschaftsforschung.

Scharpf, F. W. 2002. "The European Social Model." *JCMS: Journal of Common Market Studies* 40 (4): 645–70.

Scheiber, H. N. 1971. "The Road to Munn: Eminent Domain and the Concept of Public Purpose in the State Courts." *Perspectives in American History* 5: 327–402.

Scheiber, H. N. 1972. "Government and the Economy: Studies of the 'Commonwealth' Policy in Nineteenth-century America." Review of O. Handlin and M. F. Handlin, *Commonwealth: A Study of the Role of Government in the American Economy: Massachusetts, 1774–1861. Journal of Interdisciplinary History* 3 (1): 135–51.

Scheiber, H. N. 1973. "Property Law, Expropriation, and Resource Allocation by Government: The United States, 1789–1910." *Journal of Economic History* 33: 232–51.

Scheiber, H. N. 1975. "Federalism and the American Economic Order, 1789–1910." *Law and Society Review* 10 (1): 57–118.

Scheiber, H. N. 1978. "American Federalism and the Diffusion of Power: Historical and Contemporary Perspectives." *University of Toledo Law Review* 9: 619–80.

Scheiber, H. N. 1980a. "Federalism and Legal Process: Historical and Contemporary Analysis of the American System." *Law and Society Review* 14 (3): 663–722.

Scheiber, H. N. 1980b. "Public Economic Policy and the American Legal System: Historical Perspectives." *Wisconsin Law Review* 1980: 1159–89.

Scheiber, H. N. 1981. "Regulation, Property Rights, and Definition of 'the Market': Law and the American Economy." *Journal of Economic History* 41 (1): 103–9.

Scheiber, H. N. 1984. "Public Rights and the Rule of Law in American Legal History." *California Law Review* 72 (2): 217–51.

Scheiber, H. N. 1988. "Federalism and the Constitution: The Original Understanding." In *American Law and the Constitutional Order: Historical Perspectives*, ed. L. M. Friedman, and H. N. Scheiber. Cambridge, MA: Harvard University Press.

Scheiber, H. N. 1997. "Private Rights and Public Power: American Law, Capitalism, and the Republican Polity in Nineteenth-Century America." Review of W. J. Novak, *The People's Welfare: Law and Regulation in Nineteenth-Century America. Yale Law Journal* 107 (3): 823–61.

Schelkle, W. 2009a. "Monetary Union." In *Research Agendas in EU Studies: Stalking the Elephant*, ed. M. Egan, N. Nugent, and W. E. Paterson. London: Palgrave Macmillan.

Schelkle, W. 2009b. "Regulatory State Building in Fiscal Surveillance: The US and EU Compared." Paper presented at the EUSA Biennial Conference, Los Angeles, March 25–27. Available at <http://www.euce.org/eusa2009/papers/schelkle_10B.pdf> accessed February 17, 2014.

Schelkle, W. 2009c. "The Contentious Creation of the Regulatory State in Fiscal Surveillance." *West European Politics* 32 (4): 829–46.

Schelkle, W. 2010. "Good Governance in Crisis or a Good Crisis for Governance? A Comparison of the EU and the US." LSE Europe in Question Discussion Paper Series No. 16/2009. London: London School of Economics and Political Science. <http://www.lse.ac.uk/europeanInstitute/LEQS/LEQSPaper16.pdf> accessed December 29, 2013.

Schepel, H. 2005. *The Constitution of Private Governance: Product Standards in the Regulation of Integrating Markets*. Oxford: Hart Publishing.

Schermers, H. G., C. Flinterman, and A. E. Kellermann et al. (eds) 1993. *Free Movement of Persons in Europe: Legal Problems and Experiences*. Dordrecht, the Netherlands: Martinus Nijhoff.

Schimmelfennig, F. 2001. "The Community Trap: Liberal Norms, Rhetorical Action, and the Eastern Enlargement of the European Union." *International Organization* 55 (1): 47–80.

Schimmelfennig, F. 2009. "Integration Theory." In *Research Agendas in EU Studies: Stalking the Elephant*, ed. M. Egan, N. Nugent, and W. E. Paterson. Basingstoke: Palgrave Macmillan.

Schlomach, B. 2012. "Six Reforms to Occupational Licensing Laws to Increase Jobs and Lower Costs." Goldwater Institute Policy Report No. 247. Phoenix AZ. Available at <http://goldwaterinstitute.org/sites/default/files/Policy%20Report%20247%20Licensing.pdf> accessed July 4, 2014.

Schmidhauser, J. R. 1961. "Judicial Behavior and the Sectional Crisis of 1837–1860." *Journal of Politics* 23: 615–40.

Schmidt, L. B. 1939. "Internal Commerce and the Development of National Economy before 1860." *The Journal of Political Economy* 47 (6): 798–822.

Schmidt, S. K. 2000. "Only an Agenda Setter: The European Commission's Power over the Council of Ministers." *European Union Politics* 1 (1): 37–61.

Schmidt, S. K. 2002. "The Impact of Mutual Recognition—Inbuilt Limits and Domestic Responses to the Single Market." *Journal of European Public Policy* 9 (6): 935–53.

Schmidt, S. K. 2005. "Reform in the Shadow of Community Law: Highly Regulated Economic Sectors." *German Politics* 14 (2): 157–73.

Schmidt, S. K. 2008. "The Internal Market Seen from a Political Science Perspective." In *The EU Internal Market in Comparative Perspective: Economic, Political and Legal Analyses*, ed. J. Pelkmans, D. Hanf, and M. Chang. Brussels: Peter Lang.

Schmidt, S. K. 2009. "When Efficiency Results in Redistribution: The Conflict over the Single Service Market." *Western European Politics* 32 (4): 847–65.

Schmidt, S. K. 2013. "A Sense of Déjà Vu? The FCC's Preliminary European Stability Mechanism Verdict." *German Law Journal* 14: 1–20.

Schmidt, V. A. 1996. *From State to Market? The Transformation of French Business and Government*. New York: Cambridge University Press.

Schmidt, V. A. 1999. "European 'Federalism' and Its Encroachments on National Institutions." *Publius* 29 (1): 19–44.

Schmidt, V. A. 2001. "Federalism and State Governance in the European Union and the United States: An Institutional Perspective." In *The Federal Vision: Legitimacy and Levels of Governance in the United States and the European Union*, ed. K. Nicolaïdis and R. Howse. Oxford and New York: Oxford University Press.

Schmidt, V. A. 2002. *The Futures of European Capitalism*. Oxford: Oxford University Press.

Schmidt, V. A. 2004. "The European Union: Democratic Legitimacy in a Regional State?" *JCMS: Journal of Common Market Studies* 42 (5): 975–97.

Schmitt, H. O. 1968. "Capital Markets and the Unification of Europe." *World Politics* 20 (2): 228–44.

Schmitter, P. C. 2000. *How to Democratize the European Union . . . and Why Bother?* Lanham, MD: Rowman & Littlefield.

Schofield, W. 1908a. "Uniformity of Law in the Several States as an American Ideal: I. Case Law." *Harvard Law Review* 21 (6): 416–30.

Schofield, W. 1908b. "Uniformity of Law in the Several States as an American Ideal: II. Statute Law, and III. Case Law versus State Law." *Harvard Law Review* 21 (7): 510–26.

Schofield, W. 1908c. "Uniformity of Law in the Several States as an American Ideal: IV. State Courts versus Federal Courts." *Harvard Law Review* 21 (8): 583–94.

Schultz, S. K. 1989. *Constructing Urban Culture: American Cities and City Planning, 1800–1920.* Technology and Urban Growth series. Philadelphia, PA: Temple University Press.

Schütze, R. 2009. *From Dual to Cooperative Federalism: The Changing Structure of European Law.* Oxford and New York: Oxford University Press.

Scitovsky, T. 1956. "Economies of Scale, Competition, and European Integration." *The American Economic Review* 46 (1): 71–91.

Sedelmeier, U., and H. Grabbe. 2009. "The Future Shape of the Union." In *Research Agendas in EU Studies: Stalking the Elephant,* ed. M. Egan, N. Nugent, and W. E. Paterson. Basingstoke: Palgrave Macmillan.

Servais, D. 1988. *The Single Financial Market.* Brussels: Commission of the European Communities.

Shapiro, M. 1968. *The Supreme Court and Administrative Agencies,* ii. New York: Free Press.

Shapiro, M. 1992. "The Giving Reasons Requirement." *University of Chicago Legal Forum* 1992: 179–220.

Shapiro, M., and A. Stone Sweet. 2002. *On Law, Politics, and Judicialization.* Oxford: Oxford University Press.

Sheridan, J. W. 1996. "The Déjà Vu of EMU: Considerations for Europe from Nineteenth Century America." *Journal of Economic Issues* 30 (4): 1143–61.

Shonfield, A. 1965. *Modern Capitalism: The Changing Balance of Public and Private Power.* Oxford: Oxford University Press.

Shryock, R. H. 1967. *Medical Licensing in America, 1650–1965.* Baltimore, MD: Johns Hopkins University Press.

Sidjanski, D. 1967. "Pressure Groups and the European Economic Community." *Government and Opposition* 2 (3): 397–416.

Siedentop, L. 2001. *Democracy in Europe.* New York: Columbia University Press.

Siendentopf, H., and J. Ziller (eds) 1988. *Making European Policies Work: The Implementation of Community Legislation in the Member States.* 2 vols. London: Sage Publications.

Simon, S. 2011. "A License to Shampoo: Jobs Needing State Approval Rise." February 7. *The Wall Street Journal.* Available at <http://online.wsj.com/news/articles/SB10001424052748703445904576118030935929752> accessed September 2, 2014.

Sklar, M. J. 1988. *The Corporate Reconstruction of American Capitalism, 1890–1916: The Market, the Law, and Politics.* Cambridge, UK: Cambridge University Press.

Skocpol, T. 1992. *Protecting Soldiers and Mothers: The Political Origins of Social Policy in the United States.* Cambridge, MA: The Belknap Press of Harvard University Press.

Skowronek, S. 1982. *Building a New American State: The Expansion of National Administrative Capacities, 1877–1920.* Cambridge, UK: Cambridge University Press.

Skowronek, S. 1997. *The Politics Presidents Make: Leadership from John Adams to Bill Clinton*. Cambridge, MA: The Belknap Press of Harvard University Press.

Slot, P. J. 1975. *Technical and Administrative Obstacles to Trade in the EEC*. Leiden: A. J. Ninjhoff.

Smith, D. L., and J. L. Ray (eds) 1992. *The 1992 Project and the Future of Integration in Europe*. Armonk, NY: M. E. Sharpe.

Smith, M. P. 2005. *States of Liberalization: Redefining the Public Sector in Integrated Europe*. New York: SUNY Press.

Smith, R. M. 1993. "Beyond Tocqueville, Myrdal, and Hartz: The Multiple Traditions in America." *American Political Science Review* 87 (3): 549–66.

Smyrl, M. E. 1997. "Does European Community Regional Policy Empower the Regions?" *Governance* 10 (3): 287–309.

Smyrl, M. E. 1998. "When (and How) Do the Commission's Preferences Matter?" *JCMS: Journal of Common Market Studies* 36 (1): 79–99.

Snell, J. 2002. *Goods and Services in EC Law: A Study of the Relationship Between the Freedoms*. Oxford: Oxford University Press.

Snell, J. 2011. "Free Movement of Capital: Evolution as a Non-Linear Process." In *The Evolution of EU Law*, 2nd edn. ed. P. Craig and G. De Búrca. Oxford: Oxford University Press.

Spaak Report, 1956. "Rapport des Chefs de Délégations aux Ministres des Affaires Etrangères." Secretariat of the Intergovernmental Conference, April. Brussels.

Stampp, K. M. (ed.) 1965 [1959]. *The Causes of the Civil War*. Englewood Cliffs, NJ: Prentice Hall.

Staniland, M. 2008. *A Europe of the Air? The Airline Industry and European Integration*. Lanham, MD: Rowman & Littlefield.

Stehmann, O., and H. Zenger. 2011. "The Competitive Effects of Rail Freight Mergers in the Context of European Liberalization." *Journal of Competition Law & Economics* 7 (2): 455–79.

Stein, E. 1981. "Lawyers, Judges, and the Making of a Transnational Constitution." *American Journal of International Law* 75 (1): 1–27.

Stevens, H. 2004. *Transport Policy in the European Union*. Basingstoke: Palgrave Macmillan.

Still, B. 1936. "An Interpretation of the Statehood Process, 1800 to 1850." *The Mississippi Valley Historical Review* (1936) 23 (2): 189–204.

Stone Sweet, A. 2005. "European Integration and the Legal System." Political Science Series 101 Vienna: IHS. Available at <http://aei.pitt.edu/3006/1/pw_101.pdf> accessed July 30, 2014.

Story, J., and I. Walter. 1997. *Political Economy of Financial Integration in Europe: The Battle of the Systems*. Cambridge, MA: MIT Press.

Strange, S. 1996. *The Retreat of the State: The Diffusion of Power in the World Economy*. Cambridge, UK: Cambridge University Press.

Straubhaar, T. 1988. "International Labour Migration within a Common Market." *JCMS: Journal of Common Market Studies* 27 (1): 45–62.

Sun, J.-M., and J. Pelkmans. 1995. "Regulatory Competition in the Single Market." *JCMS: Journal of Common Market Studies* 33 (1): 67–89.

Sushka, M. E. 1976. "The Antebellum Money Market and the Economic Impact of the Bank War." *Journal of Economic History* 36 (4): 809–35.

Sushka, M. E., and W. B. Barrett. 1984. "Banking Structure and the National Capital Market, 1869–1914." *Journal of Economic History* 44 (2): 463–77.

Sylla, R. 1969. "Federal Policy, Banking Market Structure, and Capital Mobilization in the United States." *Journal of Economic History* 29 (4): 657–86.

Sylla, R. 1976. "Forgotten Men of Money: Private Bankers in Early U.S. History." *Journal of Economic History* 36 (1): 173–88.

Sylla, R. 2002. "United States Banks and Europe: Business Strategy and Attitudes." In *European Banks and the American Challenge: Competition and Cooperation in International Banking under Bretton Woods*, ed. S. Battilossi and Y Cassis. Oxford: Oxford University Press.

Tarr, G. A. 2008. "Symmetry and Asymmetry in American Federalism." Paper delivered at Queen's University, Kingston, Ontario, Canada.

Taussig, F. W. 1888. *The Tariff History of the United States*. London: Putnam and Sons. Republished and typeset, available at <http://mises.org/books/tariff_history_taussig.pdf> accessed September 2, 2014.

Taylor, G. R. 1951. *The Transportation Revolution, 1815–1860*. New York: Holt, Rinehart, and Winston.

Taylor, G. R. 1964. "American Economic Growth Before 1840: An Exploratory Essay." *The Journal of Economic History* 24 (4): 427–44.

Taylor, G. R., and I. D. Neu. 1956. *The American Railroad Network, 1861–1890*. Cambridge, MA: Harvard University Press.

Temin, P. 1968. "The Economic Consequences of the Bank War." *Journal of Political Economy* 76 (2): 257–74.

Terry, L. 2001. Interview with CrossingtheBar.com, *CrossingtheBar*. Available at <http://www.personal.psu.edu/faculty/l/s/lst3/Electronic%20Interview%20of%20Professor%20Laurel%20Terry.pdf> accessed July 30, 2014.

Tesser, L. M. 2003. "The Geopolitics of Tolerance: Minority Rights under EU Expansion in East-Central Europe." *East European Politics & Societies* 17 (3): 483–532.

The Economist. 1964. "Too Many Unit Trusts?" *The Economist Historical Archive, 1843–2010*. July 4.

The Economist. 2001. "Towards a bigger, simpler Europe." December 15 [print edition].

The Economist, 2012. "Notaries: Breaking the Seals." August 11 [print edition].

Tiebout, C. M. 1956. "A Pure Theory of Local Expenditures." *Journal of Political Economy* 64 (5): 416–24.

Tilford, S. 2010. "How to Save the Euro." London: Center for European Reform.

Tilford, S. 2011. "Europe's Competitiveness Trap." Project Syndicate. Available at <http://www.project-syndicate.org/commentary/europe-s-competitiveness-trap> accessed July 30, 2014.

Tilford, S. 2012. "Workers Must Get a Bigger Slice of the Pie." *New York Times*. Available at <http://www.nytimes.com/2012/11/23/opinion/european-workers-must-get-a-bigger-slice-of-the-pie.html> accessed February 14, 2014.

Tilly, C. 1992. *Coercion, Capital, and European States, AD 990–1992*. Cambridge, MA: Blackwell.

Tinbergen, J. 1954a. *Centralization and Decentralization in Economic Policy.* Contributions to Economic Analysis, VI. Amsterdam: North Holland.

Tinbergen, J. 1954b. *International Economic Integration.* New York: Elsevier.

Trescott, P. B. 1955. "Federal-State Financial Relations, 1790–1860." *Journal of Economic History* 15: 227–45.

Tsoukalis, L. 1997. *The New European Economy Revisited.* Oxford and New York: Oxford University Press.

Tufano, P. 1997. "Business Failure, Judicial Intervention, and Financial Innovation: Restructuring U.S. Railroads in the Nineteenth Century." *Business History Review* 71 (1): 1–40.

Ugur, M. 2007. "Liberalisation of Network Industries in the European Union: Evidence on Market Integration and Performance." Paper presented at the European Union Studies Association Conference [unpublished mimeo]. Available at <http://www .unc.edu/euce/eusa2007/papers/ugur-m-05a.pdf> accessed July 30, 2014.

Urofsky, M. I. 1985. "State Courts and Protective Legislation during the Progressive Era: A Reevaluation." *Journal of American History* 72 (1): 63–91.

Urwin, D. W. 1991. *The Community of Europe: A History of European Integration Since 1945.* London and New York: Longman.

U.S. Congress, House, Department of the Treasury. 1888. "Report on the Internal Commerce of the United States, 1887." W. F. Switzler, Part 2 of *Commerce and Navigation.* House Executive Document No. 6, Serial 2552, 50th Congress, 1st Session. Washington, DC.

Vachudova, M. A. 2005. *Europe Undivided: Democracy, Leverage, and Integration After Communism.* Oxford: Oxford University Press.

Van Gerven, W. 1966. "The Right of Establishment and Free Supply of Services within the Common Market." *Common Market Law Review* 3 (3): 344–62.

Viner, J. 1950. *The Customs Union Issue.* Studies in the Administration of International Law and Organization 10. New York: Carnegie Endowment for International Peace.

Vinocur, N., and L. Thomas. 2013. "Hollande Shuns Fight with Protected Jobs as EU Pressure Builds." July 5. *Reuters.* Available at <http://www.reuters.com/article/2013/ 07/05/us-france-liberalisation-idUSBRE96403420130705> accessed July 30, 2014.

Vipond, P. 1995. "European Banking and Insurance: Business Alliances and Corporate Strategies". In *European Casebook on Business Alliances,* ed. J. Greenwood. Hemel Hempstead: Prentice Hall.

Vipond, P. A. 1993. "Rules, Economics, and Strategies: The Process of European Financial Market Integration." Paper presented at the EUSA Biennial Conference, Washington DC [mimeo] Available at <http://aei.pitt.edu/7126/1/002360_1.PDF> accessed February 19, 2014.

Von der Groeben, H. 1987. *The European Community, the Formative Years: The Struggle to Establish the Common Market and the Political Union (1958–66).* Luxembourg: Office for Official Publications of the European Communities.

Walker, J. L. 1969. "The Diffusion of Innovations among the American States." *The American Political Science Review* 63 (3): 880–99.

Wallace, H. 1983. "Distributional Politics: Dividing up the Community Cake." In *Policy-making in the European Communities*, 2nd edn. ed. H. Wallace, W. Wallace, and C. Webb. London: John Wiley.

Wallace, H. 2000. "Europeanisation and Globalisation: Complementary or Contradictory Trends?" *New Political Economy* 5 (3): 369–82.

Wallace, H., and W. Wallace (eds) 2000. *Policy-making in the European Union*, 4th edn. New York: Oxford University Press.

Wallace, H., W. Wallace, and C. Webb (eds) 1983. *Policy-making in the European Communities*, 2nd edn. New York: Wiley.

Wallace, W. 2002. "Where Does Europe End? Dilemmas of Inclusion and Exclusion." In *Europe Unbound: Enlarging and Reshaping the Boundaries of the European Union*, ed. J. Zielonka. London: Routledge.

Wallis, J. J. 2005. "Constitutions, Corporations, and Corruption: American States and Constitutional Change, 1842–1852." *Journal of Economic History* 65 (1): 211–56.

Wallis, J. J., R. E. Sylla, and A. Grinath III. 2004. "Sovereign Debt and Repudiation: The Emerging-market Debt Crisis in the U.S. States, 1839–1843." NBER Working Paper No. 10753. Cambridge, MA: National Bureau of Economic Research.

Wallis, J. J., R. E. Sylla, and J. B. Legler. 1994. "The Interaction of Taxation and Regulation in Nineteenth Century Banking." In *The Regulated Economy: A Historical Approach to Political Economy*, ed. C. Goldin and G. D. Libecap. Chicago, IL: University of Chicago Press.

Walton, G. M., and H. Rockoff. 1990. *History of the American Economy*, 6th edn. San Diego: Harcourt Brace Jovanovich.

Ward, B. 1976. "National Economic Planning and Policies in Twentieth Century Europe, 1920–1970." In *The Fontana Economic History of Europe: The Twentieth Century*, v: Part 2, ed. C. M. Cipolla. Glasgow: Fontana/Collins.

Weatherill, S. 2012. "The Constitutional Context of (Ever-wider) Policy-making." In *The Oxford Handbook of the European Union*, ed. E. Jones, A. Menon, and S. Weatherill. Oxford: Oxford University Press.

Weiler, J. H. H. 1981. "The Community System: The Dual Character of Supranationalism." *Yearbook of European Law* 1 (1): 267–306.

Weiler, J. H. H. 1991. "The Transformation of Europe." *Yale Law Journal* 100 (8): 2403–83.

Weiler, J. H. H. 2012a. "Editorial: 60 Years since the First European Community–Reflections on Political Messianism." *European Journal of International Law* 22 (2): 303–11.

Weiler, J. H. H. 2012b. "Europe in Crisis - On 'Political Messianism', 'Legitimacy' and the 'Rule of Law'." *Singapore Legal Studies* 2012: 248–68.

Weingast, B. R. 1995. "The Economic Role of Political Institutions: Market-preserving Federalism and Economic Development." *Journal of Law, Economics, & Organization* 11 (1): 1–31.

Welch, D. 1983. "From 'Euro Beer' to 'Newcastle Brown', A Review of European Community Action to Dismantle Divergent 'Food' Laws." *JCMS: Journal of Common Market Studies*, 22 (1): 47–70.

Wendt, I. E. 2012. *EU Competition Law and Liberal Professions: An Uneasy Relationship.* Leiden: Martinus Nijhoff Publishers.

Whaples, R., and D. C. Betts. 1995. *Historical Perspectives on the American Economy: Selected Readings.* Cambridge and New York: Cambridge University Press.

White, E. N. 1982. "The Political Economy of Banking Regulation, 1864–1933." *Journal of Economic History* 42 (1): 33–40.

Whitelegg, J. 1988. *Transport Policy in the EEC.* London: Routledge.

Whitney, E. B. 1885. "Commercial Retaliation between the States." *American Law Review* 19: 62–72.

Whittington, K. E. 2007. *Political Foundations of Judicial Supremacy: The Presidency, the Supreme Court, and Constitutional Leadership in U.S. History.* Princeton, NJ: Princeton University Press.

Wibbels, E. 2003. "Bailouts, Budget Constraints, and Leviathans: Comparative Federalism and Lessons from the Early United States." *Comparative Political Studies* 36 (5): 475–508.

Wiebe, R. H. 1967. *The Search for Order, 1877–1920.* New York: Hill and Wang.

Wiecek, W. M. 1969. "The Reconstruction of Federal Judicial Power, 1863–1875." *American Journal of Legal History* 13 (4): 333–59.

Williamson, J. G. 1974. "Watersheds and Turning Points: Conjectures on the Long-Term Impact of Civil War Financing." *Journal of Economic History* 34 (3): 636–61.

Wolfram, C. W. 1995. "Sneaking around in the Legal Profession: Interjurisdictional Unauthorized Practice by Transactional Lawyers." *South Texas Law Review* 36: 665–713.

Woll, C. 2008. *Firm Interests: How Governments Shape Business Lobbying on Global Trade.* Ithaca, NY: Cornell University Press.

Woll, C. 2013. "Lobbying under Pressure: The Effect of Salience on European Union Hedge Fund Regulation." *JCMS: Journal of Common Market Studies* 51 (3): 555–72.

Woolridge, F. 1977. "Free Movement of EEC Nationals: The Limitation Based on Public Policy and Public Security." *European Law Review* 2 (3): 190–207.

World Trade Organization. 1994. General Agreement on Trade in Services (GATS). 1869 U.N.T.S. 183.

Wright, G. 1978. *The Political Economy of the Cotton South: Households, Markets, and Wealth in the Nineteenth Century.* New York: W. W. Norton.

Wright, G. 1984. "Rethinking the Postbellum Southern Political Economy: A Review Essay." *Business History Review* 58 (3): 409–16.

Yannopoulos, G. N. 1989. "The Management of Trade-induced Structural Adjustment: An Evaluation of the EC's Integrated Mediterranean Programmes." *JCMS: Journal of Common Market Studies* 27 (4): 283–301.

Young, A. R. 1995. "Ideas, Interests and Institutions: The Politics of Liberalisation in the EC's Road Haulage Industry." In *The Evolution of Rules for a Single European Market, Part I: Industry and Finance*, ed. D. Mayes. Luxembourg: Office for Official Publications of the European Communities.

Young, A. R., and H. Wallace. 2000. *Regulatory Politics in the Enlarging European Union: Weighing Civic and Producer Interests.* Manchester: Manchester University Press.

Zacchia, C. 1976. "International Trade and Capital Movements, 1920–1970." In *The Fontana Economic History of Europe: The Twentieth Century*, v: Part 2, ed. C. M. Cipolla. Glasgow: Collins/Fontana.

Ziblatt, D. 2004. "Rethinking the Origins of Federalism: Puzzle, Theory, and Evidence from Nineteenth-century Europe." *World Politics* 57 (1): 70–98.

Zimmerman, J. F. 1996. *Interstate Relations: The Neglected Dimension of Federalism.* Westport, CT: Praeger Publishers.

Zimmerman, J. F. 2002. *Interstate Cooperation: Compacts and Administrative Agreements.* Westport, CT: Praeger Publishers.

Zimmerman, J. F. 2003. "How Perfect Is the U.S. Economic Union? Interstate Trade Barriers." Paper presented at the annual meeting of the American Political Science Association, Philadelphia, PA [unpublished].

Zimmerman, J. F. 2006. *Interstate Relations: The Neglected Dimension of Federalism.* Westport, CT: Praeger Publishers.

Zimmerman, J. F. 2010. "Generating Economic Growth by Harmonizing State Regulatory Laws." Paper presented at the American Political Science Association, September 1–5. Washington, DC.

Zimmerman, J. F., and M. Wendell. 1976. *The Law and Use of Interstate Compacts.* Lexington, KY: The Council of State Governments.

Zimmerman, K. F. 2009. "Labor Mobility and the Integration of European Labor Markets." IZA Discussion Paper 3999. Bonn, Germany: Institute for the Study of Labor.

Zysman, J. 1983. *Governments, Markets, and Growth: Financial Systems and the Politics of Industrial Change.* Ithaca, NY: Cornell University Press.

EU Legislation

Directive 2001/12/EC relating to market opening and integration

Directive 2001/13/EC Licensing of Railway Undertakings

Directive 2001/14/EC Railway Safety Directive

Directive 2003/6/EC Market Abuse Directive

Directive 2003/71/EC Prospectus Directive

Directive 2004/109/EC Transparency Directive

Directive 2004/39/EC Markets in Financial Instruments Directive

Directive 2005/36/EC on the recognition of professional qualifications

Directive 2009/65/EC Updated UCITS Directive

Directive 2011/61/EU Alternative Investment Fund Managers Directive

Directive 2013/36/EU Capital Requirements Directive IV

Directive 2013/55/EU Updated Directive on the Mutual Recognition of Professionals

Directive 2014/59/EU Directive on Bank Recovery and Resolution

Directive 64/240/EEC on the abolition of restrictions on the movement and residence of Member States' workers and their families within the Community

Directive 70/50/EEC on the abolition of measures which have an effect equivalent to quantitative restrictions on imports

Directive 75/362//EEC on the mutual recognition of qualification in medicine

Directive 75/363/EEC concerning the activities of doctors
Directive 77/249/EEC Lawyers' Services Directive
Directive 77/780/EEC First Banking Directive
Directive 85/384/EEC Sectoral Directive for Architects
Directive 85/611/EEC Original UCITS Directive.
Directive 88/361/EEC Capital Movement Directive
Directive 89/229/EEC Own Funds Directive
Directive 89/48/EEC First Diplomas Directive
Directive 89/646/EEC Second Banking Directive
Directive 89/647/EEC Solvency Ratio Directive
Directive 91/308/EEC Money Laundering Directive
Directive 92/51/EEC Second Diplomas Directive
Directive 93/16/EEC Sectoral Directive for Doctors
Directive 96/26/EEC on admission to the occupation of road transport operator
Directive 98/5/EC Lawyers' Establishment Directive
Directive 99/42/EC on the recognition of professional qualifications
Directive 73/183/EEC Directive on the abolition of restrictions on freedom of establishment and freedom to provide services in respect of self-employed activities of banks and other financial institutions
Directives 77/452/EEC and 77/453/EEC Sectoral Directives for Nurses
Directives 78/1026/EEC and 78/1027/EEC Sectoral Directives for Veterinary Surgeons
Directives 78/686/EEC and 78/687/EEC Sectoral Directives for Dental Practitioners
Directives 80/154/EEC and 80/155/EEC Sectoral Directives for Midwives
Directives 85/432/EEC and 85/433/EEC Sectoral Directives for Pharmacists
Regulation 15/61 of 16 August 1961 on initial measures to realize free movement of workers within the Community
Regulation 3118/93/EEC on road cabotage (goods)
Regulation 38/64/EEC relating to the freedom of movement or workers within the Community
Regulation 575/2013 Capital Requirements Regulation
Regulation 648/2012 European Market Infrastructure Regulation
Regulation 881/92/EEC on market access in the carriage of goods by road within the Community

Court Cases

US Supreme Court
Baldwin v. Seelig, 294 U.S. 511 (1935)
Bank of Augusta v. Earle, 38 U.S. 519 (1839)
Bronson v. Kinzie, 42 U.S. 311 (1843)
Brown v. Maryland, 25 U.S. 419 (1827)
Charles River Bridge v. Warren Bridge, 36 U.S. 420 (1837)
Dent v. West Virginia, 129 U.S. 114 (1889)
Gibbons v. Ogden, 22 U.S. 1 (1824)
John Swift v. George Tyson, 41 U.S. 1 (1842)

Knox v. *Lee*, 79 U.S. 457 (1871)
Lochner v. *New York*, 198 U.S. 45, (1905)
Mandeville & Jameson v. *Joseph Riddle & Co.*, 5 U.S. 1 290 (1803)
Munn v. *Illinois*, 94 U.S. 113 (1877)
Norris v. *Boston*, 48 U.S. 283 (1849) (Passenger Cases)
Robbins v. *Shelby County Taxing District*, 120 U.S. 489 (1887)
Smith v. *Turner*, 48 U.S. 283 (1849) (Passenger Cases)
Smyth v. *Ames*, 171 U.S. 361 (1898)
United States v. *E. C. Knight Co.*, 156 U.S. 1 (1895) (Sugar Trust)
Veazie Bank v. *Fenno*, 75 U.S. 533 (1869)
Virginia v. *Tennessee*, 148 U.S. 503 (1893)
Welton v. *State of Missouri*, 91 U.S. 275 (1876)
Wabash, St. Louis & Pacific Railway Company v. *Illinois*, 118 U.S. 557 (1886)
Ward v. *Maryland*, 79 U.S. 418 (1871)
Wilson v. *Black-Bird Creek Marsh Co.*, 27 U.S. (2 Pet.) 245 (1829)

EU Court Cases
Andrea Francovich and Danila Bonifaci and others v. *Italian Republic*, Joined cases C-6/90 and C-9/90 (1991) ECR I-5357
Angelo Alberto Torresi and Pierfrancesco Torresi v. *Consiglio dell'Ordine degli Avvocati di Macerata*, Joined Cases C-58/13 and C-59/13 (2014)
Arduino, Criminal Proceedings against Manuele Arduino, Case C-35/99 (2002) ECR I-1529
Bernard Keck and Daniel Mithouard, C-267/91 and C-268/91 (2003) ECR 1–6097
B.N.O. Walrave and L.J.N. Koch v. *Association Union cycliste internationale, Koninklijke Nederlandsche Wielren Unie and Federación Española Ciclismo*, Case 36/74 (1974) ECR 1405
Brugnoni (Luigi) and Roberto Ruffinengo v. *Cassa di risparmio di Genova e Imperia*, Case 157/85 (1986) ECR I–2013
Commission v. *France* (French Merchant Seamen Case), Case 167/73 (1974) ECR 359
Commission v. *Denmark*, Case C-302/86 ECR 4607
Établissements Consten S.à.R.L. and Grundig-Verkaufs-GmbH v. *Commission of the European Economic Community*, Joined cases 56 and 58/64 (1966) ECR 299
European Commission v. *Federal Republic of Germany*, Case C-54/08 (2011) ECR I-4360
European Commission v. *French Republic*, Case C-50/08 (2011) ECR I-4199
European Commission v. *Grand Duchy of Luxembourg*, Case C-51/08 (2011) ECR I-4235
European Commission v. *Hellenic Republic*, Case C-61/08 (2011) ECR I-4403
European Commission v. *Kingdom of Belgium*, Case C-47/08 (2011) ECR I-4156
European Commission v. *Portuguese Republic*, Case C-52/08 (2011) ECR I-4290
European Commission v. *Republic of Austria*, Case C-53/08 (2011) ECR I-4314
European Parliament v. *Council of the European Communities*, Case 13/83 (1985) ECR 1513
Graziana Luisi and Giuseppe Carbone v. *Ministero del Tesoro*, Joined Cases 286/82 and 26/83 (1984) ECR 377
Irene Vlassopoulou v. *Ministerium für Justiz Bundes- und Europaangelegenheiten Baden-Württemberg*, Case 340/89 (1991) ECR I-2357

International Transport Workers' Federation and *Finnish Seamen's Union* v. and OÜ Viking, Case C-438/05 (2007) ECR I-10779

J. C. J. Wouters, J. W. Savelbergh and Price Waterhouse Belastingadviseurs BV v. *Algemene Raad van de Nederlandse Orde van Advocaten*, C-309/99 (2002) ECR I-1577

Johannes Henricus Maria van Binsbergen v. *Bestuur van de Bedrijfsvereniging voor de Metaal-nijverheid*, Case 33/74 (1974) ECR 1299

Laval Un Partneri Ltd v. *Svenska Byggnadsarbetareförbundet*, Case C-341/05 (2007) ECR I-11767

Nouvelles Frontières Case, Case 209-213/84 (1986) ECR–1425

Procureur du Roi v. *Benoît and Gustave Dassonville*, C-8/74 (1974) ECR 837

Public Prosecutor v. *Guerrino Casati*, Case 203/80 (1981) ECR 2595

Reinhard Gebhard v. *Consiglio dell'Ordine degli Avvocati e Procuratori di Milano*, Case 55/94 (1996) ECR 1–4165

Rewe-Zentral AG v. *Bundesmonopolverwaltung für Branntwein*, C-120/78 (1979) ECR 649 (Cassis de Dijon)

Reyners v. *Belgian State*, Case 2/74 (1974) ECR 631

Rüffert v. *Niedersachsen Case*, C-346/06, (2008) ECR I-1989

Sandoz GmbH v. *Finanzlandesdirektion für Wien, Niederösterreich und Burgenland*, Case C-439/97 (1999) ECR I-07041

Thieffry v. *Conseil de l'Ordre des Avocats à la Cour de Paris* (Paris Bar Council), Case 71/76 (1976) ECR 765

Index